Praise for

THE DAILY DISCIPLER

What does systematic theology have to do with our daily lives?
Most believers, if they are honest, would say, "Not much."
In *The Daily Discipler*, Neil Anderson does a superb job of showing
how theology can inform life's most difficult issues. From overcoming
sin bondages to dealing with anxiety and depression, Neil Anderson
connects the miracle work of God in Christ Jesus to our daily
lives. This book will bless you in making theology a transformative
experience instead of an intellectual exercise.

Fernando Garzon, Psy.D.
ASSOCIATE PROFESSOR, REGENT UNIVERSITY,
SCHOOL OF PSYCHOLOGY AND COUNSELING

Through his life and writings, Neil Anderson has been a genuine point
man in Christ's "army," leading believers toward the God-given objective of presenting every man free and fully mature in Christ. In *The
Daily Discipler*, Neil has encapsulated his life's work and provided a tool
that will assist many in moving from the skin-deep Christian maturity
that is so typical of our day to the genuinely transformed life that consistently exemplifies and is worthy of the Savior whose name we wear.

Michael D. Jacobson, D.O.
AUTHOR, *THE WORD ON HEALTH*
DIRECTOR, PROVIDENT MEDICAL INSTITUTE
ASSISTANT PASTOR, BETHEL BAPTIST TEMPLE

THE DAILY DISCIPLER

Neil T. Anderson

Regal

From Gospel Light
Ventura, California, U.S.A.

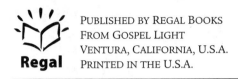

PUBLISHED BY REGAL BOOKS
FROM GOSPEL LIGHT
VENTURA, CALIFORNIA, U.S.A.
PRINTED IN THE U.S.A.

Regal Books is a ministry of Gospel Light, a Christian publisher dedicated to serving the local church. We believe God's vision for Gospel Light is to provide church leaders with biblical, user-friendly materials that will help them evangelize, disciple and minister to children, youth and families.

It is our prayer that this Regal book will help you discover biblical truth for your own life and help you meet the needs of others. May God richly bless you.

For a free catalog of resources from Regal Books/Gospel Light, please call your Christian supplier or contact us at 1-800-4-GOSPEL or www.regalbooks.com.

Library of Congress Cataloging-in-Publication Data
Anderson, Neil T., 1942-
  The daily discipler / Neil T. Anderson.
    p. cm.
  Includes bibliographical references.
  ISBN 0-8307-3721-9 (hardcover); 0-8307-3720-0 (trade paperback)
  1. Bible—Meditations. 2. Devotional calendars. I. Title.
BS491.5.A53 2005
242'.5—dc22   2005006356

Rights for publishing this book in other languages are contracted by Gospel Light Worldwide, the international nonprofit ministry of Gospel Light. Gospel Light Worldwide also provides publishing and technical assistance to international publishers dedicated to producing Sunday School and Vacation Bible School curricula and books in the languages of the world. For additional information, visit www.gospellightworldwide.org; write to Gospel Light Worldwide, P.O. Box 3875, Ventura, CA 93006; or send an e-mail to info@gospellightworldwide.org.

CONTENTS

First Quarter: Rooted in Christ

Second Quarter: Built Up in Him

Third Quarter: Living in Christ

Fourth Quarter: Forces Opposing Our Sanctification

INTRODUCTION

Most of us get up every morning, only to face a very busy day. We want to present ourselves appropriately to others, so we spend a measure of time showering and grooming. Those who are more physically disciplined will find time for exercise. Bodily discipline is important for our health and for successful living in this world. Once we've finished our morning routine, we have a quick bite to eat; and then it's off to work, school or play.

Where and how we spend our time reflects our values and reveals what we have chosen to believe. It is easy to overlook the need for spiritual disciplines because we don't always see immediate benefits. Temporal gratification often takes precedence over long-term commitments. Humanly we ask, *What's in it for me?* That seems so unrighteous, but in reality there is no sure commitment without any sure reward. The apostle Paul addresses this issue when he tells us, "Train yourself to be godly. For physical training is of some value, but godliness has value for all things, holding promise for both the present life and the life to come" (1 Tim. 4:7-8). Paul is saying that spiritual disciplines are more profitable than physical disciplines and that our lives will be more fruitful if we spend time with the Lord and seek to be transformed by the renewing of our minds to the truth of His Word.

Without capitulating to the *tyranny of the urgent,* I believe there is a need for a practical, systematic theology book that can be digested in daily nuggets. What you are holding in your hand is the result of 25 years of formal education, 60 plus years of living and 35 years of Christian service. The contents first appeared in the *Freedom in Christ Bible,* a one-year study bible published by Zondervan. They have graciously given permission for this volume to be published as a discipleship tool for busy Christians who want to be all that God created them to be.

In working through *The Daily Discipler,* you will discover who you are in Christ, what it means to be a child of God and how to live a responsible and liberated life "in Him." This yearlong study is divided into four quarters. The first three-quarters relate to God's will for your life, i.e., your sanctification (see 1 Thess. 4:3). The basis for your sanctification is your new life in Christ. As a Christian, you are in the process of conforming to the image of God, and the necessary foundation is your identity and position in Christ. The apostle Paul explains the order of growth in Colossians 2:6-10:

> So then, just as you received Christ Jesus as Lord, continue to live *in Him,* rooted and built up *in Him,* strengthened in the faith as you were taught, and overflowing with thankfulness. See to it that no

one takes you captive through hollow and deceptive philosophy, which depends on human tradition and the basic principles of this world rather than on Christ. For *in Christ* all the fullness of the Deity lives in bodily form, and you have been given fullness *in Christ*, who is the head over every power and authority (emphasis added).

Every new believer must first be rooted "in Him" in order to be built up "in Him." Being spiritually alive "in Christ" means that your soul is in union with God. Just as you encounter challenges as you grow physically, there are hurdles to overcome and lessons to learn in order to grow spiritually. In the first three-quarters you will discover what it means to be firmly rooted in Christ, to grow in Christ and to live free in Christ. The following diagram shows "Levels of Conflict" and "Levels of Growth." The first diagram illustrates what needs to be overcome at various stages of growth spiritually, rationally, emotionally, volitionally, and relationally. The second diagram illustrates the maturity that should be evident at each level.

Levels of Conflict

	Level One	Level Two	Level Three
Spiritual	"Rooted in Christ" Lack of salvation or assurance (Eph. 2:1-3)	"Built up in Christ" Living according to the flesh (Gal. 5:19-21)	"Living in Christ" Insensitive to the Spirit's leading (Heb. 5:11-14)
Rational	Pride and ignorance (1 Cor. 8:1)	Wrong belief or philosophy (Col. 2:8)	Lack of knowledge (Hos. 4:6)
Emotional	Fearful, guilty and shameful (Matt. 10:26-33; Rom. 3:23)	Angry, anxious and depressed (Eph. 4:31; 1 Pet. 5:7; 2 Cor. 4:1-18)	Discouraged and sorrowful (Gal. 6:9)
Volitional	Rebellious (1 Tim. 1:9)	Lack of self-control (1 Cor. 3:1-3)	Undisciplined (2 Thess. 3:7,11)
Relational	Rejected and unloved (1 Pet. 2:4)	Bitter and unforgiving (Col. 3:13)	Selfish (1 Cor. 10:24; Phil. 2:1-5)

Levels of Growth

	Level One	**Level Two**	**Level Three**
Spiritual	"Rooted in Christ" Child of God (Rom. 8:16)	"Built up in Christ" Lives according to the Spirit (Gal. 5:22-23)	"Living in Christ" Led by the Spirit (Rom. 8:14)
Rational	Knows the truth (John 8:32)	Correctly uses the Bible (2 Tim. 2:15)	Adequate and equipped (2 Tim. 3:16-17)
Emotional	Free (Gal. 5:1)	Joyful, peaceful and patient (Gal. 5:22)	Contented (Phil. 4:11)
Volitional	Submissive (Rom. 13:1-5)	Self-controlled (Gal. 5:23)	Disciplined (1 Tim. 4:7-8)
Relational	Accepted and forgiven (Rom. 5:8; 15:7)	Forgiving (Eph. 4:32)	Loving and unselfish (Phil. 2:1-5)

The course begins by considering God's creation and the subsequent fall of Adam and Eve. Because of the Fall, we were all born physically alive but spiritually dead in our transgressions and sins (see Eph. 2:1). The good news is we can be born-again and be new creations in Christ (see 2 Cor. 5:17). We are free from our past and free to be all that God created us to be. We will sequentially work through each level of conflict and learn how to live liberated lives in Christ.

The fourth quarter will consider the enemies of our sanctification, namely the world, the flesh and the devil. We will study the eternal battle between the kingdom of God and the kingdom of darkness, between the Spirit of Truth and the father of lies, between true prophets and false prophets, between the real and the counterfeit. The battle between good and evil is a dominant theme of Scripture, which begins in the Garden of Eden and ends in the book of Revelation. Every believer is involved in spiritual warfare, "For our struggle is not against flesh and blood, but against the rulers, against the authorities, against the powers of this dark world and against the spiritual forces of evil in the heavenly realms" (Eph. 6:12).

You will learn the believer's position in Christ, which ensures the Church's power and authority over the kingdom of darkness. Your spiritual protection in Christ will be explained; and you will be able to identify and resist temptation, accusation and deception. You will learn how the truth will set you free and how you can help others be established alive and free in Christ. Like any spiritual discipline, you will be tempted not to finish this study. You should begin and end each daily lesson with prayer. Start with praise by acknowledging the attributes of God. Your loving heavenly Father is the one and only omniscient, omnipresent and omnipotent God. Thank Him for sending Jesus to die in your place in order that your sins might be forgiven and for giving you new life in Him. Then ask the Lord to guard your heart and your mind from any distracting thoughts. Personally interact with the truth revealed in God's Word.

The *Steps to Freedom in Christ* will be mentioned several times throughout the study. This booklet can be purchased at any Christian bookstore or from Freedom in Christ Ministries. The Steps is a repentance process that helps people resolve their personal and spiritual conflicts. The theology and application of the Steps is explained in the text of my book *Discipleship Counseling*.

Take the time to read the Bible passage listed with each lesson. Truth will not set you free if it is only acknowledged and intellectually discussed. Truth must be personally believed and appropriated in the heart. Only in the heart do the mind, emotion and will converge into one life-transforming whole. You can trust the Holy Spirit to lead you into all truth and enable you to be the person God has created you to be. Finally, decide to live what you have chosen to believe, and the grace of God will enable you to do His will and glorify Him by bearing much fruit (see John 15:8).

—Dr. Neil T. Anderson

First Quarter:
Rooted in Christ

July 26/08

THE CREATION

Genesis 1:1-31

"In the beginning God created the heavens and the earth" (Gen. 1:1). These opening words of the Bible reveal that there is only one Creator God who is eternally existent. The Bible makes no attempt to prove the existence of God, only stating, "Since the creation of the world God's invisible qualities—his eternal power and divine nature—have been clearly seen, being understood from what has been made, so that men are without excuse" (Rom. 1:20).

The Old Testament prophets consistently credited God as the only creator and source of all existence. There is a contingent relationship between God and His creation, for it is the Lord "who has made all things, who alone stretched out the heavens, who spread out the earth by [Himself]" (Isa. 44:24). God's handiwork is absolutely dependent upon Him for its ordering and survival. Whenever Old Testament prophets wrote about creation, they were making a religious affirmation that God was the one and only sovereign Lord of the universe. They never entertained the thought of more than one God set forth by other religions.

Although Scripture makes clear that Earth has been created by God alone, the Word does not specify its age. As a result, scholars have differing views on the subject. Many conservatives hold to a literal 7-day creation. Recognizing that there are gaps in the genealogies given in the book of Genesis, they would propose a "young earth" theory which holds that our world has been around for 10,000 to 20,000 years. Others understand "day" to mean an age and consider that the earth is much older, possibly millions of years. However, the Hebrew word for "day" when used elsewhere in the Bible with a numerical adjective always refers to a solar 24-hour day.

Another possible explanation is the "gap" theory. According to this theory, a gap of time exists between verses 1 and 2 of Genesis. In other words, although in the beginning of time, God created the heavens and the earth, "the earth was formless and empty, darkness was over the surface of the deep, and the Spirit of God was hovering over the waters" (Gen. 1:2). Therefore, God could have created the earth thousands or millions of years before the re-creation (or restoration) of earth with a new creation of humanity to rule over it. This would account for the appearance of Satan in the garden who had previously been created and subsequently fallen from heaven.

It is interesting to note that "in the beginning" literally means, "by way of beginning," or "to begin with." The creation narrative is the starting point of history as we know it, not necessarily the absolute start to creation. While it unfolds in a manner consistent with observations made by scientists (i.e., the creation of vegetables had to come before the animals, since the study of photosynthesis has shown that green plants furnish the oxygen necessary for animal existence), the creation narrative provided the necessary stage for the creation of humanity and the unfolding drama of sin and redemption.

The creation account also establishes the relationship that we were intended to have with our Creator and reveals who we are and what our purpose is for being here. The first three chapters in the book of Genesis, depicting the creation of Adam and Eve and their subsequent fall, provide the singular backdrop that sets the stage for the rest of Scripture.

> For by him all things were created: things in heaven and on earth, visible and invisible, whether thrones or powers or rulers or authorities; all things were created by him and for him (Col. 1:16).

Thought for the day: *How should we relate to God?*

We should relate to Him as our Creator & the Creator of heaven + earth. We should relate to Him as God - with respect + honor. We should also come to understand that He has full control of this world + everything in it. Without Him nothing would exist. I love Col. 1:16 (above) because it reminds me that even though things around us + in this world can be evil + unjust - God is still in control. And as we see prophecies of the end times unfold before our eyes we can take comfort + not be so afraid because God is in control of all this too.

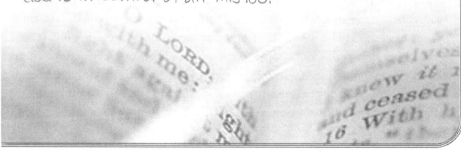

July 26/08

DIVINE REVELATION

Psalm 19:1-14

God has chosen to reveal Himself in three primary ways. The first is commonly referred to as general revelation, as illustrated in Psalm 19, verse 1: "The heavens declare the glory of God; the skies proclaim the work of his hands." The beauty and order of all things created reflect the glory of God and reveal the divine architect of the universe. What humanity discovers empirically through scientific observation is never at odds with divine revelation, since God created what science can only discover and use. ✳

God has also revealed Himself and His plan for the universe through the divinely inspired prophets and apostles who wrote the books of this Bible. The written word is referred to as special revelation, which is what the psalmist is referring to in verses 7 to 11. Special revelation interprets and explains general revelation.

✳ The ultimate revelation of God, however, is revealed in Jesus, who declared, "Anyone who has seen me has seen the Father" (see John 14:7). The Word of God is considered by Christians to be the sole authority for faith and practice because the Creator is the only One who can define Himself and explain who we are and why we are here. In creation, there is no separation between the secular and the sacred. The Bible speaks expansively to all of life and experience—to matters of faith as well as to matters of everyday practice; to the spiritual and sacred, as well as to the physical and secular; to the eternal as well as the temporal. It declares that all of life derives from God Himself. There are not two realities, but only one reality, and the ultimate reality is God. ✳

God is the Creator and His Word speaks to a lot more than just our faith and practice. It speaks to every essential discipline of society. The statement, "In the beginning God created the heavens and the earth" (Gen. 1:1) speaks directly to matters of theology and philosophy. God's prohibition to eat from the tree of knowledge of good and evil (see Gen. 2:9) is the starting point for ethics. The mention of animals "according to their kind" (Gen. 1:21) recognizes the importance of biology. The statement that "man became a living being" (Gen. 2:7) suggests our physical, psychological and spiritual nature. The command to "be fruitful and increase in number; fill the earth and subdue it" (Gen. 1:28) speaks to matters of sociology and the relationship of humans to the natural order. The statement, "Whoever sheds the blood of man by man shall his blood be shed" (Gen. 9:6) sets legal and political precedents. God's gift of grains and fruit for food (see Gen. 1:29) speaks to economic relationships. The statement, "I will put enmity between you and the woman," (Gen. 3:15) foreshadows misunderstandings that will occur between men and women throughout history.

God underlines the significance of all the above disciplines in the ultimate revelation of Jesus Christ. In theology, Jesus is the fullness of the Godhead (see Col. 2:9). In philosophy, Jesus is the Logos (Word) of God (see John 1:1). In ethics, Jesus is the true light (see John 1:9). In biology, Jesus took on the form of a man (see Phil. 2:7), and became our source for physical and spiritual life (see John 1:4). In psychology, Jesus is the true and perfect man who saves and transforms us (see Luke 1:46-47). In sociology, Jesus is our example for social relationships (see 1 Pet. 2:21). In law and politics, Jesus came to fulfill the Law (see Matt. 5:17) and is the Lord of lords and King of kings (see Rev. 19:16). In economics, Jesus is the owner of all things (see 1 Cor. 10:26). All things were created by Christ and for Christ (Col. 1:16). Finally, in history, Jesus is the Alpha and Omega (the beginning and the end; see Rev. 1:8).

The heavens declare the glory of God; the skies proclaim the work of his hands (Ps. 19:1).

Thought for the day: *How has God made Himself known to you?* God has made Himself known to me through many ways:
- The beauty of the world
- The 4 Seasons
- I remember watching Dudley as a puppy & marveled at how he used his paws to grab & hold things
- Conception (blows my mind!)
- migration (how do they know when to leave & when to return?)
- THE BEES (how they communicate to tell each other where the flowers are - how some bee's job is to keep the hive at the consistent perfect temperature with their wings
- the ants
- babies - the changes they go through in the 1st 2 years.
- through the many ways He shows us His grace & mercy - also through the artifacts, etc. that have been uncovered now & throughout the ages to prove He is real,

- Parenting = God's love for us
  - unconditional love
  - discipline
  - boundries & rules
  - wanting the very best for our kids
  - our anguish when they stray
  - having to let go just as God has let us go with a free will
  - letting them learn by their mistakes
- through His Word
- through the prophecies
- through Jesus Christ
- through the Holy Spirit
- through prayer
- through Ancient Paths
- for clearly directing me to babysit Daniel, etc.
- through testimonies of others
- through sermons

July 28/08

THE NATURE OF HUMANITY

Psalm 8

The psalmist asks, "What is man that you are mindful of him?" (v. 4). The uniqueness of humanity is revealed in creation. "God created man in his own image, in the image of God he created him; male and female he created them" (Gen. 1:27). Being created in the image of God is what sets humanity apart from the animal kingdom. Our souls have the ability to think, feel and choose. Consequently, we have the capacity to participate with God in the shaping of our own lives. The temptation is to act independently of God and determine for ourselves who we are and what we shall become.

"The LORD God formed the man from the dust of the ground and breathed into his nostrils the breath of life, and the man became a living being" (Gen. 2:7). This combination of dust (natural) and divine breath (spiritual) is what constitutes the nature of humanity who are created in the image of God. The original creation of man could be depicted as follows:

Some believe we are composed of body, soul and spirit (trichotomous), with the mind, will and emotion constituting the soul. Others understand the human soul and spirit to be essentially the same (dichotomous). Most would agree that part of our human existence is material and the other part immaterial—that each of us possesses an inner person and an outer person (see 2 Cor. 4:16).

Adam was created to be both physically and spiritually alive. To be physically alive means that our soul/spirit is in union with our bodies. We will remain physically alive as long as our soul is in union with our bodies. When Christians die physically, they will be absent from their bodies and present with the Lord (see 2 Cor. 5:6). To be spiritually alive means that our soul/spirit is in union with God. Adam and Eve were created by God to be both physically and spiritually alive.

We have a physical body that enables us to relate to the natural world through five senses. Consequently, we can taste, smell, feel, hear and see. The mind, will and emotion come together in the heart, which is the core of our inner being. "As water reflects a face, so a man's heart reflects the man" (Prov. 27:19).

Since we are not the source of our own life, the heart is inherently open to external influence. What the heart takes in also becomes its master, stamping the heart with its character. In the original creation, God was at the center of Adam's and Eve's lives, and they naturally took on His character. Even though we were created to be a little lower than heavenly beings and crowned with glory and honor, and given dominion over the animal kingdom (see Ps. 8:5-6), we are still dependent creatures who are called to worship God as the Creator and Sustainer of life.

> God created man in his own image, in the image of God he created him; male and female he created them (Gen. 1:27).

Thought for the day: *Are you spiritually alive?* Yes!

AUGUST 1, 2008

THE SIGNIFICANCE OF HUMANITY

Genesis 2

Genesis chapter 2 is an expansion of the creation account in chapter 1, depicting the uniqueness of humanity. In the presence of God, Adam's physical needs as well as his psychological needs of acceptance, security and significance were divinely met. He didn't have to search for significance. Adam was significant because he had been created in God's image; and he had been given a divine purpose, which was to rule over the birds of the sky, the beasts of the field and the fish of the sea (see Gen. 1:28). His first assignment was to tend the Garden of Eden (see Gen. 2:15), and his first act of dominion over the creatures was to name them (see v. 20).

At that time Satan was not the ruler of this world, nor did he have any sense of dominion over it. That responsibility was given to Adam and his descendants. In the center of the garden was the tree of life, and Adam could freely eat from it and any tree of the garden, except he could not eat from the tree of the knowledge of good and evil (see vv. 15-17). Had Adam and Eve chosen to live dependently upon God, they would have lived forever.

All that God had made was good (see Gen. 1:31) except for one thing. He said, "It is not good for the man to be alone" (2:18). Adam found no suitable companion when he named the animals. So God created a "helper suitable for him" (v. 18), and she and Adam were naked and unashamed (see v. 25). There was no sin in their lives and they had nothing to hide. Adam and Eve could have an intimate sexual relationship in the presence of God. They were unconditionally loved and accepted and had a sense of belonging not only to God but also to each other.

They were also safe and secure in the presence of God, both physically and psychologically. They were children of God who were intimately related to their heavenly Father. Their assignment was to "Be fruitful and increase in number; fill the earth and subdue it" (Gen. 1:28). No other creature has been created in God's image. The birds of the sky, the beasts of the field and the fish of the sea all operate according to divine instinct. Adam and Eve had the capacity to think, feel and choose. It was the intention of God that the descendants of Eve, "the mother of all the living" (Gen. 3:20), would form a human culture that would be an expression of humanity bearing the image of their Creator and sharing as God's servants in His kingly rule. No other created being had such significance.

All creation in its original form is only a reflection of the Creator. The Bible clearly teaches that there is an unseen, spiritual world from which the visible world draws its significance. "So we fix our eyes not on what is seen, but on what is unseen. For what is seen is temporary, but what is unseen is eternal" (2 Cor. 4:18). Our existence has meaning, and we maintain our significance as long as we stay intimately connected to the unseen source of life. Our faith in the invisible God is the only means by which we can withstand the seductive powers of the visible world.

> So we fix our eyes not on what is seen, but on what is unseen. For what is seen is temporary, but what is unseen is eternal (2 Cor. 4:18).

Thought for the day: *Where do you draw your significance from?*

- I'm sad to say that it is not always of God but of many other things: - being a mom, especially when the kids were young
  - being a wife
  - being a good sister, daughter + friend
  - being accepted.

- This chapter is a great reminder of WHO WE ARE - WE ARE CREATED IN GOD'S IMAGE (the only ones who are living beings), We are to have an INTIMITE RELATIONSHIP WITH GOD.

THE WAY OF LIFE

2 Samuel 22

God designed humanity to live a certain way and "his way is perfect" (2 Sam. 22:31). God is also the source of strength that enabled the children of God to live the way He prescribed. David said, "It is God who arms me with strength and makes my way perfect" (v. 33). The mind of the Hebrew believer was so ingrained with this concept that it was said of the Early Church believers that they "belonged to the Way" (Acts 9:2), and they knew that Jesus was the only way (see John 14:6; Acts 4:12).

Nonbelievers struggle with the Christian notion that there is only one way. However, every man-made object has been designed to function only one way. A computer can perform incredible calculations and be of tremendous service to humanity, but only if it is used the way it has been designed by the manufacturer. A tractor can pull a heavy load, but it can only be operated the way the designers intended it to function.

As believers we will be tempted to live another way in our own strength and resources. It is the nature of pride and a fatal flaw of human reasoning that cause us to think we know what is best for our own lives and to believe we don't need the help of God and others. "There is a way that seems right to a man, but in the end it leads to death" (Prov. 16:25).

We will also be tempted to question God's wisdom for creating us the way we are and for not giving us more favorable circumstances in which to live. (I know I do this & I believe it is wrong but I keep doing it).

But who are you, O man, to talk back to God? "Shall what is formed say to him who formed it, 'Why did you make me like this?'" Does not the potter have the right to make out of the same lump of clay some pottery for noble purposes and some for common use (Rom. 9:20-21)?

Further, "Does the clay say to the potter, 'What are you making?'" (Isa. 45:9).

The key to successful living is to know God and learn His ways and then live accordingly by faith in the power of the Holy Spirit. That is why Scripture permits us to boast in only one thing.

Let not the wise man boast of his wisdom or the strong man boast of his strength or the rich man boast of his riches, but let him who boasts boast about this: that he understands and knows me, that I am the LORD who exercises kindness, justice and righteousness on earth, for in these I delight (Jer. 9:23-24; see also 1 Cor. 1:31).

We can only fulfill our purpose if we are dependent upon God for our strength and learn to live in a manner that is consistent with how we have been designed. The prophet Samuel wrote, "For I have kept the ways of the LORD; I have not done evil by turning from my God" (v. 22). What a world this would be if all God's creation could say that.

The LORD lives! Praise be to my Rock! Exalted be God, the Rock, my Savior (2 Sam. 22:47)!

Thought for the day: *What are the results of living your way as opposed to living God's way?*
- fear
- miss opportunities.
- worry
- anxiousness
- doubt
- unhappiness
- unfulfillment
- hopelessness
- selfishness
- anger when things don't go my way.
- no peace
- no joy
- short lived happiness
- a desire to get more + more to fill the gap + never being satisfied with it
- no faith

I've lived most of my life this way + it is not fulfilling. Life is so exciting + wonderful when I live for God. He is using me in ways I never would have dreamed of + I anxiously await to see what He will do next.

THE FALL

Genesis 3

Adam and Eve's God-given dominion over this earth was immediately challenged by the serpent in the Garden of Eden. Throughout Church history, the serpent has been identified as Satan, or at least as a beast possessed by Satan. The New Testament writers referred to Satan as the tempter (see Matt. 4:3; 1 Thess. 3:5). The ancient serpent who leads the whole world astray is clearly identified by the apostle Paul as the devil, or Satan (see Rev. 12:9).

Satan immediately questioned God's Word: "Did God really say, 'You must not eat from any tree in the garden'?" (Gen. 3:1). Eve responded by saying, "We may eat from the trees in the garden, but God did say, 'You must not eat fruit from the tree that is in the middle of the garden, and you must not touch it, or you will die'" (v. 3). Notice that Eve added the words, "and you must not touch it" (v. 17). "'You will not surely die,' the serpent said to the woman. 'For God knows that when you eat of it your eyes will be opened, and you will be like God, knowing good and evil'" (vv. 4-5).

To have knowledge of good and evil means to be the origin or determiner of what is good and evil and what is true or untrue. Thus when Adam and Eve chose to eat the forbidden fruit, they were saying in effect, "We reject God as the One who determines what is right or wrong. We will determine for ourselves what is good for us." In a distorted way, Satan was right. Adam and Eve acted like gods when they chose to believe it was their prerogative to determine what was right and wrong. They played right into the hands of the devil, who is the deceiver and the father of lies.

All sin is the inevitable consequence of rebellion toward God, and every temptation is an attempt to get us to live our lives independently of God. Adam and Eve sinned and they died spiritually. Their souls were no longer in union with God and they were banished from the Garden of Eden (see v. 23). Since they could no longer eat from the tree of life (see v. 22), physical death would also be a consequence of sin.

There were two immediate consequences of the Fall. First, Adam and Eve forfeited their right to rule, allowing Satan to become the rebel holder of authority, the god of this world (see John 16:11; 2 Cor. 4:4). Second, every descendant of Adam and Eve would be born physically alive but spiritually dead (see Eph. 2:1). They would have neither the presence of God in their lives nor the knowledge of His ways.

Satan thought he had thwarted the plans of God, but the Lord responded with the first mention of the Gospel by cursing the serpent and promising that a future descendant of Eve would crush him: "And I will put enmity between you and the woman, and between your offspring and hers; he will crush your head, and you will strike his heel" (Gen. 3:15). The devil would inflict damage upon the covenant people of God, but the seed of the woman would strike the fatal blow by crushing the serpent's head, a promise fulfilled in Christ's victory over Satan.

Consequently, just as the result of one trespass was condemnation for all men, so also the result of one act of righteousness was justification that brings life for all men (Rom. 5:18).

Thought for the day: *Have you ever felt alienated from God?*

Many times. I believe it is because I turned my back on Him not Him on me.
I'm very much like the Israelites - I never seem to learn. It is like Paul says, "When I want to do good I do evil." It's that struggle.
Another problem I have is wanting to trust myself more than God. How stupid! God knows me inside out + knows what is best for me.
He made me + has a plan for me - I just need to trust Him! Sounds easy but it isn't.

THE DECEPTION OF EVE

1 Timothy 2:11-15

Like Adam, the woman was not spoken into existence as was the rest of creation. Unlike Adam, however, she was not an independent creature taken from the dust. God formed the woman from a part of the man. Adam knew the difference instantly, proclaiming, "This is now bone of my bones and flesh of my flesh" (Gen. 2:23). The man is honored by the acknowledgment that the woman was created for him. The woman is honored by the acknowledgment that the man is incomplete without her. In humility, the woman acknowledges that she was made for man. In humility, the man acknowledges that he is incomplete without the woman. They were not created to be in competition with one another. Eve came into being by the power of God, from man, for whom she is called to be a helpmate in a complementary relationship with him.

That fact that Satan could deceive Eve, which led her to believe a lie, is a sobering reality of life. Good people and even innocent people can be deceived. Deception is the major tool of Satan, because if people knew they were being deceived, they no longer would be. Deception occurs when people believe something to be true when it is not. Believing the lies of Satan brought swift judgment upon Eve: "I will greatly increase your pains in childbearing; with pain you will give birth to children. Your desire will be for your husband, and he will rule over you" (Gen. 3:16).

Any mother could testify to the first part of the curse being true. The second part of the curse has been far harder to work out in our homes, churches and societies. The apostle Paul wrote, "I do not permit a woman to teach or to have authority over a man" (1 Tim. 2:12). The order of creation is the basis for this instruction to the churches. The issue is one of authority, not inferiority, nor the stifling of a woman's contribution to the Church. Every child of God is gifted regardless of gender, and every child of God should be encouraged to use his or her gifts and talents to the glory of God. Not permitting a woman to teach (see v. 12) refers more to the establishment of doctrine, rather than proclaiming the truth in love, which we are all commanded to do.

Taking this commandment to one extreme has caused undue hardship to the women of this world and prohibited them from making a valuable contribution to the Church and society. The other extreme is for women to rebel against this commandment, resulting in the Word of God being dishonored (see Titus 2:5). Being under spiritual authority is for our own protection and being submissive does not imply inferiority. The image of God is equally present in women and men. Women have been afforded equal status with men wherever Christianity has flourished.

> This is now bone of my bones and flesh of my flesh; she shall be called "woman," for she was taken out of man (Gen. 2:23).

Thought for the day: *Is your relationship with the opposite sex complementary or competitive?*

For the most part it is complimentary. I love that Rob takes care of me & is the bread winner. I love that he does the yard work, the cars, the fixing of things. He's a real man! I love that he did not force me to work; that I could stay home & raise the kids; that I'm responsible for the housework, meals, groceries, taking the kids to their appointments, etc. (Although help with cooking & cleaning is always nice)

I am thankful that Rob sees his money as ours & that we have one bank account together & that he trusts me with the money.

Unfortunately I have an extremely hard time working with Rob on projects such as painting, etc. because of his stupid temper. That has been the hardest part of this marriage - his temper. We're getting better at working together now. If he gets angry I walk away.

- I believe a woman she stay home with the kids, she should be the nurturing one. A man is stronger & there are things that he can do that I can't & that is okay. There are things that only a woman can do & that's okay too.

THE SIN OF ADAM

Ezekiel 3:16-19

In the creation account, Eve was deceived, but Adam sinned. He knew what he was doing and he made a conscious choice to disobey God. "Therefore, just as sin entered the world through one man, and death through sin, and in this way death came to all men, because all sinned" (Rom. 5:12). The clear message of the Bible is that "the wages of sin is death" (Rom. 6:23). Sin separates us from a holy God, resulting in spiritual death; without His life to sustain us, we will also die physically. Because all have sinned, "Man is destined to die once, and after that to face judgment" (Heb. 9:27).

God had clearly warned Adam what the consequences would be if he disobeyed (see Gen. 2:15-17), but he disobeyed anyway. God continued to warn Adam's fallen descendents by providing spiritual watchmen. In the days of the prophet Ezekiel, watchmen were stationed on the highest parts of the city to warn or inform the inhabitants of coming danger. In the same way, the prophets were watchmen who relayed God's Word to the people and warned them against disobeying His law. The fact that God would hold each person responsible for his or her own behavior was the central part of the message of the prophets.

Ezekiel was a watchman who had been given the task of warning others that the wages of sin is death. If wicked men died in their sins without a word of warning from Ezekiel, God would hold Ezekiel accountable for their blood. But if Ezekiel did warn them and they did not turn from their wicked ways, then their blood was on their own hands.

In order to understand holiness, we must understand sin. But it is difficult to grasp the true nature of sin for several reasons. First, we have all sinned and lived in an environment conditioned by sin. We can't fully understand the difference between living in sin and living in righteousness because we have never experienced perfect holiness. Second, our awareness of what is sinful can easily grow dull with tolerance of and exposure to sin. Third, no living human has yet experienced the full weight of sin's consequence. Had Adam fully known what the consequences would be, he may not have chosen to sin. The same holds true for Adam's descendants, hence the need in the Old Testament for prophetic messages from God to warn them and admonish them to turn from their wicked ways.

The full responsibility for the presence and consequences of sin in the world falls upon man. Man sinned; therefore, man must die. Death itself silences every attempt to transfer, even partially, man's guilt to Satan in whom sin arose and by whom man was tempted. The devil did not make Adam sin. Adam was created in the image of God, and he had the capacity to choose as we all do.

God has authentic freedom and He cannot sin. Adam and Eve were created with a freedom that was morally qualified and whose continuance depended on refraining from sin. Freedom for humanity is the capacity not to sin and should not be understood as the morally unqualified faculty to do one or the other. Freedom does not simply lie in the capacity to choose as though it were unrelated to the consequences of the choice. "Everything that does not come from faith is sin" (Rom. 14:23).

Adam and Eve lost their freedom and their lives because of the lies they believed and the sin they willfully committed. Thankfully, neither sin nor death has the final word.

> For as in Adam all die, so in Christ all will be made alive (1 Cor. 15:22).

Thought for the day: *Do you sense your new life and freedom in Christ?*
Absolutely!

THE PERSONAL EFFECTS OF THE FALL

Genesis 4

What Adam and Eve lost in the Fall was their spiritual life and their knowledge of God, which was intrinsic to their relationship. They were now spiritually dead. Their souls were no longer in union with God, and it had an immediate effect upon their capacity to think, feel and choose. Lacking an intimate relationship with God, they had no true perception of reality. To illustrate, how does one hide from an omnipresent and omniscient God as Adam tried to do (see Gen. 3:7-8)? Adam and Eve's distorted perception of reality fits Paul's description of mental depravity of those who don't know God: "They are darkened in their understanding and separated from the life of God" (Eph. 4:18). "The man without the Spirit does not accept the things that come from the Spirit of God, for they are foolishness to him, and he cannot understand them, because they are spiritually discerned" (1 Cor. 2:14).

Adam and Eve were also emotionally distraught and became fearful and anxious. The first emotion expressed by Adam was fear (see Gen. 3:10). (To this day, anxiety disorders are the number one mental health problem in the world!) They were filled with guilt and shame. Before the Fall they were naked and unashamed. Now they wanted to hide and cover up. Just so, if we don't know of God's love and forgiveness, we will often mask our inner selves in fear that others may find out what is really going on inside us.

Adam and Eve's descendants were also emotionally plagued by anger and depression. Cain and Abel brought their offerings, but God wasn't pleased with Cain's.

> So Cain was very angry, and his face was downcast. Then the Lord said to Cain, "Why are you angry? Why is your face downcast? If you do what is right, will you not be accepted? But if you do not do what is right, sin is crouching at the door; it desires to have you, but you must master it" (Gen. 4:5-7).

In other words, you don't feel your way into good behavior. You behave your way into good feeling.

Before the Fall, Adam and Eve had only one bad choice. Afterward they were plagued by choices every moment of every day, just as we all are. Apart from God's presence in our lives, the greatest power we possess is the right and the responsibility to make choices. We can choose to pray or not to pray. We can choose to believe or not to believe.

Before the Fall, Adam and Eve had personal attributes that became glaring needs. First, they had a sense of belonging to God and each other. They were accepted, but now they were struggling with a sense of rejection. Ever since Adam and Eve's sin alienated them from God and introduced strife into human relationships, we have experienced a deep need to belong. We will never fully overcome the power of peer pressure and the fear of rejection until the legitimate need to belong is met in Christ. Second, their innocence, which was replaced by guilt and shame, precipitated an identity crisis and a search for significance. Third, their loss of spiritual life left them weak and helpless. Separated from God, they had no choice but to seek their identity in the natural order of this fallen world, find their purpose and meaning in life independent of God, and try to meet their own needs by their own strength and resources.

> The man without the Spirit does not accept the things that come from the Spirit of God, for they are foolishness to him, and he cannot understand them, because they are spiritually discerned (1 Cor. 2:14).

Thought for the day: *How has God opened your eyes to see and understand what you could not before?* I pray before I read God's Word - before I do this study + ask the Holy Spirit to reveal new things to me - to show me what God is saying. It is so amazing. I can read the same thing over + over again - and then I read it again + I understand it totally + I wonder why I didn't see it before. It is so awesome when God reveals Himself to me in a new way.

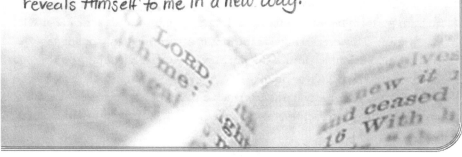

MEANINGLESS LIVING

Ecclesiastes 1

After Adam and Eve lost their relationship with God, they and all their descendants had little choice but to try to meet their own needs in a fallen world. Even though God's plan for redemption was slowly unfolding, they struggled to find purpose and meaning in life without an intimate relationship with God.

If it were humanly possible to adequately meet one's own personal needs, Solomon would have had the best chance. As king during the time Israel enjoyed its greatest prominence, he could do almost anything he wanted. He had accumulated immense personal wealth and military strength (see 1 Kings 10:14-29). He also had more God-given wisdom than any other mortal to interpret all his findings and observations (see 1 Kings 3:12). Yet with all these riches and power at his disposal, when Solomon sought to find purpose and meaning in life independent of God, he could only summarize his conclusions in the book of Ecclesiastes by writing, "Meaningless! Meaningless! . . . Utterly meaningless! Everything is meaningless" (Eccles. 1:2).

Having no relationship with God, humankind has likewise struggled with its personal identity and purpose for being here. Being a man or a woman may describe one's sexuality, but it doesn't define one's identity. As a result of the curse, women will bear their children in pain and men shall work by the sweat of their brow (see Gen. 3:16-19). Consequently, women have historically tried to find their identity in their role as mother, and men have tried to find their identity in their careers. But what if a woman never gets married or is unable to bear children? What if the man loses his job or the ability to work? Do those men and women lose their primary identity in Christ, or their God-given purpose for being here?

Trying to be our own "god" has driven people to improve their appearance, to perform better and to seek a higher social status as a means of self-verification. However, whatever pinnacle of self-identity we manage to achieve soon crumbles under the pressure of hostile rejection or criticism, introspection or guilt, fear or anxiety. Somebody will eventually look better, perform at a higher standard and reach a greater social status. Everything we have managed to achieve or possess by human effort we shall one day lose. We are incomplete without Christ, and nothing we can do by way of self-help will make us whole.

The natural person senses that something is missing but fails to fill the void by human effort. There is a longing for wholeness and a deep inner groaning as a result of its absence, but we are not alone in our groaning. "We know that the whole creation has been groaning as in the pains of childbirth right up to the present time" (Rom. 8:22). All of creation was affected by the Fall and longs for the day of redemption.

> For the creation was subjected to frustration, not by its own choice, but by the will of the one who subjected it, in hope that the creation itself will be liberated from its bondage to decay and brought into the glorious freedom of the children of God (Rom. 8:20-21).

Thought for the day: *How has your life taken on new meaning since you came to Christ?*

- Life has taken on even more meaning for me since Ancient Paths *+ the things I went through in 2007*. I believe God has a purpose for everything – I just need to be "awake" + aware of what He is doing.
- I now think about God + how I can please Him – I think about the consequences of what my sin may cause.
- I think of things in terms of ETERNITY not just the here + now. What I do here + now will effect eternity.
- I remember when Aunty Friedeborg was dying + we would go over + help – my thoughts were on how we live our lives + how we accumulate things throughout our lives, which is okay, but in the end, those things that were important before are no longer important. It made me realize how short life is + how those things will some day not matter. The things that really matter are:
  - my relationship with God
  - family + friends
  - things that will not burn in the fire.

THE GOSPEL

Philemon

The apostle Paul's letter to Philemon portrays his passion for the gospel and is a testimony of those who believe it. Paul had been imprisoned in Rome for preaching the gospel. Onesimus was someone who gladly received this "good news." His life was transformed. Onesimus was useless before Paul shared the gospel with him, but then he became useful to Paul and Philemon (see Philem. 11). Before he had been a slave, but afterward he was a brother in Christ. His identity and character had changed.

Paul prays that every believer would share this good news of salvation in Christ and that they would fully understand all that they have in Him (see v. 6). To understand the gospel, one has to understand the plight of fallen humanity, which the apostle Paul summarizes in Ephesians 2:1, "As for you, you were dead in your transgressions and sins, in which you used to live when you followed the ways of this world and of the ruler of the kingdom of the air."

To overcome the effects of the Fall, three primary issues have had to be resolved. First, the sin that separates humanity from a Holy God had to be atoned for. "For all have sinned and fall short of the glory of God, and are justified freely by his grace through the redemption that came by Christ Jesus" (Rom. 3:23-24). Jesus died for our sins in order that we may be forgiven.

Second, it is not enough that our sins are forgiven if we are still spiritually dead. To save people who have already died, you first have to cure the disease that caused them to die. Because of Christ's death on the cross, we are forgiven and because of His resurrection we have eternal life. "For the wages of sin is death, but the gift of God is eternal life in Christ Jesus our Lord" (Rom. 6:23). What Adam and Eve lost was spiritual life and Jesus came to give us life (see John 10:10). As children of God, we have received a glorious inheritance in Christ (see Eph. 1:18) and have become new creations in Christ (see 2 Cor. 5:17).

Paul wrote, "Now, brothers, I want to remind you of the gospel I preached to you . . . . If there is no resurrection of the dead, then not even Christ has been raised. And if Christ has not been raised, our preaching is useless and so is your faith" (1 Cor. 15:1,13-14). Because of the Resurrection we have new life in Christ, and eternal life is not something we get when we die physically. We receive eternal life the moment we are born again. "He who has the Son has life; he who does not have the Son of God does not have life" (1 John 5:12). Jesus said, "I am the resurrection and the life. He who believes in me will live, even though he dies" (John 11:25). In other words, those who believe in Jesus will continue to live spiritually even when they die physically.

Third, "The reason the Son of God appeared was to destroy the devil's work" (1 John 3:8). Jesus defeated the devil and disarmed him (see Col. 2:15), and we are no longer subject to him because every believer is now seated with Christ in the heavenly realms (see Eph. 2:6).

I am the resurrection and the life. He who believes in me will live, even though he dies (John 11:25).

Thought for the day: *Which has greater value, your physical life or your spiritual life?* -My spiritual life.
- My body will some day die but my spirit will continue to live for all eternity (which is so hard to comprehend) + where that will be, heaven or hell, will be determined by my decision to accept Christ as my Savior or deny Him as my Savior.
- This life - all the good things & all the bad things will end. It doesn't matter who I know, how much money I have, the possessions I have, in the end it won't matter. It won't get me to heaven. It won't come with me. It is only my relationship with Christ + what I do with my life here + now that will matter in the end. Everything else is a blessing from God.

FORGIVENESS OF SINS

Hebrews 9:11-28

After the Fall, God's plan of redemption began to unfold when He established the Abrahamic covenant (see Gen. 12:1-3). The descendants of Abraham would multiply and from his seed would come the Messiah who would be a blessing to all the peoples of the earth (see Matt. 1:1). Then God made a covenant with Israel through Moses (see Exod. 19:3). He gave them the Ten Commandments and set up a sacrificial system by which atonement could be made for sins. But a man-made sanctuary was only a copy (see Heb. 9:24), and the blood of bulls and goats (see v. 23) could not spiritually cleanse the sinner.

The sacrificial system set the stage for the coming of Jesus, who was the perfect sacrifice to atone for the sins of people for all times. "He did not enter by means of the blood of goats and calves; but he entered the Most Holy Place once for all by his own blood, having obtained eternal redemption" (Heb. 9:12). "For Christ did not enter a man-made sanctuary that was only a copy of the true one; he entered heaven itself" (Heb. 9:24).

> How much more, then, will the blood of Christ, who through the eternal Spirit offered himself unblemished to God, cleanse our conscience from acts that lead to death, so that we may serve the living God! For this reasons Christ is the mediator of a new covenant, that those who are called may receive the promised eternal inheritance—now that he has died as a ransom to set them free from the sins committed under the first covenant (Heb. 9:14-15).

Forgiveness of sins required a perfect sacrifice without spot or blemish, which no animal could qualify for, and neither can any person qualify on the basis of his or her own righteousness, because, "All of us have become like one who is unclean, and all our righteous acts are like filthy rags" (Isa. 64:6). Jesus was the perfect sacrifice for our sins. "God made him who had no sin to be sin for us, so that in him we might become the righteousness of God" (2 Cor. 5:21).

Christ has died "once for all" our sins (Heb. 9:12,26; see also Rom. 6:10). Our past, present and future sins have been forgiven. There will be no other sacrifice for our sins and none is needed. It is faulty logic to think, *I know that Christ has died for the sins that I have already committed, but what about the sins I commit in the future.* When Christ died once for all your sins, how many of your sins were future? All of them! Nor is it correct to think that our sins are forgiven because we confessed them. Our sins are forgiven because Christ died for them. We confess our sins in order to walk in the light as He is in the light (see 1 John 1:5-9) and to live in moral agreement with God. Knowing that our sins are forgiven is not a license to continue sinning; rather, it is a gracious means by which we can approach God. Our sin no longer separates us from God: "Therefore, brothers, since we have confidence to enter the Most Holy Place by the blood of Jesus, let us draw near to God with a sincere heart in full assurance of faith, having our hearts sprinkled to cleanse us" (Heb. 10:19,22).

> How much more, then, will the blood of Christ, who through the eternal Spirit offered himself unblemished to God, cleanse our conscience from acts that lead to death, so that we may serve the living God! (Heb. 9:14).

Thought for the day: *How should the truth that Christians are forgiven affect how they live?* – I think we should be living victorious lives, although I don't always feel that way.
– I should be living a life of gratitude instead of a life of ingratitude + ungreatfulness.
– I should want to share this with others so they also may understand + accept Jesus' sacrifice for us.
– I should never live a life where I do something I know is sin because I know, Jesus will forgive me anyways – that's not fully understanding His sacrifice for us + I believe it is kind of mocking Him.

NEW LIFE IN CHRIST

John 6:25-59

The blood of Jesus Christ has cleansed us from all our sins, but the gospel would not be complete without Jesus also being for us "the bread of life" (John 6:35,48; see also v. 51). Bread has been referred to as the "staff of life." Under the Law, God sustained the Israelites in the wilderness by providing them with a daily portion of manna, or "bread from heaven" (Exod. 16:4). Now Jesus claims to be the "bread of life." Most of those who heard this claim immediately protested, because they identified Him as only the son of Joseph (see John 6:42), not even to be compared with Moses.

Jesus countered by saying that Moses didn't give the Israelites the bread. It came from heaven; and although it did sustain their physical lives in the wilderness, it could not give them eternal/spiritual life. Like the manna, Jesus came from heaven, but unlike the manna that was temporal, the life of Jesus is eternal.

> "For the bread of God is he who comes down from heaven and gives life to the world." Then Jesus declared, "I am the bread of life. He who comes to me will never go hungry, and he who believes in me will never be thirsty. I tell you the truth, he who believes has everlasting life" (vv. 33,35,47).

What Adam and Eve lost was life and Jesus came to give us life (see John 10:10).

But how can we receive that gift? The answer Jesus gives to Nicodemus, a member of the Jewish ruling council, is meant for us as well. Knowing full well what was in Nicodemus's heart, Jesus replied, "I tell you the truth, no one can see the kingdom of God unless he is born again" (John 3:3). We were all born physically alive, but in order to have eternal/spiritual life we must be "born again," and the only way to do that is by believing in Jesus and by trusting in the works of Christ to give us eternal life. "The work of God is this: To believe in the one he has sent" (John 6:29). "For it is by grace you have been saved, through faith—and this not from yourselves, it is the gift of God—not by works, so that no one can boast" (Eph. 2:8-9).

Always keep in mind that eternal life is not something we get when we physically die. We are eternally and spiritually alive the moment we are born again. If you we not born again before we physically die, all we have to look forward to is an eternity without Christ. Jesus is our life (see Col. 3:4). Jesus is the way, the truth and the *life* (see John 14:6). He is the resurrection and the *life* (see John 11:25). If we have been born again, our names are written in the book of *life* (see Phil. 4:3; Rev. 20:15).

To be spiritually alive means that our souls are in union with God. It means that we are "in Christ," and that Christ is in us. The life of Christ is not just some historical account of the 33 years that He appeared in the flesh. The life of Christ is what every born again believer has right now within them. It not only means that we are again united with God, but we also have the power of His presence to live a righteous life.

> God has chosen to make known among the Gentiles the glorious riches of this mystery, which is Christ in you, the hope of glory (Col. 1:27).

Thought for the day: *Would you live differently if you fully understood that Christ is always present within you?*

- That's just it! Who can fully understand with our finite minds.
- I try to live my life pleasing to God but I now can see that I need to also look at it as Christ is always present within me. That should make us all stop & think about what we say, do, think, watch, etc.

* Lord God, I ask that You make us more aware of this. That we will not grieve the Holy Spirit by forgetting that Christ lives in us. I pray for this for Scott, Jenny & Francesco, Rob & I. Oh Lord God, make us aware of this at all times. Let it sink in deep.

* I thank You Father, Son & Holy Spirit. You are so much more than I can understand.

New Identity in Christ

John 1:1-14

There had been no new revelation from heaven for over 400 years when "the Word became flesh and made his dwelling among us. We have seen his glory, the glory of the One and Only, who came from the Father, full of grace and truth" (v. 14). To the Greek philosophers, the "word" (*logos*) was the ultimate of intellectual pursuit, the rational principal that governs the universe. God was now revealing that this highest of philosophical notions had become incarnate, that is, had taken on a human form. Jesus not only spoke the truth, He also made it clear that He is the truth and in Him there is no darkness at all (see 1 John 1:5). "In him was life, and that life was the light of men" (John 1:4). Notice that light does not produce life, rather the eternal life of God is the light of the world.

The first Adam was born both physically and spiritually alive, but he sinned and died spiritually. This last Adam was born of a virgin and was also physically and spiritually alive. Unlike the first Adam, He never sinned, even though He was tempted in every way. By His life He accomplished two tasks. First, He gave us an example to follow in His steps. He showed us how a spiritually alive person should live on planet earth. What He modeled was a life totally dependent upon His heavenly Father. He said, "By myself I can do nothing" (John 5:30); "I live because of the Father" (John 6:57); "I came from God and now am here. I have not come on my own; but he sent me" (John 8:42); "The words I say to you are not just my own. Rather, it is the Father, living in me, who is doing his work" (John 14:10); "Now they know that everything you have given me comes from you" (John 17:7).

Second, Jesus came that we might have life, and receiving that life by faith brings us a completely new identity. "Yet to all who received him, to those who believed in his name, he gave the right to become children of God—children born not of natural descent, nor of human decision or a husband's will, but born of God" (John 1:12). Further, Paul tells us, "The Spirit himself testifies with our spirit that we are God's children" (Rom. 8:16). Believers are not in the process of becoming children of God; rather, they are children of God who are in the process of becoming like Christ. Who we are determines what we do, and God wants us to know that we are His children.

How great is the love the Father has lavished on us, that we should be called children of God! And that is what we are! The reason the world does not know us is that it did not know him. Dear friends, now we are children of God, and what we will be has not yet been made known. But we know that when he appears, we shall be like him, for we shall see him as he is. Everyone who has this hope in him purifies himself, just as he is pure (1 John 3:1-3).

Christ Jesus is the only one who can meet all our needs, and the "being" needs are those most wonderfully met in our relationship with God. In Christ we have a new life, a new identity, acceptance, security and significance (see the table "In Christ" on p. 46).

And my God will meet all your needs according to his glorious riches in Christ Jesus (Phil. 4:19).

Thought for the day: *How has Christ met all your needs?*

- He has given me a new life in Him.
- He has given me hope
- He has given me purpose
- He has given me a future

- Unfortunately I let life get in the way & I lose all sight of this. I need to constantly keep my eyes on Him & remember these things.

- When I read this today I got excited. What we have in Christ is amazing. And what really excites me is that when He appears we shall be like Him - for we shall see Him.

In Christ

I Am Accepted

John 1:12	I am God's child.
John 15:15	I am Christ's friend.
Rom. 5:1	I have been justified.
1 Cor. 6:17	I am united with the Lord and one with Him in spirit.
1 Cor. 6:20	I have been bought with a price—I belong to God.
1 Cor. 12:27	I am a member of Christ's body.
Eph. 1:1	I am a saint.
Eph. 1:5	I have been adopted as God's child.
Eph. 2:18	I have direct access to God through the Holy Spirit.
Col. 1:14	I have been redeemed and forgiven of all my sins.
Col. 2:10	I am complete in Christ.

I Am Secure

Rom. 8:1-2	I am free from condemnation.
Rom. 8:28	I am assured that all things work together for good.
Rom. 8:31f	I am free from any condemning charges against me.
Rom. 8:35f	I cannot be separated from the love of God.
2 Cor. 1:21	I have been established, anointed and sealed by God.
Col. 3:3	I am hidden with Christ in God.
Phil. 1:6	I am confident that the good work that God has begun in me will be perfected.
Phil. 3:20	I am a citizen of heaven.
2 Tim. 1:7	I have not been given a spirit of fear, but of power, love and a sound mind.
Heb. 4:16	I can find grace and mercy in time of need.
1 John 5:18	I am born of God and the evil one cannot touch me.

I am significant in Christ

Matt. 5:13	I am the salt and light of the earth.
John 15:1,5	I am a branch of the true vine, a channel of His life.
John 15:16	I have been chosen and appointed to bear fruit.
Acts 1:8	I am a personal witness of Christ's.
1 Cor. 3:16	I am God's temple.
2 Cor. 5:17f	I am a minister of reconciliation.
2 Cor. 6:1	I am God's coworker.
Eph. 2:6	I am seated with Christ in the heavenly realm.
Eph. 2:10	I am God's workmanship.
Eph. 3:12	I may approach God with freedom and confidence.
Phil. 4:13	I can do all things through Christ who strengthens me.

THE DEFEAT OF SATAN

1 John 3:7-8

The fact that Christ died for our sins and gave us eternal life is good news, but the gospel would not be complete if Jesus had not defeated the devil. "The reason the Son of God appeared was to destroy the devil's work" (v. 8). After God cursed Satan, He promised that the Messiah would come through the seed of the woman and crush Satan's head (see Gen. 3:14-15). Satan tried to thwart God's plan by destroying the bloodline from which the Messiah would come. So he influenced Cain, "who belonged to the evil one" (1 John 3:12), to kill Abel. But God granted Eve another child named Seth (see Gen. 4:25), which means "restitution," and the Messianic line descends from him. Satan would later try to eliminate Moses and Jesus by having all children of their respective ages in the vicinity killed, but God provided a way for them to be spared.

John calls Satan the "evil one" (1 John 2:13-14; 3:12; 5:18-19), and credits him for being the instigator of human sin and depravity. "He who does what is sinful is of the devil, because the devil has been sinning from the beginning" (v. 8). The term "from the beginning" refers to Satan's rebellion against God before the fall of Adam and Eve (see also John 8:44). According to John, those who continue to sin belong to the devil (see 1 John 3:8,12), and are his children (see 1 John 3:10). Even though the whole world is under the control of the evil one, we know that we are children of God (see 1 John 4:1-4) and Satan cannot touch us (see 1 John 5:18-19).

John categorizes believers as little children, fathers of the faith and young men (see 1 John 2:12-14). Little children have a knowledge of who their heavenly Father is and their sins are forgiven. In other words, they have overcome the penalty of sin by the blood of the Lord Jesus Christ. The fathers of the faith have a much deeper and experiential knowledge of God. Young men are those who have overcome the evil one. In other words, they have learned to overcome the deceptive power of sin.

Satan has been defeated, but Peter warns, "Be self-controlled and alert. Your enemy the devil prowls around like a roaring lion looking for someone to devour" (1 Pet. 5:8). He is like a deadly wasp, but true believers don't belong to him and they know that his stinger has been removed. For their protection, John admonishes the children of God to walk in the light (see

1 John 1:7), confess their sins (see 1 John 1:9), obey God's Word (see 1 John 2:5) and love one another (see 1 John 4:7).

John also warns us not to love the world or anything in it (see 1 John 2:15). The same channels of temptation that deceived Eve and caused Adam to sin are the same ones that Satan used to tempt Jesus—the same ones which he is now using against the children of God (see v. 16). We must also be aware that there will be many antichrists in the world (see v. 18). Therefore we must not "believe every spirit, but test the spirits to see whether they are from God" (1 John 4:1).

The battle for the souls of mankind will continue until the Lord returns, but we have the assurance of eternal life (see 1 John 5:13) and answered prayer (see v. 15). "We know also that the Son of God has come and has given us understanding, so that we may know him who is true. And we are in him who is true—even in his Son Jesus Christ. He is the true God and eternal life" (v. 20).

The reason the Son of God appeared was to destroy the devil's work (1 John 3:8).

Thought for the day: *How should Satan's defeat affect the battle between good and evil?* The way Satan's defeat should affect the battle between good & evil would be for Christians to have the power to defeat Satan in our lives. We should be standing strong & recognizing Satan's attempts to make us fall, but I think that most of us allow Satan to defeat us instead of us defeating Satan. I often think we, including myself, are beaten down Christians. Instead of turning to God's truths we instead allow Satan's lies to take control of us. FORGIVE OF LORD GOD! FORGIVE ME!! How many times do I turn to my own strength instead of God's?! And how many times do I fail because of it! Oh how foolish I am. Thank You Jesus for DEFEATING SATAN! Thank You that we can also DEFEAT him! LORD GOD, open our eyes to his deceptions & help us (ME) to turn to Your TRUTH & Your STRENGTH for triumphing over him. Amen.

SOUND DOCTRINE

2 Timothy 3:10-17

There will be many hardships on the journey from Pentecost to the second coming of Christ for the children of God. "In fact, everyone who wants to live a godly life in Christ Jesus will be persecuted, while evil men and impostors will go from bad to worse, deceiving and being deceived" (vv. 12-13). Just before Jesus departed this earth to be with the Father, He prayed for all the believers whom He will be leaving behind: "My prayer is not that you take them out of the world but that you protect them from the evil one. They are not of the world, even as I am not of it. Sanctify them by the truth; your word is truth" (John 17:15-17). God's Word is the only infallible truth that can set us free, serve as the basis for our sanctification and protect us from deception.

Using himself as an example, Paul urges every believer to have personal knowledge of "the holy Scriptures, which are able to make you wise for salvation through faith in Jesus Christ. All Scripture is God-breathed and is useful for teaching, rebuking, correcting and training in righteousness, so that the man of God may be thoroughly equipped for every good work" (2 Tim. 3:16-17). "God breathed" means inspired by God. The written word of God was given through men superintended by the Holy Spirit so that their writings were without error.

Above all, you must understand that no prophecy of Scripture came about by the prophet's own interpretation. For prophecy never had its origin in the will of man, but men spoke from God as they were carried along by the Holy Spirit (2 Pet. 1:20-21).

God's Word is first profitable for teaching (*didache*). The emphasis of "didache" is on the content and authority of what is taught rather than the act of teaching. "Didache" has been translated as doctrine. Having "sound doctrine" relates primarily to ethical instruction (see 1 Tim. 1:9-20), and it is a requirement for those who wish to mature in Christ. "He must hold firmly to the trustworthy message as it has been taught, so that he can encourage others by sound doctrine and refute those who oppose it" (Titus 1:9).

When correctly taught and appropriated, the Word of God will rebuke, correct, train us to live righteously and thoroughly equip us for every good work. Sin will keep us from God's Word, but God's Word will keep us from sinning. His Word will rebuke us when we are wrong and correct us so we don't do it again, with the purpose of enabling us to live righteously. God never intended His Word to be intellectually discussed without appropriation, nor does He consider our walk with Him to be an intellectual exercise: "For the word of God is living and active. Sharper than any double-edged sword, it penetrates even to dividing soul and spirit, joints and marrow; it judges the thoughts and attitudes of the heart" (Heb. 4:12).

Sound doctrine and righteous living are prerequisites for every good work. The Word of God emphasizes being before doing, character before career and maturity before ministry. We can't be the people God created us to be unless His Word penetrates our hearts and transforms our lives. "For we are God's workmanship, created in Christ Jesus to do good works, which God prepared in advance for us to do" (Eph. 2:10).

> All Scripture is God-breathed and is useful for teaching, rebuking, correcting and training in righteousness, so that the man of God may be thoroughly equipped for every good work (2 Tim. 3:16-17).

Thought for the day: *What happens in our lives if the Word of God is only discussed or acknowledged and not personally appropriated?*

What happens is we take on our own view point or someone elses rather than Gods. We can be persuaded to believe anything if we don't have sound doctrine. Look at the church leaders who have been taken astray + who have lead others astray by their own beliefs or by not accepting God's Word to be unchanging. They've added in their own doctrine. I think of the United Church + others. IF YOU DON'T HAVE GOD'S WORD IN YOUR HEART + SOUND DOCTRINE - THAN IT IS EASY TO BELIEVE ANYTHING.

Thank You LORD GOD FOR YOUR WORD. GIVE ME A HUNGER FOR YOUR WORD - FOR SOUND DOCTRINE. THANK YOU FOR A CHURCH WHO LOOKS TO YOUR WORD FOR TRUTH!

JUSTIFICATION

Romans 3

In Romans 3, Paul answers the question, *How is a sinful person justified before a holy God?* "Justification" is a judicial term; however, the biblical idea of being justified is different from the modern use of the term. Human courts of justice may pronounce a person innocent if it were determined that the person's behavior was consistent with manmade laws. We, on the other hand, are accountable to God, and "No one will be declared righteous in his sight by observing the law; rather, through the law we become conscious of sin" (v. 20). How then do we obtain a favorable judgment or acquittal?

Paul clearly teaches that no human being will be justified in God's sight by the works of the law (see vv. 10,19-20,23). Apart from Christ, we are all sinful and cannot do sufficient good works to gain acquittal. We cannot render judgment on ourselves because we are always guilty, and a just God cannot render us just by our works. This is the threefold dilemma of all humanity, and the atonement of Christ is the answer.

The word "justification" is derived from two Latin words, *justus* and the verb *facere*, which together mean "to make righteous" or "to do righteousness." We are justified by the righteousness of God, not by our righteousness. "This righteousness from God comes through faith in Jesus Christ to all who believe. For we maintain that a man is justified by faith apart from observing the law" (vv. 22,28).

Justification does not mean that God overlooks our sin or fails to judge us as sinners. For us to assert that it does is to deny the integrity of God and destroy the concept of justification. God's justice and holiness demands payment for sin. Jesus paid the penalty in full at the Cross. By making Christ a substitute for man, God, God preserves His own justice and achieves salvation for the sinner (see v. 26). In justification, God's attributes of justice and love are both satisfied and given full meaning.

The concept of atonement is closely related to the issue of justification. Atonement signifies a harmonious relationship or that which brings one about. In the Old Testament, the fundamental idea of atonement was to wipe away one's sin, making possible a reconciliation with God. Christ's atonement covered, or took away, the sins of all humankind: "The death he died, he died to sin once for all" (Rom. 6:10). It is important to note here that the doctrine of justification does not mean universal salvation, but rather universal grace and forgiveness. "Justification" is a legal term for the forgiveness of sins. God pronounced that all can be forgiven in Christ, but not everyone will receive this free gift of salvation and some may never hear of it (see Rom. 10:14-17). Jesus said, "I told you that you would die in your sins; if you do not believe that I am the one I claim to be, you will indeed die in your sins" (John 8:24).

Every believer is justified before God and forgiven the moment they put their faith in Him. "Therefore, since we have been justified through faith, we have peace with God through our Lord Jesus Christ, through whom we have gained access by faith into this grace in which we now stand." (Rom. 5:1). In justification, we are joined together with God through faith in Jesus Christ. We are clothed in His righteousness and thereby stand justified before God. "Therefore, there is now no condemnation for those who are in Christ Jesus" (Rom. 8:1).

Therefore, since we have been justified through faith, we have peace with God through our Lord Jesus Christ, through whom we have gained access by faith into this grace in which we now stand (Rom. 5:1).

Thought for the day: *What does it mean to you that you have access to Almighty God?*

- It's overwhelming to know that we have access to God after reading this. I don't think about it. After reading this I realize how much I don't deserve this. I still sin - I still do things displeasing to God - sometimes purposely (which is downright rebellion), but mostly unknowingly.
- I also realize that I try to please God & have Him accept me by my "good" works but I know it is not by my good works but by my faith in Jesus Christ. The "good works" come from my faith which produces fruit, not because I do good, but by my faith.
- Before Ancient Paths I thought God would love me more if I did "good" things for Him. I couldn't get past the do's + don'ts of my growing up in the church. I was always trying to do good because I could not understand God's unconditional love for me.

Thank You Heavenly Father that it is not by what I do but by the sacrifice of Jesus Christ that gives me a relationship with You!

SANCTIFICATION

1 Thessalonians 4:1-12

In justification, God declares the believer righteous because of the righteousness of Christ, which is accounted to the believer. Justification is the act of a judge. Through justification, the condemnation that sinners deserve because of their guilt is removed. Sanctification is more the act of a priest. Through sanctification, the pollution of sin is removed from the sinner's life. The doctrine of sanctification is a process that begins at our new birth in Christ and is completed in heaven, whereas justification has fully happened at our new birth and is always referred to in the past tense for believers.

Paul says, "It is God's will that you should be sanctified" (1 Thess. 4:3). God will guide us in career choices and decision making, but the primary will of God is that we conform to His image, which is the process of sanctification. Sanctification is the gracious work of God by which He progressively delivers us—justified believers—from the pollution of sin, transforms our character to be like His and enables us to bear fruit to the glory of God. We are called to be holy just as God is holy (see 1 Pet. 1:15). To be sanctified means we are to be set apart from sin and sinful behavior, and to be righteous and live a righteous life.

Sanctification, like salvation, can be a difficult doctrine to understand unless we know that both are presented in Scripture as past, present and future verb tenses. We have been saved (see Eph. 2:4-5,8; 2 Tim. 1:8-9); we are being saved (see 1 Cor. 1:18; 2 Cor. 2:15); and someday we shall be fully saved from the wrath that is to come (see Rom. 5:9-10; Heb. 1:13-14). Even though we haven't experienced all that salvation will bring, God wants us to have the assurance of salvation (see 1 John 5:13), and the presence of the Holy Spirit in our lives is our guarantee. "Having believed, you were marked in him with a seal, the promised Holy Spirit, who is a deposit guaranteeing our inheritance until the redemption of those who are God's possession—to the praise of his glory" (Eph. 1:14).

In a similar fashion, we have been sanctified (see Acts 20:32; 1 Cor. 1:2; 6:19); we are being sanctified (see Rom. 6:22; 2 Cor. 7:1; Heb. 12:14); and someday we shall be fully sanctified in heaven (see Eph. 5:25-27; 1 Thess. 3:12-13; 5:23-24). When sanctification is referred to in the past tense, it has been commonly called positional sanctification. Present-tense uses are referred to as progressive sanctification.

It is counterproductive to our growth process to emphasize one aspect of sanctification over another. If we consider sanctification only in the past tense, then sanctification is a completed action and it could lead some to think they are perfectly righteous when they are not.

Positional sanctification is the basis for progressive sanctification. We are not trying to become children of God—we are children of God who are becoming like Christ. Progressive sanctification is the process of working out our salvation (see Phil. 2:12) and making real in our experience our new life in Christ. In this passage in First Thessalonians, Paul shows how our sanctification should be worked out in the context of relating to others.

> For God did not call us to be impure, but to live a holy life (1 Thess. 4:7).

Thought for the day: *In what way are you now sanctified (holy)?*

- living a godly life - to be holy + living my life pleasing to Him.
- being aware of + caring about what I am doing to please or displease God.
- living a life with heaven in mind
- growing in God + producing fruit
- Seeing the fruit of the Spirit develop in me:
  - Love
  - Joy
  - peace
  - patience
  - kindness
  - goodness
  - long suffering
  - self control

THINK ABOUT IT!

Through justification the condemnation that I a sinner deserves because of my guilt is removed.

POSITIONAL SANCTIFICATION

Acts 26:18

Paul brings out the truth of positional sanctification when he greets the church in Corinth: "To the church of God in Corinth, to those sanctified in Christ Jesus and called to be holy" (1 Cor. 1:2). In making a contrast between the sanctified and those who would not inherit the kingdom of God, Paul says, "But you were washed, you were sanctified, you were justified in the name of the Lord Jesus Christ and by the Spirit of our God" (1 Cor. 6:11). The status of those who have been sanctified is also prominent in the book of Hebrews, in which Jesus is portrayed as the great High Priest. Through His priestly ministry, "We have been made holy through the sacrifice of the body of Jesus Christ once for all" (Heb. 10:10; see also Heb. 10:29; 13:12).

As an apostle and missionary to the Gentiles, Paul was commissioned by God "to open their eyes and turn them from darkness to light, and from the power of Satan to God, so that they may receive forgiveness of sins and a place among those who are sanctified by faith in [God]" (Acts 26:18). Every believer has been forgiven and rescued from the dominion of darkness and brought into the kingdom of God (see Col. 1:13). Safely in the hands of their heavenly Father, sinners become saints, failures become victories, and the common is made holy.

Just as the "past tense" reality of salvation is the basis for the "present tense" working out of our salvation, so also is our position in Christ the basis for our growth in Christ. At the moment of our salvation, we are set apart, or separated, unto God and thus participate in God's holiness. Notice how Peter shows this cause-and-effect relationship:

His divine power has given [past tense] us everything we need for life and godliness through our knowledge of him who called us by his own glory and goodness. Through these he has given [past tense] us his very great and precious promises, so that through them you may participate in the divine nature and escape the corruption in the world caused by evil desires (2 Pet. 1:3-4).

Positional sanctification does not mean that as believers we are sinless and perfect. Our positional holiness is based on the fact that we are new creations in Christ (see 2 Cor. 5:17). By faith we are joined to Christ and we share in all that Christ is, including His holiness. "It is because of him that you are in Christ Jesus, who has become for us wisdom from God—that is our righteousness, holiness and redemption" (1 Cor. 1:30). Positional sanctification means that we are spiritually alive in Christ. We have been brought into fellowship with a holy God. Scripture says that only those who are clean and holy can enter His presence. As sinners we couldn't do that. But by faith in Christ, who sacrificed Himself to cleanse us of all our sins, we are joined to Him and have been invited into the "holy of holies" of heaven to have fellowship with God. It is from this lofty position in Christ that we grow in grace.

> To open their eyes and turn them from darkness to light, and from the power of Satan to God, so that they may receive forgiveness of sins and a place among those who are sanctified by faith in [God] (Acts 26:18).

Thought for the day: *What personal value do you sense in being positionally sanctified?*

Right now all I can think of is how unworthy I am. I think of Isaiah who realizes that he is unclean + unworthy when he stood before God. Wow! THIS IS WHAT I'VE BEEN ASKING GOD TO SHOW ME. I DIDN'T FEEL I WAS UNDERSTANDING WHAT CHRIST'S DEATH REALLY MEANS + TODAY HE OPENED MY EYES + ANSWERED MY PRAYER. WHAT AN UNDESERVED TREASURE WE HAVE! THANK YOU GOD! THANK YOU JESUS! THANK YOU HOLY SPIRIT FOR OPENING MY EYES!

PROGRESSIVE SANCTIFICATION

1 Peter 1

God performed a gracious work when He called us out of darkness into His marvelous light and granted us the status of holiness by virtue of our union with Christ. He did this so that we can be holy as He is holy (see 1 Pet. 1:15-16). The process of growing from carnality to Christlikeness is commonly called progressive sanctification. Paul says, "But now that you have been set free from sin and have become slaves to God, the benefit you reap leads to holiness, and the result is eternal life" (Rom. 6:22). The *Westminster Catechism* defines sanctification as, "The work of God's free grace, whereby we are renewed in the whole man after the image of God and are enabled more and more to die unto sin and live unto righteousness."

Although the Bible speaks of "past tense," or positional, sanctification more frequently than "present tense," or progressive sanctification, the concept of progressively being made holy is a dominant theme in the New Testament. Terms like "growth," "renewing," "edification," "building up," "transformation," "purification" and "renewing" are all related: they refer to the process of conforming to the image of God.

Paul shows the process of conforming to the image of God in Colossians 2:6-7, "So then, just as you received Christ Jesus as Lord, continue to live in him, rooted and built up in him, strengthened in the faith as you were taught, and overflowing with thankfulness." The primary agent of our sanctification is God Himself "through the sanctifying work of the Spirit" (1 Pet. 1:2). We have to first be rooted "in Christ," which refers to our positional sanctification, before we can be built up "in Him," which is progressive sanctification. Terms like "in Christ," "in Him" and "in the beloved" are among the most repeated prepositional phrases in the New Testament. These terms convey that children of God are spiritually alive and their souls are in union with Christ, who is our life. If there is no spiritual life, then we cannot grow spiritually.

We are also agents of our own sanctification.

Therefore, prepare your minds for action; be self-controlled; set your hope fully on the grace to be given you when Christ is revealed. As obedient children, do not conform to the evil desires you had when you lived in ignorance (1 Pet. 1:13-14).

However, as believers we must not fall into the Galatian heresy (see Gal. 3:1-5). We have not received the Holy Spirit by the works of the Law. Our salvation has come by way of faith and so does our sanctification. Paul asks, "After beginning with the Spirit, are you now trying to attain your goal by human effort?" (Gal. 3:3). We are saved by faith, and we are sanctified by faith in God through the power of the Holy Spirit. That is why Jesus prayed, "Sanctify them by the truth; your word is truth" (John 17:17). Scripture presents progressive sanctification as a challenge to us as believers. The world, the flesh and the devil oppose the will of God and therefore are enemies of our sanctification. Therefore, "Let us purify ourselves from everything that contaminates body and spirit, perfecting holiness out of reverence for God" (2 Cor. 7:1), and let us "Make every effort to live in peace with all men and to be holy; without holiness no one will see the Lord" (Heb. 12:14).[1]

Therefore, prepare your minds for action; be self-controlled; set your hope fully on the grace to be given you when Jesus Christ is revealed (1 Pet. 1:13).

Thought for the day: *What is the Galatian heresy?*

[Handwritten note:] I think the Galatian heresy is putting their faith in the work of the Law + by keeping the law they will get to heaven. They try by their human efforts rather than their faith in God. It doesn't work! God didn't plan it that way. WHEREAS, WE ARE SANCTIFIED BY FAITH IN GOD THROUGH THE POWER OF THE HOLY SPIRIT.

[Margin note:] for years + years I did this. How foolish. It does not work. It is futile + did not give me peace or hope. Only FEAR + Worry of not being good enough

CONFORMING TO THE IMAGE OF GOD

Colossians 1:9-14

It is God's will for our lives that we conform to His image (see 1 Thess. 4:3). Growing in Christ would not even be possible if God had not "qualified [us] to share in the inheritance of the saints in the kingdom of light. For he has rescued us from the dominion of darkness and brought us into the kingdom of the Son he loves, in whom we have redemption, the forgiveness of sins" (Col. 1:12-14).

The growth process is like a spiral that is ever reaching toward heaven. Paul explains this cycle of growth in verses 9-12.

The Cycle of Growth

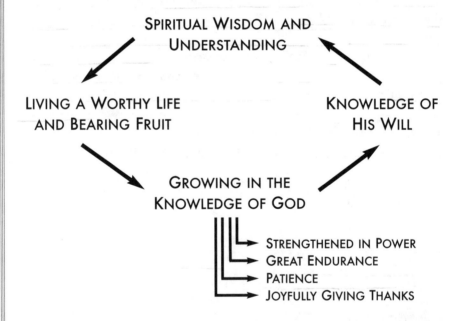

SPIRITUAL WISDOM AND UNDERSTANDING

LIVING A WORTHY LIFE AND BEARING FRUIT

KNOWLEDGE OF HIS WILL

GROWING IN THE KNOWLEDGE OF GOD

- STRENGTHENED IN POWER
- GREAT ENDURANCE
- PATIENCE
- JOYFULLY GIVING THANKS

It begins with a knowledge of God's will, which we find in His Word. His truth must enter our hearts in order for us to understand how it applies to life in all wisdom and understanding. The cycle isn't complete, however, until we choose to *live* according to what we have chosen to *believe*. We exercise our will when we choose to walk by faith and submit to God through humble obedience. When we step out in faith, we grow in the knowledge of God, and the cycle comes full circle. We will receive greater knowledge when we act upon what we already know to be true. The spin-offs of this growth cycle are increased spiritual strength, endurance, patience, joy and thankfulness, which become increasingly evident in our character.

We can block the process of growth at any one of the four points in the diagram. At the first stage, we can stop the growth process if we read the Bible as an academic exercise but never seek to apply it to our lives. When we harden our hearts we have intellectual knowledge but no spiritual wisdom or personal understanding of how God's Word applies to our lives.

At the second stage, we have allowed God's Word to penetrate our hearts and consequently convict us of sin, giving us discernment and direction for life. But the growth process could still be stymied if we never actually repented, acted upon our discernment or stepped out in faith.

At the third stage, we grow and bear fruit because we are living by faith according to what God says is true in the power of the Holy Spirit. Maturity gained through living causes us to understand the Word of God in a way that we didn't before. If we fail to live by faith, however, we will not bear fruit.

Finally, at the fourth stage, we can stop the process of growth by failing to come back to His Word. One of the great dangers of successfully bearing fruit or experiencing victory is to rest on our laurels, thinking that we have arrived. That is why Paul's words in Philippians 3:12-14 are so helpful: "Not that I have already obtained all this, or have already been made perfect, but I press on to take hold of that for which Christ Jesus took hold of me. Brothers, I do not consider myself yet to have taken hold of it. But one thing I do: Forgetting what is behind and straining toward what is ahead, I press on toward the goal to win the prize for which God has called me heavenward in Christ Jesus."

And we pray this in order that you may live a life worthy of the Lord and may please him in every way: bearing fruit in every good work, growing in the knowledge of God (Col. 1:10).

Thought for the day: *Where are you most likely to break the Colossians Cycle?*

Stage 3! Often my faith is weak. I worry about things I have no control of + lose faith + trust in God because of it. But God is working on that + my faith is getting stronger but sometimes I can worry so much that I get into a full panic. I hate it when I do this. But thank God I recognize it + can give it to Him when I get this way.

CONFESSION

1 John 1:1-11

The word "confess" (*homolegeo*) literally means "to speak the same thing" (*homos*, same, and *lego*, to speak) or "to agree with." It is the opposite of denial, whether spoken or unspoken. It can mean a public confession of faith as in Matthew 10:32, "Whoever acknowledges [confesses] me before men, I will also acknowledge [confess] him before my Father in heaven." In Romans 15:9, it is used as a praise to God, "Therefore I will praise [confess] you among the Gentiles." It can also mean the acknowledgment of sin (see 1 John 1:9).

John's concern is that we have fellowship with God and one another (see 1 John 1:2-4), but we cannot have fellowship with God and live in denial or cover up our sin. Since "God is light; in him there is no darkness at all" (v. 5), believers must also walk in the light. Walking in the light does not mean moral perfection, because, "If we claim to be without sin, we deceive ourselves" (v. 8). Walking in the light is very similar in concept to confession. It means to live in moral agreement with God. Walking in the light is to confess sin, and walking in the darkness is to deny sin.

Jesus said, "Light has come into the world, but men loved darkness instead of light because their deeds were evil. Everyone who does evil hates the light, and will not come into the light for fear that his deeds will be exposed" (John 3:19-20). Sin hinders the relationship believers have with God and others. Acknowledging, or confessing, the truth is the first step in any recovery program. We can walk in the light because we have already been forgiven and accepted by God, and we will have fellowship with one another if we walk in the light (see 1 John 1:7). If we walk in the light and speak the truth in love, God has made provision to cleanse us from whatever sin would otherwise mar our fellowship with Him and each other (see also Eph. 4:15,25).

"If we confess our sins, he is faithful and just and will forgive us our sins and purify us from all unrighteousness" (1 John 1:9). As believers, our sins are not forgiven because we confess them; our sins are forgiven because "the blood of Jesus, his Son, purifies us from all sin" (v. 7). The Cross is the only moral ground on which God can forgive us. Conversely, as believers, we are not unforgiven if we fail to confess all known sin. He is faithful to for-

[handwritten margin note:] I need to put more emphasis on this! It's not just my confession but that THE BLOOD OF JESUS PURIFIES US FROM ALL SIN.

give us because He has promised to do so, and He is just because His Son died for our sins.

"If we claim we have not sinned, we make him out to be a liar and his word has no place in our lives" (v. 10). Those who claim that they have never sinned probably haven't come to Christ in the first place, because they don't see that they have any need of salvation or a Savior. But as far as believers are concerned, John wants them to walk in the light and live a confessional life whereby God not only removes the guilt of sin (forgives) but also the stain of sin (cleanses). James, too, urges us to confess our sins one to another (see Jas. 5:16) in order to be healed. Confession brings healing to the soul and provides a breakthrough to community so that we can have fellowship with God and one another.

> If we confess our sins, he is faithful and just and will forgive us our sins and purify us from all unrighteousness (1 John 1:9).

Thought for the day: *Why do we need to confess our sins if we have already been forgiven?* Even as Christians we still sin. We will never be sinless on this earth no matter how hard we try. I believe we need to confess our sins for the following reasons:
- It keeps us in total communion with God
- It allows God to work in our life because our unconfessed sin is not separating us.
- It gives us the freedom from the bonds of that sin and gives God the freedom to work in us.
- Unconfessed sin will bog us down & draw us away from God. It will grow + grow + before we know it we won't see it as sin + the enemy will then have a foot hold.
- God wants His church to live in unity & so we need to confess our sins to one another so there can be healing in our lives + theirs.

YOU ARE AWESOME FATHER, SON + HOLY SPIRIT! THANK YOU THAT YOU ARE FAITHFUL TO FORGIVE ME, SHIRLEY GIVEN, OF MY SINS + CLEANSE ME, SHIRLEY GIVEN, FROM ALL UNRIGHTEOUSNESS!

YOU ARE AMAZING!!

REPENTANCE

2 Chronicles 7:14

People could feel sorry for their sins but still seek to conceal them or live in denial and never confess them. Confession is the first step to repentance, but it is possible for people to admit they are wrong and never change. "Repentance" literally means "a change of mind resulting in a change of living." In other words, we all hold certain attitudes and beliefs toward God and ourselves, and consequently we live a certain way. Then one day we are enlightened by the truth or come under the conviction of sin and we decide to change. If we have truly repented, we have had a change of mind and attitude and therefore no longer live the way we did before. On the other hand, we have not really repented unless we have changed the way we live.

God calls His covenant people to repent in 2 Chronicles 7:14, "If my people, who are called by my name, will humble themselves and pray and seek my face and turn from their wicked ways, then will I hear from heaven and will forgive their sin and will heal their land." Repentance is always a turning away from sin toward God, which was the primary message of John the Baptist, "Repent, for the kingdom of heaven is near" (Matt. 3:2). Those who responded to his message were baptized. "But when he saw many of the Pharisees and Sadducees coming to where he was baptizing, he said to them: 'You brood of vipers! Who warned you to flee from the coming wrath? Produce fruit in keeping with repentance'" (Matt. 3:7-8). John insisted that repentance be accompanied by the fruit of repentance: a changed life.

Paul reaffirmed the necessity of repentance: "I have declared to both Jews and Greeks that they must turn to God in repentance and have faith in our Lord Jesus" (Acts 20:21). Later he wrote, "I preached that they should repent and turn to God and prove their repentance by their deeds" (Acts 26:20). Repentance means you are renouncing sin and false beliefs and turning toward faith in God. The members of the Early Church would literally face the West and say, "I renounce you, Satan, and all your works and all your ways." Then they would face the East and make a public profession of faith. Saving faith and genuine repentance resulted in the believers changing the way they lived. If you really believe in God, it will affect your walk and your talk.

Genuine repentance for the Christian is not just a matter of human decision with the idea that we can change or save ourselves from the judgment of God. Such was the attitude of some believers in the Early Church who would say they had repented, and then they continued to do the same things they judged others for. Paul responded, "Do you think you will escape God's judgment? Or do you show contempt for the riches of his kindness, tolerance and patience, not realizing that God's kindness leads you to repentance?" (Rom. 2:3-4). God is actually the One who grants "them repentance leading to a knowledge of the truth, and that they will come to their senses and escape the snare of the devil, who has taken them captive to do his will" (2 Tim. 2:25-26).

God desires that all men and women be saved (see 2 Pet. 3:9). "For I take no pleasure in the death of anyone, declares the Sovereign LORD. Repent and live!" (Ezek. 18:32).

9/08/08
Getting this prayer group started with Pam & Nancy

If my people, who are called by my name, will humble themselves and pray and seek my face and turn from their wicked ways, then will I hear from heaven and will forgive their sin and will heal their land (2 Chron. 7:14). *is hard for me because my pride keeps me from doing it. IT IS CAUSING ME TO FIGHT AGAINST WHAT I know GOD WANTS ME TO DO. THEREFORE I NEED TO HUMBLE MYSELF + CONFESS + START THE PRAYER GROUP.*

Thought for the day: *What happens if we have faith without repentance?*

- We would still be lost in our sin. You can't have faith without repentance.
- We would still be under the snare of Satin.
- there would be no change in our life.
- Our lives would not produce fruit.

God calls us to repent, then He can work.

* Many people have faith or belief in God and believe that if they are baptized as babies they are secured in the faith. They don't understand they need to make the choice to repent and change their lives as "proof" of their true repentance + to see growth as a Christian. They have no idea that they need a relationship with God through Jesus Christ.
- You also would not have the Holy Spirit to guide you + make you concious of your sin + the desire to repent.

RECONCILIATION

Psalm 32

David committed adultery with Bathsheba while her husband was on the battlefield. After discovering she was pregnant, David brought her husband home from the field to lie with her in order to cover up David's sin, but Bathsheba's husband refused to play a part in David's charade. So David put him on the front lines where he would likely be killed, and he was. The Lord gave David plenty of time to repent, but when he didn't, the Lord sent Nathan, who was a prophet, to confront him. The guilt tore David up, and he became physically sick (see Ps. 32:3-4) until he finally confessed his transgressions to the Lord and he was forgiven (see v. 5).

I wonder if David was blind to his sin. Was he so concerned to cover it up that his heart became so hardened + he no longer recognized sin?

Many people, like David, are physically sick with psychosomatic illnesses caused by guilt and shame. Confession and repentance bring reconciliation with God and a tremendous sense of relief. "Blessed is he whose transgressions are forgiven, whose sins are covered. Blessed is the man whose sin the LORD does not count against him and in whose spirit is no deceit" (v. 1-2).

Paul reveals the process of our reconciliation with God in Romans 5:8-11:

> But God demonstrates his own love for us in this: While we were still sinners, Christ died for us. Since we have now been justified by his blood, how much more shall we be saved from God's wrath through him! For if, when we were God's enemies, we were reconciled to him through the death of his Son, how much more, having been reconciled, shall we be saved through his life! Not only is this so, but we also rejoice in God through our Lord Jesus Christ, through whom we have now received reconciliation.

God proves His love by initiating this reconciliation toward us while we are still sinners. But it is not enough to know that God loves us if we have still not embraced His forgiveness. He loves us enough to sacrifice His only Son for our sins in order that we would be saved from His wrath. But it is not enough to know that we have been saved from hell if we are still spiritually dead. Salvation in Christ brings us much more than the forgiveness

THE DAILY DISCIPLER 67

of sins; it brings us spiritual life in Christ. It is not enough to know that we are forgiven and spiritually alive; we also have been reconciled to God. We are no longer alienated from Him: "In him and through faith in him we may approach God with freedom and confidence" (Eph. 3:12).

We may never get to be in the presence of today's leaders or celebrities or have an audience with them, but as children of God we have access to our heavenly Father 24 hours of every day. Criminals can have their sentences reduced and their lives spared, but "good" people wouldn't want to associate with them—but our Holy Father wants to have a relationship with us.

All of this is from God, who reconciled us to himself through Christ and gave us the ministry of reconciliation: that God was reconciling the world to himself in Christ, not counting men's sins against them. And he has committed to us the message of reconciliation. We are therefore Christ's ambassadors, as though God were making his appeal through us. We implore you on Christ's behalf: Be reconciled to God (2 Cor. 5:18-20).

What amazing love!

Blessed is he who transgressions are forgiven, whose sins are covered. Blessed is the man whose sin the LORD does not count against him and in whose spirit is no deceit (Ps. 32:1-2).

Thought for the day: *Why doesn't every believer sense God's forgiveness?*

When I first accepted Christ I knew my sins were forgiven. But I didn't put down roots. I had a hard time reading my Bible + didn't grow like I should have. I had no self-confidence + terribly lacked self-esteem. I also never felt that I could please God + that God could not love me unconditionally. So I believed if I did this + that God would approve of me. But that is not salvation! Then when I went to the ANCIENT PATHS Seminar I saw God's unconditional love + for the first time ever I truly understood this. As we approached the end I started laughing in the Spirit + I had a picture or vision of Jesus standing beside me with His arm around my shoulder laughing with me + saying, "See! Aren't I good?" And from there I've grown deeper in my faith + know that God loves me unconditionally. I still have my times though when I doubt this but God is good + faithful + brings me away from Satan's attack. THANK YOU FATHER GOD!

9/10/08

THE GOAL OF INSTRUCTION

1 Timothy 1:1-11

Paul warns his "true son in the faith" (1 Tim. 1:2) and the Church about getting off track in their walk with God. There will be teachers of false doctrines (see vv. 3-4); some will fall back under the law, which was made for the unrighteous (see vv. 8-11); others will fall away from the faith, paying attention to deceiving spirits (see 4:1) and the deceitfulness of riches (see 6:6-18). Timothy was exhorted to maintain sound doctrine, stay under authority and develop godly character. "The goal of this command is love, which comes from a pure heart and a good conscience and a sincere faith" (1:5).

The goal of our instruction is not knowledge that makes one arrogant, but love that edifies others (see 1 Cor. 8:1). Paul says,

> If I speak in the tongues of men and of angels, but have not love, I am only a resounding gong or a clanging cymbal. If I have the gift of prophecy and can fathom all mysteries and all knowledge, and if I have a faith that can move mountains, but have not love, I am nothing (1 Cor. 13:1-2).

We have a tendency to extol the virtues of the theologian and the apologist, but Scripture teaches, "He who wins souls is wise" (Prov. 11:30) and "By this all men will know that you are my disciples, if you love one another" (John 13:35).

Going a step further, Jesus, in his reply to the religious leaders of the day who had asked Him which commandment of the Law was the greatest, said: " 'Love the Lord your God with all your heart and with all your soul and with all your mind.' This is the first and greatest commandment. And the second is like it: 'Love your neighbor as yourself' " (Matt. 22:37-39). Good instruction and sound doctrine should result in the children of God falling in love with God and one another.

It is easier to understand *agape* (godly love) when you realize that it can occur in Scripture as a noun and as a verb. When used as a noun, "agape" refers to the character of God. For example, "agape" is used as a noun in the following passages: "God is love" (1 John 4:16) and "Love is patient, love is kind" (1 Cor. 13:4). The goal of biblical instruction is to enable ourselves and others to progressively take on the character of God, which is love. There is one critical difference between agape (godly love) and *phileo* (brotherly love). The love of God is not dependent upon its object, God loves us not because we are lovable, but because God is love. It is His nature to love us. That is why the love of God is unconditional. Every child of God has been called to participate in the divine nature (see 2 Pet. 1:4) and to become like Him. Jesus said, "If you love those who love you, what credit is that to you? Even 'sinners' love those who love them. And if you do good to those who are good to you, what credit is that to you? Even 'sinners' do that" (Luke 6:32-33).

When "agape" is used as a verb, it calls us out of the goodness of our new nature to give to others what they need: "For God so loved the world that he gave his one and only Son, that whoever believes in him shall not perish but have eternal life" (John 3:16). "This is how we know what love is: Jesus Christ laid down his life for us. And we ought to lay down our lives for our brothers" (1 John 3:16). Those who have the character of love have the capacity to do the loving thing.

The goal of this command is love, which comes from a pure heart and a good conscience and a sincere faith (1 Tim. 1:5).

Thought for the day: *What happens if we make knowledge the goal of our instruction instead of love?*

- Then it is only knowledge, It's all in the head — it doesn't reach down to the soul + change one to God's character. We are to be ever changing into the character of God.

"We ought to lay down our lives for our brothers." How many of us would do that? Instead, we (I) would rather stab the person in the back by gossiping about them or criticize them—write them off. FORGIVE ME LORD — I DON'T WANT TO BE LIKE THAT! I KNOW IT'S DISPLEASING TO YOU + I know I FAIL YOU. HELP ME LORD TO STOP THIS + start praying for them instead. AMEN!!

KNOWING GOD

Philippians 3:1-14

If anybody could qualify to have a relationship with God on the basis of the Old Covenant and their Jewish heritage, Paul would be the leading candidate. He was a "Hebrew of Hebrews" (Phil. 3:5) and "as for legalistic righteousness, faultless" (v. 6). Paul was a zealous defender of the faith and knew all about God, but until the Lord struck him down on the Damascus road, he didn't know Him at all. He had an Old Covenant relationship with God, but not a personal one. After his conversion, Paul reflects on his lost status in the Jewish community. "But whatever was to my profit I now consider loss for the sake of Christ. What is more, I consider everything a loss compared to the surpassing greatness of knowing Christ Jesus my Lord, for whose sake I have lost all things" (vv. 7-8).

The most important belief that we can have is a true knowledge of God and of who we are in relationship to Him. Who is God? The Westminster Confession says, "God is a Spirit, infinite, eternal, and unchanging in His being, wisdom, power, holiness, justice, goodness and truth." Can we actually know Him? Scripture declares that God is incomprehensible: "How great is God—beyond our understanding! The number of his years is past finding out" (Job 36:26). Being finite, we cannot fully comprehend the infinite, yet we can truly know Him. Paul prays, "that the God of our Lord Jesus Christ, the glorious Father, may give you the Spirit of wisdom and revelation, so that you may know him better" (Eph. 1:17).

God has made Himself known to us through His Word, but the written Word by itself can only give us a theology about God. The ultimate revelation of God is Jesus, His Son. Jesus said, "Anyone who has seen me has seen the Father" (John 14:9). It is through Christ that we personally know our heavenly Father: "No one knows the Son except the Father, and no one knows the Father except the Son and those to whom the Son chooses to reveal him" (Matt. 11:27). The triune nature of God is fully revealed in our relationship with our heavenly Father—we are His children and He dwells within us. Scripture reassures us that although "No one has ever seen God; . . . if we love one another, God lives in us and his love is made complete in us. We know that we live in him and he in us, because he has given us of his Spirit" (1 John 4:12-13). Because we have a personal relationship with God, we know Him as Father, Son and Holy Spirit.

As children of God, we can personally petition our heavenly Father (see Matt. 6:9-13) because there is only one mediator between God and men, and that is Jesus Christ (see 1 Tim. 2:5). "This is the confidence we have in approaching God: that if we ask anything according to his will, he hears us" (1 John 5:14). As our heavenly Father, He "disciplines us for our good, that we may share in his holiness" (Heb. 12:10). God knows us better than we know ourselves (see Heb. 4:12-13), and He has made the ultimate sacrifice in order that we may know Him and have a personal relationship with Him through Jesus Christ.

> What is more, I consider everything a loss compared to the surpassing greatness of knowing Christ Jesus my Lord, for whose sake I have lost all things (Phil. 3:8).

Thought for the day: *What is the difference between knowing about God and knowing God?*

- Knowing about God is just head knowledge. There is no relationship and no salvation.
- Knowing God means we have the Holy Spirit within us - we have a relationship with Him through Christ. We are taking on His characteristics more & more. We are producing fruit.

THE GLORY OF GOD

Psalm 99

Of all the words used to describe God, "holy" speaks most directly to His deity. Hosea 11:9 says, "For I am God, and not man—the Holy One among you." To speak of God's holiness is first of all to speak of His distinctiveness or His separateness from all other things. "He is exalted over all the nations" (Ps. 99:2). As the Holy One who lives above and beyond all creation, He is also separate from all evil and moral pollution that defiles His creation.

The fact that God is morally perfect flows from the first meaning that God is separate (transcendent) as the Creator from the rest of His creation, which is fallen and sinful. "The holy God will show himself holy by his righteousness" (Isa. 5:16).

"God is light; in him there is no darkness at all" (1 John 1:5). It is humanly impossible for us to grasp the glory of God since no man has fully seen Him. Apparently, we will need a resurrected body before we can see Him face to face. Moses said to God, "Show me your glory" (Exod. 33:18), and the Lord put him in the cleft of a rock and the glory of God passed before Moses while God covered Moses' face since "no one may see [God] and live" (Exod. 33:20). When Moses came down from the mountain, "his face was radiant" (see Exod. 34:29) from the glory of God, which slowly faded away.

No mortal can fully look upon God, because of His holiness. Yet God does reveal Himself to us. Isaiah was given a vision of God seated on a throne and above Him were seraphs calling out to one another: "Holy, holy, holy is the LORD Almighty; the whole earth is full of his glory" (Isa. 6:3). Realizing God's holiness caused Isaiah to immediately cry out: "'Woe to me!' I cried. 'I am ruined! For I am a man of unclean lips, and I live among a people of unclean lips, and my eyes have seen the King, the LORD Almighty'" (Isa. 6:5). Such would be our reaction if we were suddenly confronted with the glory of God. We see a clear example of this when Peter realized who was in the boat with him: "[Peter] fell at Jesus' knees and said, 'Go away from me, Lord; I am a sinful man!'" (Luke 5:8). If we became more aware of God's glorious presence, the only sin we would be aware of is our own.

In the New Testament, believers are called to be sanctified (see John

17:19) and to be holy (see 1 Pet. 1:16). The root word of "sanctification" and "holiness" is the same. As new creations in Christ, we have been set apart to live righteous lives. When we appreciate the glory of God, the gospel is even more amazing to us. Paul said,

> We ought always to thank God for you, brothers loved by the Lord, because from the beginning God chose you to be saved by the sanctifying work of the Spirit and through belief in the truth. He called you to this through our gospel, that you might share in the glory of our Lord Jesus Christ (2 Thess. 2:13-14).

Someday we shall see God face to face with the acquired glory of our Lord Jesus Christ (see 1 John 3:2).

> Exalt the LORD our God and worship at his holy mountain, for the LORD our God is holy (Ps. 99:9).

Thought for the day: *Why do you think we cannot look fully upon God?*

- Because of our sin. We would fully see how sinful + how unworthy we our. I think His holiness would kill us - it would be too much for our sinful selves to see.

* I get so excited when I read this. With my finite mind I can only imagine what it would be like. How wonderful it will be to be in the presence of God where there is only His Holiness + Righteousness. No more living in an evil, sinful + fallen world! No more temptations + sin. THANK YOU HEAVENLY FATHER! THANK YOU JESUS FOR PAYING THE PRICE FOR ME SO I CAN SOMEDAY BE WITH YOU!

- The times I have felt God's presence is only a glimpse of what is to come. Wow!

THE OMNIPRESENT GOD

Psalm 139:3-10

"In the beginning, O Lord, you laid the foundations of the earth, and the heavens are the work of your hands" (Heb. 1:10). God is the Creator. He is not the creation. Every created thing is present somewhere, but God is everywhere present. "The heavens, even the highest heavens cannot contain him" (2 Chron. 2:6). God is not a tree or a rock, but He does sustain all things by His powerful Word (see Heb. 1:3). If God ceased to exist, so would all creation: "For in him we live and move and have our being" (Acts 17:28). We cannot think of God as being in one place or another.

> Where can I go from your Spirit? Where can I flee from your presence? If I go up to the heavens, you are there; if I make my bed in the depths, you are there. If I rise on the wings of the dawn, if I settle on the far side of the sea, even there your hand will guide me, your right hand will hold me fast (Ps. 139:7-10).

For those who are seeking the security of His presence, these are comforting words. On the other hand, it is impossible to flee from God if we are trying to hide from Him. " 'Can anyone hide in secret places so that I cannot see him?' declares the LORD. 'Do not I fill heaven and earth?' declares the LORD" (Jer. 23:24). Even the cover of darkness cannot hide us from God because darkness is as light to Him (Ps. 139:11-12).

We cannot think of God in human terms because we are finite creatures who live in a finite world. Even the expanse of space cannot contain Him, because He contains space. When we think of God as being remote, it is not because He resides in some far-off galaxy. When we sense that He is far from us, it is because of the dissimilarity of nature, not any distance that can be measured. Sin has alienated us from God, and there is nothing we can do to reconnect with Him apart from the saving work of Christ.

For those who have been reconciled to God, it is meaningless to invoke God's presence, because He is everywhere present. Instead, we ought to acknowledge that God is always present and pray that He will grant us an awareness of His omnipresence. It is also incorrect to ask God to "be with" our missionaries when God has said He would never leave or forsake them.

We should follow David's example in Psalm 16:8: "I have set the LORD always before me. Because he is at my right hand, I will not be shaken."

To worship God is to ascribe to Him the divine attributes that only He possesses. If we sense the presence of an evil spirit, we should immediately acknowledge God's presence. It is an act of worship to acknowledge that God is also present. There is no time when God is not here. We don't worship God because He needs affirmation from us concerning who He is. He is fully secure within Himself. We worship God because we need to bring His divine attributes continuously to mind. We will never be alone as long as we acknowledge that our heavenly Father is always with us.

The heavens, even the highest heavens, cannot contain him (2 Chron. 2:6).

Thought for the day: *Is it comforting or distressing to know that God is always present?*

It is comforting to know God is always present, even in those times when He seems so far away and distant, He is always present! I don't understand fully why there are times when He is silent + seems so distant but I do know that when He seemed distant + silent last March (07) when I was crying out to Him from a hopeless + dark situation that if I hung onto the faith that He was there - and I could trust Him even though He was silent, that I would get through it. And He was there and I did get through it. Thank You Heavenly Father.

THE OMNIPOTENT GOD

Revelation 19

"Hallelujah! For our Lord God Almighty reigns" (Rev. 19:6). Such will be the praise of God's people at the final judgment when God has proven to everyone that He is "KING OF KINGS AND LORD OF LORDS" (v. 16). The adjective "omnipotent" is rendered "Almighty" in Scripture and—with one exception (see 2 Cor. 6:18), occurs only in the book of Revelation (see Rev. 1:8; 4:8; 11:17; 16:7,14; 19:6,15; 21:22). The Almighty God alone has the power to create something out of nothing. In addition to His original creation, the Bible records many "mighty acts" that no other created being can accomplish. He continues to express His power by creating new things (see Matt. 3:9; Rom. 4:17), according to His pleasure, because nothing is too hard for God (see Gen. 18:14). In God resides the power to bring about and control everything that comes to pass.

The power of God is demonstrated in His ability to ensure that all prophecies are fulfilled. To do that, God must have the ability to orchestrate whatever events are necessary in order for His word to come true. This power is demonstrated in His granting the barren Elizabeth to be pregnant with John the Baptist and in the Holy Spirit's causing the Virgin Mary to be with child so that Jesus could rightfully sit on the throne of David (see Luke 1:26-38). When the astonished Mary asked how this could be, "The angel answered, 'The Holy Spirit will come upon you, and the power of the Most High will overshadow you. For nothing is impossible with God'" (Luke 1:35,37).

The omnipotence of God is only limited by His Word and nature because His power originates from His own essence. For instance, God cannot lie (see Heb. 6:18). God cannot be self-contradictory by sinning or dying. He cannot make right that which is by nature wrong. God cannot pretend that what has happened has not happened. God cannot use His power in an unwise or unholy way and therefore He cannot abuse His power. Absolute authority corrupts absolutely for those who are corruptible, but God is incorruptible. God's omnipotence is in perfect harmony with His unconditional love.

Knowing the omnipotence of God is a tremendous blessing for the children of God. First, we are assured of His protection. "He who dwells in the shelter of the Most High will rest in the shadow of the Almighty. I will say of the LORD, 'He is my refuge and my fortress, my God, in whom I trust'" (Ps. 91:1-2). Second, we are confident that God can provide for all of our needs. "My God will meet all your needs according to his glorious riches in Christ Jesus" (Phil. 4:19). Third, it is incredible to think, but highly profitable to know, that God has extended His power to those who believe (see Eph. 1:19). "I can do everything through him who gives me strength" (Phil. 4:13). As believers, we don't have the power to do whatever we want; we have God's power to do His will. We can do everything through Christ that is consistent with God's nature and will.

God is far more than an impersonal force that creates mountains and controls the forces of nature. He is the all-powerful God within us who lovingly uses His power to transform us from sinners to saints. "For the message of the cross is foolishness to those who are perishing, but to us who are being saved it is the power of God" (1 Cor. 1:18).

Hallelujah! For our Lord God Almighty reigns (Rev. 19:6).

Thought for the day: *How should the omnipotence of God give you confidence for living?*

IF ONLY I COULD FULLY OR EVEN PARTIALY GRASP THIS I WOULD BE A DIFFERENT PERSON!

- *I do understand this and I pray that I will allow God instead of my stupid worries + fears to take control + live in full confidence of God + His omnipotence.*
- *As His Word says, "Where can I go where God cannot find me. If I'm in the depths of the earth You are there ...." (My own version)*
- *LORD GOD, PLANT THAT IN MY HEART! LET IT TAKE ROOT O GOD, LET ME UNDERSTAND THAT THIS APPLIES TO MY FAMILY TOO, SO THAT I MAY LET GO OF WORRYING + HANGING ON TOO TIGHT + TRUST YOU INSTEAD. THANK YOU FATHER! I PRAISE YOU + WORSHIP YOU. AMEN!*

Sept 17/08

THE OMNISCIENT GOD

1 Chronicles 28:9

Scripture clearly reveals that God is omniscient—all-knowing. "Great is our Lord and mighty in power, his understanding has no limit" (Ps. 147:5). He has perfect knowledge of the past (see Mal. 3:16) and of the future (see Isa. 46:9-10). He has known us from eternity past (see Rom. 8:29; Eph. 2:10). It was because of God's omniscience that David admonished Solomon to serve God wholeheartedly, "for the LORD searches every heart and understands every motive behind the thoughts" (1 Chron. 28:9). This truth is also taught in Hebrews 4:13: "Nothing in all creation is hidden from God's sight. Everything is uncovered and laid bare before the eyes of him to whom we must give account." Secret sin on Earth is open scandal in heaven.

God's omnipresence partly explains His omniscience. Since He is everywhere always, His awareness is complete. Whereas humankind is bound by time, God is eternal. We understand the successive events of time and reason accordingly, but God sees the past, present and future simultaneously. For God everything is "one eternal now." That which the finite mind sees in sequence, over time, is seen by God all at once, in its totality.

It is impossible to know the future without having control over it. This creates a logical problem for the finite mind. How can Scripture teach both the sovereignty of God (see Rom. 8:29) and the free will of humanity (see 2 Cor. 5:10)? God's eternal knowledge of the future necessitates some degree of predetermination. In ways we cannot fully understand, God participates with humanity in making legitimately free choices in such a way that God can know for certain the outcome.

That God knows all things is clear from Scripture, but how He can know all things cannot be understood by us. "'For my thoughts are not your thoughts, neither are your ways my ways,' declares the LORD. 'As the heavens are higher than the earth, so are my ways higher than your ways and my thoughts than your thoughts'" (Isa. 55:8-9).

Francis Bacon said, "We cannot too often think there is a never-sleeping eye which reads the heart and registers our thoughts." Those who present a righteous face to the world but who lead sinful lives in private are usually ignorant of the fact that they are always living in full view of God. Knowing this truth about God could produce tremendous guilt if we didn't also

This statement makes me realize again that God is in control + I need to trust Him in every-thing

know "there is now no condemnation for those who are in Christ Jesus" (Rom. 8:1). If we don't want God to know what we are thinking or doing, then we shouldn't think it or do it!

The omniscience of God is a tremendous blessing for believers. First, we can know that what God has said will certainly come to pass. Second, we can be led by the Holy Spirit who knows the future. Third, we don't have to worry about tomorrow when our future is safely in the hands of God.

> "For my thoughts are not your thoughts, neither are your ways my ways," declares the LORD. "As the heavens are higher than the earth, so are my ways higher than your ways and my thoughts than your thoughts" (Isa. 55:8-9).

Thought for the day: *Do we have to fully comprehend the nature of God in order to believe that what Scripture says of Him is true?*

Absolutely not! With my finite mind there is no way that I can fully comprehend who He is or His thoughts. But thank God that He gives us enough comprehension to understand somewhat which makes me love Him more, serve Him more, fear Him, etc. It is faith and also by what He has revealed to me already. Reading the Old Testament reveals to me God's power, His love, His mercy, His longing for us to follow Him + live our lives for Him. How many times did He call Israel to come back to Him but their hearts were too hardened + He had to bring judgement down on them. It's all got to do with faith + trust.

GOD IS LOVING AND COMPASSIONATE

Nehemiah 9:17

Whether or not there is a God is not the burning question on most people's minds. There are very few people who believe that God doesn't exist, but quite a few who believe that whether He exists or not has any impact on their lives. "What difference does it make if there is a God?" and "Does He really care?" are the primary questions these people are asking. Those who have no personal knowledge of God usually have a distorted concept of Him, as do many people who profess to believe in Him.

Nobody is born with a true knowledge of God, and we won't have one until we establish a relationship with Him and learn from Scripture His true nature. Until then, our understanding of God is filtered through the grid of ignorance, false prophets and teachers, blasphemous mental thoughts, unhealthy interpersonal relationships, and some less-than-perfect role models and authority figures—especially parents.

True	**False**
Loving and caring	Hateful and unconcerned
Good and merciful	Mean and unforgiving
Steadfast and reliable	Unpredictable and untrustworthy
Offers unconditional grace	Only provides conditional approval
Present and available	Absent when needed
Gives good gifts	Takes away, a killjoy
Nurturing and affirming	Critical and never pleased/satisfied
Accepting	Rejecting
Just, fair and impartial	Unjust, unfair and partial

Many people intellectually know the truth about God, which is shown on the left column of the chart above, but their feelings toward God are often on the right side of the chart. Just telling them the truth is often not enough to resolve their deep feelings toward God.

To have a true knowledge of God, we have to have a personal relation-

THE DAILY DISCIPLER 81

ship with Him, then the Spirit of God is able to lead us into all truth. This often requires submission to God and resistance of the devil (see Jas. 4:7) in humble repentance. It is very common to see emotional healing come to those who have had their eyes opened when the truth has set them free.

And what is the truth about God? That He is compassionate and patient with us. Nehemiah testifies to this reality as he recalls the time when Aaron got tired of waiting for Moses to return from the mountain, so he and others created their own god by building a golden calf (see Exod. 32:1-6; Neh. 9:18). Even in their rebellion, God did not desert them, and Nehemiah is praising Him: "But you are a forgiving God, gracious and compassionate, slow to anger and abounding in love" (v. 17).

Throughout the Gospels, we read of instances in which God was moved by compassion. "When he saw the crowds, he had compassion on them" (Matt. 9:36). "Jesus called his disciples to him and said, 'I have compassion for these people'" (Matt. 15:32). Jesus said, "Go and learn what this means, I desire mercy [*hesed*, i.e. compassion], not sacrifice" (Matt. 9:13). "Hesed" in the Old Testament is translated as "God's loving kindness." We all benefit from the truth that God's nature is compassionate.

> But you are a forgiving God, gracious and compassionate, slow to anger and abounding in love (Neh. 9:17).

Thought for the day: *Do your feelings toward God match the truth?*

- I hate to admit it but I do have a problem with fully trusting God - that's why I worry about what could happen today or in the future. I need to really trust Him no matter my fears or the situation. I am so thankful to say He is working on me and I am coming along but I still have a long way to go.
- If I am honest with myself I sometimes still believe that God is partial but again it is not true. One reason I think this is because I don't trust Him or I haven't given Him control or my heart or motives are not right which prevents Him from working in me + therefore I see Him being partial + not caring enough about me.
- * But God is changing that in me. Thank You Heavenly Father.

GOD IS MERCIFUL AND GOOD

Psalm 100

"For the LORD is good and his love endures forever" (Ps. 100:5). Jesus said, "There is only One who is good" (Matt. 19:17), and that of course is God. Therefore, everything He does is good and we are the benefactors of His goodness. "And we know that in all things God works for the good of those who love him, who have been called according to his purpose" (Rom. 8:28). Although we are thankful, our finite minds struggle in two principal ways with the concept of the infinite goodness of God.

First, we don't really know what is good for us. What tastes good often proves to be unhealthy. What looks good may be so in appearance only. What feels good has led many people astray. Even the treacherous act of Joseph's brothers eventually brought about a greater good. Joseph said to them, "You intended to harm me, but God intended it for good to accomplish what is now being done, the saving of many lives" (Gen. 50:20). Still, when we read about how God has utterly destroyed the Amalekites (see 1 Sam. 15:2-3), it doesn't seem as if His actions are consistent with His goodness—but that view is from our limited human perspective, which may be overlooking God's justice. If we knew that there is cancer in the body, the loving thing to do is to cut it out. And if there is a rotten apple in a barrel, the good thing to do is get rid of it. We have a very tiny role in the larger drama of life, and we only see a tiny portion of the big picture that God is painting. When we are fully transformed by the renewing of our minds, "Then [we] will be able to test and approve what God's will is—his good, pleasing and perfect will" (Rom. 12:2).

Second, if God is all-powerful and good, why do bad things happen to good people? It is impossible to answer that question unless you understand that there are evil forces in this world that are actively opposing the will of God. God created Lucifer to be a light bearer. Lucifer (the beautiful angel of light) turned his back on God and became Satan, the deceiver and the accuser. God created Adam and Eve and by their choice they lost their relationship with God, which made it possible for Satan to have dominion in this world.

THE DAILY DISCIPLER   83

Consequently, evil forces are at work in this world—forces that oppose the will of God. "Yet you say, 'The way of the Lord is not just.' Hear, O house of Israel: Is my way unjust? Is it not your ways that are unjust?" (Ezek. 18:25). "Do I take any pleasure in the death of the wicked? declares the Sovereign LORD. Rather, am I not pleased when they turn from their ways and live?" (Ezek. 18:23). God is the author of life, not death; and He is in the process of making right what His rebellious creation has made wrong. The goodness of God will overcome this present evil—if not in our lifetime, then surely in the future.

God is also merciful. "But when the kindness and love of God our Savior appeared, he saved us, not because of righteous things we had done, but because of his mercy" (Titus 3:4-5). To be merciful to others is to not give them what they deserve. We deserved hell, but God was merciful and gave us eternal life. David said, "Taste and see that the LORD is good" (Ps. 34:8) and "Surely goodness and love [mercy] will follow me all the days of my life, and I will dwell in the house of the LORD forever" (Ps. 23:6).

For the LORD is good and his love endures forever (Ps. 100:5).

Thought for the day: *Why is it incorrect to blame God for all the calamity in this world?*

Because it is not God who has this calamity on the earth but man. It is our choices. I can't understand it all. Sickeness & death → a part of life. Hurricanes, earthquakes, etc. — a part of life. } Living in a fallen world

War, poverty, hunger, etc. → MAN! They say there is enough food in this world to feed everyone but I believe it is man + politics! Poverty — some by their own doing, some by oppression. WAR — Man! Man's need for power. After being in Romania + seeing what Communism does all because MEN want control. They oppress. After seeing Dachau → Man! Man's corruption brought this on! Man's desire for control. To lead through fear!

GOD IS GRACIOUS AND KIND

Hebrews 4:14-16

God is righteous and cannot be unjust at any time. To administer justice is to give people what they deserve. If justice were served, we would all have to face eternity in hell. But God is also merciful and because of His love, He did not want to give us what we deserved. Instead, Jesus satisfied the righteous demands of God by paying the price for our sins. Mercy is not giving people what they deserve. "But when the kindness and love of God our Savior appeared, he saved us, not because of righteous things we had done, but because of his mercy" (Titus 3:4-5).

Grace is giving people what they don't deserve. Because of God's mercy, He looked for another way to satisfy His justice so that we would not have to pay our own wages for sin, which is death. Because of His gracious nature, He gave us eternal life. "For it is by grace you have been saved, through faith—and this not from yourselves, it is the gift of God—not by works, so that no one can boast" (Eph. 2:8-9). Grace is unwarranted favor. It cannot be purchased and it cannot be earned. We can only respond to a gracious gift by humbly receiving it and by saying thanks and then praising the character of the giver.

In order to bear the sins of all humanity, Jesus "made himself nothing, taking the very nature of a servant, being made in human likeness" (Phil. 2:7). He became one of us in order to be our "kinsman redeemer." He became our scapegoat (substitute) by taking our place on the cross. There is another benefit of Jesus' becoming one of us: He can relate to us in every way. He faced every temptation, suffered every hardship and was totally rejected. He spoke the truth and loved sacrificially. "For we do not have a high priest who is unable to sympathize with our weaknesses, but we have one who has been tempted in every way, just as we are—yet was without sin" (Heb. 4:15).

Being omniscient, God fully understood the suffering and hardship of fallen humanity. He didn't have to become one of us in order to feel our plight. God already knew what we thought and how we felt, and His plans were in place long before Jesus came. The limitation is in our understanding, not His. It would be harder to believe that Jesus actually does "sympathize with our weaknesses" if Jesus had never suffered or been tempted as we are.

People don't want to share their burdens with someone they don't think can relate to them nor understand their situation. Nor do people unburden themselves to others who are unable to help them. Jesus not only understands, He also responds to us kindly, because He is kind and loving by nature. God gives us what we need, not what we deserve, because He is by nature gracious.

> Let us then approach the throne of grace with confidence and find grace to help us in our time of need (Heb. 4:16).

Thought for the day: *Why has the coming of Jesus made it easier for us to approach God?*

- For one thing, He was tempted + knows our temptations
- He experienced everything that we do - misunderstood, betrayed, rejection, etc.
- Number 2 which is we no longer need a High Priest to do so. Jesus is our High Priest.

GOD IS FAITHFUL

Psalm 89

It is hard to relate to somebody you can't trust or count on when needed. But you can count on God, because it is His nature to be faithful, and He is perfectly reliable. The Psalmist says, "I will declare that your love stands firm forever, that you established your faithfulness in heaven itself" (Ps. 89:2). The fact that God made the world and all that is in it and demonstrates His faithfulness by providing for His creatures is abundantly illustrated in the "nature psalms," such as Psalm 104. His faithful provision for His Chosen People is best seen in His plan for redemption as evidenced in His promises and covenants.

The Old Testament is a record of God's faithfulness in redeeming His people, from the call of Abraham to the establishment of the Israelites in the Promised Land. The Exodus from Egypt demonstrated God's faithfulness (see Exod. 15:1-17), and it caused those who had been delivered to believe in Yahweh and His servant Moses (see Exod. 14:31). For generations, even up to our own day, the Jewish people have commemorated the deliverance from Egypt and the Passover in remembrance of God's faithfulness.

From the time God made a covenant with Abraham in Genesis 12:1-3, His unlikely promises were slowly but progressively fulfilled even when it looked to be humanly impossible and in spite of overwhelming odds. The Messianic line begins with Sarah, who gave birth to Isaac when she no longer humanly could, and then God provided a scapegoat to take the place of Isaac when he was ordered to be sacrificed, preserving Abraham and Sarah's posterity. God promised that the seed of the woman would continue through the house of David and that the Messiah would sit on the throne of David. "Once for all, I have sworn by my holiness—and I will not lie to David—that his line will continue forever and his throne endure before me like the sun; it will be established forever like the moon, the faithful witness in the sky" (Ps. 89:35-36).

The first two chapters of Luke's Gospel paint a vivid picture of people who were waiting expectantly for God to fulfill His promises made under the Old Covenant (see Luke 2:25-38). Simon saw the fulfillment in the birth of Jesus and rejoiced in God's faithfulness: "Sovereign Lord, as you have promised, you now dismiss your servant in peace. For my eyes have seen your salvation, which you have prepared in the sight of all people" (Luke 2:29-30).

From the days of Abraham, many people probably thought that God was unfaithful and so lost their faith in Him when His Word was not fulfilled in their lifetime. "But do not forget this one thing, dear friends: With the Lord a day is like a thousand years, and a thousand years are like a day. The Lord is not slow in keeping his promise, as some understand slowness" (2 Pet. 3:8-9). There was a faithful remnant, however, who chose to believe in God in spite of incredible hardships and persecution (see Heb. 11). "These were all commended for their faith, yet none of them received what had been promised. God had planned something better for us so that only together with us would they be made perfect" (Heb. 11:39-40).

> But as surely as God is faithful. . . . No matter how many promises God has made, they are "Yes" in Christ (2 Cor. 1:18,20).

Thought for the day: *Do you believe that you can personally count on God to be faithful?*

- I do.... BUT.... I don't always show it with my stupid worry + fear... but God is working on that!
- I love reading the Old Testament because it shows that we can count on God's faithfulness!
- It also shows our impatience + how we don't always wait for God + mess things up because it! Things haven't changed from then to now.
- Also, as I read the Bible + see God's faithfulness in fulfilling prophecy + now as I see prophecy of the End Times being fulfilled before my eyes it re-inforces God's faithfulness.

GOD IS IMMUTABLE

Numbers 23:19

"The grass withers and the flowers fall, but the word of our God stands forever" (Isa. 40:8). The Word and character of God never changes, which is in stark contrast to that of humanity, which is in a constant state of change. This changeless nature of God is what makes Him the ultimate object of our faith. The writer of Hebrews says, "Remember your leaders, who spoke the word of God to you. Consider the outcome of their way of life and imitate their faith. Jesus Christ is the same yesterday and today and forever" (Heb. 13:7-8).

The writer doesn't say that we should necessarily imitate the behavior of those who lead us. Our faith is not based on humanity, no matter how well they behave. We should consider the lives of teachers who profess to know God and live by faith, imitating what they believe if their lives are bearing the fruit of righteousness. When we see the fruit of righteousness in the lives of our leaders, we know that the object of their faith is God and His Word, which never change.

Fallen humanity has "worshiped and served created things rather than the Creator" (Rom. 1:25). Trusting only in ourselves or others has led many believers astray, because there are no perfectly faithful people. We have not been able to solve our own problems, much less save ourselves. Humanity has found some stability by trusting in the fixed order of the universe, especially the solar system. We set our watches by it and plan our calendars. What would happen tomorrow if the sun rose two hours later than it was supposed to? The whole world would be thrown into chaos, and everyone would be extremely anxious. It takes months or years for us to establish faith in someone or something. One act of unfaithfulness or inconsistency can destroy that trust, and it will take months or years of consistent, faithful behavior to rebuild trust. In fact, we would be foolish to put our trust in someone or something which is unfaithful or unreliable. That is one reason why our human relationships are so fragile.

That is not the case concerning our relationship with God. Knowing that God is faithful and never changes is what gives us stability in our lives. We can rest in confidence knowing that the Creator who sustains the fixed order of the universe will also sustain us.

"What if some choose not to believe God? Will their lack of faith nulli-fy God's faithfulness? Not at all! Let God be true, and every man a liar" (Rom. 3:3-4). God's Word is true whether or not we believe it, and He will never change. He keeps His Word and His Covenant, being faithful to Himself. He is the rock of our salvation who changes not.

God is not a man, that he should lie, nor a son of man, that he should change his mind. Does he speak and then not act? Does he promise and not fulfill? (Num. 23:19).

Thought for the day: *What confidence can we draw from the fact that God and His Word never change?*

We can be fully confident that what God says about providing for our needs He will do. Every promise, every prophecy, etc. will happen - maybe not when we think it should - but in God's timing. This should make me realize that I need to wait on God + trust Him in everything & not end up giving up on God + then doing my own solution instead of trusting. PATIENCE + TRUST ARE HARD FOR ME!

* AS THE U.S. IS IN A FINANCIAL CRISIS I HAVE BEEN ABLE TO SEE HOW MUCH WE PUT OUR TRUST IN MONEY AND THE PANIC WE FEEL WHEN IT FAILS. WE HAVE PUT OUR TRUST IN THAT MONEY FOR RETIREMENT + IT COULD ALL BE GONE NOW. HOW SAD THAT IT TAKES SOMETHING LIKE THIS TO MAKE ME REALIZE THIS. BUT, THIS HAS NOT AFFECTED US IN ANY WAY [YET] AND SO I'M NOT PANICING BUT EVEN THOUGH I KNOW IT IS GOD WHO I NEED TO TRUST. NOT ME! NOT MONEY! NOT ROB! GOD!! (The memories of 25 years ago when there were no jobs to be had are still ceased fresh in my mind + even though I didn't trust God then He was still faithful + He met all of our needs!

THE TRINITY

Acts 2:32-36

"Hear O Israel: The LORD our God, the LORD is one" (Deut. 6:4). Old Testament Judaism and New Testament Christianity both stress monotheism (one God) as opposed to polytheism (many gods), pantheism (all is God) or atheism (no god or gods). Only Christianity recognizes the divine three-in-oneness, the eternal coexistence of the Father, Son and Holy Spirit in the inner personal life of the Godhead.

The plural nature of the Godhead is revealed in the first chapter of the Bible through the use of the plural pronoun: "Then God said, 'Let us make man in our image, in our likeness' " (Gen. 1:26). Jesus explicitly revealed the doctrine of the Trinity in the baptismal formula, which was stated by Christ Himself: "Therefore go and make disciples of all nations, baptizing them in the name of the Father and of the Son and of the Holy Spirit" (Matt. 28:19). The Epistles are saturated with the revelation of the triune Godhead, uniting all three as the agents of our salvation and sanctification. Notice how Paul unites the believer with the Father, Son and Holy Spirit in Romans 8:9, "You, however, are controlled not by the sinful nature but by the Spirit, if the Spirit of God lives in you. And if anyone does not have the Spirit of Christ, he does not belong to Christ."

Although the Father, Son and Holy Spirit work in unity, everything flows from the Father. Jesus said He could do nothing on His own initiative (see John 5:30; 8:42) and modeled a life that was totally dependent upon the Father (see John 17:7). In this way, He left us an example that we ought to follow in His steps (see 1 Pet. 2:21), for we too are called to live a life dependent upon God. Likewise, the Holy Spirit comes from the Father (see John 15:26), and He will not speak on His own (see John 16:13). As we approach the Father, we do so in the name of the Lord Jesus Christ as led by the Holy Spirit. The sacrificial death and the resurrection of Jesus Christ is the only basis by which we can approach our heavenly Father, and it is the unique work of the Holy Spirit to bear witness with our spirit that we are children of God (see Rom. 8:16) and to lead us into all truth (see John 16:13).

After Pentecost, Peter's message brought together the finished work of Christ and the outpouring of the Holy Spirit. The coming of the Holy Spirit was the evidence that Jesus has been exalted to the right hand of the heavenly Father. During the three-year public ministry of Jesus, "the Spirit had not been given, since Jesus had not yet been glorified" (John 7:39). "Therefore let all Israel be assured of this: God has made this Jesus, whom you crucified, both Lord [*kurios*] and Christ" (Acts 2:36). "Kurios" (Lord) is used to refer to Jesus in Jude 4 and is used to refer to God the Father in Jude 5.

The Athanasian Creed, which was formulated by the Early Church, reaffirmed the triune nature of God: "We worship one God in Trinity, and Trinity in Unity, neither confounding the Persons, nor dividing the substance, for there is one Person of the Father, another of the Son, and another of the Holy Ghost; but the godhead of the Father, of the Son and of the Holy Ghost is one, the glory equal, the majesty co-eternal."

> Therefore go and make disciples of all nations, baptizing them in the name of the Father and of the Son and of the Holy Spirit (Matt. 28:19).

Thought for the day: *Why is the co-deity of Christ and the Holy Spirit so important?*

Christ is our Savior. It is through His death + resurrection that we have salvation. And when we receive Jesus as our Savior the Holy Spirit comes + lives in us – guiding us + directing us.

I AM WHO I AM

Exodus 3:13-15

God called Moses to deliver His people out of bondage in Egypt and lead them to the Promised Land. How was he going to tell the people that God had sent him? God responded to this dilemma by saying to Moses,

> "I AM WHO I AM. This is what you are to say to the Israelites: I AM has sent me to you." God also said to Moses, "Say to the Israelites, 'The LORD God of your fathers—the God of Abraham, the God of Isaac and the God of Jacob—has sent me to you.' This is my name forever, the name by which I am to be remembered from generation to generation" (Exod. 3:14-15).

The name "I AM" means that what God was in the past, He is in the present, and He will also be in the future. Yahweh (Jehovah) is the most distinctive name that God was known by Israel, which comes from the same root as "I AM." This name was given to Moses to convince the children of Israel that God was faithful to His covenant and that He would lead them out of bondage through His servant Moses. The name does not primarily disclose who He is in Himself. Rather, it discloses who He is, was and will be in relationship to the people of God.

The name is mentioned in the New Testament when Jesus responded to the Jews: "'I tell you the truth,' Jesus answered, 'before Abraham was born, I am!'" (John 8:58, emphasis added). Whereas Moses was the lawgiver who led God's people from slavery in Egypt to the Promised Land, Jesus fulfilled the Law and led God's people from slavery to sin to freedom in Christ and eternal life. The God of Abraham, Isaac and Jacob is the same God who now delivers us from the kingdom of darkness to the kingdom of His beloved son (see Col. 1:13). Jesus said, "I told you that you would die in your sins; if you do not believe that I am the one I claim to be" (John 8:24, emphasis added).

John also records a number of other "I am" statements made by Jesus.

- "I am the bread of life" (John 6:48, emphasis added). Like the manna from heaven that sustained the physical life of the

[Handwritten margin notes: I hate how Molson's Brewery's slogan is "I AM Canadian." Does that not mock God? Does that not say that beer is God? What a mockery. Open our eyes Holy Spirit]

Israelites, Jesus also came from heaven to give us spiritual life.
· "*I am* the resurrection and the life. He who believes in me will live,
even though he dies; and whoever lives and believes in me will
never die" (John 11:25-26, emphasis added). In other words, if we
believe in Jesus, we will continue to live spiritually even when we
die physically.

· "I tell you the truth, *I am* the gate for the sheep" (John 10:7,
emphasis added), and later He said, "*I am* the way and the truth
and the life. No one comes to the Father except through me" (John
14:6, emphasis added). Jesus is the only means by which we can
receive eternal life and enter into God's presence. "Salvation is
found in no one else, for there is no other name under heaven
given to men by which we must be saved" (Acts 4:12).

· "*I am* the good shepherd. The good shepherd lays down his life for
the sheep" (John 10:11, emphasis added). "We are his people, the
sheep of his pasture" (Ps. 100:3).

I told you that you would die in your sins; if you do not believe that
I am the one I claim to be (John 8:24, emphasis added).

Thought for the day: *Why is Jesus the only way?*

- There is no other name under heaven given
  to men by which we must be saved.
- Jesus is the only One who paid the price
  for our sins - He was the blood offering!
- He is the only One who rose again after
  death - revealed Himself to others - and
  ascended into heaven in full view of many
  eye witnesses.
- HE IS THE ONLY ONE WHO CLAIMS TO
  BE THE ONLY WAY - ALL OTHER
  RELIGEONS SAY THEY ALL LEAD TO GOD,
  BUT IT IS BY WHAT YOU
  DO ON THIS EARTH
  THAT WILL DETERMINE
  IF YOU
  GO TO
  HEAVEN!

THE LAST ADAM

Isaiah 7:14

The first Adam was born both physically and spiritually alive. Because Adam sinned, he died spiritually and was separated from God. Physical death was also a consequence of sin, although Adam did not physically die until many years after the Fall. From that time on, every descendant of Adam and Eve has been born physically alive but spiritually dead (see Eph. 2:1).

Yet God had a plan for restoring life. He promised that redemption for His people would come through the seed of a woman (see Gen. 3:15; 17:19; Gal. 3:16). As the years passed, the Israelites became impatient and wondered how they would know the Messiah when He finally did come. "Therefore the Lord himself will give you a sign: The virgin will be with child and will give birth to a son, and will call him Immanuel" (Isa. 7:14).

There would be 400 silent years from the end of Old Testament revelation (and 750 years from the prophecy found in Isaiah 7:14) before "the Word became flesh and made his dwelling among us" (John 1:14). The prophecy was fulfilled concerning Immanuel, which means "God is with us." The prophecy of Jesus being born of a virgin was also fulfilled, which greatly amazed Mary (see Luke 1:34-35). Nobody can fully explain the mystery of the Incarnation, but Scripture clearly teaches that the eternal Son became flesh. So critical is the doctrine of the Incarnation that Scripture makes it a primary test of orthodoxy (core Christian doctrine):

> This is how you can recognize the Spirit of God: Every Spirit that acknowledges that Jesus Christ has come in the flesh is from God, but every spirit that does not acknowledge Jesus is not from God. This is the spirit of the antichrist, which you have heard is coming and even now is already in the world (1 John 4:2-3).

The Incarnation is what sets Christianity apart from the cults and all the other religions of the world. They may believe in the historical Jesus, but they do not believe that God became man. They believe that God could appear as a man, like an apparition, and suffer in appearance only, but unless they have the Holy Spirit they cannot say that Jesus was fully God while also fully human.

This union between divinity and humanity was necessary in order to bring us spiritual life. "In him was life, and that life was the light of men" (John 1:4). Notice that light does not produce life. The light of believers is the radiation of the eternal life of God. The last Adam—Jesus—like the first Adam, was also born physically and spiritually alive. But unlike the last Adam, Jesus never sinned, even though He was tempted in every way (see Heb. 4:15).

Jesus said, "I have come that they may have life, and have it to the full" (John 10:10). What Adam and Eve lost in the Fall was eternal life, and that is what Jesus came to restore. He did not come to give us a more fulfilling physical life with material blessings. Rather, He came to give us a fulfilling spiritual life filled with spiritual blessings, which are love, joy, peace, patience, kindness, goodness, faithfulness, gentleness and self-control—the fruit of the Spirit (see Gal. 5:22-23). Jesus didn't just come to give us life. He is our life (see Col. 3:4).

In him was life, and that life was the light of men (John 1:4).

Thought for the day: *How does the life of God bring light to the world?*

- The life of God brings light to the world through us – His people (or so it should).
- We show God's light in the things that we do – helping someone in need
  - caring for the widows & the orphans
  - Sharing God's love & salvation through Jesus.
  - living a godly life. I don't think I really fully understand this – our actions, whether good or bad speaks volumes. People are watching us whether we know it or not. We have to be the light because this world is pitch black otherwise. And people will come to know Jesus because of our light.

THE DEITY OF CHRIST

Philippians 2:6-11

The claim that Jesus was the promised Messiah and the eternal Son of God infuriated the Jewish leaders (see John 5:18) and caused them to accuse Jesus of blasphemy (see John 10:33). Now Paul carefully stresses the deity of Christ. Jesus is by His very nature (*morphe*) God, and in His incarnation, He embraced perfect humanity.

The key word is "morphe," which is translated as "nature" or "form." It stresses the inner essence or reality of that with which it is associated. Jesus "did not consider equality with God something to be grasped" (Phil. 2:6). In other words, Jesus did not have to strive to be God or even be like Him, because He was and is God. He voluntarily surrendered independent use of His own divine attributes. When the devil tempted Jesus to turn the rocks into bread, He simply responded, "Man does not live on bread alone, but on every word that comes from the mouth of God" (Matt. 4:4). The devil wanted Jesus to use His own divine attributes independently of the Father to save Himself. He could have called upon 10,000 angels to save Him from death on the cross, but He did not, because He came to do His Father's will.

Jesus "made himself nothing, taking the very nature [morphe] of a servant, being made in human likeness" (Phil. 2:7). "Made himself nothing" literally means "He emptied Himself." He divested Himself of His self-interest, but not of His deity. Jesus humbled Himself and took on the very nature of man. He was truly God and also truly man. "Likeness" means similar but different. He differed from the rest of humanity in that He was sinless. His self-renunciation was necessary if He were to have an authentic human experience that included geographical limitations, human development in mind and body, and the need for food and sleep. He had to totally depend on the heavenly Father.

The phrase "being found in appearance as a man" (v. 8) refers to a temporary and outer appearance in contrast to "morphe," which signifies a permanent inner quality. The condescension of Jesus included not only His birth, but also His death, which was the worst possible "death—even death on a cross!" (v. 8). Martin Luther said, "The mystery of the humanity of Christ, that he sunk Himself into our flesh, is beyond all human understanding." He left His exalted position to be like us in order to die for us. To a similar but far lesser degree, we are called to humble ourselves under God's mighty hand, so that He might lift us up in due time (see 1 Pet. 5:6).

St. Irenaeus, an Early Church father said, "The Word of God, Jesus Christ, on account of His great love for mankind, became what we are in order to make us what He is Himself." His life was the epitome of humble submission leading to death and exaltation. Jesus' example is ours to follow.

> Therefore God exalted him to the highest place and gave him the name that is above every name, that at the name of Jesus every knee should bow, in heaven and on earth and under the earth, and every tongue confess that Jesus Christ is Lord, to the glory of God the Father (Phil. 2:9-11).

Thought for the day: *What can you learn from the example of Jesus?*

Lots + Lots + Lots!
To give up our rights in order to do what God is calling us to do. It's a hard thing to do because I want to be in control so I know what where + what I am doing — OR SO I THINK I DO WHICH IS A LIE BECAUSE WE OURSELVES HAVE ABSOLUTELY NO WAY TO PREVENT WHAT A DAY HOLDS.

I know that when I let go + waited on God as to what He wanted me to do with my life, that He provided me with something far more better than I could have ever hoped for. AND YET I STILL STRUGGLE WITH THIS CONSTANTLY. HOW FOOLISH! I'm no different then the Israelites wandering in the desert. It is no wonder God calls us SHEEP! WE—I AM SO STUPID!!! LORD GOD—Forgive me of my stubborn ways + my hard headedness. Your ways are so much better than mine. Help me to remember Jesus to

this + to empty myself + to do Your will. Thank You that You remember we are but dust. Thank You Jesus for showing us the way. Amen.

THE HOLY SPIRIT

Acts 1:2-11

John baptized believers with water, but one greater than John would baptize with the Holy Spirit (see Matt. 3:11; Mark 1:8; Luke 3:16; John 1:33). The coming of the Holy Spirit, which was prophesied by Joel, happened at Pentecost (see Joel 2:28-32 and Acts 2:17-21). Jesus said,

> If anyone is thirsty, let him come to me and drink. Whoever believes in me, as the Scripture has said, steams of living water will flow from within him. By this he meant the Spirit, whom those who believed in him were later to receive. Up to that time the Spirit had not been given, since Jesus had not yet been glorified (John 7:37-39).

The promised coming of the Holy Spirit happened when Jesus was exalted at the right hand of the Father (see Acts 2:33).

The resurrected Jesus appeared to many of His followers over the course of 40 days and instructed them, "Do not leave Jerusalem, but wait for the gift my Father promised. . . . [Y]ou will receive power when the Holy Spirit comes on you; and you will be my witnesses in Jerusalem, and in all Judea and Samaria, and to the ends of the earth" (Acts 1:4,8). The Church Age began the moment believers received the Holy Spirit at Pentecost. Even though they had seen the resurrected Christ, they could not be witnesses until the resurrected life of Christ came to dwell within them through the power of the Holy Spirit. At Pentecost, they were filled and empowered by the Holy Spirit.

The Holy Spirit is not a cosmic force—He is the Third Person of the Trinity. God's Holy Spirit had inspired the Old Testament prophets, moved among God's people, had been present with them in the Person of Christ, but now He dwells within us as the Spirit of Christ. The Church, or the Body of Christ, is comprised of those believers who are born again spiritually by the action of the Holy Spirit, the Holy Spirit bearing witness with their spirit that they are children of God (see Rom. 8:16). Every believer upon the simple condition of faith in Christ is reborn (i.e., regenerated, see Titus 3:5); baptized by the Holy Spirit into the Body if Christ (see 1 Cor. 12:13); indwelt perpetually (see Rom. 8:38-39); sealed (see Eph. 1:13-14); and given the priv-

THE DAILY DISCIPLER 99

ilege of being filled by the Holy Spirit continuously (see Eph. 5:18).

Jesus promised, "I will ask the Father, and he will give you another Counselor to be with you forever—the Spirit of truth" (John 14:16-17). The Holy Spirit is first and foremost the Spirit of truth, and "he will guide you into all truth" (John 16:13), and that truth will set you free (see John 8:32). Jesus said, "He will bring glory to me by taking from what is mine and making it known to you" (John 16:14). The primary work of the Holy Spirit is to communicate God's presence to us. Because of the indwelling Holy Spirit, we have the power to live a righteous life. The Holy Spirit will also lead those who are born again, "because those who are led by the Spirit of God are sons of God" (Rom. 8:14).

The Early Church was persecuted for their belief in God, and discovered their need to maintain an intimate relationship with Him. They had been baptized into Christ, and now they needed to be continuously filled with the Spirit. "After they prayed, the place where they were meeting was shaken. And they were all filled with the Holy Spirit and spoke the word of God boldly" (Acts 4:31).

Those who are led by the Spirit of God are the sons of God (Rom. 8:14).

Thought for the day: *How are you led by the Spirit of God?*

- I'm led through listening + paying attention to Him+ when He speaks clearly to me.
- Through God's Word
- When He reveals new things to me through God's Word.
- Through a sermon
- Through prayer

A New Position "in Christ"

Colossians 2:6-10

Every Christian is alive "in Christ." The prepositional phrases "in Christ," "in Him," or "in the beloved" are some of the most often used expressions in the Epistles. These phrases occur nearly 40 times in the book of Ephesians alone. They mean that our soul is in union with God. For every verse that says Christ is in us (see Col. 1:27), there are 10 verses saying we are "in Christ." "In Christ" we are called to salvation (see 1 Cor. 7:22); regenerated (see Eph. 1:3; 2:10); and justified (see Rom. 8:1-2). "In Christ" we die (see 1 Thess. 4:16), and "in Him" our bodies will be raised up again (see 1 Cor. 15:22).

Every stage of our sanctification is made possible because we are spiritually alive "in Christ." We are to be firmly rooted "in Him," in order to be built up "in Him," which makes it possible to live "in Him" (Col. 2:6-7). Being alive and free "in Christ" is the basis for Paul's understanding of how to live the Christian life. In sending Timothy to Corinth, Paul said, "He will remind you of my way of life *in Christ Jesus,* which agrees with what I teach everywhere in every church" (1 Cor. 4:17, emphasis added).

"God has given us eternal life, and this life is *in his son*" (1 John. 5:11, emphasis added) and Paul speaks of "the promise of life that is *in Christ Jesus*" (2 Tim. 1:1, emphasis added). *"In Christ"* are "faith and love" (1 Tim. 1:14); "grace" (2 Tim. 2:1); "salvation" (2 Tim. 2:10); "all the treasures of wisdom and knowledge" (Col. 2:3); and God's "glorious riches" (Phil. 4:19). Paul says that it is because of God's work that Christians are *"in Christ Jesus,* who has become for us wisdom from God—that is, our righteousness, holiness and redemption" (1 Cor. 1:30, emphasis added). We can only say, "Praise be to the God and Father of our Lord Jesus Christ, who has blessed us in the heavenly realms with every spiritual blessing *in Christ*" (Eph. 1:3, emphasis added).

Because our lives are inseparably connected to Christ Himself, the Holy Spirit gives us the blessings that Christ alone has merited. "Now if we are children, then we are heirs—heirs of God and co-heirs with Christ" (Rom. 8:17). Further, "If we belong to Christ, then we are Abraham's seed, and heirs according to the promise" (Gal. 3:29).

It is important for us to realize that if we have accepted Christ as Savior, then we are in Christ every moment of our lives. "For in Christ all the fullness of the Deity lives in bodily form, and you have been given fullness in Christ, who is the head over every power and authority" (Col. 2:9-10). "Have been given" is past tense. Every believer is already "in Christ." Being rooted in Christ refers to our positional sanctification, which is the basis for our progressive sanctification. As believers, we are not trying to become children of God; rather, we are already children of God who are in the process of becoming like Christ.

Paul is contrasting the means by which we grow in Christ with the human traditions of the world. "Hollow and deceptive philosophy, which depends on human tradition and the basic principles of this world" (Col. 2:8) cannot reproduce in us what only the life of Christ can. Paul says, "I can do everything *through him* who gives me strength" (Phil. 4:13, emphasis added); and Jesus tells us, "Apart from me you can do nothing" (John 15:5).

Now if we are children, then we are heirs—heirs of God and co-heirs with Christ (Rom. 8:17).

Thought for the day: *Summarize what it means to be "in Christ."*

For me, "In Christ" means:
- I am in Him
- I am striving to be like Him through the help of the Holy Spirit, God's Word, etc.
- I have faith + love, grace, salvation + wisdom + knowledge
- In Christ I have died + in Him I will be raised up again.
- I am a heir of God + a co-heir with Christ (Blows me away!)

CRUCIFIED "IN CHRIST"

Galatians 2:19-20

Paul said, "I died to the law" (Gal. 2:19) because "I have been crucified with Christ and I no longer live, but Christ lives in me" (v. 20). This is possible because of our union with Christ. As believers we are no longer "in Adam," we are "in Christ." The apostle Paul identified every believer with Christ:

In His death	Romans 6:3,6; Colossians 3:1-3
In His burial	Romans 6:4
In His resurrection	Romans 6:5,8,11
In His ascension	Ephesians 2:6
In His life	Romans 6:10-11
In His power	Ephesians 1:19-20
In His inheritance	Romans 8:16-17; Ephesians 1:11-14

When Paul said, "I have been crucified with Christ," he literally meant "I have been and continue to be crucified with Christ." The eternal life we received at salvation was the eternal life of Christ, which included eternity past and eternity future. We are identified with every aspect of Christ's eternal life because we are united with Him. Because we are eternally connected to God, we can be crucified with Christ and at the same time be seated with Him in the heavenly realms (see Eph. 2:6).

Before we came to Christ, we were under the law and in bondage to sin, which can only lead to death. We had to be crucified with Christ "so that the body of sin might be done away with" (Rom. 6:6). The "body of sin" refers to the person or self (living in bodily form) under the law and the rule of sin. This person was "done away with" by being crucified with Christ. The Greek term "done away with" can mean "rendered ineffective or powerless," "destroyed," "brought to an end" or "released from." Our old self was in bondage to sin and therefore utilized all of our bodily existence in servitude to sin and its mastery. That old self has died with Christ. Now, a new self exists, which is no longer under the mastery of sin.

Sin reigns through death; therefore, the way to freedom from sin is through death (see Rom. 6:6). Therefore, if a person dies to sin, sin loses its mastery over that person. Because the believer has died with Christ (participated with Him in His death to sin), that believer is free from the mastery of sin and lives a new life of freedom. Notice how Paul expresses this new freedom from sin in Romans:

> Just as you used to offer the parts of your body in slavery to impurity and to ever-increasing wickedness, so now offer them in slavery to righteousness leading to holiness. When you were slaves to sin, you were free from the control of righteousness. But now that you have been set free from sin and have become slaves to God, the benefit you reap leads to holiness, and the result is eternal life (6:19-20,22).

Note that death is the end of a relationship, not the end of existence. According to Paul we are alive in Christ and dead to sin (see Rom. 6:11). In Christ, sin and death have no mastery over us. Physical death is still imminent, but we shall continue to live spiritually even if we die physically. Sin is still present and appealing, but we don't have to yield to it. Faith in God is our victory.

> The life I live in the body, I live by faith in the Son of God, who loved me and gave himself for me (Gal. 2:20).

Thought for the day: *How are you crucified with Christ?*

- I've died to self → no longer live for myself but for Christ - to do God's will
- I will die physically as Christ died but have eternal life.
- I am no longer in bondage to sin

A NEW IDENTITY "IN CHRIST"

Genesis 32:28-32

The name "Jacob" means "supplanter." He cheated his brother out of his birthright and then ran for his life (see Gen. 27). Twenty years later he is wrestling with God on the wrong side of the Jordon. Suddenly, the dawn breaks and Jacob sees the face of God, and the whole battle changes. Jacob wouldn't let go until this "man" blessed him. This encounter with God forever changed Jacob: "Your name will no longer be Jacob, but Israel, because you have struggled with God and with men and have overcome" (Gen. 32:28). Jacob limps across the Jordan, but his name is now Israel, which means, "God strives."

Our encounter with God has forever changed us. We are no longer "by nature objects of wrath" (Eph. 2:3), we are children of God (see 1 John 3:1-3). "For you were once darkness, but now you are light in the Lord. Live as children of light" (Eph. 5:8).

But you are a chosen people, a royal priesthood, a holy nation, a people belonging to God, that you may declare the praises of him who called you out of darkness into his wonderful light. Once you were not a people, but now you are the people of God; once you had not received mercy, but now you have received mercy (1 Pet. 2:9-10).

ONCE I WAS NOT A PEOPLE BUT NOW I AM A PEOPLE OF GOD

WOW!

All people struggle with their identity. When we were little children, we knew that we were the sons and daughters of earthly parents, and we accepted this physical heritage as our identity. When we became teenagers, we began to search for our own identity. As adults, we try to make a name for ourselves in the world. The tendency is for us to find our identity in the things we do, places we live and the roles we play.

It is different for believers who are being conformed to the image of God. "Here there is no Greek or Jew, circumcised or uncircumcised, barbarian, Scythian, slave or free, but Christ is all, and is in all" (Col. 3:11). In other words, there are no racial, religious, cultural or social distinctions. We are all children of God and share the same status in the family of God.

Paul says, "So from now on we regard no one from a worldly point of view" (2 Cor. 5:16). Literally, it means that Paul no longer recognizes believers according to the flesh, i.e., their natural identity or who they were in Adam. He recognizes believers as new creations in Christ (see 2 Cor. 5:17). Paul asks, "Don't you know that all of us who were baptized into Christ Jesus were baptized into his death?" (Rom. 6:3). Knowing who we are in Christ is the foundation for living free in Christ. Don't we know that we have been united with Christ in His death and resurrection? Don't we know that we are new creations in Christ? We have to keep asking ourselves until we reply, "Yes, I do know who I am: a new person in Christ, and by the grace of God I shall live accordingly."

Use the following list to renew your mind to the truth of who you are in Christ:

In Christ You Are:

The salt of the earth (Matt. 5:13).
The light of the world (Matt. 5:14).
A child of God (John 1:12).
A part of the true vine, a channel of Christ's life (John 15:1,5).
Christ's friend (John 15:15).
Chosen and appointed by Christ to bear His fruit (John 15:16).
A slave of righteousness (Rom. 6:18).
Enslaved to God (Rom. 6:22).
A son of God; God is spiritually your Father (Rom. 8:14-15).
A joint heir with Christ, sharing His inheritance with Him (Rom. 8:17).
A temple—a dwelling place—of God. His Spirit and His life dwell in you
    (1 Cor. 3:16; 6:19).
United to the Lord and one spirit with Him (1 Cor. 6:17).
A member of Christ's Body (1 Cor. 12:27; Eph. 5:30).
A new creation in Christ (2 Cor. 5:17).
Reconciled to God and a minister of reconciliation (2 Cor. 5:18-19).
A son of God and one in Christ (Gal. 3:26,28).
An heir of God, since you are a son of God (Gal. 4:6-7).
A saint (Eph. 1:1; 1 Cor. 1:2; Phil. 1:1; Col. 1:2).
God's workmanship—His handiwork—born anew in Christ to do His work
    (Eph. 2:10).
A fellow citizen with the rest of God's family (Eph. 2:19).
A prisoner of Christ (Eph. 3:1; 4:1).
Righteous and holy (Eph. 4:24).

A citizen of heaven, seated in heaven right now (Phil. 3:20; Eph. 2:6).

Hidden with Christ in God (Col. 3:3).

An expression of the life of Christ because He is your life (Col. 3:4).

Chosen of God, holy and dearly loved (Col. 3:12; 1 Thess. 1:4).

A son of light and not of darkness (1 Thess. 5:5).

A holy partaker of a heavenly calling (Heb. 3:1).

A partaker of Christ; you share in His life (Heb. 3:14).

One of God's living stones, being built up in Christ as a spiritual house (1 Pet. 2:5).

A member of a chosen race, a royal priesthood, a holy nation and a people for God's own possession (1 Pet. 2:9-10).

An alien and stranger to this world in which you temporarily live (1 Pet. 2:11).

An enemy of the devil (1 Pet. 5:8).

A child of God and will resemble Christ when He returns (1 John 3:1-2).

Born of God, and the evil one cannot touch you (1 John 5:18).

Not the great "I Am" (Exod. 3:14; John 8:24,28,58), but by the grace of God, you are what you are (1 Cor. 15:10).

There is neither Jew nor Greek, slave nor free, male nor female, for you are all one in Christ Jesus (Gal. 3:28).

Thought for the day: *What do you believe is your primary identity?*

- Child of God + a partaker of Christ.

IN CHRIST I AM....

- salt
- light
- child of God
- part of the True vine, Christ's friend + channel of His life.
- chose + appointed by Christ
- fruit bearer
- slave of righteousness
- enslaved to God
- Son of God
- joint heir with Christ
- A temple - a dwelling place of God.
- one spirit with Him
- a member of Christ's body
- a new creation
- reconciled to God
- one in Christ
- heir of God
- A saint
- God's handi-work
- a fellow citizen
- prisoner of christ
- righteous + holy
- citizen of heaven
- hidden with Christ
- an expression of the life of Christ
- one of God's living stones.
- a member of a chosen race
- a royal priesthood
- a holy nation
- a people for God's own possessions
- an alien + stranger in this world.
- an enemy of the devil
- A child of God
- Born of God
- ONE IN CHRIST → neither Jew nor Greek, slave nor free, male no female

A NEW PERSON "IN CHRIST"

Colossians 3:9-10

Paul wrote in Romans 6:6 that our old self was crucified with Christ. This was a decisive and definite act in the believer's past. In Colossians 3:9-10, Paul exhorts believers to stop living in the old sins of their past life, "Since you have taken off your old self with its practices and have put on the new self." Paul makes a similar point in Ephesians 4:22-24:

> You were taught, with regard to your former way of life, to put off your old self, which is being corrupted by its deceitful desires; to be made new in the attitude of your minds; and to put on the new self, created to be like God in true righteousness and holiness.

In Romans 6:6 and Colossians 3:9-10, Paul clearly teaches a definitive past action, which happened the moment we were born again, but the Ephesians passage implies a continuous action on our part. The old self was crucified with Christ (positional sanctification), but as believers we have to do our part in putting off the old self and putting on the new self (progressive sanctification). This is not an exhortation to do again for ourselves what Christ has already done for us; rather, Paul is saying that we are new people in Christ who must become in practice what God has already made us. We must have the resolve to not let our "former way of life" impinge on who we now are.

In Galatians 3:27, Paul says, "For all of you who were baptized into Christ have clothed yourselves with Christ." The term "clothed yourselves" is the same word translated "put on" in the above passages and means that we are to "put on Christ." To clothe oneself with or to put on a person means to take on the characteristics of that person and become like him or her. Paul says we are to "clothe ourselves with the Lord Jesus Christ" (Rom. 13:14). This spiritual transformation has a decisive beginning, but it is not final or complete. The process of putting off the old self who was in Adam and putting on the new self who is in Christ is the sanctifying process that makes real in our experience what has already happened at salvation. In other words, we are to become by God's grace the people He has already made us.

This spiritual metamorphosis is illustrated by the caterpillar. This earthbound little creature is led by instinct to climb as high as it can by its own strength—usually on the limb of a tree. There it sows a little button that forms an attachment for the cocoon that it spins around itself as it hangs upside down. The caterpillar then ceases to exist, and a miraculous transformation takes place. The caterpillar has "crucified" itself in order to be "resurrected" a butterfly. The caterpillar gave up all that it was in order to become all that the Creator designed it to be.

The caterpillar can't take any credit for becoming a butterfly any more than we can take credit for the work of Christ, which is imputed to us by the grace of God. Imagine what would happen to the growth of the new butterfly if it chose to believe that it was still a caterpillar and kept on crawling instead of flying. The butterfly would never reach its potential, and neither will we—if we fail to put aside the old self and embrace our new life in Christ.

For all of you who were baptized into Christ have clothed yourselves with Christ (Gal. 3:27).

Thought for the day: *How can you clothe yourself in Christ, or are you already clothed in Christ?*

- Turn away from my old life whether is be lying, manipulating, everthing that is opposite of Christ + learn to live like Christ through prayer + reading God's Word, sermons, etc.

WE ARE NOW SAINTS "IN CHRIST"

Romans 1:7

Believers are "called to be saints" (Rom. 1:7), i.e., we are saints by His calling and not by our hard work. Notice that Paul writes "to the saints" in Ephesus (see Eph. 1:1) and Philippi (see Phil. 1:1). Saints are not those who have earned their lofty titles by living a magnificent life or achieving a certain level of maturity. In the Bible, all believers are described as "saints," which means "holy ones" (see 1 Cor. 1:2; 2 Cor. 1:1). Being a saint does not necessarily reflect any present measure of growth in character, but it does identify those who are rightly related to God. In Scripture, believers are called "saints," "holy ones" or "righteous ones" more than 200 times. In contrast, unbelievers are called "sinners" over 300 times. Clearly, the term "saint" is used in Scripture to refer to the believer and "sinner" is used in reference to the unbeliever.

Although the New Testament teaches that believers can and do sin, it never clearly identifies the believer as a "sinner." Paul's reference to himself as "the worst of sinners" (1 Tim. 1:16) seems to contradict his teaching. Despite the use of the present tense by the apostle, Paul is actually referring to his pre-conversion opposition to the Gospel.

First, the reference to himself as "sinner" is in support of the first half of the verse, "Christ Jesus came into the world to save sinners" (1 Tim. 1:15). The reference to "the ungodly and sinful" a few verses earlier (1 Tim. 1:9) along with the other New Testament uses of the term "sinners" for those who are outside salvation show that the "sinners" whom Christ came to save were outside of salvation.

Second, Paul's reference to himself as a "sinner" is immediately followed by the statement: "But for that very reason I was shown [past tense] mercy" (1 Tim. 1:16), clearly pointing to the past occasion of his conversion. Paul, the worst of sinners, uses himself as an example of God's unlimited patience. Because of his past action, Paul considered himself unworthy of what by God's grace and mercy he presently was, an apostle who was in no respect "inferior to the 'super-apostles' " (2 Cor. 12:11).

Third, although declaring that he was the "worst" sinner, the apostle at the same time declares that Christ had strengthened him for the ministry, having considered him "faithful" and trustworthy for the ministry to which he was called (see 1 Tim 1:12). The term "sinner," therefore, does not describe him as a believer, but is rather used in remembrance of what he was before Christ took hold of him.

As believers, we are not trying to become saints; we are saints who are becoming like Christ. Being saints is part of our positional sanctification. In no way does this deny the continuous struggle with sin. Christians can choose to sin, and many are dominated by the flesh and deceived by the devil. Because believers sin, we want to call them sinners, but what we do does not determine who we are. Telling Christians they are sinners and then disciplining them if they don't act like saints is counterproductive at best and inconsistent with the Bible at worst. Believing who we really are in Christ determines what we do.

> Dear friends, now we are children of God. . . . Everyone who has this hope in him purifies himself, just as he is pure (1 John 3:2-3).

Thought for the day: *What effect would it have on believers if they were instructed to believe they were only sinners?*

- There would be no grace + no forgiveness.
- no sense in who we are in Christ.

A NEW RELATIONSHIP

Galatians 4:1-7

Slavery in the United States was abolished by the Thirteenth Amendment on December 18, 1865. How many slaves were there on December 19, 1865? In reality, none, but many still lived like slaves. Some did so because they had never learned the truth that they were indeed free. Some didn't believe the truth and continued to live as they had been taught. Others reasoned that they were still doing the same thing that slaves did, so they must still be slaves. They maintained their slave identity because of the things they did.

One former slave, however, heard the good news and received it with great joy. He checked out the validity of the amendment and found out that the highest of all authorities had originated the decree. Not only that, but it also had personally cost that authority a tremendous price. As a result, the slave's life was transformed. He correctly reasoned that it would be hypocritical to believe that he was still a slave rather than believe the truth that he was free. Determined to live by what he knew to be true, his experiences began to change rather dramatically. He realized that his old taskmaster had no authority over him and did not need to be obeyed. He gladly served the one who had set him free.

In Galatians 4, Paul says that we were all like little children (*nepios*, "child" [v. 1], in contrast with *huios*, "son" [v. 7]) who are subservient to our guardians and trustees, similar to the way that slaves are under the authority of their masters. Even though we had a birthright, we could not become heirs until the time appointed by our Father. "But when the time had fully come, God sent his Son, born of a woman, born under law, to redeem those under law, that we might receive the full rights of sons" (vv. 4-5). We were enslaved to the "basic principles of the world" (v. 3) until Christ came and set us free. We were in bondage to the Mosaic Law or other religious systems.

Christ did two things for those who were under the yoke of slavery (see Gal. 5:1). First, He redeemed those under the Law. The Jews were enslaved to the whole Mosaic system. It was the bondage of legalism. Second, the incarnation, death and resurrection of Christ secured for all believers their birthright as sons and daughters: "Because you are sons, God sent the Spirit of his Son into our hearts, the Spirit who calls out, 'Abba, Father.' So you are no longer a slave, but a son; and since you are a son, God has made you also an heir" (Gal. 5:6-7). As believers we may not feel free from sin and we may not feel like children of God, but in reality we are. Our position in Christ is real truth, and we must choose to believe it.

The Holy Spirit resides in our hearts, ensuring our position in God's family. The Spirit moves us to pray, "Abba, Father." The word "Abba" is the Aramaic word for "father." It was used by small children who addressed their father. It would be similar to the English word "Daddy." "Abba" implies intimacy and trust as opposed to slavery and legalism.

> So you are no longer a slave, but a son; and since you are a son, God has made you also an heir (Gal. 4:7).

Thought for the day: *What does it mean to be an heir?*

- It means I belong to the family of God
- I am not a slave to sin any longer but a heir with Jesus.
- I have an intimate relationship with God

A RIGHT STANDING

Jeremiah 52:31-34

After the fall of Jerusalem, Jehoiachin, king of Judah, was exiled to Babylon and imprisoned. Evil-Merodach was the son of Nebuchadnezzar and king of the Babylonian empire. (Evil-Merodach actually means the son or servant of the god Murduk.) Out of kindness, Evil-Merodach set Jehoiachin free, placed him in a position of honor, fellowshiped with him daily and provided for all his needs. This kingly act of grace is an Old Testament type of what has been perfectly fulfilled in Christ.

Israel had a covenant relationship with God, which was conditional. Had they trusted God and been obedient, they would have enjoyed prosperity in the Promised Land. The Lord had said to His Covenant People,

> Maintain justice and do what is right, for my salvation is close at hand and my righteousness will soon be revealed. Blessed is the man who does this, the man who holds it fast, who keeps the Sabbath without desecrating it, and keeps his hand from doing any evil (Isa. 56:1-2).

But the Chosen People were unable to keep the Law. The nation divided into Israel and Judah. Because of their disobedience, God raised up Assyria to defeat Israel. Finally Judah fell along with Jerusalem in 586 B.C. Because of Adam's sin, they had no legal relationship with God, causing them to stand guilty and under condemnation. Sin had severed their personal, moral relationship with Him, causing their nature to be impure and at odds with God's holiness as follows:

	Pre-fall man	**Post-fall man**
Natural	Righteous	"By nature objects of wrath" (Eph. 2:3)
Rational	Truthful and Right	"Darkened in their understanding" (Eph. 4:18)
Spiritual	Alive	"Separated from the life of God" (Eph. 4:18)

	Pre-fall man	Post-fall man
Emotional	Safe, secure, free	"Having lost all sensitivity" (Eph. 4:18f)
Volitional	Free to choose	"Given themselves over to sensuality" (Eph. 4:19)

Through Christ and by the grace of God, our relationship and right standing with God can be restored. We can be justified by faith. Justification is a judge's pronouncement of a person's right standing before the law. We are no longer condemned (see Rom. 8:1). When a judge condemns someone, he does not make the person a sinner; rather, he simply declares that such is the case. In justification, God is not making us inherently righteous; He is declaring that we are in a right standing before His law. This change of legal relationship is totally a gift from God, because of Christ's sacrifice on our behalf.

Out of the kindness of our Lord, our relationship has been restored. We have been set free from our sins. We are no longer children of wrath; we are children of God. We are no longer darkened in our understanding; we have been given the mind of Christ and the Holy Spirit will lead us into all truth. We are no longer spiritually dead; we are alive in Christ. We are no longer hardened in our hearts; we have been given a new heart and a new spirit. Finally, we are no longer given over to sensuality; we have been given the freedom to live a morally pure life by the grace of God.

> And God raised us up with Christ and seated us with him in the heavenly realms in Christ Jesus (Eph. 2:6).

Thought for the day: *What are the personal implications of being in a right standing with authority?*

- we are free from imprisionment
- we can live in total freedom
- We can live without fear of condemnation

Think about this! I do not have to fear God's wrath! Though I don't deserve it He has justified me! He has given me a clean heart. I AM A CHILD OF GOD - A HEIR! THINK ABOUT IT!

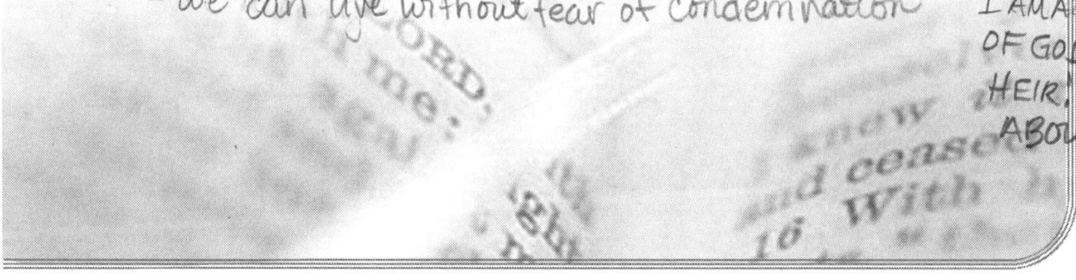

PEACE WITH GOD

Judges 6:1-24

"When the angel of the LORD appeared to Gideon, he said, 'The LORD is with you, mighty warrior'" (Judg. 6:12). The angel of the Lord was probably a *theophany* (a manifestation of God) or a pre-incarnate appearance of Christ. Like Moses, Gideon had been commissioned by God to deliver Israel. To make sure this word was from God, Gideon asked for a sign (see Judg. 6:17).

So it was that when Gideon brought his offering as instructed, an amazing miracle occurred:

Fire flared from the rock, consuming the meat and the bread. . . . When Gideon realized that it was the angel of the LORD, he exclaimed, "Ah, Sovereign LORD! I have seen the angel of the LORD face to face!" But the Lord said to him, "Peace! Do not be afraid. You are not going to die'" (Judg. 6:21-23).

Any unregenerate person would respond as Gideon did if suddenly confronted by the presence of God. If that be the case, then why would anybody want to draw near to a holy God who is perceived as a consuming fire?

That is the unfortunate perspective of many defeated Christians. They live as though God were out to get them. If they make just one mistake, then the hammer of God will surely fall on them.

Dear child of God, the hammer fell. It fell on Christ, once and for all. You are not a sinner in the hands of an angry God. You are a saint in the hands of a loving God who has called you to come before His presence. "In him and through faith in him we may approach God with freedom and confidence" (Eph. 3:12). AMEN!

"So Gideon built an altar to the LORD there and called it The LORD is Peace" (v. 24). Jesus is the Prince of Peace, and His primary work has been to mediate peace between fallen humanity and God. "Now in Christ Jesus you who once were far away have been brought near through the blood of Christ" (Eph. 2:13). Peace is now no longer out of reach: "Therefore, since we have been justified through faith, we have peace with God through our Lord Jesus Christ" (Rom. 5:1). Notice that Paul describes this justification, this peace between God and humankind, using the past tense. It has already been accomplished. There is nothing more that needs to be done. We will not die in the presence of God, as Gideon feared; we are already in the presence of God, because we are alive "in Him."

As the Peacemaker, Jesus also reconciles Jew and Gentile.

For he himself is our peace, who has made the two one and has destroyed the barrier, the dividing wall of hostility, by abolishing in his flesh the law with its commandments and regulations. His purpose was to create in himself one new man out of two, thus making peace, and in this one body to reconcile both of them to God through the cross, by which he put to death their hostility. He came and preached peace to you who were far away and peace to those who were near. For through him we both have access to the Father by one Spirit (Eph. 2:14-18).

When the barrier between God and us is torn down in Christ, it also brings down the barrier between those who are committed to Him. Trying to negotiate peace in this world without first having peace with God has not proven successful. Peace between religious and philosophical factions can only happen when both find their peace with the same God.

He came and preached peace to you who were far away and peace to those who were near (Eph. 2:17).

Thought for the day: *Do you have peace with God and others?*

I do have peace with God but I cannot say I have total peace with others. Maybe I do. It's not that I hate anyone, it's that we may have our differences & choose not to be close — I don't believe that we don't have peace with others. There won't be complete peace until heaven.

ACCESS TO GOD

Hebrews 10:19-25

"Who may ascend the hill of the LORD? Who may stand in his holy place? He who has clean hands and a pure heart" (Ps. 24:3-4). David asked for a pure heart so that he could live in the presence of God and His Holy Spirit (see Ps. 51:10-11). Isaiah's uncleanness needed the cleansing touch of an angel's burning coal (see Isa. 6:5-7). James commands, "Come near to God and he will come near to you." But then he adds what is necessary: "Wash your hands . . . and purify your hearts" (Jas. 4:8). Jesus said it is the "pure in heart" who will "see God," who will experience fellowship with Him (see Matt. 5:8). Since we have all sinned and fallen short of the glory of God (see Rom. 3:23), who can possibly approach Him?

In the Old Testament, everything about the Temple was set up to emphasize the near-unapproachable holiness and power of God. Only priests could enter the Temple, and only the High Priest, on one day a year—the Day of Atonement—could go into the Holy of Holies behind a thick veil or curtain that separated God from the priests. This was a day of great fear, reverence and awe. The High Priest entered only after going through a great deal of ceremonial cleansing. Even then, he probably entered with fear and trepidation, not knowing if he would come out alive. The other priests actually tied a rope around his ankles to pull him out of God's presence if it appeared to others that he had expired, because nobody else wanted to go in after him.

In the New Testament there is a radical shift in access to God. The moment Jesus died for our sins on the cross, "The curtain of the temple was torn in two from top to bottom" (Mark 15:38). The relationship between God and humankind had been restored. As the writer of Hebrews says:

> Therefore, brothers, since we have confidence to enter the Most Holy Place by the blood of Jesus, by a new and living way opened for us through the curtain, that is, his body, and since we have a great priest over the house of God, let us draw near to God with a sincere heart in full assurance of faith, having our hearts sprinkled to cleanse us from a guilty conscience and having our bodies washed with pure water (Heb. 10:19-22).

O that the Jews could see + understand this. Open their hearts, eyes + ears Lord Jesus that they may see + understand.

Suppose you petitioned for weeks and months to have an audience with the President of the United States, who is arguably the most powerful person on this planet. Finally, you were granted your request, and you were given 15 minutes alone with him. Since you have no personal relationship with him, what would you hope to gain by such a visit?

Now suppose that you had access to the God who created the President of the United States. He has even taken the initiative to invite you into His presence (see Matt. 11:28). Not only that, you know this God personally, and He has known you from the foundations of the world. Plus, you can have an audience with Him 24 hours of every day, and He listens to you. "This is the confidence we have in approaching God: that if we ask anything according to his will, he hears us" (1 John 5:14).

Knowing that we have access to God, let us never lose hope (see Heb. 10:23). We have a God of all hope and with Him all things are possible. So if you are discouraged, draw near to God and you will find mercy and grace in time of need (see Heb. 4:16). Because we have access to God, "Let us consider how we may spur one another on toward love and good deeds" (Heb. 10:24). Knowing that we have access to God, let us continue meeting with one another for the sake of encouragement (see Heb. 10:25).

In him and through faith in him we may approach God with freedom and confidence (Eph. 3:12).

Thought for the day: *What is keeping Christians from approaching God daily?*

I believe there is:
- lack of discipline → I have to be intent on praying - no excuses!
- busyness → put too many other things first
- lack of faith → not taking God at His Word
- laziness → not willing to take the time.
- Self-reliance → we think we can do it on our own.
- pride → keeps us from laying down our lives to God.
- put other things first → t.v., etc.

* I go through stages which I don't understand. Sometimes praying is so easy + other times it's the last thing I want to do. Why? Is it all the above? Not so much busyness but all of the rest. Lord God forgive me. I...

Want to be a woman of prayer - a woman of faith - for You are my Hope. Help me Lord Jesus as I struggle with this. I know I fall short of what You have for me because of this.

THE COMING OF THE HOLY SPIRIT

Joel 2:28-32

"Suddenly a sound like the blowing of a violent wind came from heaven and filled the whole house where they were sitting. They saw what seemed to be tongues of fire that separated and came to rest on each of them. All of them were filled with the Holy Spirit and began to speak in other tongues as the Spirit enabled them" (Acts 2:2-4). When the Holy Spirit came at Pentecost, Peter immediately associated those spiritual manifestations with the fulfillment of Joel's prophecy (see Acts 2:14-21).

The coming of the Holy Spirit at Pentecost is what distinguishes the Old Covenant from the New Covenant. Prior to Pentecost, the presence of God was *with* His people. In the Church age after Pentecost, the presence of God is *within* believers in the Person of the Holy Spirit. Old Testament believers had a legal relationship with God, but New Testament believers have a personal relationship with their heavenly Father. The primary work of the Holy Spirit is to testify "with our spirit that we are God's children" (Rom. 8:16). Peter wrote, "Once you were not a people, but now you are the people of God; once you had not received mercy, but now you have received mercy" (1 Pet. 2:10).

Through the prophet Joel, God said, "I will pour out my Spirit on all people" (Joel 2:28). This universal inclusion of all people is also a marked difference between the Old and the New Testament. "All peoples on earth will be blessed" (Gen. 12:3) through the seed of Abraham. This will be true regardless of race, age, gender or social class (see Joel 2:29). "And everyone who calls on the name of the LORD will be saved" (Joel 2:32; see also Rom. 10:13).

In the Old Testament, God spoke through the prophets to the people, but in the Church age, God personally leads every one of His children, "because those who are led by the Spirit of God are sons of God" (Rom. 8:14). In the Old Testament, Moses said, "I wish that all the LORD's people were prophets and that the LORD would put his Spirit on them" (Num. 11:29). God has put His Spirit in every New Testament believer; and according to the prophecy of Joel, "Your sons and daughters will prophesy, your old men will dream dreams, your young men will see visions" (2:28). Because of our personal relationship with Him, God will uniquely equip all His children.

Generally speaking, "the day of the LORD" (Joel 2:31) is an idiom used to emphasize the decisive nature of God's victory over His enemies. Prior to Pentecost, Jesus defeated the devil; and according to Paul, it is the eternal purpose of God to make His wisdom known through the Church to the rulers and authorities in the heavenly realms, which is the spiritual kingdom of darkness (see Eph. 3:10-12). The enemy knows he is defeated when the children of God speak the truth in love through the power of the Holy Spirit.

I will pour out my Spirit on all people (Joel 2:28).

Thought for the day: *What would happen if the entire Church were empowered and led by the Spirit of God within them?*

- The church already is but as humans we tend to look to ourselves instead of God & often live as though we are powerless.

If we would just understand & allow the Holy Spirit to work in and through us, & keep our eyes on Christ & live our lives for His Kingdom the church would be a different thing & thousands would be saved as it was in the New Testament.

O Lord God, let me not do anything to turn people away from You but let Your love flow through me that others may see You & want to know You in a personal way. O Lord the time is short! You Lord God would want none to parish & my heart cries out to You that those people whom You have brought into my (our) lives will not perish & that I will be your light that will draw them to You.

LORD GOD — ANNOINT ME WITH YOUR HOLY SPIRIT & WITH BOLDNESS.

A NEW HEART
AND A NEW SPIRIT

Ezekiel 36:26-27

We were all born into this world physically alive but spiritually dead—our hearts were deceitful and there was nothing we could do about it. There was no way that we could create for ourselves a new spiritual life, and our hearts were beyond human cure. Jeremiah wrote, "The heart is deceitful above all things and beyond cure" (Jer. 17:9). Such is the depravity of fallen humanity.

Ezekiel prophesied that God would give us a new heart and put a new spirit within us (see Ezek. 36:26). This foretaste of the Gospel promised far more than the forgiveness of sins and an external change of master. It also included a transformation within us. Our very being is changed at its deepest level so that we now have new desires and new prevailing dispositions toward life. This change of nature refers to a fundamental change in the orientation, propensities, desires and direction of our person, including our thoughts and actions. We have not become gods, but we now have God within us. All humans have the same human nature, but that nature can have different propensities and forces at work within it.

The newness of our person, or self, is clearly seen in the fact that we have been given a new heart. According to Scripture, our heart is the inner core of our personhood: "As water reflects a face, so a man's heart reflects the man" (Prov. 27:19). Just as gazing into still water reflects what we look like, so does looking into the heart provide an accurate reflection of who we really are. God knows who we really are, because He looks at the heart. "The LORD does not look at the things man looks at. Man looks at the outward appearance, but the LORD looks at the heart" (1 Sam. 16:7).

We have been given a new heart because we have been made a new creation in Christ. In fact, it is the new heart that makes a new person. Our new birth means "a new heart" (see Deut. 30:5-6; Ezek. 11:19). Proverbs 4:23 reads, "Above all else, guard your heart, for it is the wellspring of life." The last phrase literally means "for out of it are the issues of life." The heart is the fountain of our life, and it controls the course of our life. This is seen in Ecclesiastes 10:2, "The heart of the wise inclines to the right, but the heart of the fool to the left." Jesus taught that what we do comes from our heart:

"Out of the overflow of the heart the mouth speaks. The good man brings good things out of the good stored up in him, and the evil man brings evil things out of the evil stored up in him" (Matt. 12:34-35). Our new life stems from our heart. <u>Godly thoughts, motives, words, feelings, attitudes and actions all originate in our heart.</u> It is the mission control center of human life. The believer in Christ, through death and resurrection with Him, has received God's Spirit and a new heart, and thus a new control center of life.

> I will give you a new heart and put a new spirit in you; I will remove from you your heart of stone and give you a heart of flesh. And I will put my Spirit in you and move you to follow my decrees and be careful to keep my laws (Ezek. 36:26-27).

Thought for the day: *What hope does it give you knowing that the core of your being has changed?*

I have a hope that I will Continue to grow spiritually + Continue to Change+ become more like Christ.

A NEW COVENANT

Jeremiah 31:31-34

God made a covenant with the nation of Israel at the time of the Exodus from Egypt. This conditional Mosaic Covenant, which is detailed in the books of Exodus, Leviticus, Numbers and Deuteronomy, stipulated that the nation of Israel would receive God's blessings if they obeyed, but they would be punished if they didn't (see Lev. 26; Deut. 28). Since they disobeyed and rebelled against the Law, final judgment came with the fall of Jerusalem in 586 B.C., resulting in the destruction of the Temple and the deportation of the Jewish people to Babylon, where they remained in captivity for 70 years.

But God had not forgotten His people. Through the prophet Jeremiah, God made a new covenant with His people. God said, "I will put my law in their minds and write it on their hearts. I will be their God, and they will be my people" (Jer. 31:33). According to this New Covenant, God's law would be written on their hearts rather than on stone tablets (see Exod. 34:1). Then they would have the ability to live up to His righteous standards and thus enjoy His blessings. We learned from Ezekiel 36:24-32 that this inner ability to live a righteous life was due to the indwelling presence of the Holy Spirit. The Holy Spirit was present throughout the Old Testament, but He did not universally indwell all believers. Under the New Covenant, the Holy Spirit would indwell every believer, enabling each and every one to be holy as God is holy.

This New Covenant also made a provision for our sin. God said, "I will forgive their wickedness and will remember their sins no more" (Jer. 31:34). By making this covenant, God was not overlooking our sin nor was He forgetting it. God couldn't forget, because He is omniscient. "I will remember your sins no more" means "I will not take the past and use it against you in the future." Scripture says, "As far as the east is from the west, so far has he removed our transgressions from us" (Ps. 103:12).

Yet in order for the New Covenant to be efficacious, a sacrifice would be required. Before His crucifixion, Jesus announced in the Upper Room that the New Covenant would be inaugurated through the shedding of His blood (see Matt. 26:27-28; Luke 22:20). The permanence of this New Covenant was underscored by the promise that the descendants of Israel will continue to exist (see Jer. 31:35-36). The power God displayed in creating the universe was the same power that would ensure the preservation of His Chosen People. Although this covenant was made with Israel and Judah (see Jer. 31:31), the Church would also receive the benefits of this covenant (see Heb. 8:8-12). The New Covenant was inaugurated on the day of Pentecost when all the Jewish believers were gathered to celebrate the fiftieth day after the Sabbath of Passover week. Thus the Early Church believers were all Jewish.

John wrote, "Salvation is from the Jews" (John 4:22). The unconditional covenant that God had made with Abraham ensured that "all peoples on earth [would] be blessed through [Abraham]" (Gen. 12:3). As the book of Acts tells us, the gospel first came to the Jews and then to the Gentiles.

The Church has been grafted into the original branch (i.e., Israel; see Romans 11). All New Testament believers, both Jew and Gentile, live under the New Covenant that guarantees spiritual life and the forgiveness of sins. Consequently, believers no longer relate to God on the basis of the Old Mosaic Covenant that required strict observance of the Law. The New Covenant is one of grace that calls for believers to live by faith in the power of the Holy Spirit.

> I will put my law in their minds and write it on their hearts. I will be their God, and they will be my people (Jer. 31:33).

Thought for the day: *What does it mean to live under the New Covenant?*

It means that we do not live under the Mosaic law with all the rules & regulations that were impossible to keep. God made it so easy for us through Christ Jesus. Thank You Heavenly Father & thank You Jesus.

A NEW CREATION

2 Corinthians 5:16-18

As born-again believers, we are all new creations in Christ. We may not always feel like it or act like it, but Scripture clearly teaches that we are children of God (see 1 John 3:1-3) and no longer children of wrath (see Eph. 2:1-3). This immediate spiritual transformation and continuing growth is easier to understand if we are familiar with a particular agricultural technique that is used in the semitropical climate zones where a frost can severely damage citrus crops. Horticulturists have learned to use the bitter-tasting ornamental orange as rootstock because it can take a moderate freeze without damage. When the ornamental orange tree has grown to the right stage, the stem is cut just above the ground and a sweet orange, such as a navel orange, is grafted in. The new growth above the graft has a new nature.

Yet nobody looks at a navel orange grove and says, "Actually all those trees are nothing but rootstock." They were at one time, but they no longer are. The orchard is now identified by the type of fruit the trees are bearing. The same is true for us. Jesus said, "By their fruit you will recognize them" (Matt. 7:16). Believers are identified for who they are "in Christ," not for who they were "in Adam."

Suckers can continue to grow from the old roots, but they need to be trimmed off. If they are allowed to grow, they will divert the growth of the tree away from the new graft. In the same way, the gardener cuts off every branch that does not bear fruit and prunes every branch that is bearing fruit in order that it may bear even more (see John 15:2).

We have been grafted into Christ and He will prune away our old nature that doesn't bear fruit. This transformation from who we were "in Adam" to who we are now "in Christ" may be summarized as follows:

In Adam		In Christ
Old Self	*By Birth*	New Self
(Col. 3:9)		(Col. 3:10)
Sin Nature	*By Nature*	Participate in the
(Eph. 2:1-3)		Divine Nature
		(2 Pet. 1:4)

| Live According to the Sinful Nature (Flesh) (Rom. 8:5a) | *By Choice* | Live in Accordance with the Spirit or the Flesh (Rom. 8:5b; Gal. 5:13-23) |

The apostle Paul consistently identifies the believer according to the new life that has been grafted in. "So from now on we regard no one from a worldly point of view" (2 Cor. 5:16). In other words, we shouldn't perceive other believers as natural people who derive their identity from their physical origin and natural existence. Returning to the tree illustration, that which grows above the graft has only one nature, but the total tree has two natures (rootstock and navel). The believer still lives in a mortal body and is confronted with the choice of living according to the old sinful nature (flesh) or living according to the Spirit. However, the apostle Paul says, "Those who belong to Christ Jesus have crucified the sinful nature with its passions and desires" (Gal. 5:24). We are new creations in Christ, and we belong to Him. Someday, we will leave our physical body, receive a resurrected body and live forever—with only one righteous nature—in the presence of God.

> All this is from God, who reconciled us to himself through Christ (2 Cor. 5:18).

Thought for the day: *How should believers respond to this gift of new life?*

We should be grateful + thankful and realize the cost Christ paid for us + truly change - not have one foot in the world nor be sitting on the fence.. If our old nature is crucified with Christ then we should see changes in our life, in thoughts, actions, desires, etc.

A NEW HEART

Proverbs 4:23

Ezekiel prophesied, "I will give them an undivided heart and put a new spirit in them; I will remove from them their heart of stone and give them a heart of flesh. Then they will follow my decrees and be careful to keep my laws. They will be my people, and I will be their God" (Ezek. 11:19-20). A new heart and a new spirit are clearly gifts from God. Jeremiah prophesied, "I will give them a heart to know me, that I am the LORD. They will be my people, and I will be their God, for they will return to me with all their heart" (Jer. 24:7). This is a heart to know and experience God.

Contrary to popular thinking, the dominant function of the heart is not emotional. The heart, according to Scripture, is primarily the place where human beings think; secondly, where they will; and thirdly, where they feel. This was confirmed by H. Wheeler Robinson. He counted 822 uses of the word "heart" in Scripture for some aspect of human personality. According to his categorization, 204 of the 822 uses refer to our intellect, 195 to our will and 166 to our emotions.[1] It is better to think of our heart as the center of self and the seat of reflection, rather than the seat of our emotions.

The essential business of the heart is stated in Proverbs 15:14: "The discerning heart seeks knowledge." The word for "heart" occurs most frequently in the portions of the Bible known as the wisdom literature (for example, 99 times in Proverbs and 42 times in Ecclesiastes) as well as the highly instructional book of Deuteronomy (51 times). These portions of Scripture instruct us in the way of God's wisdom, which we are to know and understand with our hearts. Thus the goal of life is to gain a heart of wisdom (see Ps. 90:12).

In order to direct our ways and transform our lives, the truth of God's Word must penetrate our hearts. It is possible to intellectually know the truth and yet not allow it to have an impact on how we feel or what we do. Only in the heart do the mind, emotion and will come together in holistic unity. When we allow the truth to penetrate our hearts, it immediately stirs the emotions, which drive the will. The Biblical idea of knowing God and knowing the truth that will set us free involves our emotions and our will, not just our intellect. To grow and live righteous lives, we must experience

God, not just have an intellectual knowledge of His attributes.

Many believers are not experiencing God's presence or the liberating benefits of knowing Him, because they have never gotten beyond an intellectual understanding of who He is. The greatest commandment is to "Love the Lord your God with all your heart and with all your soul and with all your mind" (Matt. 22:37). To obey this commandment requires our total being. We must enter into the experience of worship, and the experience of living with God on a daily basis.

Love the Lord your God with all your heart and with all your soul and with all your mind (Matt. 22:37).

Thought for the day: *How do you love God with all your heart?*

My selfish ways often get in the way of loving God with all of my heart but I love to learn more about God through scripture reading, Bible study, praise + worship, etc. As I do this I see His great love not only for me but for all mankind. God is so awesome + so amazing + He sent Jesus who obeyed Him + showed us how to live + then died for ME. It is mind boggling + overwhelming. What an AWESOME GOD WE SERVE.

A NEW SPIRIT

John 3:1-15

Nicodemus was a Pharisee and a member of the Sanhedrin. Not wanting his colleagues to know of his association with Jesus, Nicodemus went to see Him under the cover of darkness to inquire about the kingdom of God. He recognized that Jesus taught with authority and knew that no one could have performed the miracles that Jesus had unless God were with Him (see John 3:1-2). Jesus turned the conversation to the doctrine of regeneration. "I tell you the truth, no one can see the kingdom of God unless he is born again" (v. 3). Nicodemus did not understand—he wondered how a child could again enter into the womb of his mother. But Jesus was not talking about going through the natural birth process again; rather, He was talking about a new birth.

What distinguishes the natural birth from this new spiritual birth is its origin. "Flesh gives birth to flesh, but the Spirit gives birth to spirit" (John 3:6). The term "born again" in verse 3 literally means "born from above." In regeneration, the supernatural origin is just as important as the newness of the birth. The ideas of "newness," "regeneration" and a supernatural origin are all joined together in Titus 3:5: "He saved us through the washing of rebirth and renewal by the Holy Spirit, whom he poured out on us generously through Jesus Christ our Savior." In salvation, there is a washing and a renewing, a change in the innermost attitudes and inclinations of our hearts of such a nature that it can only be compared with the generation and birth of life. Unlike natural birth, however, this birth does not have its origin in the will of humankind but in the sovereign power of God. It is a birth that is not of the flesh, nor of blood, but of the Spirit.

In regeneration, the Holy Spirit indwells every believer. His coming produces a radical change from pollution and death to holiness and life. The coming of the Holy Spirit produces a new creation in Christ. The newly "born from above" believer is exhorted to "put on the new self, created to be like God in true righteousness and holiness" (Eph. 4:24). Even as a newly born child cannot orchestrate his or her own conception and birth, neither can any believer take any credit for the transformation of him or herself. The power to change comes from above.

Unregenerate people are like dry sponges wrapped in plastic. In that state, they serve no useful purpose. Then one day, God strips away the plastic wrapping, puts the squeeze on them and plunges them into a pool of His living water. While they are submerged, God loosens His grip and every pore of their being is filled with His presence. Now they are complete in Christ and able to fulfill the purpose for which they were created. Should these sponges decide to pull away from the water, they would soon dry out and fail again to fulfill their purpose, even though they are forever free from that which originally bound them.

Good Analogy

Born-again believers are Holy Spirit possessed—the Holy Spirit has taken up residence in their bodies and made them temples of God.

> Do you not know that your body is a temple of the Holy Spirit, who is in you, whom you have received from God? You are not your own; you were bought at a price. Therefore honor God with your body (1 Cor. 6:19-20).

Thought for the day: *What does it mean to you that your body is a temple of God, a dwelling place for the Almighty?*

- To start with, it is so hard for my finite mind to fully grasp this. I know it is true but if I could fully comprehend it I know God would be able to do so many amazing things. I'm going to pray that the Holy Spirit will reveal this TRUTH in a new way.
- There has been so much commotion with many of the changes in our church — i.e. coffee shop... coffee brought into the sanctuary Sunday mornings, etc. But when Pastor Glen explained that we are the Temple of God not the church building; it made sense to me + I wasn't so upset about these things, although I still have a few struggles with it all.
- Anyways, it makes me think twice before I do and say things — see things such as movies + tv., etc.

ASSURANCE OF SALVATION

1 John 5:1-13

Salvation is a definitive experience. When we receive Jesus into our lives (see John 1:12), we are born again (see John 3:3). At that very moment, we are rescued from the dominion of darkness, brought into the kingdom of God, redeemed and forgiven of our sins (see Col. 1:13-14). We are no longer "in Adam." We are new creations "in Christ," and our names are recorded in the "Lamb's book of life" (Rev. 21:27). "And this is the testimony: God has given us eternal life, and this life is in his Son. He who has the Son has life; he who does not have the Son of God does not have life" (1 John 5:11-12).

God wants His children to be assured of their salvation. "I write these things to you who believe in the name of the Son of God so that you may know that you have eternal life" (1 John 5:13). Essentially, there are three means by which we can be assured of our salvation. The first is the witness of Scripture. God has taken the initiative to provide for our salvation, established the criteria by which we can experience it and revealed the plan for both in His authoritative Word.

God secured our salvation by sacrificing His only Son to die in our place for our sins. Then by His power, God resurrected Christ in order that we may have eternal life in Him. The means by which we can experience salvation is by believing in the finished work of Christ. "Everyone who believes that Jesus is the Christ is born of God" (1 John 5:1). We are not saved by how we behave; we are saved by how we believe. Saving faith, however, is not just giving mental assent to what one chooses to believe. Saving faith is relying on the death and resurrection of Christ as the only means for salvation. The apostle Paul wrote, "If you confess with your mouth, 'Jesus is Lord,' and believe in your heart that God raised him from the dead, you will be saved. For it is with your heart that you believe and are justified, and it is with your mouth that you confess and are saved" (Rom. 10:9-10). People can mentally acknowledge that a historical person named Jesus died for their sins and rose again and yet not be born again. Believing that Jesus is Lord is not the same as believing that Jesus is "my Lord." Jesus is the Savior, but those who are saved confess Jesus as the Lord of their lives and live accordingly. What we choose to believe affects our walk and our talk; and if it doesn't, we really don't believe.

[Handwritten margin note: Oh how we get caught up in believing we must do this or we are not saved. It is only through Christ]

s - breast cancer (Maxines friend diagnosed a month ago)
(Stage 3)

Vonna Love - breast cancer.
& family

Matthew 5:43.... He causes
~~the~~ His sun to rise on the
evil and the good, & sends
rain on the righteous &
unrighteous.

THE DAILY DISCIPLER 133

John teaches that those who are born again love the Father and the Son (1 John 5:1), and those who love the Father "obey his commands. And his commands are not burdensome, for everyone born of God overcomes the world" (vv. 3-4). To emphasize the point, John asks, "Who is it that overcomes the world? Only he who believes that Jesus is the Son of God" (v. 5). The two additional means by which we can be assured of our salvation is the evidence of a changed life and the internal witness of the Holy Spirit (see v. 6), which we will cover the next two days. Every believer needs to understand that Christ has brought us salvation and that He wants all His children to be assured of their salvation. *I struggled with doubts for too long.*

> And this is the testimony: God has given us eternal life, and this life is in his Son. He who has the Son has life; he who does not have the Son of God does not have life (1 John 5:11-12).

Thought for the day: *Do you have eternal life? Do you want to have eternal life?*

Yes I have eternal life. And once I got passed my doubts + fears which gripped me I can be excited + not be so fearful of all the things we see going on in the world. It is so amazing!

THE WITNESS OF THE SPIRIT

Revelation 2:1-7

God has made it possible for us to have a relationship with Him and He wants us to have the assurance that we are His children, if indeed we have been born again. We may think we are saved, and those around us may agree that we are; but only God has the authority to confirm our status before Him, and He does. For every true believer, "The Spirit himself testifies with our spirit that we are God's children" (Rom. 8:16). If we have been born again, our human spirit is in union with God, providing an internal confirmation that we are indeed children of God. "Because you are sons, God sent the Spirit of his Son into our hearts, the Spirit who calls out 'Abba, Father'" (Gal. 4:6).

This inner witness is far more than a subjective feeling. The presence of the Holy Spirit in our lives brings a new love for God and a progressive detachment from the sinful attractions of this world. "For everyone born of God overcomes the world" (1 John 5:4). The true believer cannot continue in sin without being convicted by the Holy Spirit. Those who are struggling to overcome the entrapment of sin often question their salvation—yet the very fact that their sinful behavior bothers them may be the best evidence that they have been born again. The Holy Spirit cannot take up residence in our lives and silently sit by while we continue to defile our bodies, which are temples of the Holy Spirit. If we as believers continue to live in sin, we will be miserable, and we will hate the sin that holds us in bondage. "The world and its desires pass away, but the man who does the will of God lives forever" (1 John 2:17).

Becoming a new Christian is like getting married. We fall in love with our spouse and nothing else matters. We do things to please the other person. This newly established relationship is the most important thing in our lives, and everything else revolves around it. But any relationship can easily degenerate into ritualistic routines. Doing church work and observing religious rituals are not the same as loving God. Our service *for* God could actually become the greatest hindrance to our devotion *to* God. The Apostle John rebukes the Church in Ephesus for having lost their first love; he calls them to repent and to do again the deeds they did when they were new believers. John concludes by saying, "He who has an ear, let him hear what the Spirit says to the churches. To him who overcomes, I will give the right to eat from the tree of life, which is in the paradise of God" (Rev. 2:7). The presence of the Holy Spirit in the lives of believers is what defines the Church, and "those who are led by the Spirit of God are sons of God" (Rom. 8:14).

The presence of the Holy Spirit also brings a new desire to read God's Word—together with the ability to understand it. "The man without the Spirit does not accept the things that come from the Spirit of God, for they are foolishness to him, and he cannot understand them, because they are spiritually discerned" (1 Cor. 2:14). The Holy Spirit is the Spirit of truth (see John 14:17) and "He will guide you into all truth" (John 16:13). That truth will confirm your status with your heavenly Father and set you free (see John 8:32).

The Spirit himself testifies with our spirit that we are God's children (Rom. 8:16).

Thought for the day: *Why should believers who continue in sin and do not feel convicted question their salvation?*

The Holy Spirit living in us will convict us when we are sinning – but often I think we can come to a point where we will not listen + this becomes a dangerous place to be. Pretty soon we can find ourselves fallen away.

Being a Christian I seem to be in constant battle – growing + then bang! Something or my selfishness will overcome me + pull me down. Or sometimes I will do something knowing I shouldn't but do it anyways + then ask for forgiveness which is so wrong.

It would be so nice if we the church would take our masks off + quit pretending that all is well + confess that we are struggling in a certain area – then maybe we could have others pray for us + help us instead of worrying what others will say.

THE WITNESS OF A CHANGED LIFE

3 John

Salvation brings a definitive change at the very core of our being. We are new creations in Christ; and this becomes evident in the way we think, feel and behave. Our desires change and our language begins to clean up. Others begin to sense a difference in our demeanor as well as our behavior. John says, "Anyone who does what is good is from God. Anyone who does what is evil has not seen God" (3 John 11). James writes, "What good is it, my brothers, if a man claims to have faith but has no deeds?" (Jas. 2:14). We are saved by faith, but "faith by itself, if it is not accompanied by action, is dead . . . Show me your faith without deeds, and I will show you my faith by what I do" (Jas. 2:17-18). James is not challenging the doctrine of justification by faith. He is simply saying that if we really believe God and trust Him for our salvation, it will affect our walk and our talk.

It is important to understand the difference between having a relationship with God and living in harmony with Him. When you were physically born, you became a child of your natural father through no choice of your own. Is there anything you can do to change that biological fact? What if you ran away from home or disavowed that he was ever your father? Nothing you do or say can ever change the fact that you are blood related. However, what you say or do does affect whether or not you live in harmony with your earthly father. If you trust and obey your father, you will live in harmony with him. But even if you don't, he is still your father, although a life of disobedience will not be a very pleasant experience for you.

The same holds true in our relationship with God. We are spiritually related to God through the blood of our Lord Jesus Christ (see 1 Pet. 1:18-19). "For you have been born again, not of perishable seed, but of imperishable, through the living and enduring word of God" (1 Pet. 1:23). Our new birth means that we are "children born not of natural descent, nor of human decision or a husband's will, but born of God" (John 1:13). "For we are God's workmanship, created in Christ Jesus to do good works, which God prepared in advance for us to do" (Eph. 2:10). He chose us, adopted us into His family and made us children of God. "Having believed, you were marked in him with a seal, the promised Holy Spirit, who is a deposit guaranteeing our inheritance until the redemption of those who are God's possession—to the praise of his glory" (Eph. 1:13-14).

As children of God, is there anything we can do that would affect the harmony of our relationship with our heavenly Father? Yes, and just like our relationship with our earthly father, it is an issue separate from that of our relatedness. We will live in harmony with our heavenly Father if we trust and obey Him. If we fail to perfectly trust or obey Him, we will not lose our salvation, but we will lose our daily victory and rob ourselves of His blessings. "Dear friend, I pray that you may enjoy good health and that all may go well with you, even as your soul is getting along well" (3 John 2).

> Anyone who does what is good is from God. Anyone who does what is evil has not seen God (3 John 11).

Thought for the day: *What defines a relationship?*

1st. – family – those who you are related to even if you don't have much to do with them.

2nd. – relationship with God – who created us & called us to be His through Jesus Christ.

- How we live according to our relationship to Him. Do we love Him & seek to know Him better. Do we do what He calls us to do.

- Or do we accept a relationship where we live for ourselves not obeying God or not letting our lives be really changed because of Him.

THE SINNER'S PRAYER

Ephesians 2:8-9

Salvation is a gift from God. It is free because Jesus paid the price. He did for us what we could not do for ourselves. "For it is by grace you have been saved, through faith—and this not from yourselves, it is the gift of God—not by works, so that no one can boast" (Eph. 2:8-9). Grace is God's unmerited, free, spontaneous love for the spiritually dead and sinful inhabitants of this fallen world—a love that was revealed and made effective through Jesus Christ. We can't earn grace; we can only humbly receive it as a free gift.

In our sinful state, we can only throw ourselves upon the mercy of God. If by the grace of God we receive mercy in this lifetime, we shall not have to face what we justly deserve in eternity. If God were to give us what we deserve, we would all reap eternal damnation. The good news is, "He saved us, not because of righteous things we had done, but because of his mercy" (Titus 3:5).

Have you ever reflected on the fact that "Everyone who calls on the name of the Lord will be saved" (Rom. 10:13)? You can receive Christ right now by choosing to believe that Jesus died for your sins on the Cross and was resurrected in order that you might have eternal life. "Yet to all who received him, to those who believed in his name, he gave the right to become children of God" (John 1:12). You can express your choice to trust only in Christ and receive Him into your life by saying the following prayer:

> *Dear heavenly Father, I confess that I have sinned and that I am
> a sinner by nature. I know that I am spiritually dead because of my
> sin and not worthy to be your child. I am in great need of your grace
> and I throw myself upon your mercy. I am sorry for my sins, and I humbly
> ask for your forgiveness. I choose to believe that Jesus died for my sins on the
> Cross, and I choose to believe that He came to give me eternal life. As an act
> of faith, I receive you into my life, and I pray that You would enable me to
> be the person that You created me to be. I choose from this day forward to
> repent by turning away from sin and to live a righteous life by faith in the
> power of the Holy Spirit. I ask all this in the wonderful name of Jesus,
> whom I confess to be my Lord and my Savior. Amen.*

Did you call upon the name of the Lord? Do you believe in your heart that Jesus died for your sins and that He was raised from the dead in order that you may have eternal life? Is Jesus the Lord of your life? If you can say yes to these questions, then you are a child of God and a member of the body of Christ. Welcome to the family of God! There is nothing more that you can do to ensure your salvation, because you have not been saved by your good deeds. Salvation is a free gift from God—a gift that you have just received. All God asks of you is that you be the person He created you to be and that you glorify Him by living a righteous life. Why don't you take a moment to thank Him for sending Jesus to die in your place in order that you might be forgiven and have eternal life.

Everyone who calls on the name of the Lord will be saved (Rom. 10:13).

Thought for the day: *Who wouldn't throw themselves upon the mercy of God if they knew the truth?*

THE TEST OF SALVATION

2 Corinthians 13:5

If you died tonight, where would you spend eternity? Would you be with God in heaven? The apostle Paul admonishes you to "examine yourselves to see whether you are in the faith; test yourselves. Do you not realize that Christ Jesus is in you—unless, of course, you fail the test?" (2 Cor. 13:5). Attending religious services won't save you. Trying to live a righteous life won't save you. Practicing spiritual disciplines won't save you. Participating in Christian ordinances won't save you. Only by the grace of God can you be saved, and there is only one definitive test for determining whether you have been born again: "He who has the Son has life; he who does not have the Son of God does not have life" (1 John 5:12). If you have received Christ into your life by faith, you have eternal life and you may claim the following for yourself:

Since I am in Christ, by the grace of God:

I have been justified—completely forgiven (Rom. 5:1).
I died with Christ and died to the power of sin's rule over my life (Rom. 6:1-11).
I am free from condemnation (Rom. 8:1).
I have been placed into Christ by God's doing (1 Cor. 1:30).
I have received the Spirit of God that I might know the things freely given to me by God (1 Cor. 2:12).
I have been given the mind of Christ (1 Cor. 2:16).
I have been bought with a price; I am not my own; I belong to God (1 Cor. 6:19-20).
I have been established, anointed and sealed by God in Christ (2 Cor. 1:21).
I have been given the Holy Spirit as a pledge guaranteeing my inheritance in Christ (Eph. 1:13-14).
I have died with Christ and I no longer live for myself, but for Christ (2 Cor. 5:14-15).
I have been crucified with Christ and it is no longer I who live, but Christ lives in me (Gal. 2:20).

I have been blessed with every spiritual blessing (Eph. 1:3).

I was chosen in Christ before the foundation of the world to be holy and blameless before Him (Eph. 1:4).

I was predestined—determined by God—to be adopted as God's son (Eph. 1:5).

I have been redeemed and forgiven and I am a recipient of His lavish grace (Eph. 1:7)

I have been made alive together with Christ (Eph. 2:5).

I have been raised up and seated with Christ in heaven (Eph. 2:6).

I have direct access to God through the Spirit (Eph. 2:18).

I may approach God with boldness, freedom and confidence (Eph. 3:12).

I have been rescued from the domain of Satan's rule and transferred to the kingdom of Christ (Col. 1:13).

I have been redeemed and forgiven of all my sins. The debt against me has been canceled (Col. 1:14).

I have Christ within me (Col. 1:27).

I am firmly rooted in Christ and am now being built up in Him (Col. 2:7).

I have been spiritually circumcised (Col. 2:11).

I have been made complete in Christ (Col. 2:10).

I have been buried, raised and made alive with Christ (Col. 2:12-13).

I died with Christ and I have been raised up with Christ. Christ is now my life (Col. 3:1-4).

I have been given a spirit of power, love and self-discipline (2 Tim. 1:7).

I have been saved and set apart according to God's doing (2 Tim. 1:9; Titus 3:5).

I am sanctified and I am one with the Sanctifier. He is not ashamed to call me brother (Heb. 2:11).

I can come boldly before the throne of God to find mercy and grace in time of need (Heb. 4:16).

I am a partaker of God's divine nature (2 Pet. 1:4).

Praise be to the God and Father of our Lord Jesus Christ, who has blessed us in the heavenly realms with every spiritual blessing in Christ (Eph. 1:3).

Thought for the day: *What effect would it have on the Church if every child of God knew and believed the Scripture listed above?* [1] I BELIEVE ALL OF THIS BUT IT IS A MATTER OF IT TAKING ROOT. then we would not only see a huge change in us but a huge change in the world.

OVERCOMING GUILT

Romans 8:1-4

When theologians talk about guilt, they are talking about an objective deviation from an ethical standard. To *feel* guilty and to *be* guilty are not the same thing. Apart from Christ, we all stand guilty before the Law whether we feel like it or not. The Law is God's ethical standard, but the Law could not be kept by any of us because we were "weakened by the sinful nature" (Rom. 8:3). Therefore, we all stood condemned by the Law. According to the Gospel, Jesus came in our likeness and became a sin offering so that the righteous requirements of the Law might be fully met in us (see v. 4). "Therefore, there is now no condemnation for those who are in Christ Jesus" (v. 1).

As children of God, we have been justified by faith (see Rom. 5:1). We are no longer guilty before God, because we are no longer "under law, but under grace" (Rom. 6:14). God will not condemn us because Christ has met His righteous demands. Because of our position in Christ, we are to consider ourselves to be "dead to sin but alive to God in Christ Jesus" (Rom. 6:11). Death is the end of a relationship, not the end of existence. We are now rightly related to God, and we are no longer *in Adam* nor are we in the kingdom of darkness. We are *in Christ*, and the law of life in Christ Jesus has set us free from the law of sin and death (see Rom. 8:2).

The law of sin and death is still operative because we cannot do away with a law. Sin is still appealing and powerful, and physical death is still imminent for all of us. As regards the latter, even though physical death is imminent for believers, we shall continue to live spiritually even after we die physically (see John 11:25-26). As regards the former, if Jesus didn't do away with the law of sin, then how can we be free from it? Jesus overcame that law with a greater law, which is "the law of the Spirit of life" (Rom. 8:2).

For the sake of illustration, let's compare the law of sin to the law of gravity. Now, let me ask, Can we fly? Can we, by our own self-effort, overcome the law of gravity? We can momentarily overcome the pull of gravity by jumping, but even the greatest high jumpers fail to overcome the law of gravity. However, we can fly "in" an airplane, because the airplane has enough power to overcome the law of gravity. If we stepped out of the plane or if the plane were to lose power while in the air, we would crash and burn.

In the same way, as long as we live in Christ, we can overcome the attraction of sin. But when sin makes an appeal, we can say, "I don't have to sin. I am alive in Christ and dead to sin. I have a power within me greater than the power of sin."

My dear children, I write this to you so that you will not sin. But if anybody does sin, we have one who speaks to the Father in our defense—Jesus Christ, the Righteous One. He is the atoning sacrifice for our sins, and not only for ours but also for the sins of the whole world (1 John 2:1-2).

We also have an adversary who accuses the brethren day and night before God (see Rev. 12:10). As believers, if we ever feel guilty, we can say with confidence, "There is now no condemnation for those who are in Christ Jesus."

Through Christ Jesus the law of the Spirit of life set me free from the law of sin and death (Rom. 8:2).

Thought for the day: *How has the law of the Spirit of life set you free from the power of sin and death?*

It has set me free from death - spiritual death. It has given me life.
I can be assured that no matter what I do I can humbly come to God + ask for forgiveness of my sins through Jesus Christ.

Overcoming Shame

Micah 7:7-10

Christians are forgiven but not perfect. Jesus paid the penalty for all our sins and assumed responsibility for their eternal consequences. As a result, the Lord will not condemn us and He will remember our sins no more. We, however, have to live with the temporal consequences of our own attitudes and actions. If God had eradicated all the temporal consequences of sin, there would be no motivation to stop sinning. We would party on weekends, confess our sins on Sunday and falsely believe that our actions have no negative consequences.

To illustrate, suppose you have been consuming alcohol for years and have become chemically addicted. At first you were able to cover up your indiscretions, but now your sinful lifestyle has been exposed. Your job performance has become substandard, you have embarrassed yourself publicly, your spouse has left and your health is deteriorating. Finally, you throw yourself upon the mercy of God. He forgives you and makes you a new creation in Christ. However, alcohol has taken its toll on your body, the job is over, and your wife is gone, and you find out that society is less forgiving than God. Still, you are able to find a successful recovery ministry that helps the fallen turn to God, seek His forgiveness, ask the forgiveness of others, repair what they can and build a new life in Christ. Your shame is eventually overcome by the grace of God.

This was the case for Micah who spoke to the sinful conditions of Israel and Judah. He looked forward to God's redemption—the coming of the Savior (see Mic. 7:7) even though he lived under the Mosaic Law. At the time of Micah the enemy of the Israelites was gloating over these "chosen people" who had sinned and incurred the judgment of God. Their enemy was taunting them, asking, "Where is the LORD your God?" (v. 10). Micah responds, "Though I have fallen, I will rise. Though I sit in darkness, the LORD will be my light" (v. 8). The shame the Israelites felt because of their sin caused them to hide and cover up, but the Lord always leads His people into the light. When they faced the truth and turned to God, their enemy was covered with shame, and her downfall was certain (see v. 10).

Many cultures of this world are shame based. They punish sinners by shaming them publicly. They make the point that something is wrong with them. Other cultures are guilt based. They punish sinners because they have done something wrong. The kingdom of God is grace based. There was something wrong with us, but now we are new creations in Christ. We have sinned and fallen short of the glory of God, but Christ has died for our sins. Now we can live righteous lives as children of God. We are what we are by the grace of God. We can still choose to sin, and our loving heavenly Father will discipline us, but that just proves that we are His children (see Heb. 12:8).

As children of God, we are not motivated by guilt and shame. Neither guilt nor shame contributes to our mental health, nor do they promote righteous living. We are motivated by the love of God. We don't condemn others when they sin; we discipline them for their good. The Christian ministry is one of reconciliation, not condemnation. We don't shame one another; we build up one another. *I think that Christians including myself are good at condemning instead of building up. How we fail!

Hatred stirs up dissension, but love covers over all wrongs (Prov. 10:12).

Thought for the day: *Should we seek to expose the sins of others, or should we not count their sins against them?*

- We should do at Nathan did with David - exposed David's sin to David. God forgave David + he punished him for his sin and there were also natural consequences too that he had to live with too.
- When a person truly repents God forgives BUT MAN (INCL. ME) ARE NOT SO FORGIVING - we keep them knocked down instead of helping them back up.
- But I do think that we have a responsibility to keep an eye on those who may continue to struggle + warn others as a protection - not as gossip - such as in the case of a pedophile.

Oh Lord - help me to help lift those up who have fallen and have truly repented instead of keeping them down. Give me the wisdom + discernment I need.
Thank you for your mercy
+ love Lord God + that you remember no more.

CONVICTION OF SIN

2 Corinthians 7:9-11

Paul makes a distinction between godly sorrow for our sins and worldly sorrow (see 2 Cor. 7:9-11). Worldly sorrow can be due to a faulty conscience, the guilt trip we put on one another or the accusations of the devil, which will be dealt with in a later study). Guilt is not a feeling—it is a judicial term relating to law. We have all sinned and broken the moral law of God, and therefore we are all guilty. In Christ, our sins are forgiven and we have been pardoned. Still, many Christians retain a psychological guilt that is based on an emotional feeling or an insufficient understanding of God's grace. We may feel guilty due to worldly sorrow, but that cannot change the fact that we stand forgiven before God.

Nonbelievers and believers alike feel guilty if they violate their conscience. Our conscience is a function of our mind, and it will always be true to itself, but not necessarily to God. Before we came to Christ, our conscience was formed as we assimilated values from our home, school and social environments. Observing role models and learning right from wrong from others has shaped our conscience. Yet it is important to remember that our human resources and role models have not been infallible. When we come to Christ, our conscience begins to change as we are transformed by the renewing of our mind. Letting our conscience be our guide is not the same as letting the Holy Spirit be our guide.

Nonbelievers come under the conviction of sin and turn to Christ. "Godly sorrow brings repentance that leads to salvation and leaves no regret, but worldly sorrow brings death" (2 Cor. 7:10). The apostle Paul says he is happy when that happens, because that is the work of God (see v. 9). Should we sin as born-again believers, we will also have a sense of sorrow for what we have said or done. That is the convicting (not condemning) work of the Holy Spirit. You will know godly sorrow by the end result. "See what this godly sorrow has produced in you: what earnestness, what eagerness to clear yourselves, what indignation, what alarm, what longing, what concern, what readiness to see justice done" (v. 11).

Worldly sorrow may feel the same as godly sorrow, but the end results are radically different. Many people are sorry they got caught sinning, but such sorrow seldom leads to repentance. Others may feel sorry for their sins and have an emotional catharsis and confess their sins to others. But if there is no genuine repentance, they will regret this action later. Godly sorrow leads to repentance without regret. People don't regret finding their freedom in Christ through genuine repentance. They are thankful for their newfound freedom.

Peter and Judas provide an example of the difference between godly sorrow and worldly sorrow. In a moment of crisis, Peter, fearing for his life, denied Christ three times (see Luke 22:60). However, he then came under the conviction of the Holy Spirit, repented and became the first spokesperson for the Early Church (see Luke 22:61-62; Acts 2:14-41). Jesus reinstated Peter and gave him the opportunity to share three times that he loved Him (see John 21:15-19). Judas would have had the same chance to repent, but he did not. After his betrayal of Jesus, Judas came under the sorrow of the world and hung himself (see Matt. 27:1-5). His actions did not demonstrate God-centered sorrow over the wickedness of sin that leads to death. His actions demonstrated a self-centered sorrow over the temporal consequences of sin that had negatively affected him.

As we seek to transform lives in Christ through godly sorrow, let us remember the lesson of Good Friday: One thief hung on a cross by Jesus and experienced the sorrow of the world and died. The other thief "became sorrowful as God intended" (2 Cor. 7:9) and joined Jesus in paradise (see Luke 23:40-43).

Godly sorrow brings repentance that leads to salvation and leaves no regret, but worldly sorrow brings death (2 Cor. 7:10).

Thought for the day: *How can you tell the difference between godly sorrow (conviction of sin) and the devil's accusations?*

- Satan constantly accuses — trying to make us believe we still bear that sin which robs us of peace with Christ.
- WE DOUBT THAT GOD COULD FORGIVE US — a ploy of Satan.
- Godly sorrow brings true repentance + we know we are forgiven + never want to do it again.

OUR INHERITANCE IN CHRIST

Hebrews 1:1-4

God has spoken to our forefathers through His prophets, but now He is speaking to us through His Son (see Heb. 1:1). The fact that Jesus is the ultimate revelation of God is demonstrated by the following seven descriptive statements about Him (see vv. 2-4):

- Jesus has been appointed heir of all things (see also Rom. 8:17).
- Through Jesus, the universe was made (see also John 1:3; Col. 1:18).
- Jesus is the radiance of God's glory (see also John 1:14,18).
- Jesus is the exact representation of the Father (see also John 14:9; Col. 1:15).
- By His powerful word, Jesus sustains all things (see also Col. 1:17).
- Jesus provided the purification of our sins (see also Titus 2:14; Heb. 7:27).
- Jesus is seated at the right hand of the Majesty in heaven (see also Heb. 8:1; 10:12).

The destiny of Christians is bound up in the destiny of Jesus. "Christ has indeed been raised from the dead, the firstfruits of those who have [died]" (1 Cor. 15:20). Jesus was the first to receive the birthright. As born-again believers, we also have a birthright since we are all children of God. "Now if we are children, then we are heirs—heirs of God and co-heirs with Christ" (Rom. 8:17). All this is possible because we are spiritually alive "in Christ."

And God raised us up with Christ and seated us with him in the heavenly realms in Christ Jesus, in order that in the coming ages he might show the incomparable riches of his grace, expressed in his kindness to us in Christ Jesus (Eph. 2:6-7).

As grateful believers we say with Paul, "Praise be to the God and Father of our Lord Jesus Christ, who has blessed us in the heavenly realms with every spiritual blessing in Christ" (Eph. 1:3). According to Ephesians 1:4-14, our inheritance in Christ includes:

- Being chosen in Christ before the creation of the world to be holy and blameless (see v. 4).
- Being predestined to be adopted as His sons and daughters through Jesus Christ (see v. 5).
- Being redeemed through Christ's blood, the forgiveness of sins (see v. 7).
- Being knowledgeable of the mystery of His will (see v. 9).
- Being chosen and predestined according to His plan (see v. 11).
- Being included in Christ when we heard the word of truth (see v. 13).
- Being marked in Jesus with a seal, the promised Holy Spirit (see vv. 13-14).

[handwritten margin note: This is hard to comprehend + I pray that God will take this + root it in my heart so that I may live a life that is Holy + powerful.]

According to God's Word, we have a rich inheritance in Christ. The problem is many Christians may not know it, or they fail to comprehend this incredible truth about being a joint heir with Jesus. So Paul prays that we would know God better and that our hearts would be enlightened in order that we may know the riches of our inheritance in Christ (see Eph. 1:17-19). God's promises need to be claimed, and His truth needs to be believed in order for it to be effective in our lives.

As you close your study today, make this your prayer:

Glorious Father and God of my Lord and Savior Jesus Christ, I ask that You would give me the spirit of wisdom and revelation so that I may know You better. I pray also that the eyes of my heart may be enlightened in order that I may know the hope to which You have called me, the riches of Your glorious inheritance in the saints and Your incomparably great power that You have extended to all of us who believe. In Jesus' name I pray. Amen.

Now if we are children, then we are heirs—heirs of God and co-heirs with Christ, if indeed we share in his sufferings in order that we may also share in his glory (Rom. 8:17).

Thought for the day: *To what are you a spiritual heir?*

[handwritten: I am a heir of God + co-heir with Christ. I am CHOSEN - PREDESTINED - REDEEMED - KNOW the MYSTERY of His will - CHOSEN + PREDESTINED TO HIS PLAN - INCLUDED IN CHRIST - Have the HOLY SPIRIT.]

Dec 2/08

THE LOVE OF CHRIST

Ephesians 3:14-21

Does God love you? If you performed better, would God love you more? Does God love one person more than another? Do you really know the rich inheritance that you have in Christ? Such questions trouble every defeated Christian.

Paul addresses these issues in the book of Ephesians by modeling how we should pray for all the saints, and possibly ourselves. Paul first prays that our knowledge of God would increase and that we would know the rich inheritance that we have in Christ (see Eph. 1:17-18). Then in Ephesians 3:14-21, Paul asks that we be filled with the power to comprehend the love of Christ that goes beyond knowledge. He desires that all believers be rooted in the love of Christ, established and "filled to the measure of all the fullness of God" (v. 19). *This is what I long for. The Holy Spirit just spoke to me— it is my worry that keeps me from this.*

Lord God I pray for this.

The two dominant Greek words in Scripture translated as love are *agape* and *phileo*. Phileo is brotherly love. It represents the natural affection we show among family, friends and countrymen. Agape is God's love. It reflects the nature of God, because "God is love" (1 John 4:16). God loves us, not because we are lovable, but because it is His nature to love us. The love of God is not dependent upon its object. That is why the love of God is unconditional.

It is imperative that every believer knows that God loves him or her and why. If you performed better, God wouldn't love you any more than He does now. If you performed poorly, He would still love you the same. He may discipline you for your sake, "because the Lord disciplines those he loves" (Heb. 12:6). Further, "If you are not disciplined (and everyone undergoes discipline), then you are illegitimate children and not true sons" (Heb. 12:8).

Jesus said, "A new command I give you: Love one another" (John 13:34). Before salvation we loved one another as well as we humanly could. But with Christ in us, we have a new capacity to love because we have become a partaker of His divine nature (see 2 Pet. 1:4). "We love because he first loved us" (1 John 4:19). Our ability to love others is due to the presence of God in our lives and is the measure of our maturity. Paul says, "The goal of this command is love, which comes from a pure heart and a good conscience and a sincere faith" (1 Tim. 1:5). As we grow in Christ, our nature takes on more and more the nature of love, and our capacity to love others also increases.

To further your own understanding of God's love, personalize Paul's prayer for yourself as follows:

> *Dear heavenly Father, I pray that out of Your glorious riches*
> *You would strengthen me with power through Your Spirit in my inner*
> *being, so that Christ may dwell in my heart through faith. I pray that I may*
> *be rooted and established in Your love. Grant me the power with all the*
> *saints to grasp how wide and long and high and deep Your love is. Enable*
> *me to know Your love that is beyond my mental ability to understand.*
> *I pray that You would fill me to the measure of Your fullness. You are able*
> *to do immeasurably more than I could ask or imagine, according to Your*
> *power that is at work within me. May You be glorified in Your Church*
> *throughout all generations forever and ever. Amen.*

I pray also that the eyes of your [MY] heart may be enlightened in order that you [I] may know the hope to which he has called you [ME], the riches of his glorious inheritance in the saints (Eph. 1:18).

Thought for the day: *Why don't we fully understand our inheritance in Christ?*

SIN – DOUBT – IMMATURITY IN CHRIST.
I struggled so much with this until Ancient Paths where God revealed His love for me. My life has gradually changed since then. But after being at Hannah's for Hanukkah + seeing the power + authority that Denise + Hannah prayed with I realize I am lacking so much of what God has for me due to my lack of faith, doubt + not allowing Him to do more. If we all lived + prayed with that authority (which made me think of the disciples after Christs Pentecost + Paul) the world would be a different place because of it.
Lord God – I LONG FOR THIS.

SECOND QUARTER:
BUILT UP IN HIM

THE TRUTH SHALL SET YOU FREE

John 8:31-36

Truth is an attribute of God and is unlimited, unchanging and absolute. All truth is God's truth, and the idea of absolute truth stems from His perfection and from His omniscience (all-knowing). God not only *is* truth, but he *knows* all truth. He is the Creator, and our ability to comprehend truth is dependent upon Him. We can only know the truth as He has revealed it. "Grace and truth came through Jesus Christ" (John 1:17), who is the ultimate revelation of God.

Jesus said, "If you hold to my teaching, you are really my disciples. Then you will know the truth, and the truth will set you free" (John 8:31-32). The Jews were puzzled by this statement since they perceived themselves to be free already, having "never been slaves of anyone" (v. 33). But Jesus wasn't talking about being subject to another person. He was talking about the freedom that comes from being His disciple. Jesus is, "The way and the *truth* and the life" (John 14:6, emphasis added). Knowing Jesus and His Word liberates us from the law of sin and death and sets us free from our past so that we can be the people God created us to be.

Cognitive truth is something we can intellectually know to be true by reason and observation. It is true that you are reading this right now, and it is true that two plus two equals four. Biblical truth is moral truth because it reflects the nature of God. Truth, in the moral sense, is far more than intellectual awareness or the ability to reason logically. When believed, God's eternal truth transforms the heart and affects the whole inner character of a true disciple of Jesus. Paul refers to this as "knowledge of the truth that leads to godliness" (Titus 1:1). Contrast this with the devil who did not hold "to the truth, for there [was] no truth in him" (John 8:44). Wicked men suppress the truth by means of their wickedness (see Rom. 1:18), and those who don't know and believe God have exchanged the truth of God for a lie (see Rom. 1:25).

Jesus said, "I tell you the truth, everyone who sins is a slave to sin" (John 8:34). But there is a way to be free of sin. In Luke 4:16-21, Jesus makes it clear that He has come in fulfillment of Isaiah 61:1-2, which refers to the Messiah who came to deliver us from sin. "Through Christ Jesus the law of the Spirit of life set [us] free from the law of sin and death" (Rom. 8:2). As liberated children of God, we are no longer subject to the law of sin and death. We are free in Christ to live righteous lives.

The only thing that we as Christians ever have to admit to is the truth. Truth is not something we fear. It is the liberating agent by which those who are in bondage are set free from the law of sin and death. We are instructed to speak the truth in love (see Eph. 4:15,25) and to walk in the light (see 1 John 1:7) in order to experience the freedom that Christ purchased for us on the cross. The Holy Spirit is "the Spirit of truth" (John 14:17); and He will lead us into "all truth" (John 16:13), and that truth will set us free.

So if the Son sets you free, you will be free indeed (John 8:36).

Thought for the day: *How has knowing the truth (God and His Word) liberated you?* It has given me life-purpose - peace. I am not condemned - I am set free. I am forgiven as far as the east is from the west.

ABSOLUTE TRUTH

Proverbs 3:5-7

Truth is that which corresponds to reality. God is the ultimate reality, and that which He creates is real and cannot exist apart from Him. Truth corresponds to the way things really are, whereas falsehood does not correspond to reality. Christianity has always affirmed the concept of absolute truth, because truth is rooted in the absolute nature of God. In other words, truth is absolute in that it has always been true and it will always be true, regardless of whether humanity accepts or rejects it. When we believe something to be true, that does not make it true. Absolute truth is true whether or not we believe it. Truth is not conditional—it does not derive its validity from our perception of it. We cannot create truth, nor can we destroy it. We can only *choose* to believe it—and we *must* believe it if we want to remain mentally healthy people who are in touch with reality.

The various philosophies have tests to determine whether or not something is true or false. According to the coherence theory, something is true if it is logically self-consistent. Something would be considered false if it wasn't logically consistent with how the rest of reality was perceived. According to this theory, a string of lies could be logically consistent with each other, but they are not truthful. They lack an eternal standard that is consistent with the nature of God. Then there is the pragmatic view, which says that something is true if it works. Demonic activities work, but they are rooted in the father of lies.

As the world enters the twenty-first century, there are many popular philosophies that argue against the idea of absolute truth. Postmodernism is a movement that claims truth is relative; therefore, it can be whatever you choose it to be. What is true for you may not be true for another. At the heart of Postmodernism is the rejection of absolute *moral* truth as revealed by the nature of God and divine revelation. It is a philosophical rebellion against God. Postmodernists have depersonalized God because an impersonal God doesn't have to be served. They prefer to decide for themselves what is true and what is false, thereby becoming their own moral standard.

The New Age movement twists reality in a different direction. The heart of New Age teaching is that we are God or a god. We don't need a Savior to die for our sins; we just need to realize that we are gods. Since each of us is our own god, we can create reality with our own minds. Truth then becomes what we believe it to be; and if we believe hard enough, it will become true. Recall that Satan deceived Adam and Eve with the same lie in the Garden of Eden (see Gen. 3:4-5).

Christians have chosen to follow the wisdom of Solomon who wrote, "Trust in the LORD with all your heart and lean not on your own understanding" (Prov. 3:5). We reject the notion that we are gods, instead humbly choosing to submit to the One who is the truth. We accept the fact that we have a personal relationship with the "author and perfecter of our faith" (Heb. 12:2), and we choose to acknowledge Him in all our ways (see Prov. 3:6). "For the word of the LORD is right; and all His works are done in truth. For the LORD is good; his mercy is everlasting; and His truth endureth to all generations" (Ps. 33:4; 100:5, *KJV*).

You will know how people ought to conduct themselves in God's household, which is the church of the living God, the pillar and foundation of the truth (1 Tim. 3:15).

Thought for the day: *How is the Church the pillar and foundation of truth?*

We know + believe that God is Truth + Jesus came so that we may know TRUTH. We are (or should be) the moral compass that leads the world to Truth, but unfortunately we have failed + have allowed the immoral to make up "truth" for us. We have failed terribly. We're too busy with our own lives or when I grew up the church had become too separate to make an impact. (or that is how I see it).
I believe that if we lived our lives as we should the world would be a different place.

OWNING THE TRUTH

Psalm 51

We can be sorry that we have sinned, but that doesn't constitute confession. We can ask God or others to forgive us, but our request accomplishes little if we aren't specific about what we need to be pardoned from. We will not enjoy our relationship with God and others unless we own up to the truth and live accordingly. The first step in establishing a righteous relationship is to embrace the truth. We will never come to Christ unless we admit that we have sinned and are sinful by nature. Without such an admission, we fail to acknowledge that we need a Savior.

When it comes to the issue of facing our sinfulness, we can learn a lot from David, who had been chosen by God to be the King of Israel. David had a whole heart for God, but he ended up committing a hideous sin. He lusted after Bathsheba while her husband, Uriah, was away at war. When she became pregnant, David tried to cover his sin by calling Uriah home so that he could have relations with his wife, but he refused to have special privileges while the other men were away at war. So David arranged for Uriah to be on the front line where he would surely be killed (see 2 Sam. 11). David came under heavy conviction (see Ps. 32), but still he did not acknowledge his sin. So God sent Nathan to confront him (see 2 Sam. 12), and David finally threw himself upon the mercy of God and confessed his sins (see Ps. 51:1-5).

The first step in any recovery program is to stop living in denial and face the truth. You can't help someone who will not admit he or she has a problem. Most of us are like David. If we think we can get away with it, we will probably try. But if we are Christians, we can rest assured that the hand of God will be heavy upon us, as it was for David, who wrote: "When I kept silent, my bones wasted away through my groaning all day long. For day and night your hand was heavy upon me; my strength was sapped as in the heat of summer" (Ps. 32:3-4).

Some will not acknowledge their sins even under heavy conviction. In such cases, divinely sent human intervention may be necessary, as it was for David. That was the role of a prophet in the Old Testament—to bring sinners to repentance. The purpose of the gift of prophecy in the New Testament is to lay bare the secrets of the heart so the unrepentant will turn to God (see 1 Cor. 14:25). Many recovery ministries practice a process called intervention for those who are living in denial of their sinful behavior. A special meeting is arranged at which family and friends speak the truth in love to the one living in denial. The purpose is to get the loved one to acknowledge the truth and to offer the person the kind of help that will set him or her free from his or her sinful ways.

Interventions fail if the person will not admit he or she has a problem and needs help. They also fail if the confronted person only gives mental assent to what others are saying and goes along with their suggestions in order to appease them. It will only work if the truth is acknowledged in the inner person, i.e., the heart. The troubled individual has to own the truth as David did and desire the only remedy for his or her sin: a righteous relationship with God (see Ps. 51:7-13).

Surely you desire truth in the inner parts; you teach me wisdom in the inmost place (Ps. 51:6).

Thought for the day: *What is the difference between truth intellectually acknowledged, and truth revealed and personally embraced in the inner person?*

Intellectual knowledge means head knowledge whereas when truth is revealed & embraced, we know it in our heart, soul, spirit & mind & it changes us & WE LIVE IT.

EMOTIONAL TRUTH

Lamentations 3

When truth enters the heart, it immediately stimulates an emotional response. Only in the heart do the mind, emotion and will come together in holistic unity. We have little or no direct control over our emotions. We cannot willfully change how we feel, but we do have control over what we think and what we choose to believe. Our emotions are primarily a product of our thoughts. How we think and what we choose to believe affect how we feel.

Suppose your place of employment were laying off personnel. You have been a faithful employee for years and believe the current company downsizing won't affect you. On Monday you get a message from your boss that he wants to see you Friday morning at 10:30 A.M. How would you feel that week if you thought you were going to be laid off? You could get very depressed if you thought you were going to lose your job. You could get angry if you thought you were being treated unfairly. You would probably experience anxiety because of all the uncertainties. You might even be tempted to act upon some of your feelings. The truth is, you wouldn't know what the meeting is all about. You would probably be on an emotional roller coaster all week as your mind contemplates all the possibilities. Chances are you would be gripped by fear and apprehension as the moment of truth draws near.

Friday has finally arrived. As you enter the office to meet with your boss, you are greeted with applause by the management team who inform you that you have been promoted to vice president. How would your feelings change after hearing the truth? If what we believe does not conform to truth, then what we feel does not conform to reality.

Notice how the writer of Lamentations feels as he mentally recalls negative circumstances: "I remember my affliction and my wandering, the bitterness and the gall. I well remember them, and my soul is downcast within me" (v. 19). In the previous verses of chapter 3, he is blaming God for all his dismal circumstances. He believes that God has driven him from light to darkness (see vv. 1-6). He feels trapped and doesn't believe that God hears his cry for help (see vv. 7-8). Not only that, God has led him astray, pounced on him like a wild beast and pierced his heart with an arrow (see vv. 9-13). He has become a laughingstock among his peers (see v. 14). All these negative circumstances and perceptions have left him bitter and without peace (see vv. 15-18). His soul has become downcast because he mentally entertains all these dismal thoughts. *I am extremely good at being like this - not good.*

Suddenly, his whole countenance changes. "Yet this I call to mind and therefore I have hope: Because of the LORD's great love we are not consumed, for his compassions never fail. They are new every morning; great is your faithfulness" (vv. 21-23). There has been no change in his external circumstances. What has changed is his mental process. He has recalled to his mind the truth about God. It would have done no good for someone to say that he shouldn't feel that way about God because he couldn't really have changed how he felt. He could, however, change how he has been thinking—and he does. When he chose to believe the truth about God, his emotions were conformed to reality.

In just the same way, we are not emotionally impacted by our environment alone. We are emotionally impacted by how we mentally interpret the circumstances of life and by what we have chosen to believe.

For as he thinks within himself, so he is (Prov. 23:7).

Thought for the day: *Be aware today of what you are thinking and how your thoughts are making you feel.*

This is all so true! It is absolutely amazing how our emotions can mess us up! I do think that men are more level headed & don't get drawn in so much by emotion whereas we women are very emotional & live by our emotions more than what is really true. And having our hormone changes at certain times of the month does not help.

I believe the key answer is to keep my eyes on God & not on the situations & the emotions that go with it - to remember "Because of God's great love we are not consumed, for His compassions never fail. They are new every morning, great is God's faithfulness." AMEN!

DESTROYED FOR THE LACK OF KNOWLEDGE

Hosea 4:1-6

The nation of Israel was apostate. Even the land suffered from the immorality of the people (see Hos. 4:3). The priests were warned not to blame the people, since they too were guilty of sinning and they were also guilty of not teaching the truth. "My people are destroyed from lack of knowledge. Because you have rejected knowledge, I also reject you as my priests; because you have ignored the law of your God" (v. 6). Ignorance of the law may not be an acceptable excuse, but people will remain in bondage to their sins if they don't know the truth.

Paul raises the same issue concerning salvation.

How, then, can they call on the one they have not believed in? And how can they believe in the one of whom they have not heard? And how can they hear without someone preaching to them? And how can they preach unless they are sent (Rom. 10:14-15)?

That is why the Church has been commissioned to preach the gospel to the ends of the earth (see Matt. 28:19). We are saved by faith; but if we don't know what it is that we are to believe, then how can we be saved? If we don't know the truth, then how can the truth set us free?

If a local department store had a 50-percent-off sale on all its merchandise, how could you take advantage of the sale if you never heard about it? Merchants have to get the word out if they are going to stay in business, and so does the Church. The Church is "the pillar and foundation of the truth" (1 Tim. 3:15); and her members are called to speak the truth in love (see Eph. 4:15,25) and to share their faith with those who have never heard the good news. Ignorance is not bliss; it is defeat.

Even if we have heard the good news so as to believe unto salvation, we still need to have an increasing knowledge of the truth in order to live liberated lives. People are in bondage to what they have been taught or to what they have chosen to believe in the past. If truth sets people free, then lies will keep them in bondage. Many Christians are not experiencing their freedom in Christ because of past traumatic experiences. It is not the trauma experiences themselves that are keeping believers in bondage. Rather, they are in bondage to the lies they have believed as a result of those negative experiences.

Suppose the father in the home has physically abused a child. As a result of the beatings, the child could choose to believe a variety of lies such as: "I'm no good," "God doesn't love me," or "I deserved this punishment because my parents are older and they must be right." Because of abuse, children develop negative images of themselves. Even their concept of God the Father is often tainted by early childhood experiences of an abusive or neglectful father figure. Unless these misconceptions and lies are identified and replaced with truth, wounded children will grow up to be adults who are in bondage to false beliefs.

There are also active forces in this world that attempt to deceive us into believing a lie. There have been and will continue to be false prophets and teachers. Satan, who is the father of lies, "leads the whole world astray" (Rev. 12:9). We have also been clearly warned "that in later times some will abandon the faith and follow deceiving spirits and things taught by demons" (1 Tim. 4:1). So let us be on guard and cling to the truth that is ours in Christ Jesus.

My people are destroyed from lack of knowledge (Hos. 4:6).

Thought for the day: *What would happen in this world if pastors didn't preach the truth to their congregations and if the Church never took the Gospel to the world?*

Christianity would die!

There are more & more denominations that don't preach the truth. It has caused splits in the church. I.E. United & Anglican churches have allowed same sex marriages & those who stand on God's Word have left & started their own church seperate from those who believe the lie. Is it because they don't know God's Word & the Truth & have they been blinded by the Pastor's teachings? Yes! WE NEED TO STAND FIRM IN GOD'S TRUTH!

THE NATURE OF FAITH

Hebrews 11

There is no more important concept for us as Christians to understand than the nature of faith. The Creator has established faith as the means by which we live and relate to Him. We are saved by faith (see Eph. 2:8-9), and we walk, or live, by faith (see 2 Cor. 5:7). "And without faith it is impossible to please God, because anyone who comes to him must believe that he exists and that he rewards those who earnestly seek him" (Heb. 11:6). Faith is the operating principle of life. All of us walk by faith. The only difference between Christian faith and non-Christian faith is the object of our faith. The real issue is not *whether* one believes or not believes. The real issue is *in what or in whom* one believes.

To illustrate how faith works, consider how we drive our cars. When we come to an intersection and see a green light, we continue to drive through without stopping. Although we can't see the color of the light facing the other direction, we believe it is red. We also believe that the drivers of the cars coming from the other direction have seen the red light and will stop. If we didn't have faith in traffic lights, we would not proceed through the intersection—or we would do so very cautiously!

Hope is the parent of faith. The biblical idea of hope is not wishful thinking. Rather, hope is the present assurance of some future good. People don't proceed by faith if they have no hope. Suppose you want to catch a bus. You walk to the bus stop in faith, hoping the bus will be on time and that the schedule is right. If the bus never comes and the schedule has been wrong, your hope is dashed, and you lose faith in the public transportation system. If you had never had any hope of catching the bus, you would not have proceeded by faith. That would be foolish.

The writer of Hebrews said, "Now faith is being sure of what we hope for and certain of what we do not see" (Heb. 11:1). We drive confidently through the intersection with the green light because we feel certain the drivers coming the other direction see a red light. We drink soda out of a can even when we can't see the content, because we believe the manufacturer is delivering a safe product. The public in general demonstrates a lot of faith in our government and private industry, even though neither is perfect.

The object of our Christian faith is the God of all hope. The record of faithful people in Hebrews 11 is a testimony of God's faithfulness. They had great faith because they had a great God. They chose to believe God and live accordingly, even though it meant extreme hardship. By faith Noah built an ark, even though there was no body of water on which it could rest (Heb. 11:7). By faith Abraham was willing to sacrifice his own son, because he believed that God could raise Isaac from the dead (see vv. 17-19). These heroes of faith believed the promises of God—though they did not receive what was promised in their lifetime—because they looked forward to a greater eternal reward (see vv. 13-16,39-40).

And without faith it is impossible to please God, because anyone who comes to him must believe that he exists and that he rewards those who earnestly seek him (Heb. 11:6).

How about faith when we pray.

Thought for the day: *What do you demonstrate faith in every day in addition to faith in God?* - driving somewhere safely.
- getting up in the morning
- doctors

THE OBJECT OF OUR FAITH

Hebrews 13:7-8

Faith has something in common with meditation. The primary issue is what you meditate on, and in what or whom you believe. The psalmist wrote, "Blessed is the man who does not walk in the counsel of the wicked or stand in the way of sinners or sit in the seat of mockers. But his delight is in the law of the LORD, and on his law he meditates day and night" (Ps. 1:1-2). Faith is dependent upon its object. To say that you should walk by faith begs the question, Faith in what? You cannot have faith in faith.

Jesus Christ is the only legitimate object of our faith, for two reasons. First, we can trust in Jesus because of the witness of those who have chosen to believe in Him. Trusting in Christ results in our becoming new creations and believing that the truth sets us free. The writer of Hebrews says, "Remember your leaders, who spoke the word of God to you. Consider the outcome of their way of life and imitate their faith" (Heb. 13:7). He doesn't say that we should imitate what they do or say. If their lives demonstrate what they believe, then we should imitate what they believe, because what we do or say is just a product of what we have chosen to believe. People don't always live according to what they profess, but they always live according to what they believe.

The second and primary reason Jesus is the ultimate object of our faith is that He never changes. "Jesus Christ is the same yesterday and today and forever" (Heb. 13:8). We learn to trust people who are true to their word, and we come to trust in things that have proven to be consistent. The most universally accepted faith object is the fixed order of the universe. We set our clocks and make plans according to the calendars. The world would be thrown into chaos if the rotation of the sun and moon suddenly changed. If we have that much confidence in the sun, why not in the Son who spoke the universe into existence and sustains all things by His powerful Word? (See Heb. 1:3.)

It takes time to establish trust in something or someone, because the process of building faith requires consistent and continuous behavior demonstrated over time. That is why our relationships are so fragile. It may take months or years to establish a great degree of trust in one another, but one act of unfaithfulness can destroy it. We can choose to forgive those who have betrayed us, but it often takes a long time to regain the trust that has been lost.

If God were to change or if His Word proved to be false, then He would no longer be a legitimate object of our faith. Centuries of human history have proven that the nature of God is eternally consistent, as is His Word. "The grass withers and the flowers fall, but the word of our God stands forever" (Isa. 40:8). Jesus said, "I tell you the truth, until heaven and earth disappear, not the smallest letter, not the least stroke of a pen, will by any means disappear from the Law until everything is accomplished" (Matt. 5:18). In other words, heaven and earth will pass away before the smallest letter in the Hebrew alphabet will disappear from God's Word or be altered in any way. Critics have hammered on this anvil for centuries. Yet the hammers and those who wield them have fallen away, but the anvil of God's Word remains the same.

Jesus Christ is the same yesterday and today and forever (Heb. 13:8).

Thought for the day: *Why is God the ultimate object of our faith?*

God is unchanging. We can trust Him fully of this. His love never changes – His Word does not change. GOD IS THE CREATOR OF THE HEAVENS & THE EARTH. HE IS THE CREATOR OF ME. HE SENT HIS SON TO DIE IN MY PLACE + ALL PEOPLES PLACE. HIS PROPHECIES HAVE BEEN FULFILLED – WHAT HE SAYS WILL HAPPEN WILL HAPPEN. MAYBE NOT IN MY LIFETIME BUT IT WILL HAPPEN. I see & hear what is happening in the world & watch how end-time prophecies are being fulfilled.

GROWING IN FAITH

Romans 10:14-17

If faith is dependent upon its object, then how much faith you have depends upon how well you know the object of your faith. If you know seven promises from the Word of God, your faith is limited to those seven promises. If you know 7,000 promises from the Word of God, your faith will be greatly enlarged. "Consequently, faith comes from hearing the message, and the message is heard through the word of Christ" (Rom. 10:17). We grow in our faith as we increase our knowledge and understanding of God and His Word.

Suppose a father stands his young son on a table, encourages the boy to fall or jump into his arms, and the child does. As the process is repeated, the father progressively steps farther from the table, and his son continues to jump, because he trusts his father to catch him. Now suppose the father puts the boy on the limb of a tree and encourages him to jump into his arms. It is a little bigger leap of faith, but the boy jumps nevertheless, because he believes his father will catch him. Would the boy jump from the tree into his little sister's arms? Probably not; even though the leap is the same, the object of his faith has changed. The ability of the best of fathers to be the perfect object of a child's faith will diminish as he or she continues to climb the tree of life.

No matter how high we climb the tree of life, our heavenly Father will always be there for us, and we will feel safe and secure if our faith is rooted in Him. As little children, we bore our parents' name and depended on them for our daily existence, but salvation has brought a change in our identity. We are now children of God, and our heavenly Father has become the ultimate object of our faith. We hear about Him from godly parents and Christian teachers, who instruct us in the ways of God. We read and memorize God's Word, and we learn to live by faith according to what He says is true. In order to live a victorious Christian life by faith, we have to know the Word of God. It is presumptuous for us to step out in faith beyond that which we know to be truth. If we don't know the truth, we can't live the Christian life by faith.

Perhaps even worse than our not knowing the truth is our deciding for ourselves what we want to believe—this makes us the objects of our own faith. Some self-initiated arbiters of truth try to manipulate God by cleverly worded prayers and claiming false promises by "faith." That will only bring disillusionment and despair. Some are disappointed in God because He doesn't respond the way they thought He should have. It is critically important to understand that God is under no obligation to us. He is only under obligation to Himself and His Word. He is a faithful Father who keeps all His promises, and He will never deviate from His Word.

Jesus said, "I tell you the truth, unless you change and become like little children, you will never enter the kingdom of heaven" (Matt. 18:3). Little children trust their parents. They believe what their parents tell them, and well-trained children instantly obey without question. In order to mature in our faith, we need that same childlike faith.

Therefore, whoever humbles himself like this child is the greatest in the kingdom of heaven (Matt. 18:4).

Thought for the day: *How would you define "childlike faith"?*

Just as it does in this lesson. Trusting God no matter what He asks because of our faith in Him.

When I was going through all of my troubles in 2007 with recovering from the surgery, the depression, + not knowing what to do with my life — my faith was strong! I knew God would bring me through this + that He had a plan + purpose for me even though I didn't know what it was + even though I had a dark, dark week of struggle, I was able to trust Him — knowing that He would work it all out. Right now I don't feel as strong — maybe because things are going well. I guess it is when we go through struggles that is when we know if our faith is strong or weak.

Thank You Heavenly Father that we can stand in faith knowing that You are in control. I praise You + I thank You.

FAITH AND WORKS

James 2:14-25

In most of our English translations of the Bible, the words "faith," "trust" and "believe" are all translated from the same root word in the original Greek text. However, the common usage of each of these three words can be understood in quite different ways. Saying "I believe in that" doesn't often carry the same weight as saying "I trust in that." Giving mental assent to something is not the same as a demonstrated reliance upon it. To "believe in Jesus" and to "trust in Jesus" have the same meaning in Scripture. Many people say they "believe" in the historical Jesus, but they have never trusted in Him as the only means of salvation and eternal life. That is the point James is making when he writes: "You believe that there is one God. Good! Even the demons believe that—and shudder" (Jas. 2:19). Although demons acknowledge God, they have demonstrated no trust in God.

"What good is it, my brothers, if a man claims to have faith but has no deeds? Can such faith save him?" (Jas. 2:14). James is not challenging the apostle Paul's teaching that we are justified by faith and by faith alone. He is correcting the faulty notion that people can profess to believe in something when there is no evidence in their lives to verify it. To the person whose life bears no resemblance to his professed beliefs, James says, "Show me your faith without deeds, and I will show you my faith by what I do" (v. 18). Remember, people don't always live according to what they profess, but they do live according to what they truly believe in their hearts.

Everything you do is an expression of what you have chosen to believe. Jesus said, "Blessed are those who hunger and thirst for righteousness, for they will be filled [or satisfied]" (Matt. 5:6). Do you believe what Jesus said? If you believed it, what would you be doing? You would be hungering and thirsting after righteousness!

James illustrates the truth that faith in God results in good works by calling our attention to Abraham, who is often referred to as the father of our faith (see Jas. 2:23-24). Paul uses Abraham as the prime example of justification by faith: "Abraham believed God, and it was credited to him as righteousness" (Rom. 4:3; see also Gal. 3:6). James asks, "Was not our ancestor Abraham considered righteous for what he did when he offered his son Isaac on the altar?" (Jas. 2:21). It seems like Paul and James contradict each other until you continue with James's argument. "You see that his faith and his actions were working together, and his faith was made complete by what he did" (v. 22). In other words, you know that Abraham trusted God because of his willingness to sacrifice his only son, which never happened because God provided a scapegoat. So Abraham's justification came through faith, and his "work" was the fruit of that faith.

James did not say that good works are essential for faith or for salvation. He taught that our works are the evidence of our faith: "In the same way, faith by itself, if it is not accompanied by action, is dead" (Jas. 2:17). According to James, faith can only be demonstrated by what we do—actions speak louder than words.

Suppose you were jailed and put on trial for having professed to be a Christian. Other than your words, would there be enough evidence to convict you? Your life is a testimony to what you believe. Jesus said, "By their fruit you will recognize them" (Matt. 7:16).

> Show me your faith without deeds, and I will show you my faith by what I do (Jas. 2:18).

Thought for the day: *If the behavior of people you know doesn't match what they profess to believe, which one do you believe?*

I believe that they have not allowed God to work in their lives to the point where they know & understand & WANT to do good works. Or sometimes our faith is weak & we think that if we do good works we will please God or God will love us more. Sad to say that this was me for too long. I believed in Jesus but I struggled so much with Him being able to truly love me that I did works to compensate for it. And then there was a time when I had faith but my life did not show it by my actions, what I was watching, etc. My faith & my works did not line up.

LIVING BY FAITH

Galatians 3:10-14

Legalists are people who attempt to satisfy the just demands of God by their own works. They have either refused God's offer of grace; or they have never heard it, so they have never had the opportunity to understand and believe the gospel. As a result, they feel cursed or condemned because nobody has perfectly kept the law. "For whoever keeps the whole law and yet stumbles at just one point is guilty of breaking all of it" (Jas. 2:10). "Clearly no one is justified before God by the law, because, 'The righteous will live by faith' " (Gal. 3:11).

Paul says, "The law is not based on faith; on the contrary, 'The man who does these things will live by them' " (Gal. 3:12). Our understanding of law and grace affects how we live. If we choose to live under the law, we will seek to know the commandments of God as the Pharisees did and try our best to live accordingly. This usually results in a lot of rules and regulations that are enforced by the community. History has shown that traditions are added to the list of do's and don'ts in order to keep us from breaking the law. Trying our best to keep the law in our own strength can only result in defeat, frustration and burnout. The whole community feels condemned by their inability to keep the law.

The good news is, "Christ redeemed us from the curse of the law by becoming a curse for us" (Gal. 3:13). The means by which we live would radically change if we choose to receive this free gift or God. Living under the grace of God is a life concept rather than a law concept. "He redeemed us in order that the blessing given to Abraham might come to the Gentiles through Christ Jesus, so that by faith we might receive the promise of the Spirit" (v. 14). Under the grace of God, we receive new life that enables us to live in a whole different way. Under the New Covenant, we live by faith according to what God says is true in the power of the Holy Spirit.

Under the law, we try to change people's behavior. Under the grace of God, we are new creations in Christ, and we are transformed by the renewing of our minds (see Rom. 12:2). The focus shifts when we become new believers in Christ. Under the grace of God, we seek to change how we think and what we believe, because that is what determines what we do. For this reason repentance is so important for the new believer. "Repentance" literally means "a change of mind."

The grace of God is also a dynamic enablement for us as believers. We no longer try to live the Christian life in our own strength. We have received the promise of the Holy Spirit, and we live by His strength.

Trying to change our behavior without changing who we are and what we believe will produce two different types of flawed believers: those who are driven try to measure up to external standards but fail, and those who know they can't measure up to the law and so rebel against it. Regarding the former, their external conformity to the law never matches their inner turmoil. Jesus said to the teachers of the Law, "On the outside you appear to people as righteous but on the inside you are full of hypocrisy and wickedness" (Matt. 23:28). Regarding the latter, their rejection of external standards produces guilt and shame. A rule without a relationship leads to rebellion.

Clearly no one is justified before God by the law, because, "The righteous will live by faith" (Gal. 3:11).

Thought for the day: *Contrast living under the law to living under the grace of God.*

[handwritten notes in right margin: This is exactly what it was for me when growing up. All rules + nothing about relationship. I get so angry when I think of it. *]*

[handwritten notes: Living under law — rules that ... Living under the grace of God - relationship where you want to live a righteous life + a renewing of our minds. *]*

THE FEAR OF GOD

Isaiah 8:12-14

Fear is the most basic instinct of every living creature. An animal without fear will soon become some predator's dinner. Fear is the natural response when our physical safety and psychological well-being are threatened. Rational fears are rooted in truth, and they are necessary for our survival. Phobias are irrational fears that are rooted in false perceptions and lies. We categorize certain fears by their objects. Acrophobia is a fear of high places. Claustrophobia is a fear of enclosed places. Xenophobia is the fear of strangers. In order for a fear object to be legitimate, it must be perceived as imminent (present) and potent (powerful).

For most people, poisonous snakes are legitimate fear objects. You are probably experiencing no fear of snakes as you read this, because there are none present. You would be overcome immediately with fear if one suddenly appeared in your room, because it would pose a potent, imminent danger. But if the poisonous snake in your room were dead (imminent but not potent), you wouldn't have to fear it. A fear object is no longer legitimate if it loses just one of its attributes.

God is the ultimate fear object, because He is omnipresent and omnipotent. "The LORD Almighty is the one you are to regard as holy, he is the one you are to fear, he is the one you are to dread, and he will be a sanctuary" (Isa. 8:13). Normally a fear object is something or someone we want to run and hide from, but not so with God. He becomes our sanctuary when we fear Him. We revere God because we have total respect for His attributes, but the fear of God goes deeper. God has the power to judge, causing the psalmist to say, "If you, O LORD, kept a record of sins, O LORD, who could stand? But with you there is forgiveness; therefore you are feared" (Ps. 130:3-4).

It was prophesied of Jesus that "he will delight in the fear of the LORD" (Isa. 11:3). And we should, too, because Jesus took our punishment upon Himself. Consequently, "There is no fear in love. But perfect love drives out fear, because fear has to do with punishment" (1 John 4:18). Does that mean we no longer fear God? No, because "The fear of the LORD is pure, enduring forever" (Ps. 19:9); and "the fear of the LORD is the beginning of wisdom" (Ps. 111:10). The wise person fears God, because in fearing God, he or she will have no cause to fear anything else. He is the only fear object that eliminates all other fear objects, because nothing and no one else can be elevated above Him. We maintain a deep reverence for God, because of who He is and because we are accountable to Him.

So we make it our goal to please him, whether we are at home in the body or away from it. For we must all appear before the judgment seat of Christ, that each one may receive what is due him for the things done while in the body, whether good or bad. Since, then, we know what it is to fear the Lord, we try to persuade men (2 Cor. 5:9-11).

Fear is a powerful motivator, and knowing that we are accountable before God should motivate us to do everything pleasing to Him.

The wicked man flees though no on pursues, but the righteous are as bold as a lion (Prov. 28:1).

Thought for the day: *On what basis can the righteous be bold as a lion?*

- The righteous can be bold because God is our sanctuary.
- We are to fear God & not man which makes us realize that we want to do what is right in God's eyes & gives us that boldness we need whether it is to stand firm or to speak the Truth.

OVERCOMING THE FEAR OF DEATH

1 Corinthians 15:50-55

Fear was the first emotion expressed by Adam after the Fall (see Gen. 3:10); and because of the Fall, the most repeated command in Scripture is "fear not." What Adam and Eve lost in the Fall was life; and according to Scripture, "The last enemy to be destroyed is death" (1 Cor. 15:26). Because we are alive in Christ, death is no longer a legitimate fear object. Even though physical death is still imminent (see Heb. 9:27), it is no longer potent. "Death has been swallowed up in victory. Where, O death, is your victory? Where, O death, is your sting?" (1 Cor. 15:54-55).

No one looks forward to the process of dying, but there is no reason for us as believers to fear death. "We are confident, I say, and would prefer to be away from the body and at home with the Lord" (2 Cor. 5:8). The spiritual life we have in Christ is eternal. Our physical life is temporal and perishable. Paul wrote, "The perishable must clothe itself with the imperishable, and the mortal with immortality" (1 Cor. 15:53). In other words, our perishable physical life must be joined with the imperishable life of Christ so that when we physically die, "death [will be] swallowed up in victory" (v. 54). In order to be with God in heaven, we must physically die and receive a resurrected body, because "Flesh and blood cannot inherit the kingdom of God" (v. 50). When we physically die, we will be absent from the body, but present with the Lord for all eternity. If we have not received spiritual life before we physically die, we will face eternity in hell. Therefore, we should place the highest value not on our physical life, but on our spiritual life in Christ.

Paul says, "For to me, to live is Christ and to die is gain" (Phil. 1:21). Nothing else will fit in that formula: For me to live is my family, and to die would be loss. For me to live is my career, and to die would also be loss. If we are free from the fear of death, we are free to live responsible lives today. Being free from the fear of death is not a license to commit suicide, nor is it a license to needlessly throw ourselves in harm's way. Our physical life is an entrustment of which we are to be good stewards. "Now it is required that those who have been given a trust must prove faithful" (1 Cor. 4:2).

Yet even as good stewards, we must be willing to part with that over which we have stewardship. The fear of death should never prevent us from doing our duty. This point is well illustrated by the story of a fierce storm that had left a trawler in mortal danger. The Coast Guard was summoned to rescue the crew. A young seaman was paralyzed with fear at the prospect of going out to sea in such hazardous conditions. He pleaded with the captain, "We can't go out; we will never come back." The captain replied, "We must go out; we don't have to come back."

This world is not our home. We have been allowed to remain on this planet for a purpose. If we fear the Lord, we will seek above all else to fulfill our calling. Paul said, "I am torn between the two: I desire to depart and be with Christ, which is better by far; but it is more necessary for you that I remain in the body. Convinced of this, I know that I will remain, and I will continue with all of you for your progress and joy in the faith" (Phil. 1:23-25).

Precious in the sight of the LORD is the death of his saints (Ps. 116:15).

Thought for the day: *On what basis could the Author of Life say that the death of His saints is precious in His sight?*

Right now we are separated from Him but when we die we'll be with Him where we belong.

OVERCOMING THE FEAR OF PEOPLE

1 Peter 3:13-22

The early Christians were fearless, as evidenced by the record of their adventures in Acts. On one occasion it was observed, "After they prayed, the place where they were meeting was shaken. And they were all filled with the Holy Spirit and spoke the word of God with boldly" (Acts 4:31). Boldness is the mark of a Spirit-filled Christian. "For God did not give us a spirit of timidity, but a spirit of power, of love and of self-discipline" (2 Tim. 1:7). We surrender control of our lives to any fear object we elevate above God. But if we fear the Lord, we have self-control. Fearing God is an act of worship, because we are recognizing the supremacy of Him above all others.

Jesus said, "Do not be afraid of those who kill the body but cannot kill the soul. Rather, be afraid of the One who can destroy both soul and body in hell" (Matt. 10:28). Saul, the first king of Israel, sinned because "[he] was afraid of the people and so [he] gave in to them" (1 Sam. 15:24). Moses sent 12 spies into the land of Canaan (see Num. 13:1), who discovered it to be a fruitful land. But 10 spies gave a bad report because they feared the people who lived there, saying, "We seemed like grasshoppers in our own eyes, and we looked the same to them" (Num. 13:33). Fear had distorted their perspective, but Joshua and Caleb had the right one: "Do not rebel against the LORD. And do not be afraid of the people of the land, because we will swallow them up. Their protection is gone, but the LORD is with us" (Num. 14:9).

No one denies that people can do incredible emotional and physical harm to each another. But we should not give another human being the right to determine who we are. We are children of God, and only He has the right to decide who we are—and who we are meant to become. The fear of man will compromise our witness, and we will end up trying to please others and fail to please God. Paul said, "If I were still trying to please men, I would not be a servant of Christ" (Gal. 1:10). A servant of Christ will seek to do that which is good. Peter asked, "Who is going to harm you if you are eager to do good?" (1 Pet. 3:13). The unfortunate truth is that some may seek to harm us, but that cannot alter who we are, nor should that fear control us.

But even if you should suffer for what is right, you are blessed. "Do not fear what they fear, do not be frightened." But in your hearts set apart Christ as Lord. Always be prepared to give an answer to everyone who asks you to give the reason for the hope that you have. But do this with gentleness and respect, keeping a clear conscience (1 Pet. 13:14-16).

Fear of man is the number one reason why we Christians often fail to share our faith. It is an irrational fear, because it is not based in truth. The truth is we are called to be witnesses, and those who are lost need to know the truth that will save them. But many may not hear the gospel message if we allow the fear of man to control our lives. The only way to overcome the fear of man is to feel the fear, but do the right thing anyway. If we do the thing we fear the most, the death of an irrational fear is certain.

Fear of man will prove to be a snare, but whoever trusts in the LORD is kept safe (Prov. 29:25).

Thought for the day: *Why do we have nothing to fear if we are in the center of God's will?*

Because we know we are doing God's will
+ pleasing Him. He is with us + will take
care of us even in suffering. This is so easy
for me to write but if it means suffering
I may not do so well.
I really admire Hannah for her boldness.
Even though she is mocked + shunned by
her community she still carries on.

OVERCOMING THE FEAR OF FAILURE

1 Samuel 17

The fearful ask, "What do I stand to lose if I do?" The fearless ask, "What do I stand to gain if I do and lose if I don't?" Israel was confronted with those options when the Philistines sent Goliath to challenge their champion. "On hearing the Philistine's words, Saul and all the Israelites were dismayed and terrified" (1 Sam. 17:11). Their fear of failure kept them from going up against the giant. David asked, "What will be done for the man who kills this Philistine and removes this disgrace from Israel? Who is this uncircumcised Philistine that he should defy the armies of the living God?" (v. 26). David reasoned, *I would gain a lot if I do* (see v. 25), and *Israel will be disgraced if I don't.* The Israelites had seen the giant in relationship to themselves, but David saw the giant in comparison to God. The Lord had delivered David from a lion and a bear, and He believed that God would deliver him "from the hand of this Philistine" (v. 37).

The Bible is a historical account of failures. Moses struck the rock in anger and failed to reach the Promised Land. Elijah slew 450 prophets of Baal, but ran from Jezebel. Peter told the Lord to His face that he would go to prison and even be willing to die for Him; then, fearing for his life, he denied three times that he even knew Jesus. David slew Goliath, but he also slept with Bathsheba and brought great pain to his family. Many of the heroes mentioned in Hebrews 11 would be considered flops by modern-day standards. But they were not mentioned because of their accomplishments; they were commended for their faithfulness (see Heb. 11:39-40).

To stumble and fall is not failure. To stumble and fall again is not failure. Failure comes when we say, "I was pushed," and then fail to get up again. We have failed ourselves if we blame others for our lack of progress or rationalize why we can't get back up again. We have failed others when we don't assume our responsibility in the Body of Christ. There are two kinds of failures: moral failure and failure to meet certain objectives. Moral failure cannot be blamed on anyone but ourselves. If we have sinned, we need to confess it to God (see 1 John 1:9), receive His forgiveness and cleansing, and get up from where we have fallen.

We all have failed to accomplish one or more of our life objectives, but that doesn't make us failures. A mistake is never a failure unless we fail to learn from it. Those who are afraid to fail never try. They follow the path of least resistance. Letting the fear of failure control our lives is like putting the car in reverse and jamming on the break. We may reduce our losses, but we never really accomplish anything to the glory of God. We all like the security of the tree trunk, but the fruit is always out on the end of the limb!

Remember, success is 90 percent attitude and 10 percent aptitude. Every step toward maturity will be met with new challenges and obstacles to be overcome. You will feel the fear of failure if you are growing in Christ; but if you fear the Lord, you will overcome that fear. You will be able to look back and say, "It was an unshakable faith in God and persistence that got me through."

Though a righteous man falls seven times, he rises again (Prov. 24:16).

Thought for the day: *How can the grace of God help you overcome the fear of failure?*

God's grace allows us to fail – God is loving & forgiving. When I do fail I must get back up & continue forward & NOT GIVE UP BECAUSE I KNOW GOD ISN'T THROUGH WITH ME BECAUSE OF THAT ONE FAILURE

FREEDOM FROM FEAR

2 Timothy 1

Paul begins this letter by encouraging Timothy to be faithful. He knows that fear will be the chief obstacle, so he writes, "For God did not give us a spirit of timidity, but a spirit of power, of love and of self-discipline" (2 Tim. 1:7). Based on what God has given us, we can take certain steps to ensure that no fear—other than the fear of God—is controlling our lives.

The first step is to submit to God and resist the devil (see Jas. 4:7). You need to resolve any personal or spiritual conflicts. You can do this by working through "The Steps to Freedom in Christ." By doing so, you will experience the presence of the Wonderful Counselor and eliminate any possible interference by the evil one.

The second step is to analyze your fears. Start by asking God to reveal the basis for your fears. What is it that you are actually afraid of? What is controlling your life? The root of any phobia is a belief that is not based in truth. Your false beliefs need to be rooted out and replaced by God's truth. The Holy Spirit will lead you into all truth as you submit to Him and study God's Word. You may also decide to seek the godly counsel of others who can help you identify your fears. You need to discover the lies behind irrational fears, renounce each one and then choose to believe the truth.

The third step is to analyze how your fear has impacted your lifestyle. How has fear prevented you from living a responsible life, compelled you to do that which is irresponsible or compromised your Christian witness? Fear is a powerful motivator for good or for evil. If irrational fear has caused you to lead a sinful lifestyle, it is not enough for you to be sorry. Believing lies and living irresponsibly need to be confessed to God and repented of.

The fourth step is to face the fear and work out a responsible plan of action. Irrational fears are like mirages in the desert. They seem real until you move toward them. But if you back away from irrational fears, they gain an even greater control of your life. You may need the advice and assistance of a pastor or godly counselor who will help you take the first step toward resolving your fears. Long-standing fears may need to be eradicated slowly. If you are afraid to ride in an elevator, then don't start with the tallest building in town. Find a two-story building with an elevator, and gain confidence with each new step you take.

THE DAILY DISCIPLER 183

Determine in advance what your response will be to all possible reactions to your plan. What are the possible consequences of standing up to a fear object? Thinking this through will help solidify your initial plan of action and help you answer the question, Can I live with the consequences? Christians can always live with the consequences of doing what is right and living a responsible life (whereas nobody can adequately prepare for living an irresponsible life). You should be more afraid of not doing God's will, than of doing the will of another fear object.

Commit yourself to carry out the plan of action in the power of the Holy Spirit. Committing yourself to do God's will is the key to overcoming your phobias. If it is judicious, have someone pray for you and hold you accountable for the plans you have made.[1]

Do not be afraid of those who kill the body but cannot kill the soul. Rather, be afraid of the One who can destroy both soul and body in hell (Matt. 10:28).

Thought for the day: *How does knowing the truth set you free from irrational fears?*

My biggest fear is of a loved one dying or of immediately jumping to an irrational fear of what has happened & why they are late, etc. I have an over active imagination that does not help - it fuels the fear.

Thank God He is working on this & I am turning to Him when the fears starts coming instead of turning to the "What If's".

Because of these fears I sheltered my kids as they were growing up. There is a far line between common sense & irrational fear.

I NOW LAY IT BEFORE GOD & QUOTE FROM THE BIBLE. I'M EVEN ABLE TO SLEEP BEFORE SCOTT GETS HOME.

Thank You Lord Jesus for being my strength!

LIVING UNDER AUTHORITY

Romans 13:1-7

Under the Old Covenant, God intended to establish His people in the Promised Land. The Mosaic Law was both civil and ceremonial. The prophet, priest and king roughly represented the legislative, judicial and executive branches of government—resembling the governmental structure in the United States. Each branch had certain restrictions to ensure a proper check and balance. The king could not use his executive powers for personal gain (see Deut. 17:14-20). The priests avoided any conflict of interest by having no portion of the land (see Deut. 18:1-8). The prophets could not speak presumptuously (see Deut. 18:20-22). The system broke down when Solomon violated God's restrictions (compare 1 Kings 10:14—11:8 with Deut. 17:14-20).

Under the New Covenant, Christians have dual citizenship. First, "Our citizenship is in heaven" (Phil. 3:20), because of our new birth in Christ. Second, we have a citizenship in our respective countries, because of our natural birth or naturalization processes. The Word of God governs the Church, but the State has its own constitution. How then do we relate to these two governing authorities? The apostle Paul said, "Everyone must submit himself to the governing [higher] authorities, for there is no authority except that which God has established" (Rom. 13:1). The primary reason we are to submit to higher authorities is because "there is no authority except that which God has established." If we rebel against any higher authority, we are rebelling against God (see Rom. 13:3), and we bring civil and/or divine judgment upon ourselves.

The Church as a whole is never charged with the responsibility of governing the State. The Church is the conscience of the State. Individual members of the Church are citizens of the State who may be called to civil service. Civil authorities are God's servants who are instruments of justice in the land (see Rom. 13:4). Government forces, when properly used, prevent tyranny, ensure social order and execute justice. We should not fear the rulers of the State if we are submissive and living righteous lives (see vv. 3-4). The Church should never stand in opposition to another authority that God has established. We are urged to pray "for kings and all those in authority, that we may live peaceful and quiet lives in all godliness and holiness"

(1 Tim. 2:2). In doing so, we not only avoid punishment, but we also don't violate our own conscience.

Just like the priests needed to be supported by the offerings of the people (see Deut. 18:2), so do "God's servants, who give their full time to governing" (Rom. 13:6). Therefore, citizens of the country should pay their taxes. Paul admonished us to "Give everyone what you owe him: If you owe taxes, pay taxes; if revenue, then revenue; if respect, then respect; if honor, then honor" (Rom. 13:7). Paying our taxes is not optional; we owe our taxes and we owe respect to those who govern. No country can survive anarchy, and no ruler can be effective if subjects do not respect the position of those in authority over them. We respect the position of authority, not necessarily the person in it. It is not Christian to sit in judgment of rulers or publicly criticize them. There are times when we must obey God rather than people, and being submissive doesn't mean that we roll over and play dead. A faithful steward is a good citizen in both kingdoms.

> Show proper respect to everyone: Love the brotherhood of believers, fear God, honor the king (1 Pet. 2:17).

Thought for the day: *How should Christians respond to civil servants who are less than righteous?*

THE SIN OF REBELLION

1 Samuel 15

The Bible is a historical account of humankind's propensity to rebel. Adam and Eve rebelled in the Garden of Eden. Cain murderously rebelled against God's rejection of his offering. Although we have one reference in Genesis to a man who "walked with God" (see Gen. 5:24), it would appear that all the ancient people—except Noah—were in rebellion; as a result, God sent the Flood. The people were rebellious again when they built the Tower of Babel. Their prideful desire to reach heaven and make a name for themselves resulted in God confounding their languages and scattering the people throughout the land. Miriam and Aaron rebelled against Moses. Lot rebelled against Abraham. Esau rebelled against Jacob. Absalom rebelled against David. The whole world is in rebellion against God. We were all rebellious by nature, and even as believers we are continuously tempted to "do it our way."

The seriousness of rebellion can be illustrated by the life of Saul, the first king of Israel. God had given clear instructions to Saul: "Go and completely destroy those wicked people, the Amalekites; make war on them until you have wiped them out" (see 1 Sam. 15:2-3). But Saul decided on his own to keep some of the spoils of war and spare the life of Agag, the Amalekite king (see vv. 8-9). He justified his actions by saying he kept the best of the spoils in order to make sacrifices to God (see v. 15). Saul would not acknowledge his own rebellion, insisting that he had obeyed the Lord.

> But Samuel replied: "Does the LORD delight in burnt offerings and sacrifices as much as in obeying the voice of the LORD? To obey is better than sacrifice, and to heed is better than the fat of rams. For rebellion is like the sin of divination, and arrogance like the evil of idolatry" (vv. 22-23).

Rebellion may be humanity's worst sin.

Saul rebelled because he feared the people more than he did God (see 1 Sam. 15:24), and he decided for himself how he was going to worship Him. Like Saul, we may not see our own rebellion. We are rebellious when we sit in judgment of those who are over us and decide for ourselves what the right course of action should be. We criticize the government and look for ways to get around the law when we should instead be praying for and submitting to governing authorities. We go to church and critique the message and the choir. The message is supposed to sit in judgment of us, and we are supposed to "worship in spirit and in truth" (John 4:24).

Rebellion is far more than an action; it is an attitude. Rebellion is essentially a problem of the heart. Our standing up physically while sitting down spiritually will not escape God's notice, since He looks upon the heart. Going through the motions of worship is not what God is pleased with. David came to understand this after his sin with Bathsheba: "You do not delight in sacrifice, or I would bring it; you do not take pleasure in burnt offerings. The sacrifices of God are a broken spirit; a broken and contrite heart, O God, you will not despise" (Ps. 51:16-17). God does not delight in our external acts of worship when our hearts are not right.

> He has showed you, O man, what is good. And what does the LORD require of you? To act justly and to love mercy and to walk humbly with your God (Mic. 6:8).

Thought for the day: *Why is rebellion like the sin of divination (witchcraft)?*

UNDERSTANDING SUBMISSION

1 Peter 2:9-25

The Greek word for submission is a military term which means to "arrange under." If we are submissive to God, we will also be submissive to civil government (see 1 Pet. 2:13-17); parents (see Eph. 6:13); husbands (see Eph. 5:22; 1 Pet. 3:1-4) and wives (see Eph. 5:21; 1 Pet. 3:7); employers (see 1 Pet. 2:18-23); and church leaders (see Heb. 13:17). The charge to be submissive to governing authorities always comes with a promised blessing. It is for our own spiritual protection that we are called to be submissive. Scripture warns us that we are in hostile territory on planet Earth and admonishes us to fall in rank and follow God.

The world would have us believe that we are nothing; therefore, we need to scheme, maneuver, manipulate or do whatever is necessary to get ahead and make a name for ourselves. Peter shares the opposite message. We are special children of God, and should therefore be submissive.

> You are a chosen people, a royal priesthood, a holy nation, a people belonging to God, that you may declare the praises of him who called you out of darkness into his wonderful light. Once you were not a people, but now you are the people of God; once you had not received mercy, but now you have received mercy (1 Pet. 2:9-10).

It is a mature act of faith to trust God to work in our lives through less-than-perfect leaders who will undoubtedly be in positions of authority over us at some time in our lives. We submit to their authority because of their position. Should governing authorities demand that we do something that is contrary to the will of God, then we must obey God, as the Early Church did (see Acts 4:18-20). Rather than be disrespectful, we should offer them a creative alternative as Daniel did (see Dan. 1:8-16). We also don't have to obey those in authority if they have overstepped the scope of their authority. Policemen can direct traffic, but they cannot come into our church and command us to worship a certain way.

Submission never means surrendering who we are. In fact, being submissive is the only way that we can be all that God intends us to be. Our identity and our freedom are found in Christ, and are unrelated to who we report to in this world. Nobody can keep us from being the people God created us to be. "For we are God's workmanship, created in Christ Jesus to do good works, which God prepared in advance for us to do" (Eph. 2:10). We may be ridiculed for being Christians, but "it is God's will that by doing good you should silence the ignorant talk of foolish men" (1 Pet. 2:15). When, while serving under an earthly master, we suffer unjustly for doing good, it is commendable before God. "To this you were called, because Christ suffered for you, leaving you an example, that you should follow in his steps" (1 Pet. 2:21).

"Wives, in the same way be submissive to your husbands so that, if any of them do not believe the word, they may be won over without words by the behavior of their wives" (1 Pet. 3:1). Their appeal should be based on "the unfading beauty of a gentle and quiet spirit, which is of great worth in God's sight" (v. 4). Esther was such a woman; and because of her willingness to be submissive to the king, who was her husband, she saved the nation of Israel.

Submit to one another out of reverence for Christ (Eph. 5:21).

Thought for the day: *Does being submissive ever conflict with who we are in Christ?*

THE GREAT COMMANDMENT

Matthew 22:34-40

Jesus silenced the Sadducees who had questioned Him about the resurrection, which they didn't believe in (see Matt. 22:23-33). Having heard about this incident, the Pharisees wanted to test Jesus. "An expert in the law, tested him with this question: 'Teacher, which is the greatest commandment in the Law?' " (Matt. 22:36). Obviously, knowing the Ten Commandments in which the first four concern our relationship with God and the rest with how we relate to others (see Exod. 20:1-17), Jesus answered,

> "Love the Lord your God with all your heart and with all your soul and with all your mind." This is the first and greatest commandment. And the second is like it: "Love your neighbor as yourself." All the Law and the Prophets hang on these two commandments (Matt. 22:37-40).

They didn't ask Jesus for the second greatest commandment, but He gave it to them anyway. These two commandments define the whole purpose of the Word of God, which is to love God and other people. We are to love God with our entire being. The second commandment necessarily flows from the first. If we loved God with our whole being, we would also love our neighbor as ourselves. The Pharisees knew that Jesus was right, but they struggled with the second part. So another expert in the Law asked Jesus, "And who is my neighbor?" (Luke 10:29). Jesus answered by telling the parable of the Good Samaritan (see Luke 10:30-37). The Samaritans were foreigners and hated by the Jews. The Jews considered them to be half-breeds, both physically and spiritually. Both groups were openly hostile to each other. But in the parable, the Samaritan proved by his deeds that he was the good neighbor.

Love of neighbor is not limited by our national boundaries, nor does it recognize any denominational or religious differences.

> If anyone says, "I love God," yet hates his brother, he is a liar. For anyone who does not love his brother, whom he has seen, cannot love God, whom he has not seen. And he has given us this com-

mand: Whoever loves God must also love his brother (1 John 4:20-21).

Our relationship with God is inextricably bound up with our relationships with others. If we have a truly righteous relationship with God, then we will have healthy, loving relationships with our neighbors. In the Sermon on the Mount, Jesus said, "You have heard that it was said, 'Love your neighbor and hate your enemy.' But I tell you: Love your enemies and pray for those who persecute you, that you may be sons of your Father in heaven" (Matt. 5:43-45).

Jesus said, "So in everything, do to others what you would have them do to you, for this sums up the Law and the Prophets" (Matt. 7:12). At the time, the Jews practiced a negative form of the Golden Rule: "Whatever you would not wish done to you, do not yourself to another." It was the law of retaliation. The Golden Rule is based on the law of grace.

> But love your enemies, do good to them, and lend to them without expecting to get anything back. Then your reward will be great, and you will be sons of the Most High, because he is kind to the ungrateful and wicked. Be merciful, just as your Father is merciful (Luke 6:35-36).

We are to relate to others as Christ has related to us. Essentially, that means showing mercy by not giving other people what they deserve. But that doesn't go far enough. We are to give people what they don't deserve—in other words, we are to *love* one another.

> Love the Lord your God with all your heart and with all your soul and with all your mind (Matt. 22:37).

Thought for the day: *How can you keep the Great Commandment?*

THE LORDSHIP OF CHRIST

Mark 8:34-40

The number one obstacle that keeps us from being all that God has created us to be is ourselves. Self-sufficient and self-centered living keeps us from finding our sufficiency in Christ. To deny ourselves is to deny self-rule. Dying to self is the primary battle of life. The flesh scrambles for the throne and wants to play God, but Jesus is already on the throne and He graciously offers to share it.

The cross we pick up is the cross of Christ. His cross has provided forgiveness for what we have done and deliverance from what we were. We are forgiven because He died in our place; we are delivered because we have died with Him. Seeking to overcome self by self-effort is futile. Self will never cast out self, because an independent self that is motivated by the flesh still wants to rule. When we follow Christ, the Holy Spirit will lead us down the path of death to self-rule. "For we who are alive are always being given over to death for Jesus' sake, so that his life may be revealed in our mortal body" (2 Cor. 4:11). Denying ourselves, picking up our cross daily and following Jesus may sound like a dismal path to take, but it most assuredly isn't for the following three reasons.

First, you are sacrificing the lower life to gain the higher life. If you want to save your natural life (i.e., finding your identity and sense of worth in positions, titles, accomplishments and possessions, and seeking only worldly well-being), you will lose it. You may have some of it for a time, but not for eternity. Furthermore, efforts to possess temporal blessings keep you from pursuing what you could have in Christ. If you aim for this world, that is all you will get, and only for a short time. Aim for the next world, heaven, and you get it—plus the benefits of knowing Christ now.

Second, you are sacrificing the pleasure of things to gain the pleasures of life. What would you accept in exchange for the fruit of the Spirit in your life? What material possession, what amount of money, what man-made position or title would you exchange for love, joy, peace, patience, kindness, goodness, faithfulness, gentleness and self-control? The lie of this world is that temporal possessions will give us love, joy, peace and the like, but they can't. For some deceptive reason, we strive to be happy as animals instead of being blessed as children of God.

Third, you are sacrificing the temporal to gain the eternal. One of the great signs of spiritual maturity is the ability to postpone rewards. Look at the example of Moses. "He chose to be mistreated along with the people of God rather than to enjoy the pleasures of sin for a short time. He regarded disgrace for the sake of Christ as of greater value than the treasures of Egypt, because he was looking ahead to his reward" (Heb. 11:25-26).

We may encounter some hardships in following Christ, but "our light and momentary troubles are achieving for us an eternal glory that far outweighs them all" (2 Cor. 4:17). Making Jesus the Lord of our lives also makes Him the Lord of our problems. As Lord, He assumes responsibility for what we could never fulfill ourselves. Heaven is where we say to God, "Thy will be done." Hell is where God says to us, "Thy will be done."

> If anyone would come after me, he must deny himself and take up his cross and follow me (Mark 8:34).

Thought for the day: *What does it mean to deny yourself?*

RELATING TO ONE ANOTHER

Luke 6:20-42

The greatest challenge in life is learning to relate to one another in a fallen world. The Lord exhorted us to love our enemies (see Luke 6:27-36) and to restrain from judging one another (see vv. 37-42). It is only the grace of God that enables us to love those who hate us. Consider the dynamics involved when two people are at each other's throats. Chances are they will be attacking the other person's character, while looking out for their own needs. There is no way that two people can get along if that is what they are doing. Before God, we are responsible for our own character and the needs of those around us. Romans 14:4 says, "Who are you to judge someone else's servant? To his own master he stands or falls. And he will stand, for the Lord is able to make him stand." And Philippians 2:3-5 tells us,

> Do nothing out of selfish ambition or vain conceit, but in humility consider others better than yourselves. Each of you should look not only to your own interests, but also to the interests of others. Your attitude should be the same as that of Christ Jesus.

What would life be like if we all assumed responsibility for our own character and committed ourselves to loving one another? Surely that is what Scripture requires of us. Conforming to His image is God's plan for our lives, and out of this developing character we meet one another's needs. Then why doesn't this transforming love seem to be present—even in our churches and Christian homes? It will happen in heaven, but in this world we live with imperfect people, and none of us has matured to perfection. That is why we are to take the plank out of our own eye before we even consider looking at the speck in someone else's eye (see Luke 6:41-42).

Jesus has instructed us how to respond to those who don't abide by His teaching. "Do good to those who hate you, bless those who curse you, pray for those who mistreat you" (Luke 20:27). In other words, respond to their bad attitude with deeds of kindness; speak well of those who speak ill of you; and should their bad attitude and speech digress to bad behavior, then all you can do is pray for them. The point is, nobody can keep you from being the person God created you to be, so don't let immature people determine who you are and how you should respond. When treated poorly by others, do not respond in kind. Instead, "Do to others as you would have them do to you" (v. 31).

You get out of life what you put into it. If you want a friend, then be a friend. If you want someone to love you, then love someone. "Do not judge, and you will not be judged. Do not condemn, and you will not be condemned. Forgive, and you will be forgiven. Give, and it will be given to you" (Luke 20:37-38). It is one of life's great compensations to know that you cannot help another without helping yourself in the process. Whatever life asks of you, give a little more and it will come overflowing back to you: "A good measure, pressed down, shaken together and running over, will be poured into your lap. For with the measure you use, it will be measured to you" (v. 38).

Do to others as you would have them do to you (Luke 6:31).

Thought for the day: *What would life be like if everyone obeyed the "Golden Rule"?*

DISCIPLINE AND JUDGMENT

Zechariah 8:14-17

Judicial and civil judgments are made in the courts of our land when people commit crimes or fail to work out their differences with one another. Judges are to "render true and sound judgment" (Zech. 8:16), which are based on facts brought by witnesses. They aren't judging people when they settle differences and determine guilt or innocence. They are determining guilt or innocence based on the law of the land and by the testimony of witnesses. Only God can righteously judge us.

In our relationships with others, we are commanded not to judge one another, but we are instructed to discipline those caught in sin for the purpose of restoring fellowship. Knowing the difference between the two has serious implications for how we relate to others. Judgment is related to a person's character, and discipline is related to a person's behavior.

Suppose you catch your son telling a lie and you say to him, "Son, what you just said right now isn't true." You are not judging him. You are confronting him for the purpose of discipline. If you said, "Son, you are a liar," that would be judging him.

Some attempts at discipline are nothing more than character assassination. If you called me dumb, stupid or arrogant, what could I do about it? I couldn't instantly change my character. Making a negative judgment of my character is a form of rejection, and it causes you to be at odds with me. But if you pointed out a behavior problem, I could own up to my sin, confess it, repent and seek forgiveness from those I had offended. I may have to live with the consequences of the sin and make restitution, if warranted, but I would be reconciled with God and others.

Character is what we build up in one another, and we are not to tear it down. If all God's children would memorize the following verse and never violate it, many of our church and family problems would disappear. "Do not let any unwholesome talk come out of your mouths, but only what is helpful for building others up according to their needs, that it may benefit those who listen" (Eph. 4:29). When we tear each other down, we grieve the Holy Spirit (see v. 30). Let us do no evil to our neighbor. Let us speak the truth in love. In civil matters, let the judges in our courts decide our guilt or innocence based on witnesses, and let God be the judge of our character.

Discipline has to be based on observed behavior. You have to personally see or hear what another person has said or done before you can rightfully confront them. The Mosaic Law required two or three witnesses in order to carry out a capital punishment (see Deut. 19:15). Christians are likewise instructed to have two or three witnesses before bringing a sinning believer before the Church (see Matt. 18:15-20). If you catch a person in sin, confront that person with the purpose of winning him or her back. If the person refuses to repent and there are no other witnesses, the matter ends there.

Discipline is not the same as punishment. Punishment is retroactive. Discipline is future oriented. God doesn't punish us when we sin. He disciplines us so that we don't do it again. The punishment we deserved has already fallen on Christ.

God disciplines us for our good, that we may share in his holiness (Heb. 12:10).

Thought for the day: *What are the differences between discipline and judgment, and how does punishment differ from discipline?*

A PROPER DEFENSE

Isaiah 53

What should we do when someone wrongly judges us and attacks our character? Should we be defensive? Just as He did for everything else in life, Jesus has set the standard for how we should respond.

> To this you were called, because Christ suffered for you, leaving you an example, that you should follow in his steps. He committed no sin, and no deceit was found in his mouth. When they hurled their insults at him, he did not retaliate; when he suffered, he made no threats. Instead, he entrusted himself to him who judges justly (1 Pet. 2:21-23).

Isaiah 53 is one of the clearest prophecies of Christ in the Old Testament. "He was pierced for our transgressions, he was crushed for our iniquities; the punishment that brought us peace was upon him, and by his wounds we are healed" (v. 5). He suffered in silence for our sins and never once opened His mouth to defend Himself (see v. 7). Our situation is somewhat different, because we are not sinless. However, we still shouldn't defend ourselves for two reasons. First, if their judgments are right, we don't have a defense. Even though they are wrong to judge us, it would do no good to defend ourselves. Attempts to defend our character often intensify the efforts of those judging us. We should follow Christ's example by not retaliating and trust Him who judges justly. Then we must thank God that our sins are forgiven, accept the fact that we are a work in progress and learn from the experience. The wise man said, "Rebuke a discerning man, and he will gain knowledge" (Prov. 19:25). Such attacks on our character reveal how secure or insecure we are in Christ. There would be no need to defend yourself if you knew that Christ was your defense.

Second, if their judgments are wrong, we don't need a defense. This situation is actually harder to deal with than the first, because there is no truth in what they are saying. Should someone personally and falsely attack our character, we should just listen. After they have finished pointing out every little character defect, their gun is empty. The last thing we want to do is hand them some more ammunition. If we attempted to defend ourselves against any one of their allegations, they would probably become even more convinced that it was their responsibility to convince us of our imperfections. That only leads to more accusations and verbal excursions.

Suppose we responded by saying, "I'm sorry you are upset with me; what do you suggest I do?" That may create an opportunity for ministry for two reasons. First, by not trying to play the role of God in their lives, as they were trying to do in ours, we leave room for the Holy Spirit to bring conviction in their lives. When we play the role of the Holy Spirit in someone else's life, it misdirects their battle with God onto ourselves, and we are not up for the task. Second, nobody tears down another person's character from a position of strength. They are wrong to judge us, and it is helpful to know that in some way they must be hurting. There is some reason that they are angry and upset. It would be far more profitable to discover their difficulty, than to try defending ourselves.

> Here me, you who know what is right, you people who have my law in your hearts: Do not fear the reproach of men or be terrified by their insults (Isa. 51:7).

Thought for the day: *What has happened in the past when you have become defensive?*

ACCEPTANCE AND AFFIRMATION

Romans 15:1-7

Ultimately we are accountable to God, but we also need to be accountable to one another. This ensures proper care and discipline in our churches and homes. As we consider how this can happen amongst ourselves, consider the following four words and ask yourself, "From which end of the list does God come to us?"

Authority
Accountability
Affirmation
Acceptance

Your answer to that question will reveal what kind of a parent you are and how you do ministry.

Scripture leaves little room for doubt as to the answer: God first came to us with acceptance through Jesus Christ: "While we were still sinners, Christ died for us" (Rom. 5:8). Then came the affirmation: "The Spirit himself testifies with our spirit that we are God's children" (Rom. 8:16). Those who are accepted and affirmed will voluntarily be accountable to authority figures; but if authority figures demand accountability without acceptance and affirmation, they will never get full disclosure. That is why Paul admonished us to "Accept one another, then, just as Christ accepted you, in order to bring praise to God" (Rom. 15:7).

Jesus never said, "Listen, people, shape up because I am God." Jesus had no human or earthly position of authority; and yet "the crowds were amazed at his teaching, because he taught as one who had authority, and not as their teachers of the law" (Matt. 7:28-29). People recognized His authority, because it was based on His character. Jesus dined with sinners so they knew they were accepted, even when their own religious leaders had rejected them. The Gospels reveal that sinners loved to be around Jesus and that Jesus waged war against hypocritical religious leaders. Sinners who desperately need Jesus often stay away from churches because of what they per-

THE DAILY DISCIPLER 201

ceive to be religious hypocrisy on the part of churched believers.

Not only Jesus but also His followers related to others in a spirit of love and acceptance. Listen to how Paul speaks of his manner toward the Thessalonians:

> As apostles of Christ we could have been a burden to you, but we were gentle among you, like a mother caring for her little children. We loved you so much that we were delighted to share with you not only the gospel of God but our lives as well, because you had become so dear to us (1 Thess. 2:6-8).

Acceptance and affirmation are two of the most basic needs that we all have. We only need to observe little children to know this—they unashamedly ask for both. "Did I do good, Mommy?" "Do you like the picture I drew?" We don't grow out of those needs, but we all too often stop extending acceptance and affirmation to adults and to our children as they grow older.

Listen to the dialogue between an authoritarian parent and a tardy child:

"Where were you?"

"Out!"

"What were you doing?"

"Nothing!"

Does that sound familiar? It is all too common in our homes, churches and schools. Overbearing authoritarianism repels intimate disclosure. True accountability cannot be demanded; it is voluntarily given. We can force some external accountability through threats and intimidation, others will never be vulnerable to an authority figure unless they know they are loved, accepted and affirmed. As Christian leaders and parents, we may not always be able to control those under our authority, but we can always love them.

> Accept one another, then, just as Christ accepted you, in order to bring praise to God (Rom. 15:7).

Thought for the day: *Why would God be praised if we accepted one another as He has accepted us?*

OVERCOMING REJECTION

Acts 15:36-40

Everyone knows what it feels like to be unduly criticized and rejected, especially when it comes from people we want to please. Nobody can be their best at everything, and sometimes we fail to live up to other people's expectations. Paul and Barnabas wanted to embark on a second missionary journey, but they had a sharp disagreement over Mark, who had deserted Paul earlier. Paul's refusal to bring Mark resulted in a split between him and Barnabas. Paul rejected Mark (see Acts 15:36-40).

We have been born and raised in a worldly system that chooses favorites and rejects seconds. From the earliest age, we strive to please significant others in order to gain their approval. But this fallen world is a dog-eat-dog, survival-of-the-fittest system. In our natural state, we choose to adapt to this world system in one of three ways.

First, there are some who try to beat the system. These people try to earn their acceptance and strive for significance through their appearance, performance or social status. They feel driven to get to the top because winning is their passport to acceptance, security and significance. They are characterized by perfectionism and emotional insulation that usually lead to anxiety, stress and burnout. They are prone to controlling and manipulating people and circumstances for their own end, so it is difficult for them to yield control of their lives to God. Eventually, their abilities diminish—and younger, stronger and more capable controllers replace them.

Second, others give in to the system, embracing its warped standards. The strongest, prettiest and most talented are "in," and they are "out," because they don't measure up in those categories. By giving in to this worldly system, these people succumb to society's false judgment of their worth. They often find it difficult to accept themselves because others haven't. Some have trouble relating to God, because they blame Him for making them deficient in the eyes of the world.

The third group rebels against the system. They respond to rejection by saying, "I don't need you, and I don't want your love!" They need love and acceptance like everyone else, but they refuse to acknowledge their needs. They often underscore their defiance and rebellion by dressing and behaving in ways that are objectionable to the general population. Rebels are marked by self-hatred and bitterness. They are irresponsible and undisciplined. They think that God and "religious" people are trying to squeeze them into a socially acceptable mold.

All three responses to the social systems of this world eventually lead to defeat. The kingdom of God is totally different. Nobody wins in the world's system, but everybody wins in the kingdom of God. We are not in competition with one another. Paul says, "We do not dare to classify or compare ourselves with some who commend themselves. When they measure themselves by themselves and compare themselves with themselves, they are not wise" (2 Cor. 10:12). We are loved and accepted unconditionally by God. Each of us is an essential part of the Body of Christ. Helping another person succeed enhances our success. The more we build one another up, the more we build ourselves up.

Mark must have discovered this wonderful truth—because he and Paul were eventually reconciled. While doing time in a Roman prison, Paul wrote in his last epistle, "Get Mark and bring him with you, because he is helpful to me in my ministry" (2 Tim. 4:11).

You come to him, the living Stone—rejected by men but chosen by God and precious to him (1 Pet. 2:4).

Thought for the day: *How can the acceptance of God in our lives overcome the rejection by others?*

THE MINISTRY OF RECONCILIATION

Leviticus 3

All the animal sacrifices prescribed under the Old Covenant (see the book of Leviticus for the various types of offerings) are no longer needed under the New Covenant. Christ, who died once for all, has become our sin offering (see Heb. 10:10). We fulfill the burnt offering when we offer our bodies as living sacrifices, holy and pleasing to God (see Rom. 12:1). The fellowship offering was given in voluntary gratitude for past blessings, answered prayer or a bountiful harvest. It has traditionally been called the "peace offering" because the root Hebrew word *shalom* means "peace." The peace offering in the Old Testament pictures the fellowship that we now have with God on the basis of Christ's death on the cross. We worship with thanksgiving and praise, because we have been reconciled to God who has made us new creations in Christ.

As members of the Body of Christ, we have been reconciled to God.

All this is from God, who reconciled us to himself through Christ and gave us the ministry of reconciliation: that God was reconciling the world to himself in Christ, not counting men's sins against them. And he has committed to us the message of reconciliation. We are therefore Christ's ambassadors, as though God were making his appeal through us (2 Cor. 5:18-20).

Now we are His ambassadors and ministers of reconciliation. We are witnesses of Christ's resurrection, because we are new creations in Christ and we have His resurrected life within us. In the power of the Holy Spirit, we say to all who will listen, "We implore you on Christ's behalf: Be reconciled to God" (2 Cor. 5:20). Like God, we don't count their sins against them, because what they do is just symptomatic of the real problem: their separation from God.

The message of reconciliation always begins with God, but it encompasses the relationships we have with others. It begins with God, because any attempt to unite members of the fallen human race on any basis other than Christ has always failed. When we are reconciled to God, we become brothers and sisters in Christ, and that is the basis for our unity. The Body of Christ will remain fragmented as long as we associate purely on the basis of common theology, race and tradition. The basis for our unity is our common heritage in Christ. That is why Paul exhorts us:

> Be completely humble and gentle; be patient, bearing with one another in love. Make every effort to keep the unity of the Spirit through the bond of peace. There is one body and one Spirit—just as you were called to one hope when you were called—one Lord, one faith, one baptism; one God and Father of all (Eph. 4:2-6).

The ministry of reconciliation originates with God, not humanity. Reconciliation must be personally experienced by faith, but it is universally inclusive. It is voluntarily accepted and voluntarily shared. The message has been entrusted to humankind to be delivered to all, but it is owned and accredited by God. It achieves what otherwise is impossible, and it is gratefully experienced by all those who have received it. It is the greatest gift that one can receive, yet it is meant to be given away.[1]

> All this is from God, who reconciled us to himself through Christ and gave us the ministry of reconciliation: that God was reconciling the world to himself in Christ, not counting men's sins against them (2 Cor. 5:18-19).

Thought for the day: *What is the ministry of reconciliation?*

BE AT PEACE WITH EACH OTHER

Mark 9:50

When Jesus finished His work on Earth, He went to be with the Father. The eternal purpose of God is now being worked out through the Church empowered by the Holy Spirit (see Eph. 3:10-11). As children of God we are the salt and light of the world (see Matt. 5:13-16). We have no light in and of ourselves, but we have the life of Christ within us. John said of Jesus, "In him was life, and that life was the light of men" (John 1:4). Notice that light does not produce life; rather, the eternal life of God produces light. Our purpose is to glorify God in our bodies. The glory of God is a manifestation of His presence. Therefore, we glorify God when we manifest, or make known, to others the life of Christ within us. Bringing light into a dark world is what makes life meaningful. It doesn't matter what size our light is, because there is not enough darkness in the world to put out the light of one small candle. The truth spoken in love always shines through the darkness.

It has been said that you can lead a horse to water, but you can't make it drink. That may be true, but you can create a powerful thirst by putting salt in their oats. Salt enhances the flavor of life. When unbelievers see the children of God living a liberated life in Christ, they can't help but want what they have. Salt also acts as a preservative against the evil forces that would seek to corrupt us. Therefore, "Have salt in yourselves, and be at peace with each other" (Mark 9:50). Jesus said, "Blessed are the peacemakers, for they will be called sons of God" (Matt. 5:9). Any mortal can divide a fellowship, but it takes the grace of God to bring reconciliation to Himself and to establish unity among His people.

Paul says, "If it is possible, as far as it depends on you, live at peace with everyone" (Rom. 12:18). However, it may not always be possible. If another person refuses to be reconciled, there is little that we can humanly do other than to petition God. Regardless of how others respond, we must assume our responsibility to be peacemakers and continue carrying on the ministry of reconciliation. Our responsibility is to be a witness. It is God's responsibility to save them. We cannot assume responsibility for the lives of others, but we must assume responsibility for our own attitudes and actions. We cannot make others what we want them to be, and they cannot keep us from being the people God created us to be.

The enmity that exists between two parties must be removed in order for reconciliation to occur. Our reconciliation with God is now possible, because the enmity that existed between God and His children was removed when Christ sacrificed His life for our sins. "The death he died, he died to sin once for all" (Rom. 6:10). It can be argued that the sins of all people who have ever lived have been forgiven by God, but not all are reconciled to Him. That is why the Church has been given the ministry of reconciliation.

In order to establish and maintain a peaceful coexistence with each other, we have to repent, seek the forgiveness of those whom we have offended and forgive those who have offended us. What we have freely received from God, we freely extend to others.

If it is possible, as far as it depends on you, live at peace with every-one (Rom. 12:18).

Thought for the day: *When isn't it possible to live at peace with others?*

SEEKING THE FORGIVENESS OF OTHERS

Luke 7:36-50

This poignant story of the sinful woman's devotion to Christ reveals the gratitude we should feel when we realize that we are forgiven. Nobody had ever treated her like Jesus did, because nobody ever forgave her like Jesus did. She could hardly contain her love for Jesus, because she, who had been forgiven much, loved much. "But he who has been forgiven little loves little" (Luke 7:47). Apparently, the degree to which we have been forgiven has some effect on our capacity to love others. Maybe it is the degree to which we understand how much we have been forgiven that affects our capacity to love, since we have all sinned greatly and have been forgiven much. The self-righteous Pharisee had no capacity to love, because he had no sense of his need for forgiveness.

We sought the forgiveness of God, and we received it at the time of our salvation. According to Jesus, now we need to seek the forgiveness of others whom we have offended. "Therefore, if you are offering your gift at the altar and there remember that your brother has something against you, leave your gift there in front of the altar. First go and be reconciled to your brother; then come and offer your gift" (Matt. 5:23-24). In other words, if we have offended someone else, then we shouldn't attempt to worship God if we have not gone to that person first and sought reconciliation. The text is not suggesting that we practice some morbid introspection by trying to determine any and all possible ways that we may have offended someone else. It is the work of the Holy Spirit to cause us to "remember," and it is the offense known by the other party that is to be dealt with. It doesn't make any difference if the other person offended us more than we offended them. Our purpose for seeking forgiveness is not to get others to own up to their offense. We have to assume responsibility for *our* sin.

The following are the essential steps to take when seeking the forgiveness of others for the purpose of reconciliation:

1. Identify in your own mind the offense you committed and the attitude behind it.

2. Make sure you have already forgiven the person for any wrong on their part.

3. Think through the precise wording you will use when asking for their forgiveness.
   - Label your action as wrong.
   - Confess only as much detail as necessary for the offended person to understand.
   - Make no defenses, alibis or excuses.
   - Do not project blame nor confess for another.
   - Your confession should lead to the direct question, Will you forgive me?

4. Seek the right place and the right time to approach the offended.

5. Make your quest for reconciliation in person and face to face. If the offense was an immoral indiscretion that could result in legal action, then have a responsible third party present.

6. Make restitution if it is warranted.

7. Do not document your confession or write a letter. A letter can be easily misread or misunderstood, read by the wrong people and be kept when it should be destroyed.

8. If they refuse to forgive, then prayerfully commit your case to our heavenly Father and worship God with a clear conscience.

Settle matters quickly with your adversary (Matt. 5:25).

Thought for the day: *If you have sinned against another person, why should you settle matters quickly?*

FORGIVING OTHERS

Ephesians 4:29-32

It is inevitable that we will suffer at the hands of others, no matter how righteously we live. Physical and emotional abuse can leave us feeling bitter, angry and resentful, signaling the need to forgive. Our old fleshly nature seeks revenge and repayment, but the Spirit says, "Forgive them just as Christ has forgiven us." "But you don't know how badly they hurt me," we cry. The wise pastor responds, "As long as you hold on to your bitterness, they are still hurting you. Forgiveness is what sets you free from your past and stops the pain. You don't heal in order to forgive; you forgive in order to heal."

Forgiveness is not forgetting. God says, "For I will forgive their wickedness and will remember their sins no more" (Heb. 8:12). That means God will not use our past sins against us in the future. He will remove them as far from us as the east is from the west (see Ps. 103:12). Considering how God forgives us, we know that we haven't forgiven others if we continuously bring up their past and use it against them. Forgetting may be a long-term by-product of forgiving, but it is not the means by which we forgive.

Forgiving others does not mean that we tolerate sin. God forgives, but He never tolerates sins. We must forgive those who have wronged us, and then we should set up scriptural boundaries to stop future abuse.

As we begin the journey toward releasing those who have sinned against us, we need to face the reality that forgiveness is resolving to live with the consequences of another person's sin. But that's not fair! Of course it isn't fair, but we will have to anyway. Everybody is living with the consequences of somebody else's sin. We are all living with the consequence of Adam's sin. The only real choice is whether we will do so in the bondage of bitterness or in the freedom of forgiveness.

If we are required by God to forgive as Christ has forgiven us, then how did Christ forgive us? He took our sins upon Himself. We have not truly forgiven another unless we have taken that person's sin upon ourselves. As long as we refuse to forgive, we are emotionally chained to past events and the people who hurt us. The purpose of forgiveness is to set the captive free and then realize that we have been the captives. It is for our own benefit that we forgive others.

But where is the justice? The Cross is what makes forgiveness morally correct. Christ died once for all our sins: his sins, her sins, your sins and my sins. "But I want justice now!" We will never have perfect justice in this lifetime. That is why there is a coming final judgment. "But I want revenge!" "Do not take revenge, my friends, but leave room for God's wrath, for it is written: 'It is mine to avenge; I will repay,' says the Lord" (Rom. 12:19). "But why should I let them off my hook?" That is precisely why we should forgive, because we are still hooked to them. If we let them off our hook, are they off God's hook? What is to be gained in forgiving others is freedom from our past. God will make things right in the end.

Forgiving others does not mean that we don't testify in court against another. Nor does it mean that we avoid confronting a brother who is living in sin. Forgiving others makes our own heart right before God and allows us to experience our freedom in Christ. Only then can we righteously testify in court and confront others.

Be kind and compassionate to one another, forgiving each other, just as in Christ God forgave you (Eph. 4:32).

Thought for the day: *How has God forgiven you?*

FORGIVING FROM THE HEART

Matthew 18:21-35

If you have offended someone else, don't attempt to worship God when you are convicted to seek reconciliation (see Matt. 5:24). Go first to those who have something against you, seek their forgiveness, and be reconciled. If someone has offended you, don't go to that person. Go first to God and forgive that person as Christ has forgiven you. It is critical to understand the difference, because many people wrongly think that they have to go to the person who offended them in order to forgive them. Forgiveness is a prerequisite for reconciliation, but reconciliation may not always be possible. The person you need to forgive may be dead or unreachable. In some cases it would be unwise, because confronting an offender who is unrepentant may actually set you up for even more abuse.

Jesus tells us that we should continue forgiving as many times as is necessary (see Matt. 18:22), and He puts our need to forgive others in perspective. God has forgiven us a debt that could never be paid. "Ten thousand talents" was way beyond a lifetime wage (see v. 24). We simply cannot repay the debt we owe God. Therefore, we have no choice but to throw ourselves upon His mercy. In comparison, 100 denarii is equal to wages from 3 months of work (see v. 28). While it would be humanly possible to pay off that debt, the man who had received mercy from God showed no mercy to his fellow man. God requires us to be merciful as He has been merciful to us, and to forgive as He has forgiven us. The following are steps to forgiving from our hearts:

1. Ask the Lord to reveal to your mind the people you need to forgive, including all those you have negative feelings toward. Don't overlook the need to let yourself off your own hook.

2. Face the hurt and the feelings of hatred. If you are going to forgive from the heart, you have to allow the painful memories to surface. If you are unwilling to admit to the pain and the emotional damage, the forgiveness process will be incomplete. Humanly we try to suppress our emotions, but God is trying to surface those names and events so they can be faced and let go.

3. Forgiveness is a crisis of the will. You choose to bear the conse-

quences of their sin. You choose to let go of the past and grab hold of God. You choose not to seek revenge. You cannot wait until you feel like forgiving, because you will never get there. God is not asking you to like the person who offended you. He is asking you to accept His provision for your freedom and healing of your damaged emotions. He is asking you to let Him be the avenger. He is asking you to forgive from your heart every person who has offended you and for every offensive thing they did as follows:

Lord, I forgive _____ (person) for _____ (verbally express every hurt and pain the Lord brings to your mind and how it made you feel).

4. After you have forgiven every person for every painful memory, finish by praying:

Lord, I release all these people to You, and I release my right to seek revenge. I choose not to hold on to my bitterness and anger, and I ask You to heal my damaged emotions. In Jesus' name, I pray. Amen.

If you, O LORD, kept a record of sins, O Lord, who could stand? But with you there is forgiveness; therefore you are feared (Ps. 130:3-4).

Thought for the day: *Would people respect you more or less if you kept a record of their sins?*

Living by the Spirit

Galatians 5

Under the Old Covenant, the children of Israel had to learn to abide by the Law in their own strength. But they could not do it, and neither can we. "The law was put in charge to lead us to Christ that we might be justified by faith. Now that faith has come, we are no longer under the supervision of the law" (Gal. 3:24-25). As children of God, we are under the New Covenant of grace. Now we live by faith in the power of the Holy Spirit. The tension between living our way in our own strength and living God's way in His strength is explained by Paul: "For the sinful nature [flesh] desires what is contrary to the Spirit, and the Spirit what is contrary to the sinful nature" (Gal. 5:17). They are in opposition to each other, because the flesh operates independently of God, and the operation of the Holy Spirit is always dependent upon God the Father.

How do we live by the Spirit? If we answered that question by giving three steps and a formula, we would be putting you back under the law. The Holy Spirit is a "He," not an "it." Living by the Spirit is a relational concept, not a legal concept. Actually this passage tells us more what living by the Spirit is not, but that is extremely helpful, because it gives us the parameters in which we freely live. First, living by the Spirit is not legalism. "But if you are led by the Spirit, you are not under law" (Gal. 5:18).

> It is for freedom that Christ has set us free. Stand firm, then, and do not let yourselves be burdened again by a yoke of slavery. Mark my words! I, Paul, tell you that if you let yourselves be circumcised [for religious purposes], Christ will be of no value to you at all (vv. 1-2).

In other words, "Don't go back under the law."

Second, living by the Spirit is not license. We live by the Spirit, "so that you do not do what you want" (Gal. 5:17). Paul tells us, "You, my brothers, were called to be free. But do not use your freedom to indulge the sinful nature" (v. 13). In other words, living by the Spirit does not enable us to do whatever we want to do. It enables us to do God's will. So if living by the Spirit is neither legalism nor license, then what is it? It is liberty. "Now the

Lord is the Spirit, and where the Spirit of the Lord is, there is freedom" (2 Cor. 3:17).

Living by the Spirit is the only means by which we overcome the power of the flesh. "So I say, live by the Spirit, and you will not gratify the desires of the sinful nature" (Gal. 5:16). If we have a choice as to whether we live by the Spirit or by the sinful nature, then how can we know which we are choosing? Simple. What do our lives reveal?

> The acts of the sinful nature are obvious: sexual immorality, impurity and debauchery; idolatry and witchcraft; hatred, discord, jealousy, fits of rage, selfish ambition, dissensions, factions and envy; drunkenness, orgies, and the like (vv. 19-21).

"But the fruit of the Spirit is love, joy, peace, patience, kindness, goodness, faithfulness, gentleness and self-control. Against such things there is no law" (vv. 22-23). Notice the contrast between deeds and fruit. Only the latter is a living spiritual principle.

> Since we live by the Spirit, let us keep in step with the Spirit (Gal. 5:25).

Thought for the day: *How do you keep in step with the Spirit?*

OVERCOMING LEGALISM

2 Corinthians 3:5-18

Paul tells us, "Clearly no one is justified before God by the law, because, 'The righteous will live by faith'" (Gal. 3:11). That truth that believers are no longer under the law is clearly taught in Scripture, but why does the Church still struggle with legalism and why do some choose to live as though they are still under the law? Some Christians actually prefer living under the law and having someone tell them what is right and what is wrong. Others are ignorant of their spiritual life in Christ and the means by which we live under the New Covenant. Troubled by the problems of immorality, we often seek the simple solution of laying down the law.

If you want to relate to God under the law, then you need to know what Scripture has to say about legalism. First, "All who rely on observing the law are under a curse, for it is written: 'Cursed is everyone who does not continue to do everything written in the Book of the Law'" (Gal. 3:10). Trying to live by the law only produces guilt, "For all have sinned and fall short of the glory of God" (Rom. 3:23). Legalists are driven people who never reach perfection. Perfectionism is a self-destructive process.

Second, "For if a law had been given that could impart life, then righteousness would certainly have come by the law" (Gal. 3:21). The law is powerless to give life. Telling people that what they are doing is wrong does not give them to power to stop doing it. "He has made us competent as ministers of a new covenant—not of the letter but of the Spirit; for the letter kills, but the Spirit gives life" (2 Cor. 3:6).

Third, the law actually has the capacity to stimulate our desire to do what it was intended to prohibit.

> For when we were controlled by the sinful nature, the sinful passions aroused by the law were at work in our bodies, so that we bore fruit for death. But sin, seizing the opportunity afforded by the commandment, produced in me every kind of covetous desire (Rom. 7:5,8).

To illustrate that truth try telling your children, "You can go here, but you can't go there!" The moment you say that, where do they all want to go? A

Christian school published a list of movies that the students could not see. Guess which ones they all wanted to see? Adam and Eve were commanded not to eat from the tree of the knowledge of good and evil, but they did (see Gen. 2:15-17; 3:6). The forbidden fruit seem to be the most desirable, as does the grass on the other side of the fence.

The commandments of God are not restrictive; they are protective. They reflect the nature of God and are therefore good. The glory of the Lord was revealed when He engraved the law in letters on stone (see 2 Cor. 3:7-8). But trying to live a righteous life by the law can only lead to discouragement, defeat and death. "If the ministry that condemns men is glorious, how much more glorious is the ministry that brings righteousness" (v. 9). Only by the Spirit of God can we live righteous lives and not carry out the desires of the flesh. Only by faith can we be justified. Only by the grace of God can we grow in Christ.[1] "And we, who with unveiled faces all reflect the Lord's glory, are being transformed into his likeness with ever-increasing glory, which comes from the Lord, who is the Spirit" (v. 18).

> But sin, seizing the opportunity afforded by the commandment, produced in me every kind of covetous desire. For apart from law, sin is dead (Rom. 7:8).

Thought for the day: *How can the law produce covetous desires?*

OVERCOMING LICENTIOUSNESS

1 Corinthians 8

It is false reasoning to say, "If I am completely forgiven and under grace, then I don't have to live according to the law." Living by the Spirit is not a license to do whatever we want. The licentious person disregards rules and regulations. Paul asks, "Shall we go on sinning so that grace may increase? By no means! We died to sin; how can we live in it any longer?" (Rom. 6:1-2). God has delivered us from the bondage of sin, why would we want to return to living in chains? We are not under the law, but we are not lawless. We have an eternal standard, but neither legalism nor license is the means by which we live righteous lives. Living under the grace of God by faith in the power of the Holy Spirit is not a license to sin; rather, it is a gracious means not to sin.

We are free in Christ to live a moral life, but there are times when we should restrict our freedom. The first is mentioned by Paul in 1 Corinthians, " 'Everything is permissible for me'—but not everything is beneficial. 'Everything is permissible for me'—but I will not be mastered by anything" (6:12). We have the freedom to eat whatever we choose, but food can become our master if we find ourselves living to eat instead of eating to live. Our freedom becomes license when we abuse our rights and indulge ourselves. One piece of dessert can be good, but four pieces are not. We have to master our appetites, or they will master us. Let us remember that the fruit of the Spirit is self-control (see Gal. 5:23). To continue experiencing the freedom we have in Christ, we have to live responsible lives in the power of the Holy Spirit, and do all things in moderation.

The second instance in which we should restrict our freedom is when to do so is for the good of another: " 'Everything is permissible'—but not everything is beneficial. 'Everything is permissible'—but not everything is constructive. Nobody should seek his own good, but the good of others." Paul qualified our freedom with the principle of love (see 1 Cor. 8:1). "Be careful, however, that the exercise of your freedom does not become a stumbling block to the weak" (v. 9). We have to learn to restrict our freedom for the sake of a weaker brother or sister. If what we are doing is morally permissible, but offensive to others, then we shouldn't do it. We never have the right to violate another person's conscience. "When you sin against your brothers in this way and wound their weak conscience, you sin against Christ. Therefore, if what I eat causes my brother to fall into sin, I will never eat [it] again, so that I will not cause him to fall" (vv. 12-13).

License is a form of spiritual deception referred to as Gnosticism. People think they can indulge their flesh without violating their spirit. They falsely reason, "What I do in the flesh doesn't matter; it is only what I do in the Spirit that matters." The Corinthians had reasoned that food was both necessary and pleasurable. When their stomachs signaled hunger, it was to be satisfied. They also argued that sex was both necessary and pleasurable, and therefore any sex drive had to be satisfied. But Paul answered their argument when he wrote, "The body is not meant for sexual immorality, but for the Lord, and the Lord for the body" (1 Cor. 6:13). We cannot separate our bodies from who we are. Our bodies are temples of God.

Do you not know that your bodies are members of Christ himself? (1 Cor. 6:15).

Thought for the day: *Why is it wrong to indulge the flesh?*

FILLED WITH THE SPIRIT

Acts 4:31

Paul writes, "For we were all baptized by one Spirit into one body—whether Jews or Greeks, slave or free—and we were all given the one Spirit to drink" (1 Cor. 12:13). The Spirit's indwelling (see John 14:17, Rom. 8:9); sealing (see 2 Cor. 1:22; Eph. 1:13); and baptism (see Gal. 3:27) all occur at the time of regeneration and are therefore never commanded. The Church Age began with the promised coming of the Holy Spirit at Pentecost. But the Early Church soon learned that there would be an ongoing need to be filled with the Holy Spirit.

The presence of the Holy Spirit in the lives of believers is what sets them apart from the rest of humanity; a Christian is simply one in whom Christ dwells. Although the Holy Spirit has taken up residence in every true believer, not every believer is fully yielded to Him. Spirit-filled believers are yielded to God, and their lives are characterized by His presence. "Being filled" is very similar in meaning to "being controlled." Therefore, to be filled with the Holy Spirit is to be under His control. The fruit of the Spirit becomes evident in the lives of believers who are yielded to Him (see Gal. 5:22-23). Other manifestations of the Spirit-filled life are not uncommon, as evidenced by a particular Early Church prayer meeting in which "They [the believers] were all filled with the Holy Spirit and spoke the word of God boldly" (Acts 4:31). In this case, God sovereignly bestowed the filling.

According to Paul, the responsibility falls upon the believer to be filled with the Spirit. "Do not get drunk on wine, which leads to debauchery. Instead, be filled with the Spirit" (Eph. 5:18). The evidence of being filled with the Holy Spirit is revealed in the ways we communicate with each other and with God (see Eph. 5:19-20). The idea of being filled with the Spirit is not like a glass that is empty and needs to be filled. We already have the Holy Spirit. The idea is more like a balloon full of air that can become much bigger and sail much higher if it is filled with more air. In the same way we who are already temples of the Holy Spirit can be filled even more if we fully open ourselves to the divine breath of God.

Our potential to bear fruit increases as we grow in Christ. As new believers, we are like small lawn-mower engines. As we grow, we become more like tractor engines, but neither can bear fruit without gas. We never outgrow our need for God. We cannot fulfill our purpose without the enabling power of the Holy Spirit. We need to be filled with the Holy Spirit and we can be if we will confess our sin and yield to Him. Make it your daily practice to do so with a simple prayer:

> *Dear heavenly Father, I come before Your presence as Your child.*
> *I thank You for Your grace and mercy by which I am saved.*
> *I acknowledge You as my Lord and my Savior. You are the only*
> *omnipotent, omnipresent and omniscient God. You alone are worthy*
> *of praise. I confess that I have not always yielded myself to You. I have*
> *been self-willed, self-centered and self-sufficient. I choose to believe that*
> *I am alive, free and forgiven in Christ. I choose to live by faith according*
> *to what You say is true. I now yield myself to You as my Lord and my*
> *Savior, and I ask You to fill me with Your Holy Spirit in order that*
> *I may glorify You in my body. In Jesus' name I pray. Amen.*

Therefore I tell you that no one who is speaking by the Spirit of God says, "Jesus be cursed," and no one can say, "Jesus is Lord," except by the Holy Spirit (1 Cor. 12:3).

Thought for the day: *What does the presence of the Holy Spirit enable us to do and say?*

RELEASING THE HOLY SPIRIT

1 Thessalonians 5:16-22

Jesus encouraged His disciples to be persistent in prayer, "For everyone who asks receives; he who seeks finds; and to him who knocks, the door will be opened" (Luke 11:10). To assure them that God would not give them any bad gifts, Jesus said, "If you then . . . know how to give good gifts to your children, how much more will your Father in heaven give the Holy Spirit to those who ask him!" (v. 13). That promise was fulfilled at Pentecost, and it is still being received by those who seek God for salvation and the fullness of the Holy Spirit. Yielding ourselves to God is a question of trust. We are questioning God's integrity when we ask, "If He filled me with His Holy Spirit, what would He do with my life and how would He manifest His presence in me?"

We can trust God, because we know that He has our best interests at heart. Nothing but good can come from seeking God with all our heart. Jesus said, "If anyone is thirsty, let him come to me and drink. Whoever believes in me, as the Scripture has said, streams of living water will flow from within him" (John 7:37-38). Jesus was referring to the internal presence of the Holy Spirit who is waiting to be released. The Spirit-filled Christian is always joyful, prays continuously and is forever grateful (see 1 Thess. 5:16-18).

When Moses saw the burning bush, he was startled because the fire was not consuming the bush (see Exod. 3:3). If the bush had been burning because of the natural substance it was made of, it would have been consumed immediately. It continued to burn because God was in the bush. The same is true of us. If we try to serve God out of our own strength, we will burn out. We don't live our natural lives for God; He lives His eternal life through us. We serve God by His strength, not by our strength. Therefore, "Do not put out the Spirit's fire, do not treat prophecies with contempt" (1 Thess. 5:19-20). God can choose to work supernaturally through anybody—He even spoke through Balaam's donkey! (See Num. 22:28.)

When God works through us, He does not bypass our humanity nor trample on our personality. As Spirit-filled Christians we are fully human, and God works through the uniqueness of our personalities. We are fully alive and fully free to fulfill our potential, which can only be accomplished in Christ. Scripture admonishes us not to quench the Spirit or grieve the Spirit (see Eph. 4:30). It seems paradoxical, but letting God reign in our lives is the only way we can have self-control, which is a fruit of the Spirit.

On the other hand, "Test everything. Hold on to the good. Avoid every kind of evil" (1 Thess. 5:21-22), because there are many spiritual counterfeits in this world. Scripture admonishes us to avoid two extremes. First, we are to have nothing to do with those who hold to a form of godliness but deny its power (see 2 Tim. 3:5). Second, avoid those who appear to be zealous for God but whose zeal is not based on knowledge (see Rom. 10:2). To be spiritually safe, we need to be knowledgeable of the truth and be spiritually discerning. If our motives are pure, we can yield ourselves to God and trust Him to work through us in any way He chooses. In doing so, we release the Holy Spirit and manifest the presence of God within us.

> Jesus stood and said in a loud voice, "If anyone is thirsty, let him come to me and drink. Whoever believes in me, as the Scripture has said, streams of living water will flow from within him" (John 7:37-38).

Thought for the day: *How can we manifest the presence of God in our lives?*

LIVING UNDER GRACE

Romans 6:1-14

There is only one appropriate response to a command in Scripture. Obey it! There is only one appropriate response to a promise in Scripture. Claim it! There is only one appropriate response to a biblical fact or a declared truth in Scripture. Believe it! Keep this in mind as we look at Paul's argument in Romans chapter 6, which is based on our spiritual union with Christ. If Christ has triumphed over sin and death, then so have we, because we are alive "in Christ."

"We died to sin; how can we live in it any longer?" (Rom. 6:2). How can we as believers die to sin? We can't, because we already have. "Or don't you know that all of us who were baptized into Christ Jesus were baptized into his death?" (v. 3). We have also been buried (see v. 3) and raised with Christ (see v. 5). We cannot be united with Christ in His death and not be united with Him in His resurrected life. Jesus didn't just die for our sins; He also came to give us life: "Now if we died with Christ, we believe that we will also live with Him" (v. 8).

Although Scripture tells us that we died with Christ, the defeated Christian tries to put the old self to death and can't do it. Why? Because he is already dead! "For we know that our old self was crucified with him" (Rom. 6:6). It is false reasoning to ask, "What experience must we have in order for this to be true?" The only experience that had to happen, happened 2,000 years ago; and the only way we can enter into the experience is by faith. We cannot do for ourselves what Christ has already done for us. We don't make anything true by our experience, and any effort to do so will prove fruitless. We believe that what God has done and said on our behalf is true. When we choose to believe God and live accordingly by faith, it works out in our experience.

We don't do the things we do with the hope that God may someday love us. God loves us. That is why we do the good things we do. We don't labor in the vineyard with the hope that God may someday accept us. God has accepted us, and that is why we labor in the vineyard. What we do does not determine who we are. God has determined who we are, and being new creations in Christ should determine what we do. When we as believers choose to sin, that does not make us sinners any more than sneezing makes us sneezers. We are still children of God who have chosen to disobey our Father.

Christ defeated death when He was resurrected, and He defeated sin when He died once for all our sins (see Rom. 6:8-10). "In the same way, count yourselves dead to sin but alive to God in Christ Jesus" (v. 11). Counting ourselves dead to sin does not make us dead to sin. We are dead to sin because of our new life in Christ; therefore, we continue to believe it, and it will work out in our experience. When we are tempted to sin, we need to simply respond by faith and say, "I am alive in Christ and sin is no longer my master."

If we have been united with [Christ] like this in his death, we will certainly also be united with him in his resurrection (Rom. 6:5).

Thought for the day: *Why are we inclined to think that we are united with Christ in His death, but not in His resurrection?*

THE CHRISTIAN'S RELATIONSHIP TO THE LAW

Mark 2:23-28

The Pharisees were strict in keeping the law, but they added many other rules and regulations that were intended to keep believers from breaking the law. Their tactic was similar to building a fence around the law, but in practice the fence soon becomes a law. For instance, we are not to be unequally yoked (see 2 Cor. 6:14). So to keep our Christian children from marrying a nonbeliever, we establish additional rules like, "You can't date nonbelievers or associate with them." That may be wise in some cases, but it is not a law. Jesus ignored man-made rules, but He never violated the law. In fact Jesus said, "Do not think that I have come to abolish the Law or the Prophets; I have not come to abolish them but to fulfill them" (Matt. 5:17). How, then, do we as believers relate to the law?

The term "law" in Scripture is often associated with specific commands, especially the Old Testament Mosaic Law. But the concept of law is much broader. The Hebrew word *torah*, which is the basic word for "law" in the Old Testament, is related to the Hebrew word *hora*, meaning "to teach or instruct." The fundamental meaning is not "command," but "instruct." The word came to be used for the entire Word of God. The Jews use the word "Torah" to refer to the first five books of the Old Testament. Christians have used the term "law" to describe sections of Scripture and Scripture as a whole, including commandments as well as promises. The latter is what Jesus meant when He said that He came to fulfill the Law. He kept all the commandments and fulfilled all the promises.

The law of God is an expression of His will. Just as there are physical laws by which the physical world is structured, so also there are His moral and spiritual laws, which are the expression of His moral nature, which govern the personal and moral spheres of God's creation. For this reason, in the Old Testament, believers as well as unbelievers were subject to the overarching principle that following God's laws led to blessings, and disobeying them led to misery and destruction. The New Testament believer "in Christ," however, is not related to the law in the same way. The nonbeliever stands before the law in himself—that is, as a sinner and, consequently, a lawbreaker. He lives under the condemnation of the law. But the believer "in Christ" has the same relationship to the law that Christ has. God's righteous principles for life are all fulfilled in Christ. We are free from the legal bondage of the law: "Therefore, there is now no condemnation for those who are in Christ Jesus" (Rom. 8:1).

The law has become our tutor to lead us to Christ so that we may be justified by faith (see Gal. 3:24-25). Now that we are in Christ, the law is no longer our tutor. What we could not fulfill in the flesh, Christ fulfilled for us. Now that we are "in Christ," we can actually live righteous lives that are consistent with the moral laws of God. The means by which we attempt to live righteously have changed, however. We now relate to God by faith and live by the power of the Holy Spirit.

We have been released from the law so that we serve in the new way of the Spirit, and not in the old way of the written code (Rom. 7:6).

Thought for the day: *Who or what is our tutor under the New Covenant?*

WALKING WITH GOD

Matthew 11:28-30

How much can we accomplish in the kingdom of God when we operate by ourselves? Nothing! How much will be accomplished in this present Church Age if we do nothing and expect God to do everything? Nothing! God has committed Himself to work through the Church. We have the privilege to water and plant in God's kingdom, "but God [makes] it grow" (1 Cor. 3:6). Nothing grows without God, but nothing grows if we don't water and plant. The fact that nobody hears unless a preacher is sent (see Rom. 10:14-15), illustrates the same principle. God could have chosen to bypass the Church, but instead He has chosen to work through us. It is His kind intention that we walk together, and Jesus has provided the perfect example of how that works.

Jesus was a carpenter in His youth. Carpenters didn't frame houses in those days. They fashioned doors and yokes out of wood, and His own handiwork later became useful metaphors for His ministry. A yoke is a heavy wooden beam that fits over the shoulders of two oxen. The yoke can only work if two oxen are in it, and they are pulling together. For the purpose of training, a young ox is yoked to an older ox, who has "learned obedience from what he suffered" (Heb. 5:8). The young ox will be tempted to stray off to the left or to the right, but the old ox stays on the right path. The young ox may think the pace is a little slow and try running ahead, but all he gets is a sore neck. Slowly the young ox begins to realize that the old ox knows how to walk. The pace is right and the course is true, so he decides to learn from him.

Being yoked with Jesus does not mean that we sit around thinking pious thoughts, expecting God to do it all. Nor is it running around in endless activities trying to do it all by ourselves. It is a walk with the only One who knows the way, who is the truth and has the life to make it possible. In Him we find rest for our souls, for His yoke is easy and His burden is light (see Matt. 11:29-30). What would we learn from Jesus if we walked with Him? We would learn to take one day at a time and trust God for tomorrow. We would learn the priority of relationships as taught to Mary and Martha. We would learn to love people and use things—instead of loving things and using people. We would learn what it means to be compassionate. This remarkable passage is the only place in the Bible where Jesus describes Himself, and He said, "I am gentle and humble in heart" (v. 29). With all the harshness and vulgarity surrounding us in this fallen world, we have been invited to walk with the gentle Jesus. Imagine that!

> Do you not know? Have you not heard? The LORD is the everlasting God, the Creator of the ends of the earth. He will not grow tired or weary, and His understanding no one can fathom. He gives strength to the weary, and increases the power of the weak. Even youths grow tired and weary, and young men stumble and fall; but those who hope in the LORD will renew their strength. They will soar on wings like eagles; they will run and not grow weary, they will walk and not be faint (Isa. 40:28-31).

> He who walks with the wise grows wise, but a companion of fools suffers harm (Prov. 13:20).

Thought for the day: *How can you practice resting in the presence of God?*

LED BY THE SPIRIT

Exodus 13:20-22

Even in the wilderness, God led His people and provided for their needs. The Lord guided them on their way to the Promised Land with a cloud by day and a pillar of fire by night (see Exod. 13:20-22), and He never deserted them. His guidance was unfailing, constant and loving. "He brought his people out like a flock; he led them like sheep through the desert. He guided them safely, so they were not afraid" (Ps. 78:52-53). The psalmist says, "We are his people, the sheep of his pasture" (100:3), and Jesus is the good shepherd (see John 10:14). "He calls his own sheep by name and leads them out" (John 10:3).

God's children are often referred to as sheep in Scripture. For the most part, it is a comforting notion, but it also conveys our helpless nature. Sheep are not carnivorous like wolves. They sacrificially give their wool while they are living and their meat when they die. There is a lot of good to be said for sheep, but they are not the smartest animals on the farm, especially when it comes to eating. Sheep left alone in lush green pastures will eat themselves to death. That is probably why David the shepherd tells us, "The LORD is my shepherd, I shall not be in want. He makes me lie down in green pastures" (Ps. 23:1-2).

In our western world, we keep our sheep moving in green pastures by chasing them from the rear, much like Australian sheep dogs who bark at the heels of the sheep. But that is not the way shepherds led their sheep is Israel. Even to this day, the shepherd will stand up and say something as he walks away. The sheep look up and follow the shepherd. That is why Jesus says, "My sheep listen to my voice; I know them, and they follow me" (John 10:27). Paul writes, "Those who are led by the Spirit of God are sons of God" (Rom. 8:14).

Being led by the Spirit implies that we are not being pushed. So if someone asks us to make a hasty decision without prayerful reflection, the answer should be no. God doesn't lead that way. The guidance of God may come suddenly but never to the spiritually unprepared. Pentecost was sudden, but it was preceded by many days of prayer (see Acts 1:14). Being led by the Spirit also means that we are not being lured away in some underhanded manner. God does everything in the light.

We rely on the guidance of God to safeguard our lives in the same way that a pilot trusts the air traffic controller during the landing of a flight at night. To land safely, the pilot has to trust the man in the control tower whom he cannot see. The pilot is not flying the only plane in the air. Others are waiting for instructions to land and also looking to the control tower for guidance. But the voice from the tower is not enough to land the plane safely. All good pilots have spent hours reading their instruction manual, learning how to fly and land competently. They have almost committed the manual to memory, so they know how to fly instinctively. As the voice over the radio slowly guides the pilot around obstacles that he cannot see, the pilot isn't afraid. He has done his homework, and he has learned to trust the unseen man in the control tower. Just so we as God's children are led by the Spirit, and we have learned to trust His Word.

If you led by the Spirit, you are not under [the] law (Gal. 5:18).

Thought for the day: *Why is divine guidance more than just written instruction?*

ENDURING HARDSHIP

Hebrews 12:1-13

Bringing light into a dark world invites three predictable responses. First, some will run from the light because their deeds are evil. Jesus said, "Everyone who does evil hates the light, and will not come into the light for fear that his deeds will be exposed" (John 3:20). Those who live in sin feel convicted around Christians, and so they stay away from churches that preach the truth. Second, some will embrace the light as a liberating friend and gladly come to Jesus. Third, others will try to discredit the light source. This is what men tried to do to Jesus, and those who let their light shine today will suffer from similar insults and persecution.

> Remember those earlier days after you had received the light, when you stood your ground in a great contest in the face of suffering. Sometimes you were publicly exposed to insult and persecution; at other times you stood side by side with those who were so treated (Heb. 10:32-33).

With such opposition, how do we "run with perseverance the race marked out for us" (Heb. 12:1)? First, let us consider the example of Jesus who is the author and perfecter of our faith. Nobody has suffered like Jesus did for the sake of righteousness. He is our model and inspiration for endurance. "Consider him who endured such opposition from sinful men, so that you will not grow weary and lose heart" (v. 3). Second, consider the example of the heroes of faith mentioned in Hebrews 11. They are the great cloud of witnesses cheering us on to victory. If they could endure the ill treatment of others without having the life of Christ in them, imagine what we can endure with the life of Christ within us. We should always keep in mind that the will of God will never lead us where the grace of God cannot sustain us.

Third, we are to "endure hardship as discipline" (Heb. 12:7). The writer of Hebrews quotes Proverbs 3:11-12 as a word of encouragement (see Heb. 12:5-6). Being disciplined by God proves that we are children of God, "because the Lord disciplines those he loves" (v. 6). If we as imperfect parents are aware of the need to discipline our children, how much more aware is God of *our* need for discipline? We can endure hardship as discipline if we know there is a purpose behind it. "No discipline seems pleasant at the time, but painful. Later on, however, it produces a harvest of righteousness and peace for those who have been trained by it" (v. 11).

Those who prosper in life know that endurance is the key to success. It is said that success is 10 percent inspiration and 90 percent perspiration. Those who earn graduate degrees are usually no more intelligent than those who quit before they finish their progam. They graduated because they endured the process. No pain, no gain—this is true not just of the athlete but also of all those who have overcome the odds to be all that Christ created them to be.

You will never fulfill your purpose in life if you continue to choose the path of least resistance or quit before you finish the race. Too many Christians encounter a little opposition and drop out saying, "It must not be God's will!" On the contrary, it is God's will that you persevere. "You need to persevere so that when you have done the will of God, you will receive what he has promised" (Heb. 10:36).

Endure hardship with us like a good soldier of Christ Jesus (2 Tim. 2:3).

Thought for the day: *What is to be gained if we endure hardship?*

RENEWING THE MIND

Romans 12:1-2

The moment we were born again, we became new creations in Christ: "the old has gone, the new has come" (2 Cor. 5:17). We are no longer spiritually dead in Adam, we are now spiritually alive in Christ (see 1 Cor. 15:22). We have been transferred out of the kingdom of darkness into the kingdom of God's beloved Son (see Col. 1:13). Have you ever wondered, *If all that is true, then how come I still feel the way I did before and still struggle with a lot of the same issues?* Perhaps an illustration followed by a theological explanation will help clarify why we don't sense an immediate and overwhelming change in the way we think and feel after we have been born again.

To illustrate, suppose you had a vindictive soccer coach for several years. This coach belittled his athletes and ruled with fear and intimidation. In order to make the team, you had to learn how to cope, succeed and survive under his authority. Then one day you got traded to another team, and you got a new coach. The old coach was gone. You were no longer under his authority, and you no longer had any relationship with him. Your new coach is nothing like your old coach. He is kind and respectful to his team, and he motivates out of love. But how do you think you initially related to your new coach and teammates? The way you had been trained under the old coach. Your relationship with your new coach, your behavior on the field, your attitude—nothing would change until you got to know the new coach.

In this same way, since we were all born physically alive but spiritually dead in our trespasses and sins (see Eph. 2:1), we all learned to live our lives independently of God. We had neither the presence of God in our lives nor the knowledge of God's ways. So we learned how to cope, succeed and survive in this fallen world. Having no other recourse, we "followed the ways of this world and of the ruler of the kingdom of [darkness]. . . . gratifying the cravings of our sinful nature and following its desires and thoughts. Like the rest, we were by nature objects of wrath" (Eph. 2:2-3). As a result, sinful thoughts and desires were deeply ingrained in our minds.

Then one day we became new creations in Christ: We got transferred to a different team and we got a new coach, but nobody pushed the "clear" button in our memory bank. All the previous training experiences, memories and habits were still programmed into our minds. Now do you see why Paul wrote, "Do not conform any longer to this world, but be transformed by the renewing of your mind" (Rom. 12:2)? We all were conformed to this world. Even as believers we will remain conformed to this world if we continue living as we always have. So we must make a conscious decision to put aside the lifestyles of this "present evil age" (Gal. 1:4). We must continuously be transformed by the renewing of our minds. We get our English word "transformation" from the Greek word *metamorphosis*, which implies a total change from inside out. The key to this transformation is the mind, the control center of our thoughts, attitudes and actions.

> And we, who with unveiled faces all reflect the Lord's glory, are being transformed into his likeness with ever-increasing glory, which comes from the Lord, who is the Spirit (2 Cor. 3:18).

Thought for the day: *How are you being transformed into His likeness?*

TEARING DOWN MENTAL STRONGHOLDS

2 Corinthians 10:1-5

The imagery that Paul is using in 2 Corinthians 10:1-5 is not defensive armor. It is battering ram offensive weaponry. He is not using the conventional weapons of this world to tear down strongholds. He is using divine weapons that are at our disposal. These strongholds are not physical barriers that fortify a city. These are mental strongholds raised up against the knowledge of God. We can tear them down, because we have the mind of Christ (see 1 Cor. 2:16) and the Spirit of truth within us.

Research has shown that attitudes and beliefs are formed very early in our childhood. Since we are not physically born with the presence of God in our lives, we absorb these mental attitudes in two primary ways from the environment in which we were raised. First, they are assimilated into our minds through prevailing experiences such as the homes we were raised in, the schools we attended and the neighborhoods in which we played. These values and attitudes are more caught than taught. Different children respond to the same environment in different ways; therefore, every child's mental attitude is different. Second, mental strongholds are developed through traumatic experiences like the death of a parent, divorce in the home, or various kinds of mental and physical abuse.

Strongholds are habitual, mental patterns of thought. Some call them flesh patterns. These strongholds are memory traces burned into our minds over time or by the intensity of traumatic experiences. They are similar to what psychologists call defense mechanisms, and they always reveal themselves in a less than Christlike temperament. They are formed in our minds like deep tire tracks in a wet pasture: After the ruts have been established over time, the driver doesn't even have to steer anymore—and any attempt to steer out of the ruts is met with resistance. If we choose the wrong path for six consecutive weeks, we will have developed a new habit; and if the habit persists, a stronghold is formed.

For example, an inferiority complex is a stronghold. Nobody is born inferior to another; but in this competitive world, it is almost impossible not to feel inferior to someone who is smarter, faster, stronger and prettier.

Negative self-perceptions can only be torn down in Christ. In the kingdom of God, everybody has equal value. God loves each of His children the same, and we are not in competition with one another.

Exhibiting the unhealthy characteristics of an adult child of an alcoholic is another stronghold. Suppose an alcoholic father has three children. The oldest chooses to stand up to his father when he comes home drunk. The middle son accommodates his father. The youngest son runs and hides. Twenty years later, the father is long gone, and those three boys are confronted by a hostile situation. Chances are the oldest son will fight, the middle son will accommodate, and the youngest son will run and hide. We learn mental strongholds like these over time as we interact with our environment, but they can be torn down in Christ.

If we have been trained wrongly, can we be retrained? If we have believed a lie, can we now choose to believe the truth? If we have programmed our minds wrongly, can they be reprogrammed? Of course! We are transformed by the renewing of our minds, and we win the spiritual battle when we "take captive every thought to make it obedient to Christ" (2 Cor. 10:5). If we have a thought that is contrary to God's Word, we simply dismiss it and stay obedient to Christ.

We demolish arguments and every pretension that sets itself up against the knowledge of God, and we take captive every thought to make it obedient to Christ (2 Cor. 10:5).

Thought for the day: *What should you do when you have a thought that is not consistent with God's Word?*

LETTING CHRIST RULE IN OUR HEARTS

Psalm 119:1-16

Psalm 119 is a devotional on the Word of God. It is has 22 divisions—each one beginning with a different letter in the Hebrew alphabet. The psalmist asks, "How can a young man keep his way pure? By living according to your word. I have hidden your word in my heart that I might not sin against you" (vv. 9,11). Paul expands upon this instruction in Colossians 3:15, "Let the peace of Christ rule in your hearts." "Rule" means "to act as a judge or arbiter." How do we let the peace of Christ arbitrate in our hearts? By letting the Word of Christ dwell within us (see Col. 3:16).

Suppose you have stored a lot of filth in your mind. Then one day you decide to clean up your mind. The moment you make that decision, the battle for the mind gets worse. As long as you are mentally giving in to tempting thoughts, you will hardly feel the struggle. The battle begins the moment you decide to resist the tempting thoughts and choose to clean up your mind. How can you do that?

Imagine that your mind is a pot filled with coffee. Because you chose to mix coffee grounds with the water in the pot, the liquid is dark, dirty and opaque. There is no way you can filter out the coffee from the water. Now suppose there is a bowl of crystal-clear ice next to the pot. Although you can't dump the whole bowl of ice into the pot all at once, you can take one ice cube each day and put it in the pot. At first you may not notice any difference; but if you continue to add one cube per day, before long the liquid in the pot will begin to clear up. If you kept adding ice, day after day, at a certain point you wouldn't be able to taste, smell or see the coffee in the pot. Although the coffee is still there, it has been diluted by the ice. Of course, this method will only work provided you don't also keep adding a scoop of coffee every day.

In the same way, if we wish to rid our minds of filth, we must read and study the Word of God each day. Because our minds are like computers. If we put garbage in, we will get garbage out. The process of renewing our mind often begins with one step forward and one step backward. We spend time in God's Word during our devotions, but then we go back into the world for work and leisure where we are mentally assaulted again. Learning to take every thought captive in obedience to Christ takes time and commitment, but it can be done. The next day we take two steps forward and one back, then three steps forward and one back. If we stay committed to the process, it will soon become 20, 30 and 40 steps forward and one back.

The Spirit of God will lead us into all truth if we choose that path, and He will convict us if we choose the wrong path. Make a commitment to be like the psalmist, who wrote, "I rejoice in following your statutes as one rejoices in great riches. I meditate on your precepts and consider your ways. I delight in your decrees; I will not neglect your word" (Ps. 119:14-16). Someone has said, "Sin will keep us from God's Word, but God's Word would keep us from sin."

> Let the peace of Christ rule in your hearts, since as members of one body you were called to peace. And be thankful (Col. 3:15).

Thought for the day: *How can you let the peace of Christ rule in your heart?*

CHOOSING THE TRUTH

Philippians 4:4-9

Being transformed by the renewing of our minds requires a proper orientation toward God. Circumstances may not always allow us to be happy, but we can always rejoice in the Lord. Joy is a fruit of the Spirit; and this inner joy can be experienced in every circumstance, because "the Lord is near" (Phil. 4:5). Paul admonishes us to get rid of our anxious thoughts by turning to God. He uses four words to describe our communion with God: "Prayer" is a general term describing our approach to God; "Petition" is a request for a specific need; "Thanksgiving" is an attitude of the heart that should always accompany prayer; and "Requests" are specific things we ask for. If we commune with God through prayer, petition, thanksgiving and requests, "the peace of God, which transcends all understanding, will guard [our] hearts and [our] minds in Christ Jesus" (v. 7).

When we find ourselves thinking negative or immoral thoughts, we should just confess them to God. We should not try to rebuke every negative thought. Doing so would be like trying to keep 12 corks submerged while treading water in the middle of the ocean. We should ignore the corks and swim to shore! We are not called to dispel the darkness. We are called to turn on the light. We win the battle for our minds by choosing the truth. Trying not to think negative thoughts is futile, because it just reinforces the negative thought.

Being created in the image of God, we have the capacity to choose. That means we can choose to believe or not believe, and we can choose what we want to think about. It is not enough to turn to God. We have to assume responsibility for our own thoughts. God will assist us through His grace, but He will not do our thinking for us. Paul admonishes us to think about "whatever is true, whatever is noble, whatever is right, whatever is pure, whatever is lovely, whatever is admirable" (Phil. 4:8). These six objects for our thoughts are excellent and praiseworthy.

While we should choose to think good thoughts, we also cannot deny reality or live in a fantasy world where everything turns out right. Being out of touch with reality is the first sign of mental illness. A mentally healthy person is in touch with reality. And although God is the ultimate reality, this fallen world is also a reality with which we must interact.

It is in our day-to-day living in this fallen world that we have to put our positive thoughts into action. After we spend time with God away from the distractions of the world, we must return to our daily responsibilities. We cannot just sit around and try to have positive thoughts. Our thoughts must result in appropriate behavior. Everything we do is a product of our thoughts. In other words, we don't do anything without first thinking it. When we face the harsh realities of this world, we need to think, *Is this true or is it not true, and how can I live the truth and speak the truth in love? What is the noble thing to do—how can I respond in a dignified manner that is worthy of respect? What is the right thing to do? What is the morally pure thing that I could do? What could I do that would promote peace and goodwill? What could I do that would be positive and constructive rather than negative and destructive?*

> Whatever you have learned or received or heard from me, or seen in me—put it into practice. And the God of peace will be with you (Phil. 4:9).

Thought for the day: *Why isn't it enough to just think good thoughts?*

STUDYING GOD'S WORD

Ezra 7:8-10

If we are going to be transformed by the renewing of our minds, we have to study God's word. There are no shortcuts. Nobody else can study for us. Old ways of living in this world have to be replaced by new ways of living in the kingdom of God. The lies of this world have to be replaced by the truth of God's Word. God's Word sitting on the shelf will not transform us. The truth has to be in our hearts. It is not enough to think about Scripture—we have to think scripturally. Wisdom is seeing life from God's perspective.

Ezra devoted himself to studying God's Word, but he also took the next step, the most important part of learning: He observed the law of the Lord (see Ezra 7:10). We learn far more by doing than we do by just hearing. People retain only about 10 percent of what they hear, 20 percent of what they see, but 90 percent of what they do. Only when we have incorporated the Word of God into our lives are we in any position to teach others. Teachers have to walk their talk in order to be effective in ministering to others. James tells us:

> Do not merely listen to the word, and so deceive yourselves. Do what it says. Anyone who listens to the word but does not do what it says is like a man who looks at his face in a mirror and, after look-ing at himself, goes away and immediately forgets what he looks like. But the man who looks intently into the perfect law that gives freedom, and continues to do this, not forgetting what he has heard, but doing it—he will be blessed in what he does (Jas. 1:22-25).

The truth of God's Word is not supposed to be intellectually discussed without appropriation. The truth is supposed to enter our hearts, set us free and transform our lives. Interpersonal conflicts arise and our witness is compromised when people have knowledge without spiritual maturity. They will be perceived as noisy gongs or clanging cymbals (see 1 Cor. 13:1) if they have no love. Studying God's Word is not an intellectual exercise. It is an interaction with God, and His living Word transforms our lives. If our lives are going to be transformed, our time spent in God's Word must spill over into our daily activities. Nowhere is this more emphasized than in the

Jewish confession of faith known as the *Shema*. "Shema" is the Hebrew word for "hear," and it means "to hear as though to obey." It is recorded in Deuteronomy and recited daily by pious Jews:

> Hear, O Israel: The LORD our God, the LORD is one. Love the LORD your God with all your heart and with all your soul and with all your strength. These commandments that I give you today are to be upon your hearts. Impress them on your children. Talk about them when you sit at home and when you walk along the road, when you lie down and when you get up. Tie them as symbols on your hands and bind them on your foreheads. Write them on the doorframes of your houses and on your gates (6:4-9).

> Do your best to present yourself to God as one approved, a workman who does not need to be ashamed and who correctly handles the word of truth (2 Tim. 2:15).

Thought for the day: *According to the Shema, what is the correct way to handle the word of truth?*

Overcoming Anger

1 Samuel 18

Think of our emotions as being to our soul what our ability to feel is to our body. Now suppose somebody had the power to take away the sensation of physical pain and offered it to us as a gift. Would we receive it? If we lost the ability to feel pain, our bodies would become hopelessly scarred in a very short time. Our souls would also be scarred if we never felt anger, anxiety or depression. These God-given emotions are like an indicator light on the dash of a car signaling something is wrong. Covering the light with a piece of tape would be suppression. Suppressing our emotions is dishonest and unhealthy. Stuffing our emotions is what causes many psychosomatic illnesses. Smashing the light is indiscriminate expression, and venting our rage is unhealthy for the people around us. So how should we deal with our emotions?

What we should do is look under the hood. That is acknowledgment. Our emotional health is dependent upon our emotional honesty. We can't be right with God and not be real. If necessary, God may have to make us real in order to be right with Him.

When it comes to learning about how to deal with our anger, we can take away some valuable lessons from the story of Saul and David. Now Saul was angry, because he was jealous. David was getting more applause than he was. Insecure people get angry when their social status is being upstaged by others. Saul certainly didn't look under the hood, nor did he suppress his anger. He vented his anger on David. A little self-inventory may have prevented all of that. David was the best friend of Saul's son. David had saved Israel from the Philistine giant, and he had successfully done whatever Saul sent him to do (see 1 Sam. 18:5). Saul should have thanked God for David. David was secure because the Lord was with him (see v. 12). People who are secure in Christ are less prone to anger, because their identity and sense of worth are found in Christ, not in the success or failure of others, nor in the positive or negative circumstances of life.

Before he ever became angry with David, Saul was bitter as a result of his confrontation with Samuel (see 1 Sam. 15). Because of Saul's rebellion and disobedience, the Lord had rejected Saul as king of Israel and had told Samuel to anoint David as king. There is no evidence that Saul ever repented of his sin or forgave David for upstaging him. At the heart of angry people is a bitter spirit. Such unresolved anger gives the devil an opportunity. After venting his anger toward David, "The next day an evil spirit from God came forcefully upon Saul" (1 Sam. 18:10). The same could happen to us if we do not forgive from our heart. Jesus tells us that the unforgiving servant would be turned over to the jailers (tormentors) to be tortured (see Matt. 18:34). In the New Testament the Greek word for "jailer" is used almost exclusively for spiritual torment. That is why Paul says, "I have forgiven in the sight of Christ for your sake, in order that Satan might not outwit us. For we are not unaware of his schemes" (2 Cor. 2:10-11).

Paul also advises us, " 'In your anger do not sin': Do not let the sun go down while you are still angry, and do not give the devil a foothold" (Eph. 4:26-27). Our spiritual and mental health depend upon how well we learn to handle our emotions. It is not a sin to be angry, but in our anger we must not sin. If we wish not to sin, then we should be angry the way Christ was: We should be angry at sin.

Do not make friends with a hot-tempered man, do not associate with one easily angered (Prov. 22:24).

Thought for the day: *Why are angry people to be avoided if possible?*

A HUMBLE WALK WITH GOD

Micah 6:8

The long-term process of walking by faith can be illustrated by the game of golf. Suppose a 5-year-old child hits the ball 75 yards, but is 15 degrees off the center of the fairway. Because of the short distance, the ball will probably land in the fairway. Now the child is 12 years old and hits the ball 200 yards. If the ball is 15 degrees off, the ball is probably in the rough. When the child becomes an adult and hits the ball 250 yards, a 15-degree error could land the ball out of bounds. If what we believe is 15 degrees off from the Word of God, there may not be a lot of negative consequences when we are young. But there will be if we continue to believe things that are contrary to God's Word. Suddenly we find ourselves in the rough or out of bounds. This midlife crisis can leave us thinking, *I always believed if I did this or that I would be successful, satisfied or fulfilled.* As our culture drifts further away from our Judeo-Christian roots, the consequences of what our young people believe are showing up before they reach adulthood.

We don't have to wait until life falls apart to find out whether or not our walk is true. Our emotional response to what we think and believe is revealing whether we are on the right path. Remember that our emotions are predominantly a product of our thought life. Consciously or subconsciously we have certain ideas or goals in our minds for how we should live and what must happen in order for us to live satisfied, successful lives. Often, our sense of worth is tied to those goals.

Suppose you just found out that your goal to be promoted at work was being blocked by your supervisor. You would probably feel angry. What if your promotion was uncertain? You would probably feel anxious every time you thought about it. You would likely feel depressed if you thought your goal for a promotion was impossible.

We will be on an emotional roller coaster if we believe that our identity and our sense of worth are dependent upon other people and the circumstances of life. If a pastor believes that his sense of worth is dependent upon the response of his congregation, then he may try to control or manipulate them into responding the way he wants. But every member of the congregation can block that goal. Suppose a mother believes that her sense of self-worth depends on having a harmonious, happy, Christian family. Every member of that family can and will block that goal.

Paul said that the goal of our instruction is love (see 1 Tim. 1:5), and "the fruit of the Spirit is love, joy, peace, patience . . . self-control" (Gal. 5:22-23). Notice that the fruit of the Spirit is self-control, not child control or congregational control. Also notice that the fruit of the Spirit is singular (i.e., fruit not fruits). The love of God manifests itself in joy, peace, patience. If our goal in life is to become the person God created us to be, then the fruit of the Spirit becomes evident in our lives. Regardless of circumstances, we experience joy instead of depression, peace instead of anxiety, and patience instead of anger.

When life is not going your way, as it wasn't for Israel in Micah's day, then learn to act justly, love mercy and walk humbly with your God.

Make it your ambition to lead a quiet life, to mind your own business and to work with your hands, just as we told you (1 Thess. 4:11).

Thought for the day: *What is your ambition in life and why?*

GOALS AND DESIRES

Luke 12:13-21

According to Jesus, "A man's life does not consist in the abundance of his possessions" (Luke 12:15). A foolish man works toward the wrong end. To live a successful and satisfied life, we have to have the right goals. No God-given goals for our lives can be impossible, uncertain or blocked. Even the secular world knows that the authority of leaders is undermined if commands are issued that cannot be obeyed. So if God wants something done, it can be done! "For nothing is impossible with God" (Luke 1:37), and "I can do everything through him who gives me strength" (Phil. 4:13). However, "everything" has to be consistent with God's will.

To understand how we can successfully live the Christian life, we need to make a distinction between Godly goals and godly desires. *A godly goal is any specific orientation that reflects God's purpose for our lives, and that is not dependent upon people or circumstances beyond our right or ability to control.* The only person we have the right and the ability to control is ourselves. Nobody and nothing can keep us from being the person God created us to be—and for us to become that person is God's goal for our lives. If we are honest with ourselves, we will look in the mirror and say, "The only person who can keep me from reaching that goal is me!"

A godly desire is any specific result that depends on the cooperation of other people, the success of events or favorable circumstances that we have no right or ability to control. We cannot base our identity, success or sense of worth on our desires, no matter how godly they may be, because we cannot control their fulfillment. God desires that all would repent and live (see Ezek. 18:32), but not all will. God writes to His children so that they may not sin (see 1 John 2:1), but His sovereignty and His success are not dependent on whether or not we sin. God has no goals for us that can be blocked, uncertain or impossible.

If your goal as a parent is to have a happy, harmonious, Christian family, you will suffer a lot of emotional ups and downs, especially if you believe that your sense of worth is dependent upon creating that picture-perfect family. Although your desire is a worthy one, every member of your family can and will block that goal at some point. But what if you made it your goal to be the parent and spouse God called you to be? Who can block that goal? You are the only one who can.

Suppose a well-meaning pastor has one primary goal and that is to triple the size of his church and win his community to Christ. Every member of the community can block that goal. Relentless in his pursuit, the pastor starts manipulating his people and pressuring them to produce. That church will suffer a lot of pain until the pastor realizes that his goal is to become the pastor God created him to be, and that is the best way to reach the community for Christ.

There is nothing wrong with having godly desires—such as reaching our community for Christ—but we shouldn't base our identity and sense of worth on their fulfillment. We should never try to control and manipulate people in order to accomplish our goals. We shouldn't get angry, anxious or depressed if our desires are not met, but we may feel disappointed. Life is full of disappointments, but they are likely His appointments to greater maturity in Christ. Other people don't always cooperate and events don't always go our way, but these realities of life are not keeping us from conforming to the image of God.

It is God's will that you should be sanctified (1 Thess. 4:3).

Thought for the day: *What would happen to your anger if you had no blocked goals?*

A TRUE SENSE OF WORTH

2 Peter 1:3-11

How does a Christian establish a true sense of worth? As odd as it may sound, not through the possession or exercise of spiritual gifts! Spiritual gifts are important for building up the Body of Christ, but we don't all have the same gifts. Therefore, "God has combined the members of the body and has given greater honor to the parts that lacked it, so that there should be no division in the body" (1 Cor. 12:24). Our individual talents make a contribution to the kingdom of God, but God has given five talents to some, two talents to some and only one talent to others. Does that mean that only the Christian with five talents can have any legitimate sense of worth? The answer is a definite no, and those who try to find their identity and sense of worth in gifts and talents run the risk of not accomplishing God's primary goal for their lives: godly character.

Are intelligence, beauty and performance the means by which we gain a sense of worth? The answer again is no.

God chose the foolish things of the world to shame the wise; God chose the weak things of the world to shame the strong. He chose the lowly things of this world and the despised things—and the things that are not—to nullify the things that are, so that no one may boast before him (1 Cor. 1:27-29).

There is certainly nothing wrong with being an intelligent, beautiful performer especially if you use your gifts to the glory of God. After all it was God who gave you those life endowments. God has not equally distributed gifts, talents and intelligence to all, but He has equally distributed Himself. We all benefit by His promises, and we all participate in His divine nature (see 2 Pet. 1:4).

Unlike this world, the ground before the Cross is level. We all have the same standing in Christ. We find our sense of worth in our new identity and in our growth in character. "His divine power has given us everything we need for life and godliness" (2 Pet. 1:3). Those who know who they are in Christ and have a life characterized by love, joy, peace, patience, kindness, goodness, faithfulness, gentleness and self-control will have a legitimate sense of worth, and they will not be unfruitful. The good news is that every Christian has exactly the same opportunity to accomplish that goal and the same inheritance in Christ.

What is wrong if some Christians don't possess these qualities? According to Peter, they have become near-sighted and blind, and they have forgotten that they have been cleansed from all their sins (see 2 Pet. 1:9). They have taken their eyes off the Lord and have forgotten or never knew who they are in Christ. They need to take their eyes off this world and fix their eyes on Jesus, the author and perfecter of their faith. "Dear friends, now we are children of God. . . . Everyone who has this hope in him purifies himself, just as he is pure" (1 John 3:2-3).

> Therefore, my brothers, be all the more eager to make your calling and election sure. For if you do these things, you will never fall, and you will receive a rich welcome into the kingdom of our Lord and Savior Jesus Christ (2 Pet. 1:10-11).

Thought for the day: *How can we have a legitimate sense of worth and never stumble?*

RIGHTEOUS INDIGNATION

Mark 11:12-28

Anger is a God-given emotion. We are never instructed to deny our anger, but we are instructed to manage our emotional life by choosing to believe the truth and having the right goals for our lives. The basis for our emotional stability is our identity, acceptance, security and significance in Christ. Once we are established in Christ, then the trials and tribulations of the world no longer have a negative effect on us. In fact,

> We also rejoice in our sufferings, because we know that suffering produces perseverance; perseverance, character; and character, hope. And hope does not disappoint us, because God has poured out his love into our hearts by the Holy Spirit (Rom. 5:3-5).

The trials and tribulations of this world actually reveal wrong goals and at the same time make possible the goal of our lives: that we conform to the image of God.

When we think about conforming to God's image, we probably do not think about taking on His righteous wrath. Yet the Bible actually talks more about the wrath of God than it does about our anger and wrath. God's anger is not born out of His insecurity, and He doesn't have blocked goals. God's anger is a righteous indignation toward sin. Cursing the fig tree and cleansing the Temple illustrate His anger and judgment to come. Jesus didn't get mad because the fig tree had no figs when He wanted some. At that time of the year, the fig tree should have had edible buds. Yet it did not, which indicated that the tree was not going to bear any fruit. The cursing of the fig tree was a prophetic sign of God's impending judgment on Israel, not an angry reaction because Jesus was hungry. The unproductive fig tree symbolized Israel's spiritual barrenness, despite their outward appearance of religious fervor.

His anger is continuous, but His loving kindness and mercy temper it. God is incredibly patient toward those who sin. We would be much swifter about judging others and forcing them to suffer the consequences of their sin. (Remember, He turned over the table, not the moneychangers.) He has the perfect capacity to separate the sin from the sinner. If that were not so, we would all be doomed. We, too, should have a sense of righteous indignation, but we need to learn from His example how to express it.[1]

Abraham Lincoln said, "To sin by silence when they should protest makes cowards of men." Philipp Melancthon, German humanist, Reformer and contemporary of Martin Luther, said, "All that is needed for sin to abound is for good men to do nothing." Righteous indignation moves us to correct that which is wrong. The heroes of our faith in Hebrews 11 could not sit by and watch the world go to hell. They had to do something, even if it cost them their lives, and it often did. If we are going to be salt and light in this fallen world, we need to speak the truth, but we need to do it in love. We must make a stand for righteousness, but we should silently stand by if we can't do so without violating the fruit of the Spirit. To speak the truth without love would make us no different from those who represent the ideals we are standing against—and it would profit no one. Let the message spoken in love—not the messenger—be the offense.

> "In your anger do not sin": Do not let the sun go down while you are still angry, and do not give the devil a foothold (Eph. 4:26-27).

Thought for the day: *How can you be angry and not sin?*

OVERCOMING ANXIETY

Matthew 6:19-34

Jesus teaches that anxious people have two treasures and two visions, because they try to serve two masters. He also teaches in this passage that double-minded people worry about tomorrow—and they worry about their possessions. Regarding the latter, there is a lot to worry about! First, there is the decay of all things physical, which is the law of entropy. The second law of thermodynamics says that without the introduction of new energy all systems become progressively more disorderly and will decay. If rust doesn't destroy them, then moths or termites will. Second, possessing earthly treasures causes others to covet and steal, which poses a concern for our security. It is hard to be anxiety free if we are worried about our possessions. Personal security comes from relationships, not physical possessions. The critical question is, What do we treasure in our hearts?

It is important to note that there is nothing inherently wrong with owning possessions. It is the love of money, not money itself, that is the root of all sorts of evil (see 1 Tim. 6:10). Paul tells us,

> Command those who are rich in this present world not to be arrogant nor to put their hope in wealth, which is so uncertain, but to put their hope in God, who richly provides us with everything for our enjoyment. Command them to do good, to be rich in good deeds, and to be generous and willing to share. In this way they will lay up treasure for themselves as a firm foundation for the coming age, so that they may take hold of the life that is truly life (1 Tim. 6:17-19).

There will be no peace trying to serve two masters. Whichever master we choose to serve, by that master we shall be controlled.

Jesus dealt first with our possessions (see Matt. 6:19-24), then He turned to the matter of our provision. Trusting God for tomorrow is a question of worth. Birds are not created in the image of God, but we are! Birds will not inherit the kingdom of God, but we will! If God takes care of the birds, with how much more care will He take care of us! "If . . . God clothes the grass of the field, which is here today and tomorrow is thrown into the fire, will he not much more clothe you, O you of little faith?" (v. 30). God lays His own reputation on the line. It is our responsibility to trust and obey. It is His responsibility to provide. This is a question of God's integrity. Does He care for us, and will He provide for our needs? Yes and yes! Your heavenly Father knows what you need: "Therefore do not worry about tomorrow, for tomorrow will worry about itself. Each day has enough trouble of its own" (v. 34).

Do we believe that the fruit of the Spirit will satisfy us more than earthly possessions? Do we believe that if we hunger and thirst after righteousness that we will be satisfied? Do we believe that God will supply all our needs according to His riches in glory? If we do, then we will, "Seek first his kingdom and his righteousness, and all these things will be given to [us] as well" (v. 33).

A man's life does not consist in the abundance of his possessions (Luke 12:15).

Thought for the day: *What do you treasure most and whom do you trust?*

DOUBLE-MINDED THINKING

Joshua 24:14-15

In the New Testament, the primary words for anxiety are *merimna* (the noun) and *merimnao* (the verb). Of the 25 uses, 5 of them indicate a sense of caring; the other 20 refer to a distracting, negative sense of worry or dread. In the positive sense, we should feel a little anxious if we have an important responsibility to fulfill, and it should motivate us to take necessary steps to carry out our responsibility. Most of our anxious thoughts, however, are not profitable and can lead to psychosomatic illnesses. Worrying doesn't accomplish anything. People have actually believed that if they worried about something, they could prevent it from happening. But we are not going to help the plane stay in the air by worrying, and we are not going to improve the odds in our favor by fretting about all that could go wrong. Jesus tells us, "Who of you by worrying can add a single hour to his life?" (Matt. 6:27). On the other hand, excessive worrying can take some years off your life.

Recall that anxiety differs from fear, in that fear has an object whereas anxiety doesn't. We are anxious, because our goals are uncertain and we don't know what is going to happen tomorrow. The process of worrying can be more debilitating than actually experiencing the negative consequences of what we worried about. In fact, some of us feel relieved to have the anxious "waiting" period over, even if the much worried over "happening" hasn't turned out the way we wanted. It is easier for us to live with "what is" than it is to live with "what if." When we don't know what is going to happen tomorrow, we are tempted to make assumptions. It seems to be a peculiar trait of the mind to assume the worst. However, nothing good can come from making negative assumptions and then acting upon them as though they were facts.

The root of "merimna" is the verb *merizo*, which means "to draw in different directions or distract." When "merimna" is used as a verb (*merimnao*), it appears to be a conjunction of "merizo" and *nous*, which means mind. That is probably why the translators of the *King James Version* of the Bible translated "do not worry" (Matt. 6:25) as "take no thought," and "why do you worry" (Matt. 6:28) as "why take ye thought." To be anxious in a negative sense is to be double-minded, and James says a double-minded person is unstable in all their ways (see Jas. 1:8). This is clearly revealed in Matthew 6:24-25: "No one can serve two masters. Either he will hate the one and love the other, or he will be devoted to the one and despise the other. You cannot serve both God and Money. Therefore I tell you, do not worry about your life."

In today's passage, Joshua is giving his farewell address and reminding the Israelites of their great victories and of how the Lord had delivered them. The land was yet to be fully possessed, and there would be many more battles to fight. Joshua, knowing that his leaving might create uncertainties in the minds of the Israelites, advises them:

> Fear the LORD and serve him with all faithfulness. . . . But if serving the LORD seems undesirable to you, then choose for yourselves this day whom you will serve, whether the gods your forefathers served beyond the River, or the gods of the Amorites, in whose land you are living. But as for me and my household, we will serve the LORD (Josh. 24:14-15).

He is a double-minded man, unstable in all he does (Jas. 1:8).

Thought for the day: *What will be the result of trying to serve two masters?*

"Plan A" Living

Mark 7:8-9

To overcome anxiety we need to acquire a singleness of vision and purpose. The question is, Are we going to live our way or God's way? Let's call God's way Plan A, which we accept by faith. Let's call humanity's way Plan B, which is a natural product of human reason and intuition. There are times when God's ways don't make sense to us from our limited human perspective. We can never know if we are basing our decisions on all the facts, nor can we predict with precision what the consequences of our choices and actions will be. That is why God says His ways are not our ways (see Isa. 55:8).

When we come to Christ, our old ways of thinking and living are still programmed into our minds. If we don't know God's ways, we will continue to live the way we always have. Now that we have the mind of Christ (see 1 Cor. 2:16), we can learn God's ways. Until we are fully committed to live according to what God says is true, we will waffle between Plan A and Plan B. A commitment to live according to Plan A decreases our commitment and tendency to live as we always have. Mixing our ways with God's ways decreases our commitment to Plan A. That is what the Pharisees were doing by observing their man-made traditions; as a result, they set aside the commandments of God (see Mark 7:8-9). Such waffling between Plan A and Plan B creates its own anxieties for us as Christians, because we become double-minded.

A natural person often experiences less anxiety than an immature or uncommitted Christian who wants to straddle the fence and have the "best" of both worlds. The natural person creates his or her own rationalistic worldview and natural explanation of reality and can live anxiety free in this world for a time. The natural person has become his or her own god, but don't follow the natural person's example. "There is a way that seems right to a man, but in the end it leads to death" (Prov. 14:12). Therefore, don't choose Plan B because it may seem less worrisome in the present.

To illustrate this principle, consider marriage. God's Plan A for marriage is a life-time, monogamous relationship between a man and a woman who are to stay faithful and committed to each other until death separates them. A young couple should be instructed not to even mentally consider any other options, because that opens the door to temptation. Thinking about what it would be like to be married to someone else is a fantasy that will appear more attractive than the reality that we have. We can actually carry on a mental affair with someone other than our spouse, but such fantasies and mental affairs will chip away at our commitment to Plan A.

What would happen if a young couple got married with the understanding that they could always get a divorce if the relationship didn't work out? They *will* probably get divorced, because commitment is what makes the marriage relationship unique. If a wife establishes her own career because she believes the marriage won't last, she is making preparations for Plan B. If a husband is more committed to his job than his marriage, he is choosing Plan B. But choosing Plan A is choosing a way of life that is consistent with how the Creator intended us to live.

Whether you turn to the right or to the left, your ears will hear a voice behind you, saying, "This is the way; walk in it" (Isa. 30:21).

Thought for the day: *Why do some believe it is easier to fall back on their old ways of living?*

KNOWING GOD'S WAYS

Jeremiah 9

Someone speculated that every decision people make is an attempt to reduce further anxiety. To cope with their anxiety, people consume food, alcohol and drugs; have illicit sex; mindlessly repeat mantras; and escape to cabins, boats and lonely places. More prescription drugs are dispensed for the temporary "cure" of anxiety than for any other reason. But when the temporary cures wear off, we have to return to the same world—only now we have the added problem of the negative consequences of the escape mechanisms. Anxiety drains our energy today and dims our hope for tomorrow.

Anxiety arises out of a state of disconnection. Man's wisdom, strength and riches cannot comprehend, accomplish or buy the peace that comes from being rightly related to God. The only thing that we can boast about is our understanding of God and His ways (see Jer. 9:23-24). God has designed us to live a certain way; and living any other way is like swimming upstream in our own strength, or succumbing to the current and being swept helplessly along. But having the peace of God regardless of external circumstances is like floating on a pond.

Life is like a factory that has hundreds of gears all intertwined and running together. It runs smoothly as long as the gears are well oiled and perfectly centered. Should one of the gears get just a little out-of-round and start taking an elliptical path, it will no longer mesh with the other gears, and it will wear out quickly. The out-of-place gear not only does damage to itself, but it also creates friction with those gears closely connected to it. In the same way, we have to stay closely connected to God and to those in the family of God around us if we are to become the people God wants us to be. But we can't all work together as a harmonious whole unless we are Christ centered and submissive to His ways.

We need to discover the God-created harmony and rhythms of life. He is the Master Musician, and we are His orchestra. When we are filled with his Spirit, we will sing and make melody in our hearts to the Lord (see Eph. 5:19). If each of us follows the director and plays our part, the music will be a glorious expression of God's glory. But if our timing is off, or if we play a different tune, we create an awful noise. (The greatest tragedy of all would be to go to the grave with our music never expressed.)

In the time of Jeremiah, the Israelites were not living in harmony with God. So Jeremiah was disgusted with the house of Israel, and he wanted to get away from these unfaithful people (see Jer. 9:2). They were self-centered and had not followed God's ways (see vv. 13-14). Instead of living in harmony with their God, these people were wailing. God's orchestra was out of tune with Him. Their attempt to correct their own problems was at best superficial. "They dress the wounds of my people as though it were not serious. 'Peace, peace,' they say, when there is no peace" (Jer. 8:11). But God never gives bandage answers to cancerous problems.

> This is what the LORD says: "Let not the wise man boast of his wisdom or the strong man boast of his strength or the rich man boast of his riches, but let him who boasts boast about this: that he understands and knows me, that I am the Lord, who exercises kindness, justice and righteousness on earth, for in these I delight," declares the LORD (Jer. 9:23-24).

> Let him who boasts boast in the Lord (1 Cor. 1:31).

Thought for the day: *What would this world be like if everyone were in tune with the Lord?*

CASTING OUR ANXIETIES ON CHRIST

1 Peter 5:6-10

Christ has invited us to cast our anxieties on Him, because He cares for us. This means that we have to humble ourselves by surrendering our ways and submitting to His ways. The following steps will help you overcome anxiety.

1. The first thing a Christian does about anything is pray. "Do not be anxious about anything, but in everything, by prayer and petition, with thanksgiving, present your requests to God" (Phil. 4:6). *Lord, I come humbly before your presence as Your child. I acknowledge my dependence upon You, and I ask for Your divine guidance. Show me what I am responsible for and what I am not. Fill me with Your Holy Spirit and guide me into all truth. I ask for Your peace to guard my heart and my mind in Christ Jesus.*

2. Resolve all personal and spiritual conflicts by submitting to God and resisting the devil (see Jas. 4:7) through genuine repentance (see my book *Steps to Freedom in Christ*). The purpose is to make sure your heart is right with God and to eliminate any demonic influences on your mind.

3. State the problem. What are you anxious about? A problem well stated is half solved. In anxious states of mind, people can't see the forest for the trees, so put the problem in perspective. What matters for eternity? Seek godly counsel if necessary, but do not turn to ungodly counsel or temporary cures.

4. Separate the facts from the assumptions. People are not anxious about what they know; they are anxious about what they don't know. People may be fearful of the facts, but not anxious.

5. Determine what you have the right or the ability to control. Your duty in life and sense of worth are tied only to that for which you are responsible. If you aren't living a responsible life, you should feel anxious. Don't try to cast your responsibility on Christ; He will throw it back. But do cast your anxiety onto Him, because His integrity is at stake in meeting your needs—if

you are living a responsible and righteous life.

6. List everything you can do that is related to the situation that is under your responsibility. What is the noble thing to do (i.e., how can you assume your responsibility in a dignified manner that is worthy of respect)? What is the right thing to do? What is the morally pure thing to do? What could you do that would promote peace and goodwill? What could you do that would be positive and constructive rather than negative and destructive?

7. Complete everything on your list. Then commit yourself to be a responsible person and fulfill your calling and obligations in life. Take every thought captive in obedience to Christ and keep your mind focused on what is true.

8. Submit to God in prayer everything that lies outside of your responsibility and your right or ability to control. If you have fulfilled your responsibilities and you believe the truth, the rest is God's responsibility. Any residue anxiety is probably due to your having assumed responsibilities that God never intended you to have.

The fruit of righteousness will be peace (Isa. 32:17).

Thought for the day: *Why would righteous living result in peace?*

OVERCOMING DEPRESSION

Psalm 38

Every population group of the world is experiencing a blues epidemic in an age of anxiety. The number of people seeking medical treatment for depression has doubled in the last decade. Depression is often called the common cold of mental illness, because it is so prevalent. Like anxiety disorders, depression also arises out of a state of disconnection from God. After the Fall, Adam was fearful and anxious (see Gen. 3:10), and Cain was angry and depressed (see Gen. 4:5). Depression is often the response to losses in our lives, and humankind's greatest loss has been our relationship with God. In Psalm 38, verses 1 through 8 reveal the suffering of separation, and verses 9 through 14 reveal the loneliness of separation.

In Psalm 38, David records nearly every symptom of depression. Depression is a sense of helplessness and hopelessness and David wisely turns to the God of hope and help (see v. 22). Determine your state of depression by circling the numbers that best represent you in the following scale (1 for very low energy and 5 for very high energy):

1. Low energy   1 2 3 4 5   High energy
2. Difficulty sleeping or   1 2 3 4 5   Uninterrupted sleep
   interrupted sleep
3. No desire to be involved   1 2 3 4 5   Very involved in activities
4. No desire for sex   1 2 3 4 5   Healthy sex drive
5. Bodily aches and pains   1 2 3 4 5   Feel physically good
6. Loss of appetite   1 2 3 4 5   Enjoy eating
7. Sad (tearful)   1 2 3 4 5   Joyful
8. Despairing and hopeless   1 2 3 4 5   Hopeful and confident
9. Low frustration tolerance   1 2 3 4 5   High frustration tolerance
   (irritable)   (pleasant)
10. Withdrawn   1 2 3 4 5   Involved with people
11. Mental anguish   1 2 3 4 5   Peace of mind
12. Low sense of self-worth   1 2 3 4 5   High sense of self-worth
13. Pessimistic   1 2 3 4 5   Optimistic (about the future)

14. Negative perception of   1 2 3 4 5   Positive perception of self
     self and circumstances   and circumstances

15. Self-destructive   1 2 3 4 5   Self-preserving

Add up the numbers that you circled. You are severely depressed if your total is between 15 and 24; depressed if your total is between 25 and 34; mildly depressed of your total is between 35 and 44.

Depression affects our body, soul and spirit and recovery requires a physical, mental, emotional and spiritual answer. There are biological and neurological causes for depression that have to be considered in order to have a comprehensive answer. In such cases, medical treatment is necessary. However, most causes of depression are psychological and spiritual. Medical doctors and Christian caregivers need to work together in order to provide a complete answer. Taking a pill to cure your body is commendable, but taking a pill to cure your soul is deplorable. May God give you the wisdom to know the difference.

Hope deferred makes the heart sick, but a longing fulfilled is a tree of life (Prov. 13:12).

Thought for the day: *Why is hope so important for successful living?*

THE BASIS FOR OUR HOPE

Psalm 13

Someone once said, "You can live 40 days without food, seven days without water, seven minutes without air, but you can't live a moment without hope." Hope is not wishful thinking; rather, it is the present assurance of some future good. Depression is a sense of hopelessness born out of a negative and often false perception of ourselves, our present circumstances and the future. The resulting emotional state may not be based on reality nor perceived truthfully from God's perspective. Recall from an earlier study that if what we believe does not reflect truth, then what we feel does not reflect reality.

In Psalm 13, David is exhibiting many of the classic symptoms of depression including hopelessness, negative self-talk, thoughts of death and sadness. David is depressed because he is focusing on his circumstances, sees no future hope and has a false perception of himself and God. Even though David believes in God, he is depressed, because what he believes about God is not true. How can an omnipresent and omniscient God forget him for even one minute, much less forever? Depressed people often have a distorted concept of God and of themselves. If you believe that God has forgotten you, then you have no hope. If you think you have lost your salvation or never had it, then you have no hope.

"Wrest[ling] with my thoughts" (Ps. 13:2) is nothing more than David talking to himself. That, of course, is not the answer. But turning to God is the answer, and that is what David does (see Ps. 13:5-6). So does the oppressed psalmist when he repeats the following verse three times: "Why are you downcast, O my soul? Why so disturbed within me? Put your hope in God, for I will yet praise him, my Savior and my God" (Pss. 42:5,11; 43:5). David overcomes his depression by first placing his trust in God's unfailing love (see Ps. 13:5). David had always trusted in God, but he had allowed the negative circumstances of his life to draw his attention away from God. The temporal state of his condition is put in the light of God's unfailing love. We would do well to follow David's example and place our trust in the Lord. God is the only constant in this ever-changing world.

Second, David's heart rejoices in his salvation. He remembers that he has a covenant relationship with God—and so do we. God hasn't changed, and His Word hasn't changed.

Dear friends, now we are children of God, and what we will be has not yet been made known. But we know that when he appears, we shall be like him, for we shall see him as he is. Everyone who has this hope in him purifies himself, just as he is pure (1 John 3:2-3).

So when we find your hope fading, we should recall again who God is and who we are in Christ.

Third, David sings to the Lord. Singing is one of the key ways to focus our minds and stop wrestling with our thoughts. One of the main determinants of whether a depressed mood will persist or lift is the degree to which we ruminate. Worrying about what is depressing us makes the depression all the more intense and prolonged. Singing hymns of praise helps focus our minds, and singing is something we can choose to do. Plus, the spiritual dimension of music is often overlooked. When David played the harp, the evil spirit departed from Saul (see 1 Sam. 16:21-23), and the hand of the Lord came upon Elisha when the harpist played (see 2 Kings 3:15).

I will sing of your love and justice; to you, O LORD, I will sing praise (Ps. 101:1).

Thought for the day: *How can singing praise songs lift depression?*

OVERCOMING HOPELESSNESS

Hebrews 6:13-19

A newly adopted child found himself in a big mansion. His new father said, "This is yours, and you have a right to be here. I have made you a joint heir with my only begotten Son. My son paid the price that set you free from your old taskmaster, who was cruel and condemning. I purchased it for you because I love you." It seemed too good to be true, but the child was deeply grateful, and he soon began to form new relationships with the other adopted children.

He especially enjoyed the buffet table from which he freely ate. Then it happened! He accidentally knocked over a stack of glasses and a valuable pitcher crashed to the floor and broke. Some dark figure outside the mansion began to accuse him, and he thought, *You clumsy, stupid kid! You will never get away with this. What right do you have to be here anyway? You'd better hide before your new master finds out, or he will surely throw you out.* At first he was caught up with the wonder of living in the new mansion with a new family and a loving father, but now he was confused. Old tapes created in early childhood began to play again in his mind. He was filled with self-condemning thoughts. *You don't belong here. You belong in the basement.* So he descended into the basement.

The cellar was dreary, dark and depressing. The only light came from the open door at the top of the long stairway. He heard his father calling for him; but he was too ashamed to answer, and he was starting to question whether he had ever been adopted in the first place. Old friends would try to encourage him to come back upstairs, but he didn't think he would fit in. Besides, he was tired and didn't feel like being around people. He made a few half-hearted attempts to climb the stairs, but he never went far enough or stayed long enough to resolve his conflicts and learn the truth that would set him free.

Then one day a shaft of light penetrated his mind and reason returned *Why not throw myself on the mercy of this one who calls himself my father?* So he mustered his strength and climbed the stairs to face his father. "Father," he said, "I knocked over some glasses and broke a pitcher." Without saying a word, his father took him by the hand and led him into the dining room. To the boy's utter amazement, his father had prepared a banquet for him!

"Welcome home, Son," his father said. "There is no condemnation for those who are in my family."

Oh, the deep, deep love of Jesus and the matchless grace of God. If we could accept our heavenly Father's gracious love, we would never confine ourselves in the basement of depression or succumb to the grip of hopelessness. "In love he predestined us to be adopted as his sons through Jesus Christ, in accordance with his pleasure and will" (Eph. 1:5). "We who have fled to take hold of the hope offered to us may be greatly encouraged" (Heb. 6:18), because God has confirmed our inheritance by His unchangeable promise and the unchangeable oath that confirms His promise. Our hope in God is a solid anchor for our souls, and the answer to hopelessness and depression. Since God cannot lie, then the basis for our hope is found in His character and His Word, and not in our failures or in the circumstances of our lives.

We have this hope as an anchor for the soul, firm and secure (Heb. 6:19).

Thought for the day: *How is hope an anchor for our souls?*

THE PROBLEM OF HELPLESSNESS

Exodus 6:6-12

Endowed by the Creator with mental and physical powers, we have launched satellites; we have transplanted hearts, kidneys and livers, allowing people to live longer. We have climbed the highest peaks, descended into the lowest depths and probed outer space, going where no man has ever gone before. Athletes keep chopping inches and seconds off world records, but there is a limit to what finite humans can do. But if we were gods, as the false prophets of the New Age movement would have us believe, then there would be no limit to what we could do. We are not gods, and without God we will eventually find ourselves in a helpless situation. Our finite resources can help us overcome many obstacles for a time, but in the end they cannot save us.

A sense of helplessness is a primary symptom of depression, and often it is learned. Take fleas, for instance. Put them in a beaker with a glass plate over the top. After a few futile attempts to fly out, the fleas will remain in the beaker even after the glass plate has been removed. Or what about fish? Put a glass divider in an aquarium with fish on one side and their favorite food on the other. Within days, remove the glass divider, and the fish will remain on their side. Or consider baby elephants, who are chained to a stake in the ground. They will remain staked to the ground even when they are older and could easily pull up the stake, because they learned to be helpless when they were young.

The Israelites suffered from a similar kind of helplessness. They couldn't believe good news when they heard it! God instructed Moses to tell the Israelites,

> I am the LORD, and I will bring you out from under the yoke of the Egyptians. I will free you from being slaves to them, and I will redeem you with an outstretched arm and with mighty acts of judgment. I will take you as my own people, and I will be your God (Exod. 6:6-7).

When Moses shared this good news with the Israelites, they didn't listen to him, "because of their discouragement and cruel bondage" (v. 9). Years of conditioning had left them with a sense of helplessness. Even Moses felt helpless to persuade the Pharaoh since he had learned by experience that he could not even persuade his own people. It is not uncommon today to see entire people groups gripped by depression, because they feel helpless to change their circumstances.

Scientific experiments are showing that a real or perceived sense of helplessness affects our neurochemistry. Helping people overcome their sense of helplessness and hopelessness has proven to be as effective as anti-depressant medication—without the potentially negative side effects. If the precipitating cause for depression is not neurological, should we take medication? Perhaps that question is best answered by an analogy. If we are suffering from acid indigestion, should we take an antacid? Yes, why suffer needlessly? But that is not a complete answer. We should probably consider changing our eating habits and other potential causes for the upset stomach should be investigated.

Why has there been such a significant increase in depression over the last 50 years? What physical changes have we undergone that would make us so much more vulnerable to depression? It is very doubtful that our brain chemistry or our genes have changed radically. No. The answer lies in our having forgotten that abundant life comes God, not the world. Our hope has been misplaced, our beliefs have strayed from the truth, and we have failed to learn how helplessness can be overcome by turning to God.

With man this is impossible, but with God all things are possible (Matt. 19:26).

Thought for the day: *Why can't we overcome our own helplessness?*

OVERCOMING HELPLESSNESS

Numbers 13:26—14:9

A bright light suddenly awakened a man in his room, and the Lord spoke to him in the midst of it. "I have work for you to do," He said. Then the Savior showed the man a large rock and told him to push on it with all his might, and this he did. For months the man faithfully pushed on that rock, but it never moved. The man began to get the impression that the task was impossible and that he was an unworthy servant because he was unable to move the stone. "Lord," he said, "I have labored hard and long in your service, and I have not even nudged that rock one inch. What is wrong? Am I failing You?" The Lord answered,

> My son, I asked you to serve and you accepted. I told you to push on the rock, and this you have done. But never once did I mention that I expected you to move the rock, at least not by yourself. Now you come to Me discouraged, feeling like a failure and ready to quit. But is that so? Look at yourself. Your body is strong and muscled. Through opposition you have grown much and you are now better able to face the challenges before you. I, my son, will move the rock. All I asked of you was to trust Me and obey.

God saved the Israelites from Egypt and led them through the wilderness to the Promised Land. Imagine their dismay when 10 of the spies came back and gave a discouraging report of those who dwelt there: "We can't attack those people; they are stronger than we are" (Num. 13:31). Their present circumstances were bleak, and now they had no hope for the future. Their situation seemed hopeless. They felt helpless, because they were unable to do anything about it. Two of the spies didn't see it that way, however. Joshua and Caleb saw the land as exceedingly good (see Num. 14:7). As for the enemy, they could see with the eyes of faith that their protection was gone and that the Lord was with His people (see Num. 14:9). God would win their battles for them. For their part, the Israelites had to overcome their fears by trusting God and obeying His Word.

In this fallen world we all have felt helpless from time to time. How should we respond when the government turns a deaf ear to the Church, or when other people show contempt for the Lord? Is it our job to take on the government and to change those who are blasphemous? If we try, we will become angry controllers or suffer severe depression. If you want to feel helpless and depressed, try assuming God's responsibility for Him. It is not our responsibility to change the world. It is our responsibility to trust and obey, and to become the people God has called us to be. As Christians we are never helpless if we are in the will of an omnipotent God.

Henry Ford once said, "Whether you think you can or whether you think you can't; either way you are right." There is some truth to that axiom, but you don't overcome helplessness by the power of positive thinking. You overcome helplessness by the power of God and by believing the truth. Someone once said that success comes in cans and failure comes in cannots. On the following page are "Twenty Cans of Success" that will help you overcome your sense of helplessness.

I can do everything though him who gives me strength (Phil. 4:13).

Thought for the day: *Is a Christian ever truly helpless?*

Twenty Cans of Success

1. Why should I say I can't when the Bible says I can do all things through Christ who gives me strength (see Phil. 4:13)?
2. Why should I worry about my needs when I know that God will take care of all my needs according to His riches in glory in Christ Jesus (see Phil. 4:19)?
3. Why should I fear when the Bible says God has not given me a spirit of fear, but of power, love and a sound mind (see 2 Tim. 1:7)?
4. Why should I lack faith to live for Christ when God has given me a measure of faith (see Rom. 12:3)?
5. Why should I be weak when the Bible says that the Lord is the strength of my life and that I will display strength and take action because I know God (see Psalm 27:1; Dan. 11:32)?
6. Why should I allow Satan control over my life when He that is in me is greater then he that is in the world (see 1 John 4:4)?
7. Why should I accept defeat when the Bible says that God always leads me in victory (see 2 Cor. 2:14)?

8. Why should I lack wisdom when I know that Christ became wisdom to me from God and God gives wisdom to me generously when I ask Him for it (see 1 Cor. 1:30; Jas. 1:5)?

9. Why should I be depressed when I can recall to mind God's lovingkindness, compassion and faithfulness and have hope (see Lam. 3:21,23)?

10. Why should I worry and be upset when I can cast all my anxieties on Christ who cares for me (see 1 Pet. 5:7)?

11. Why should I ever be in bondage knowing that Christ has set me free and where the Spirit of the Lord is, there is freedom (see Gal. 5:1; 2 Cor. 3:17)?

12. Why should I feel condemned when the Bible says there is no condemnation for those who are in Christ Jesus (see Rom. 8:1)?

13. Why should I feel alone when Jesus said He is with me always and He will never leave me nor forsake me (see Matt. 28:20; Heb. 13:5)?

14. Why should I feel like I am cursed when the Bible says that Christ rescued me from the curse of the law that I might receive His Spirit by faith (see Gal. 3:13-14)?

15. Why should I be discontented when I, like Paul, can learn to be content whatever the circumstances (see Phil. 4:11)?

16. Why should I feel worthless when Christ became sin for me so that I might become the righteousness of God (see 2 Cor. 5:21)?

17. Why should I feel helpless in the presence of others when I know that if God is for me, nobody or nothing greater can be against me (see Rom. 8:31)?

18. Why should I be confused when God is the author of peace and He gives me knowledge through His Spirit who lives in me (see 1 Cor. 2:12; 14:33)?

19. Why should I feel like a failure when I am more than a conqueror through Christ who loved me (see Rom. 8:37)?

20. Why should I let the pressures of life bother me when I can take courage knowing that Jesus has overcome the world and its problems (see John 16:33)?

OVERCOMING LOSSES

Mark 10:32-34

Nobody likes to entertain the idea of impermanence. We live every day with the assumption that tomorrow will be the same. We make plans for the future with the thought that we will have our health, and the same old job, family and friends. James says otherwise.

> Now listen, you who say, "Today or tomorrow we will go to this or that city, spend a year there, carry on business and make money." Why, you do not even know what will happen tomorrow. What is your life? You are a mist that appears for a little while and then vanishes. Instead, you ought to say, "If it is the Lord's will, we will live and do this or that" (Jas. 4:13-15).

Only God is permanent; everything else is changing. We are time-oriented people by nature, who are in the process of learning to see life from God's eternal perspective.

Three times Jesus told His disciples that He was going to Jerusalem and there He would be betrayed and crucified. The first time, they essentially denied Jesus, and Peter even rebuked Him (see Mark 8:31-32). The second time they didn't understand and were afraid to talk about it (see Mark 9:32). On this third occasion, the disciples were terrified. Their life as usual was soon to be over (see Mark 10:32). We all go through a very predictable reaction when an established lifestyle is abruptly ended by a crisis. Usually the crisis is defined by a significant loss that can be real, threatened or imagined.

Our first response is denial, and that can last for 3 minutes or 30 years. Our initial reaction is a sense of disbelief, *No, not me!* Then we get angry and wonder, *How can this happen to me?* The anger often turns to bargaining as we think, *Maybe I can alter what happened?* Finally, we feel depressed when the consequences of the loss cannot be reversed. Reaction to losses is the primary cause for depression. No crisis can destroy us, but it can reveal who we are.

Crisis Reaction Cycle

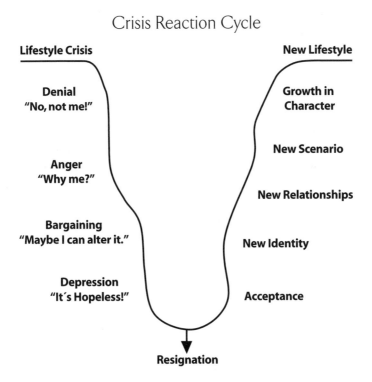

Lifestyle Crisis

Denial
"No, not me!"

Anger
"Why me?"

Bargaining
"Maybe I can alter it."

Depression
"It´s Hopeless!"

New Lifestyle

Growth in Character

New Scenario

New Relationships

New Identity

Acceptance

Resignation

Learning to overcome losses is a critical part of our growth process. Everything we now have, someday we shall lose, except for our relationship with God. The critical questions are: Are we going to choose the path of resignation and allow the loss to negatively affect us for the rest of our lives? Or are we going to accept what we cannot change and grow through the crisis? A wise person once said, "A bend in the road is not the end of the road unless you fail to make the turn."

For our light and momentary troubles are achieving for us an eternal glory that far outweighs them all (2 Cor. 4:17).

Thought for the day: *Why doesn't God see our troubles as permanent?*

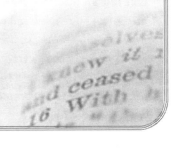

278 THE DAILY DISCIPLER

SURVIVING THE CRISIS

Job 3

Job has suffered the loss of everything except his life. He is in the pit of depression, and he wishes he had never been born. He has not accepted his present condition; instead, he has resigned or given up on life (see Job 3). Since we all experience losses in our lives, we need to learn how to accept what we cannot change and grow through the crisis. How well we handle a crisis will be determined by how we process three mental constructs.

The first is permanence. The speed of recovery is greatly affected by whether we think the consequences of the crisis will have a short-term or long-term negative effect on us. The loss is permanent, but it doesn't have to affect us permanently. There is the potential to grow through every crisis. Suppose your new employer is very irritable. It is a short-term problem if you think that it is just a passing mood and it will have little impact on you. But it is a long-term problem if you think your boss is always irritable. You can respond to this crisis as follows:

"I'm going to ignore him."	That is denial.
"I'm going to be irritable back."	That is anger.
"I'm going to try appeasing him."	That is bargaining.
"I'm stuck with this irritable person whom I can't change."	That is depression.
"I'm going to quit this job."	That is resignation.
"I'm going to love him and learn how to live with him."	That is acceptance.

The second mental construct is pervasiveness. You will recover slowly if you think your whole life has been ruined. If you experience one loss, you are not a loser. If you fail to accomplish one goal, you are not a failure. If you get laid off at work, you are not unemployable.

It is natural to grieve for what we have lost, and grieving is an important part of the recovery process. However, a prolonged depression due to losses signifies an undue and unhealthy attachment to people, places and things that we have no right or ability to control. The martyred missionary Jim Elliot said, "He is no fool who gives up what he cannot keep in order to gain what he cannot lose."

The third mental construct is personalization. Blaming yourself for every loss will keep you in rut. If you experience loss in one area, don't generalize it and create a total crisis. Keep your loss specific. If you experience a crisis today, don't allow it to affect you tomorrow. Keep short accounts. If the world is disintegrating around you, don't accept the blame when it's not appropriate. If you are suffering the consequences of a bad decision, then change what you can, minimize your losses and move on.

Such traumatic losses often cause us to reevaluate who we are, especially if our identity has been tied up with what we have lost—such as when we lose a job or spouse. A crisis can deepen our walk with God and solidify our identity in Christ. Losses also precipitate the need for new relationships and change of scenery. These changes are probably necessary for our growth in Christ, but we may not make them unless forced to do so.

I consider everything a loss compared to the surpassing greatness of knowing Christ Jesus my Lord (Phil. 3:8).

Thought for the day: *What did Paul lose when he encountered God, and why were those losses nothing compared to what he gained?*

THE ELIJAH COMPLEX

1 Kings 19

Elijah was truly a "man of God." He had just witnessed the power of God displayed against the prophets of Baal (see 1 Kings 18:16-45). When Jezebel heard of it, she responded, "May the gods deal with me, be it ever so severely, if by this time tomorrow I do not make your life like that of one of them" (1 Kings 19:2). This incredible man of God was afraid and ran for his life. He left his servant in Beersheba and went a day's journey farther into the desert. This great man of God ran because he believed a lie, just as any one of us can. Then he cried out in despair, " 'I have had enough, LORD,' . . . 'Take my life; I am no better than my ancestors.' Then he lay down under the tree and fell asleep" (vv. 4-5).

Elijah was exhibiting many of the classic signs of depression: He was afraid, fatigued, felt like a helpless failure, isolated and all alone. That can easily happen after a mountaintop experience. Brimming with confidence and flushed with victory, Elijah suddenly found himself vulnerable. Confidence in God can easily turn to self-confidence when we let our guard down. God in His mercy prescribed some food and rest for His discouraged warrior. "All at once an angel touched him and said, 'Get up and eat.' He looked around, and there by his head was a cake of bread baked over hot coals, and a jar of water" (1 Kings 19:5-6).

We can become depressed when our electrolytes are depleted and our bodies are malfunctioning for lack of nutrition, as was probably the case for Elijah. God addressed these deficiencies by prescribing food and rest. Our mental health is dependent upon a proper balance of rest, exercise and diet. In addition, Elijah was probably suffering from postadrenal exhaustion. Our adrenal glands respond to stress by secreting cortisone into our bloodstream. If the stress becomes too great, our adrenal glands can't keep up. Stress becomes distress, and our system breaks down. This often happens to driven people who work until they collapse in exhaustion and depression.

The precipitating cause of Elijah's depression was not physical, however. This faithful servant had always been obedient to God, but now the Lord had asked him twice, "What are you doing here, Elijah?" (1 Kings 19:9,13). Elijah responded:

I have been very zealous for the LORD God Almighty. The Israelites have rejected your covenant, broken down your altars, and put your prophets to death with the sword. I am the only one left, and now they are trying to kill me, too (v. 10).

Elijah ran because he believed a lie, not because God had sent him into the wilderness. Further, Elijah wasn't the only one left—there were 7,000 others who had not bowed their knees to Baal (see v. 18).

God was not asking Elijah (or us) to establish His kingdom program or bring judgment upon those who had not kept His covenant. He was asking Elijah (and us) to trust Him and follow wherever He leads. He will bring judgment in due time, establishing His kingdom—in His way and in His timing. This is neither for us to decide nor for us to accomplish. Although Elijah was very zealous for God's work, he was wrong to assume sole responsibility for getting the job done. Those who buy into the Elijah Complex are vulnerable to the enemy's lies and may end up mentally depressed and physically exhausted.

Elijah was afraid and ran for his life (1 Kings 19:3).

Thought for the day: *Why did this obedient and fearless man suddenly become fearful and run?*

GROWING THROUGH TRIALS

Romans 5:1-5

In the heat of battle, it pays to stand back and put everything in perspective. Will this matter for eternity? What are the long-term consequences? Where is God in the process, and what is He trying to accomplish? That is what Paul is doing in the beginning verses of this chapter (see Rom. 5:1-5). We have been justified, and so in the midst of any trial we have access to God. We can look with confidence to the future because we have hope in God. With that in mind, we can rejoice in our sufferings because we know that there is a divine purpose behind them.

It seems ludicrous to rejoice in our sufferings, but James gives us the same advice.

> Consider it pure joy, my brothers, whenever you face trials of many kinds, because you know that the testing of your faith develops perseverance. Perseverance must finish its work so that you may be mature and complete, not lacking anything (Jas. 1:2-4).

Persevering through trials and tribulations is what develops our character. God's will for our lives is our sanctification (see 1 Thess. 4:3), which is accomplished by the forging of our character through perseverance—and that is where our hope lies. The love of God will never allow us to suffer more than we can endure, and by His grace we can persevere.

Seeing life from our temporal perspective can lead to a false hope. People see their jobs as hopeless so they change jobs; or they see their marriages as hopeless, so they change spouses; or they see their churches as hopeless and so they change churches. Paul and James admonish us to stay on course and grow up. There may be legitimate reasons for us to change jobs or churches. But are we just running away from the pressures of life so that we can avoid our responsibility to grow up? We will have to face the same obstacles again, and each time we run away makes the process harder.

Suppose a husband shared with his pastor that his wife had just left him. How can the pastor minister hope? Saying that together they will win her back is giving a false hope. Neither person has the right or ability to control her. The husband who tries to manipulate, force or coerce her back needs to realize that such behavior is probably what caused her to leave in the first place. It would be better for the pastor to say something like this: "If you haven't made a commitment to be the husband and father that God has called you to be, would you be willing to make that commitment now?" The husband can't change his wife, but he can change himself and that is by far the best way to win her back. Even if she doesn't come back, he can grow through the crisis and be a better person in the future—and that is where his hope lies.

The test of our character is determined by how much or how little it takes to prevent us from becoming the person God created us to be. Character is the primary qualification for Christian leadership. God always places the priority of character before career, and maturity before ministry. If we don't observe that order, He may allow our careers and ministries to suffer in order to establish our character. Yet if we had God's perspective, we would rejoice, because He is in the process of conforming us to His image and that is where our hope lies.

> We also rejoice in our sufferings, because we know that suffering produces perseverance; perseverance, character; and character, hope (Rom. 5:3-4).

Thought for the day: *Why should we rejoice while going through trials and tribulations?*

COMMITMENT TO OVERCOME DEPRESSION

John 5:1-18

The Bible doesn't say what the man's illness was, but the story underscores an important question that Jesus asked: "Do you want to get well?" (John 5:6). Jesus sovereignly healed him, but the cure didn't have anything to do with the man's faith. He only offered an excuse; and when Jesus took that away, the man reported Jesus to the authorities for healing him on the Sabbath. Jesus may or may not heal physical illnesses today as He did in the Gospels, but most psychosomatic illnesses can be cured as follows:[1]

1. Commit yourself to complete recovery. The key to any cure is commitment. That means no excuses for not following through nor blaming someone else. Decide to believe that you can do all things through Christ who strengthens you (see Phil. 4:13) and then do it.

2. Commit yourself to pray first about everything. The first thing a Christian does about anything is pray. The tendency of the western world is to seek every possible natural explanation and cure first. Scripture says that Jesus told us to seek first His kingdom and His righteousness, and "all these things will be given to you as well" (Matt. 6:33).

3. Commit yourself to having an intimate relationship with your heavenly Father. This requires repentance and faith in God. You can resolve your personal and spiritual conflicts by going through the *Steps to Freedom in Christ*. To be mentally healthy, you must have a true understanding of who God is and be rightly related to Him.

4. Commit yourself as a child of God. The second basic standard for mental health is to have a biblical understanding of who you are in Christ and to know what it means to be a child of God. You cannot consistently feel or behave in a way that is inconsistent with what you believe about yourself.

5. Commit your body to God. If the previous four steps do not

cure your psychosomatic illness, then consult a medical doctor for a complete physical examination. There are many forms of biological depression that can be diagnosed and treated. Disorders of the endocrine system can produce symptoms of depression. These include the possibility of low blood sugar, malfunctioning pituitary gland, adrenal exhaustion and problems related to the female reproductive system. Work toward a proper balance of nutrition, exercise and diet. At this stage medication may be necessary to cure the body.

6. Commit yourself to the renewing of your mind. Mental depression stems from a negative view of yourself, your circumstances and the future. These false perceptions can only be overcome as we are transformed by the renewing of our minds (see Rom. 12:2) and by choosing to believe the truth (see Phil. 4:6-9).

7. Commit yourself to good behavior. Make realistic plans to be involved with your family and church members. Live a responsible life by following through on your commitments. Schedule meaningful activities and exercise.

8. Commit yourself to overcome every loss whether real, imagined or threatened. Be aware that abstract losses like reputation, social standing, friendships, etc., are harder to identify. You can choose to overcome every loss by deepening your walk with God, reaffirming who you really are in Christ, growing in character and by developing a more Christian lifestyle.

These things I [Jesus] speak in the world so that the may have My joy made full in themselves (John 17:13).

Thought for the day: *How can you make the joy of the Lord your strength?*

THIRD QUARTER:
LIVING IN CHRIST

SUFFERING FOR RIGHTEOUSNESS' SAKE

Job 1

Suffering is generally understood as the consequence of our own sin or the sin of others, and God allows it for the perfecting of our faith. When David sinned, he felt the heavy hand of God in the form of physical and mental suffering (see Ps. 32:3-5). But God allowed Job to suffer at the hands of Satan, because he was a righteous man (see Job 1:8)—although Job's three friends believed that he was suffering because he had done something wrong.

Believers have always struggled with the question, Why do bad things happen to good people? That question cannot be fully explained without taking into account the evil influences of Satan and his demons who actively oppose the will of God. If God and humanity are the only two players, then one or the other will inevitably have to take the blame for all the suffering in this world. That was the conclusion of Job's wife who responded to his suffering by saying, "Are you still holding on to your integrity? Curse God and die!" (Job 2:9).

The book of Job begins with Satan asking God, "Does Job fear God for nothing?" (Job 1:9). In other words, "Do the covenant children of God love the Lord because of who He is, or do they love God because of His blessings?" God answered by allowing Job to suffer at the hands of Satan. Job's three friends were wrong when they kept insisting that Job was suffering because he had done something wrong. Job made the mistake of defending himself. Job's defense of himself came to an end when God asked, "Who are you to question Me, Job? If I am God, I have the right to do with your life whatever I want" (see Job 38—41). Job agreed, and "the LORD made him prosperous again and gave him twice as much as he had before" (Job. 42:10).

Two valuable lessons are learned from the story of Job. First, we have the assurance that God will deliver us and speak to us in our suffering (see Job 36:15). Second, we have the assurance that God will make it right in the end. Identifying with Christ in this fallen world will include some suffering for the sake of righteousness. "In fact, everyone who wants to live a godly life in Christ Jesus will be persecuted" (2 Tim. 3:12). As children of God we share in His inheritance and His sufferings (see Rom. 8:17). "For just as the sufferings of Christ flow over into our lives, so also through Christ our comfort overflows" (2 Cor. 1:5).

Peter advised us not to be surprised by the painful trials of suffering, but rather rejoice that we are participating in the suffering of Christ (see 1 Peter 4:12-13). We shouldn't assume that others are suffering because they have done something wrong. They may be suffering because they are doing something right. "So then, those who suffer according to God's will should commit themselves to their faithful Creator and continue to do good" (2 Pet. 4:19).

> But those who suffer he delivers in their suffering; he speaks to them in their affliction (Job 36:15).

Thought for the day: *What comfort do you draw from this verse?*

SUFFERING BUILDS CHARACTER

Hebrews 2:9-10

Physical pain is necessary for our survival. If we could not feel pain, our bodies would be covered with scars. Emotional pain is just another form of suffering and is necessary for our growth in Christ. Physical, mental and emotional pain need to be acknowledged and corrective steps taken—or our survival chances are going to decrease. Suffering will certainly get our attention, as it should. Someone once said, "Small trials often make us beside ourselves, but great trials bring us back to ourselves."

Jesus is the greatest example of the reality that suffering is necessary in order to perfect our character. Apart from the suffering He endured to pay the consequences of our sin, suffering produced something in His own life. Scripture says He was made perfect through suffering (see Heb. 2:9-10). "Although he was a son, he learned obedience from what he suffered" (Heb. 5:8). These verses do not suggest that Jesus was disobedient or sinful. Rather, they refer to His growth from infancy to adulthood after He took upon the form of a man. His growth experience through suffering made Him a compassionate High Priest who could identify with and come to the aid of suffering people. The suffering of Jesus teaches us the fullness of what it means to obey our heavenly Father, no matter what the cost. We learn the chain of moral values that develop as a result of adversity. "Because we know that suffering produces perseverance; perseverance, character; and character, hope" (Rom. 5:3).

The process of putting off the old self is painful, because denying ourselves is not easy and there is no painless way to die. To surrender our right to self-govern, which we have stubbornly claimed as our right, is a painful process. Growth pains are an inevitable part of life. Our prayers are heard by our loving Father, but they may not be answered the way we thought, as the unknown author of this poem illustrates:

I asked God for strength, that I might achieve; I was made weak, that I
    might learn humbly to obey.
I asked for health, that I might do greater things; I was given infirmity,
    that I might do better things.

I asked for riches, that I might be happy; I was given poverty, that I
   might be wise.
I asked for power, that I might have the praise of men; I was given
   weakness, that I might feel the need for God.
I asked for all things, that I might enjoy life; I was given life, that I
   might enjoy all things.
I got nothing I asked for; but everything I had hoped for.
Almost despite myself, my unspoken prayers were answered.
I am, among all men, most richly blessed!

> For we do not have a high priest who is unable to sympathize with
> our weaknesses, but we have one who has been tempted in every
> way, just as we are—yet was without sin. Let us then approach the
> throne of grace with confidence, so that we may receive mercy and
> find grace to help us in our time of need (Heb. 4:15-16).

Thought for the day: *How has God made it easier for us to approach Him?*

SUFFERING DRAWS US CLOSER TO GOD

Isaiah 63:9

Our love for God is compromised when we become too attached to the good things He gives us. Suffering helps to strip away any pretense in our relationship with God. It weans us from all that is not God so that we might learn to love our heavenly Father for who He is. Augustine said, "God wants to give us something, but cannot, because our hands are full—there's nowhere for him to put it." Suffering empties our hands so that God can give us the true treasure of life. God knows that the joy of life can only be found in Him. But we may not seek Him as long as we think happiness can be found another way. If our own natural lives remain pleasant, there is no felt reason to surrender them. Suffering makes our own natural lives less agreeable.

We live in a world of moral conflict. The battle between good and evil has brought a suffering that even God shares. He suffers because of what sin has done to His creation. Isaiah said, "In all their distress he too was distressed" (Isa. 63:9). This reality of evil and the true nature of God's love for us would not be known except through the experience of suffering. The only way in which moral evil can enter into the consciousness of the morally good is in the form of suffering. A person who is both evil and happy has no understanding that his actions are not in accord with the moral laws of the universe.

Suffering has a way of binding people together. It provides opportunities for us to minister to each other. Such ministry serves to bring people together and promotes unity among believers and that is what Jesus has prayed for (see John 17:21). "The Father of compassion and the God of all comfort, who comforts us in all our troubles, so that we can comfort those in any trouble with the comfort we ourselves have received from God" (2 Cor. 1:3-4). In the midst or our suffering we need to know that:

1. God is always in control of our suffering. We may never know the full reasons for all the sufferings we endure, but we know that God will use our sufferings for our good and His. God

always has a purpose for what He does and allows.

2. God always has a limit on the amount of suffering He allows for each of us. For instance, Satan could not touch Job's life. Some saints like Job and Paul obviously have broader shoulders that enable them to suffer more for righteousness' sake.

3. God's presence will enable us to withstand the pressure of suffering if we turn to Him. If we cast our cares on Him, He will sustain us (see Ps. 55:22), but He may not remove our suffering until His perfect will is accomplished. Remember, "The will of God will not take us where the grace of God cannot sustain us."

For just as the sufferings of Christ flow over into our lives, so also through Christ our comfort overflows. If we are distressed, it is for your comfort and salvation; if we are comforted, it is for your comfort, which produces in you patient endurance of the same sufferings we suffer. And our hope for you is firm, because we know that just as you share in our sufferings, so also you share in our comfort (2 Cor. 1:5-7).

Thought for today: *How do the sufferings of Christ and our sufferings affect our ability to minister to others?*

GOD'S MINISTRY OF DARKNESS

Isaiah 50:10-11

According to this passage in Isaiah, obedient servants who fear the Lord may find themselves walking in the dark (see Isa. 50:10-11). Isaiah is not talking about the darkness of sin; he is talking about the darkness of uncertainty. In the light you know who your friends and enemies are, and the path before you is clear, as are the obstacles. It is easy to walk in the light, but in the dark every natural instinct tells you to sit down or drop out.

God called Abraham out of Ur to the Promised Land and there He made a covenant with him (see Gen. 12:1-3). God said He would multiply Abraham's descendants as the stars of the sky and the sands of the sea. So Abraham proceeded to live as though God's Word was true, but then came years of darkness. So many years went by that Abraham's barren wife matured beyond the childbearing years. So Abraham thought he would help God fulfill His covenant by creating his own light. Sarai, his wife, supplied the match by encouraging Abraham to go into Hagar, her maidservant (see Gen. 16:1-9). That act of adultery resulted in two races of people, Arab and Jew, and to this day the whole world lies down in torment.

The natural tendency during these times of darkness, when we don't see things God's way, is to do things our way. According to Isaiah, when we create our own light, God allows it, and misery follows it. While other innocent babies were being slaughtered, God ensured the safety and protection of Moses. God's plan was to use Moses to set His people free. Years later, Moses sensed the call of God and felt the burden for his people. He pulled out his sword, killed a man and was exiled to the backside of the desert. Moses walked in darkness for 40 years before God turned on the light in the form of a burning bush (see Exod. 2—3).

During these times of darkness and doubt, Isaiah admonishes us to keep on walking by faith in the light of previous revelation. Never doubt in darkness what God has clearly revealed in the light, and be mindful that is often the darkest before the dawn. When you are inclined to believe the night will never end, consider the words of Isaiah: "Someone calls to me from Seir, 'Watchman, what is left of the night? Watchman, what is left of the night?' The watchman replied, 'Morning is coming, but also the night'" (Isa. 21:11-12). No matter how dark the night or how despairing the circumstances, morning comes. When the temptation to create your own light is overwhelming, just hold on to the truth that this too will pass. During these winter seasons of your soul, you should avoid making major decisions. Disastrous choices are made by those who don't wait upon the Lord.

His ministry of darkness is a lesson in trust. We learn to rely on Him during the hard times. Yes, we thank God for the mountain top experiences, but our growth takes place in the valleys.

> I form the light and create darkness, I bring prosperity and create disaster; I, the LORD, do all these things (Isa. 45:7).

Thought for the day: *What should you do when God allows the darkness to come upon you?*

GOD'S MINISTRY OF REST

Exodus 33:12-14

Moses had no small task ahead of him. He had led the Israelites out of bondage in Egypt, but now he had the overwhelming task of leading them through the wilderness to the Promised Land. God guided them with a cloud by day and fire by night, and He supplied manna from heaven for their nourishment. But the desert was stark, and there were no modern-day camping accommodations for 5 million people who would eventually wander the desert for 40 years! Realizing the enormity of the task, Moses had two requests of God: "Who is going with me?" and "Let me know your ways" (see Exod. 33:12-13). Those may be the two most important issues in every Christian's journey. "The LORD replied, 'My Presence will go with you, and I will give you rest'" (Exod. 33:14).

Guiding 5 million complaining people across a barren desert for 40 years is not anybody's idea of a rest. But the only way to evaluate the quality of a rest is to determine how one feels at the end. It was said of Moses 40 years later, when he looked into the Promised Land: "Moses was a hundred and twenty years old when he died, yet his eyes were not weak nor his strength gone" (Deut. 34:7). God had given Moses rest! Biblical rest is neither a cessation of labor nor the abdication of responsibility. Biblical rest is living God's way by faith empowered by His presence. The alternative is to live our way in our own strength, which leads to burnout.

Under the Old Covenant, God provided rest for His people by setting aside one day per week when no work was to be done. Even the land was to lie dormant every seventh year. This need for rest is still necessary for our bodies, but the Law was a shadow of something far greater to come. In Christ we find rest for our souls. Jesus said, "Come to me, all you who are weary and burdened, and I will give you rest" (Matt. 11:28). Jesus is inviting us to come into His presence and learn from Him. We will find rest for our souls because His ways are not hard and His burden is light (see Matt. 11:29-30).

"Therefore, since the promise of entering his rest still stands, let us be careful that none of you be found to have fallen short of it. For we also have had the gospel preached to us. . . . Now we who have believed enter that rest"

(Heb. 4:1-3). God's work is finished and we have the privilege to rest in the finished work of Christ. "There remains, then, a Sabbath-rest for the people of God; for anyone who enters God's rest also rests from his own work, just as God did from his. Let us, therefore, make every effort to enter that rest" (Heb. 4:9-11).

> My soul finds rest in God alone; my salvation comes from him. He alone is my rock and my salvation; he is my fortress, I will never be shaken (Ps. 62:1-2).

Thought for the day: *Where and how can we find rest for our souls?*

OVERCOMING SEXUAL BONDAGE

2 Samuel 13

It is no sin to be attracted to the opposite sex. But innocent attraction can soon become infatuation that leads to mental obsession. David saw that Bathsheba was very beautiful, but he didn't look for God's way of escape. He stepped over a moral boundary when he sent someone to find out about her (see 2 Sam. 11:2-3). David's weakness may have contributed to his son Amnon's obsession with Tamar, "the beautiful sister of Absalom son of David" (2 Sam. 13:1). Solomon warned in Proverbs 6:25-26, "Do not lust in your heart after her beauty or let her captivate you with her eyes, for the prostitute reduces you to a loaf of bread, and the adulteress preys upon your very life." The sexual fantasy in Amnon's mind had been played out so many times that he was physically sick.

It is no sin to be tempted; and when we are tempted, God provides a way of escape (see 1 Cor. 10:13). But we miss that opportunity when we continue to entertain lustful thoughts in our mind. James says, "But each one is tempted when, by his own evil desire, he is dragged away and enticed. Then, after desire has conceived, it gives birth to sin; and sin, when it is full-grown, gives birth to death" (1:14-15). Amnon had probably carried on a sexual affair with Tamar for some time in his own mind. His obsessive thoughts screamed for expression. So Amnon and his friend Jonadab concocted a plan to get Tamar into Amnon's bed (see 2 Sam. 13:3-5).

Once a plan to fulfill the demands of lust is set in motion, it can seldom be stopped. Amnon had lost control; and where there is no self-control, all reason is gone. Amnon's sexual obsession had reduced him to a loaf of bread—powerless to stop the runaway train of his desires. Tamar tried to reason with Amnon, but he was "like one of the wicked fools of Israel" (v. 13). Amnon violated her with no regard for the damage it would do to either of them. "Then Amnon hated her with intense hatred. In fact, he hated her more than he had loved her" (v. 15).

People in bondage hate the sin that controls them. After consuming their fill, alcoholics throw their bottle against the wall in disgust, only to buy another when the cravings return. Lust cannot be satisfied. The more you feed it, the more it grows. In early development, one can be sexually stimulated by a sensual look or simple touch. The rush of a lustful thought or sexual encounter leads to a euphoric experience that doesn't last. A sense of guilt and shame follows, but inwardly there is the desire to have that euphoric experience again. Every repeated exposure leads to greater sexual degradation in order to reach that same euphoric experience. The downward spiral of guilt and shame leads to greater bondage, sickness and death.

In the year 2004, half of those who are in their 20s have a sexually transmitted disease that is essentially incurable. Type the word "sex" into an Internet search engine, and you will get 180 million hits. Half the people who stay in hotels will watch pay-per-view adult entertainment. There are 800 million DVDs or VHS adult movies available for a population of 300 million people.

Do not lust in your heart after her beauty or let her captivate you with her eyes (Prov. 6:25).

Thought for the day: *How can you keep lust from consuming you?*

FOOLISH THINKING

Proverbs 7:6-27

The simple young man in this story lacked judgment (see Prov. 7:7). He had no idea that his naiveté would cost him his life (see vv. 22-23). The woman who seduced him was dressed like a prostitute, supposedly religious (see v. 14) and married (see v. 19). The wise man would have seen the danger and discerned immediately that her intentions were not good. The simple person doesn't consider the consequences of sin. The fool wants only immediate gratification. At the beginning of the twenty-first century, acquired immune deficiency syndrome (AIDS) is the most incurable disease in the world, but it is easily the most preventable. All you have to do is abstain. Yet millions are dying every year of AIDS. To throw away your life, career, marriage and reputation for a few minutes of sexual pleasure is totally irrational.

Jesus tells us,

> You have heard that it was said, "Do not commit adultery." But I tell you that anyone who looks at a woman lustfully has already committed adultery with her in his heart. If your right eye causes you to sin, gouge it out and throw it away. It is better for you to lose one part of your body than for your whole body to be thrown into hell. And if your hand causes you to sin, cut it off and throw it away (Matt. 5:27-30).

Jesus is graphically illustrating the seriousness of sexual sin, and we should be willing to sacrifice whatever it takes to keep from paying a far greater cost for the inevitable consequences of adultery, disease and death.

Now we all know that our eyes and hands are not the culprits when we sin. We could all be cutting off body parts, and we still would not have solved the problem. Jesus explains in the previous verse that if we have looked lustfully at another, we have *already* committed adultery in our hearts. The looking is the evidence, not the cause. In the Sermon on the Mount, Jesus teaches that genuine righteousness is a matter of the heart, and not the result of external conformity. "For I tell you that unless your righteousness surpasses that of the Pharisees and the teachers of the law, you will certainly not enter the kingdom of heaven" (Matt. 5:20). The prevention of murder (see Matt. 5:21-26) and adultery (see Matt. 5:27-32) require a transformation of our hearts and a renewing of our minds.

Salvation does not improve our old nature. Salvation makes us a new creation in Christ and a partaker of the divine nature (see 2 Pet. 1:4). "Those who belong to Christ Jesus have crucified the sinful nature with its passions and desires" (Gal. 5:24). In Christ we have the potential not to sin, but there are three requirements. First, we must choose to believe the truth and repent of our sins. Second, to keep from committing sexual sins, we have to live by the Spirit and not carry out the desires of the sinful nature (see Gal. 5:16). Third, we must renew our minds and "take captive every thought to make it obedient to Christ" (2 Cor. 10:5).

Since we live by the Spirit, let us keep in step with the Spirit (Gal. 5:25).

Thought for the day: *How can we practically keep in step with the Spirit when we are tempted?*

THE ENTRAPMENT OF SIN

2 Chronicles 29

The revival under Hezekiah is a model of repentance for the Church and a foretaste of the Gospel. First, He consecrated the priests and cleaned out the Temple (see 2 Chron. 29:15-16). As New Testament believers, we are priests, and our bodies are temples of God. Then Hezekiah ordered the sin offering. The sin offering was a blood offering only. The carcass of the sacrificed animal was disposed of outside the walls of the city. Jesus is our sin offering. After shedding His blood, His body was entombed outside the walls of the city. Then Hezekiah ordered the burnt offering, which sacrificed the whole body of the animal. When Hezekiah ordered the burnt offering, the music in the temple began (see v. 27). In the New Testament, we are the burnt offering: "Therefore, I urge you, brothers, in view of God's mercy, to offer your bodies as living sacrifices, holy and pleasing to God—this is your spiritual act of worship" (Rom. 12:1). It is not enough to know that our sins are forgiven. We must yield ourselves to Him as *living* sacrifices, then the music begins in our temples as He fills us with His Spirit. We will, "Speak to one another with psalms, hymns and spiritual songs. Sing and make music in your heart to the Lord" (Eph. 5:19).

As believers we are to consider ourselves to be alive in Christ and dead to sin. "Therefore do not let sin reign in your mortal body so that you obey its evil desires" (Rom. 6:12). That is our responsibility; and the next verse tells us how, including one negative instruction and two positive instructions:

Do not offer the parts of your body to sin, as instruments of wickedness, but rather offer yourselves to God, as those who have been brought from death to life; and offer the parts of your body to him as instruments of righteousness (Rom. 6:13).

Personal revival and victory come when we clean out the temple through genuine repentance, choosing to consecrate ourselves *and* our bodies to God as instruments of righteousness.

Every sexual sin involves using our bodies as instruments of unrighteousness. When we do, we allow sin to reign in our mortal bodies. Thank God our sins are forgiven in Christ, but the music won't begin in our temple until we fully repent. Confession is the first step in repentance, but that by itself will not resolve the entrapment of sin. We need to renounce every use of our bodies as instruments of unrighteousness and then submit our bodies to God as living sacrifices. The process is complete when we have fully submitted to God *and* resisted the devil (see Jas. 4:7). See the *Steps to Freedom in Christ* for a comprehensive process of repentance. If we have dealt with sin's entrapment and yielded our bodies to God as living sacrifices (Rom. 12:1), then the process of being transformed by the renewing of our minds according to Romans 12:2 is possible.

> What is the source of quarrels and conflicts among you? Is not the source your pleasures that wage war in your members? (Jas. 4:1, *NASB*).

Thought for the day: *Why does committing a sexual sin allow sin to reign in our mortal bodies, and why won't simple confession resolve it?*

SEXUAL BONDING

1 Corinthians 6:9-20

Some Corinthians believed that the body was not important since it is transitory. Therefore, they thought that eating food and being promiscuous had no bearing on their spiritual life. Paul counters by saying, "The body is not meant for sexual immorality, but for the Lord, and the Lord for the body" (1 Cor. 6:13). As believers, our bodies are temples of God and members of Christ Himself. We have been purchased by the blood of the Lamb; therefore, our body, soul and spirit belong to Him.

Every Christian is united with God and one in spirit with Him. It creates, therefore, a tremendous sense of inner conflict to be spiritually united with God and, at the same time, be physically united to a prostitute. According to Paul, two become one flesh as the result of a sexual union (see 1 Cor. 6:16). This does not mean they are married, since marriage is a mutual commitment made in accordance with the laws of the State. For believers, marriage is also a spiritual union as they become one in Christ. Becoming one flesh in this passage means a man and a woman have joined together physically. It also implies that some kind of immoral bond has taken place. Paul explained that using our bodies as instruments of unrighteousness allows sin to reign in our mortal bodies (see Rom. 6:12-14).

The entrapments of sexual sins are manifested in commonly observed ways. First, promiscuous sex before marriage leads to a lack of sexual fulfillment after marriage. Second, a believer who is sexually united with an unbeliever becomes bonded in such a way that the Christian can't break away without genuine and complete repentance. Third, when a believer has been violated sexually before marriage against her will (rape or incest), it undermines her ability to perform freely in marriage. Women who have been sexually violated have been left with the impression that sex is dirty, and they can't stand to be touched, even by their spouses. Someone has used their body as an instrument of unrighteousness and violated their temple. But the opposite effect results for those who voluntarily had sex with family members before marriage. These people can't be sexually satisfied, and they continuously seek sexual fulfillment with multiple partners.

There are no guarantees that you will never be sexually violated in your lifetime. But the gospel ensures you that no one has to remain a victim forever. You can renounce that sexual use of your body with the other person, ask God to break that bond and then commit your body to God as a living sacrifice. And for the sake of your own freedom and relationship with God, you need to forgive that person who violated you. (See the *Steps to Freedom in Christ* for a complete process.)

People are deceived if they think they can sin sexually and suffer no eternal consequences. Secret sin on Earth is open scandal in heaven. Establishing the concept of *adults only* in America has implied that there is a different moral standard for adults than there is for children, which is not true. If something is morally wrong for children, it is morally wrong for adults.

> Flee from sexual immorality. All other sins a man commits are outside his body, but he who sins sexually sins against his own body (1 Cor. 6:18).

Thought for the day: *Why are sexual sins in a class by themselves?*

SIN DWELLING IN YOU

Romans 7:14-25

Even though Christians should consider themselves to be alive in Christ and dead to sin (see Rom. 6:11), Paul reveals the ongoing struggle that we have in overcoming the power of sin. The personal pronoun and verb "I am," taken together in Romans 7:14, imply that Paul is talking about his present Christian experience. Stating that he agrees with the law of God (see v. 16), and delights in God's law in his inner being (see v. 22) reveals his status as a true believer. Notice that every disposition of Paul's heart (mind, will and emotion) is directed toward God. The passage illustrates that human effort to fulfill the law is powerless to overcome the sin that dwells within us. Taking into account the larger context, the passage also illustrates what it would be like if we allowed sin to reign in our mortal bodies (see Rom. 6:12).

Paul knows what is right and wants to do what is right, but for some reason he cannot (see Rom. 7:15-16). Paul isn't the only player in this battle, however. There is sin living in him (see v. 17). He said, "I know that nothing good lives in me, that is, in my sinful [flesh]" (v. 18). Paul is not saying he is no good. He is saying "nothing good lives in" me. It's like he has a sliver in his finger—it is a "no good" thing in Paul, but it is not he himself. Paul carefully separates himself from the sin, even though it is his responsibility to keep sin from reigning in his mortal body (see Rom. 6:12). Evil is right there with him (see Rom. 7:21), but he does not consider himself evil.

Even though Paul feels wretched (miserable, not sinful), he inwardly delights in God's law (see Rom. 7:22). The true believer may feel defeated and discouraged, because they are not seeing the victory, but they know what is right in the inner person. The problem is, the law of sin is at work in their physical body, and it is waging war against the law of the mind. The battle is in the mind. The present-day struggle with eating disorders is an illustration of this mental battle. Eating disorders (anorexia and bulimia) have little to do with food. The problem is one of deception. Those struggling with eating disorders are obsessed with their bodies and appearance. Many will secretly cut themselves, defecate and purge. They sense there is evil present in them, but they are deceived as to what it is. Defecating, purging or cutting will not eliminate the evil that is present in them. To win the battle for their minds, they need to renounce the lie that cutting, defecating and purging are effective means of cleansing themselves, and announce that Christ is the only means by which we can be cleansed.

If we are losing the battle for our minds and using our bodies as instruments of unrighteousness, who will rescue us from our bodies of death? Jesus will! He came to set the captives free and bind up the brokenhearted. Renouncing the sinful uses of our bodies and then submitting them to God as living sacrifices lay the foundation for the transformation that comes from renewing of our minds.[1]

> Through Christ Jesus the law of the Spirit of life set me free from the law of sin and death (Rom. 8:2).

Thought for the day: *Since there is a law of sin and death that cannot be done away with, how are we to overcome them?*

UNDERSTANDING CHEMICAL ADDICTION

Proverbs 23:29-35

Some people "linger over wine" (Prov. 23:30), because they want to get rid of their inhibitions so they can party. Others turn to alcohol and drugs as a means of coping. Some rely on chemicals to give them some relief from their physical and emotional pain. They feel pain, so they reach for the pills. People feel down, so they do something to pick themselves up. They feel stressed out, so they do something to calm themselves down. It worked before, so it will work again. Many people have trained themselves to depend upon chemicals to pick them up, to stop the pain, to soothe the nerves and to feel good. Chemical users feel the rush of the onset reaction and mellow out. The resulting euphoric experience doesn't last, however. When the effects wear off, the guilt, fear and shame become more and more pronounced with each successive use. Occasional use soon becomes a habit, a means of coping.

Feeling guilty about their behavior may cause some to drink surreptitiously. Because of shame, they leave their familiar surroundings to drink or use where no one knows them. It takes more and more alcohol or a greater fix to reach the original high. With the habit comes a greater tolerance for the drug of choice. Greater consumption will never get users back to their first euphoric experience. The lows keep getting lower and lower when the effects of the drug wear off. No matter what drug they try or how often they use, it's never enough. For chemical addicts the loss of control robs them of their ability to live responsible lives. Financial problems develop as they struggle to support their habit.

The downward spiral of addiction of users leads them to greater immorality, and their sense of worth plummets. They perceive themselves as disgusting. Their eating and grooming habits deteriorate, as does their health. The vast majority of chemical abusers are also sexually addicted. They withdraw socially, not wanting their weaknesses to be seen. They fear being publicly humiliated or exposed. They become paranoid about people looking at them or talking about them. They have no mental peace. Condemning thoughts haunt them day and night. They begin to hallucinate (see Prov. 23:33). The only way to silence the voices is to continue drinking or continue using. Solomon describes the numbness of those who hit the bottom. "'They hit me,' you will say, 'but I'm not hurt! They beat me, but I don't feel it! When will I wake up so I can find another drink?'" (v. 35).

Admitting you have a problem is the first step in overcoming any addiction. Those who think they can stop drinking or using can only prove it to themselves by doing so. If you find that you can't stop, then you know you need a power greater than yourself. In Christ you have power over sin, and He alone has the capacity to meet all your needs.

> Wine is a mocker and beer a brawler; whoever is led astray by them is not wise (Prov. 20:1).

Thought for the day: *Is it wise to see the results of chemical addiction and proceed to drink excessively or use drugs anyway?*

OVERCOMING ADDICTION

Titus 3

"At one time we too were foolish, disobedient, deceived and enslaved by all kinds of passions and pleasures" (Titus 3:3). Our foolishness is evident when we think that we can overcome our enslavement to sin by human effort or by the strict enforcement of some well-intentioned program. No program can set anyone free, only Christ can do that. The key to overcoming any addiction is for us to get out from under the law and into the grace of God. Just trying to stop sinning will never work. If abstinence were the goal, then Ephesians 5:18 would read, "Do not get drunk with wine, therefore stop drinking!" Paul's answer is to be filled with the Holy Spirit. "So I say, live by the Spirit, and you will not gratify the desires of the sinful nature" (Gal. 5:16).

Before we come to Christ, we develop certain flesh patterns as a means of relating to others, dealing with pain, coping with stress and trying to succeed—or simply survive. Some will turn to alcohol and drugs. Taking away the chemical will be met with resistance, because that has been their means of coping. They become miserable "dry drunks," with glaring needs and many unresolved conflicts. Turning to chemicals to deal with their problems also arrests their mental and emotional development. They mask their problems rather than finding biblical solutions and growing through the crisis.

The first step is to admit we have a problem and come to Christ. "But when the kindness and love of God our Savior appeared, he saved us, not because of righteous things we have done, but because of his mercy" (Titus 3:4). We don't change in order to come to Christ. We come to Christ in order to change. Those who are "enslaved by all kinds of passions and pleasures" (v. 3) need the support of the Christian community where their needs can be met through their relationship with Christ and His body. That is why, "Our people must learn to devote themselves to doing what is good, in order that they may provide for daily necessities and not live unproductive lives" (v. 14). Their need for eternal life, identity, acceptance, security and significance can only be met in Christ. In Christ they are not alcoholics or addicts—they are children of God.

The next step is to resolve their personal and spiritual conflicts. See the

Steps to Freedom in Christ for the complete process. Through this process, addicts establish a righteous relationship with God and resist the influence of the devil. Those who struggle with addictive behavior have no mental peace and are being deceived (see Titus 3:3). Eliminating the accusing, tempting and blasphemous thoughts is necessary for their recovery. They need to know the truth that will set them free and start them on the path of sanctification. The final step is to be involved in trusting and accountable relationships. They need to cut off destructive relationships and behaviors and start living responsible lives in a supportive Christian community.[1]

> "Let us eat and drink for tomorrow we die." Do not be misled: "Bad company corrupts good character." Come back to your senses as you ought, and stop sinning (1 Cor. 15:32-34).

Thought for the day: *Why must we cut off relationships that are not healthy?*

OVERCOMER'S COVENANT

Revelation 21:6-8

To experience your freedom in Christ, make the following covenant with God to overcome any habitual sins in your life; and if necessary, do it daily until recovery is complete:

1. I know that I cannot save myself, nor set myself free by my own efforts and resources. Therefore, I place all my trust and confidence in the Lord, and I put no confidence in the flesh. When tempted to live my life independent of God, I will declare that apart from Christ I can do nothing.

2. I know that rebellion is as the sin of witchcraft, and insubordination is as iniquity and idolatry. Therefore, I consciously choose to submit to God and resist the devil. I will deny myself, pick up my cross daily and follow Jesus.

3. I know that God is opposed to the proud but gives grace to the humble. Therefore, I choose to humble myself before the mighty hand of God in order that He may exalt me at the proper time.

4. I know the law is unable to impart life or give me victory over sin. Therefore, by the grace of God, I choose to believe that I am alive in Christ and dead to sin. I commit myself to walk by faith in the power of the Holy Spirit.

5. I know that my actions don't determine who I am, but who I am does determine what I do. Therefore, I choose to believe the truth that I am now a child of God and am unconditionally loved and accepted.

6. As a child of God, I know that I am under the New Covenant of grace. Therefore, I choose to believe that sin is no longer master over me. I am spiritually alive, and there is no condemnation for those who are in Christ Jesus.

7. I know that I have harmfully programmed my mind and used my body as an instrument of unrighteousness. Therefore, I renounce every unrighteous use of my body. I submit my body to God as a living sacrifice, and I commit myself to be trans-

formed by the renewing of my mind.

8. I know that my thoughts have not been pure. Therefore, I commit myself to take every thought captive to the obedience of Christ, and choose to think upon that which is true, honorable, right, pure and lovely.

9. I know that I will face many trials and tribulations. Therefore, I commit myself to grow through difficult times believing that I can do all things through Christ who strengthens me.

10. I know that it is more blessed to give than to receive. Therefore, I choose to adopt the attitude of Christ, which was to do nothing from selfishness or empty conceit. With humility of mind I will regard others as more important than myself; and I will not merely look out for my own personal interests, but also the interest of others.

So then, those who suffer according to God's will should commit themselves to their faithful Creator and continue to do good (1 Pet. 4:19).

Thought for the day: *It has been said that the key to any cure is commitment. Why is this so?*

DISCIPLINE YOURSELF FOR GODLINESS

Daniel 1

Many recovery ministries and diet plans fail, because they are based on a law concept rather than grace. Just trying to stop drinking alcohol, taking drugs and eating certain foods that you crave has not proven to be very successful. Abstinence isn't easier if those in authority require you to eat food and drink wine that is forbidden by God, as was the case for Daniel. Rather than just rebel against the king and put the king's official in a tight spot, Daniel suggested a creative alternative. As a result, the official saved face, the king was pleased, and Daniel was healthier (see Dan. 1:8-20).

The secular world says, "Work the program, the program works." There is no program that can set you free. Trying to follow a law-based program that encourages abstinence is like trying to get an old bone away from a dog. If you try to grab it, you will have a dogfight. But if you throw the dog a steak, it will spit out the old bone. The gospel is a steak served on a platter of grace.

Faith-based programs focus on teaching the truth that sets us free. No matter how serious the addiction, true believers are still children of God who are alive in Christ and dead to sin. Believers are not addicts, alcoholics, coaddicts and coalcoholics; they are children of God, and their victory is found in their identity and position in Christ. It is counterproductive to label struggling Christians with a negative failure identity.

To believe that an alcoholic will always be an alcoholic or to believe that a sinner will always be a sinner is a denial of the gospel. On the other hand, the alcoholic and addict cannot deny their own sin if they want to experience the grace of God. Once they acknowledge their sin and invite Christ into their lives, they have been born again. And every born-again believer is a new creation in Christ. It is far better for the Christian to say, "I am a child of God who struggles with alcohol or drugs, but I am learning what it means to be alive and free in Christ."

Disciplining ourselves to abstain from things that are bad for us will not prove to be effective, but disciplining ourselves for the sake of godliness will be profitable now and for all eternity. "For physical training is of some value, but godliness has value for all things, holding promises for both the present life and the life to come" (1 Tim. 4:8).

Righteous people don't focus on what they shouldn't be doing, they focus on who they are in Christ and what they should be doing. "For though a righteous man falls seven times, he rises again" (Prov. 24:16). When they fall, righteous people don't say, "I'm a hopeless failure who was never called to walk." They say, "Lord, I fell again. Thank You for Your forgiveness. I'm going to get back up and learn to live by faith in the power of the Holy Spirit so that I don't have to fall again." Like Daniel, they also have creative alternatives they can easily choose when tempted to sin.

Dear friends, now we are children of God, and what we will be has not yet been made known. But we know that when he appears, we shall be like him, for we shall see him as he is. Everyone who has this hope in him purifies himself, just as he is pure (1 John 3:2-3).

Thought for the day: *Why is it so important to know who we are in Christ?*

ACCOUNTABILITY

1 Thessalonians 2:5-12

If we are going to live a righteous life, we need to be accountable to God first and then one another. We will all give an account to God some day whether we want to or not (see 2 Cor. 5:10). It is better to be honest with God now, receive His forgiveness, and live in conscious moral agreement with Him. "But if we walk in the light, as he is in the light, we have fellowship with one another, and the blood of Jesus, his Son, purifies us from all sin" (1 John 1:7). Notice that the fellowship is not only with God, but one another.

Consider the following four words and their order: "authority," "accountability," "affirmation" and "acceptance." From which end of that list did Jesus initiate His relationship to us? Did Jesus ever appeal to His divine status in the Gospels in order to bring us into accountability? He did just the opposite. First came the acceptance: "When we were still powerless, Christ died for the ungodly" (Rom. 5:6). Then came the affirmation: "Yet to all who received him . . . he gave the right to become children of God" (John 1:12).

When authority figures demand accountability without affirmation and acceptance, they will never get it. People will give some external accountability under duress, but they will not share intimately what is going on inside. But when people know they are accepted and affirmed by the authority figures, they will choose to be accountable to them. Paul could have asserted his authority since he was an apostle, but he chose instead to be gentle among them, "like a mother caring for her little children" (1 Thess. 2:7). Not only did he share the gospel with the Thessalonians, he also shared his own life.

This principle is true in our homes. When distraught parents demand to know where their children have been, their children will likely respond, "I was out!" When asked what they were doing, the children will say, "Nothing!" Nobody will openly be accountable to others unless he or she is first assured of his or her acceptance and affirmation.

We need to follow the Lord's example when it comes to trying to parent, disciple or counsel others: If we confess to God, He forgives and cleanses us (see 1 John 1:9). Those we are in authority over need to know that they are loved and accepted—unconditionally. Only then can they fully trust us. If those we are trying to help cannot share intimately with us, then we will never know how to help them. But we may be the reason they aren't sharing.

Those who are struggling to overcome addictive behaviors can always go to God and receive mercy and find grace to help in time of need. Their recovery process will be greatly helped if they have at least one person who will accept and affirm them no matter what is shared. If we want to be like Christ, then we ought to be able to say to our children, to those whom we disciple or to those we counsel: "There isn't anything you could share with me that would cause me to love you less."

> Therefore each of you must put off falsehood and speak truthfully
> to his neighbor, for we are all members of one body (Eph. 4:25).

Thought for the day: *Why can't we be honest with each other in our families and ministries?*

GROWING THROUGH COMMITTED RELATIONSHIPS

Titus 2

The sanctifying process is primarily worked out in our lives through committed relationships for two reasons. First, people can put on a public face, giving others a distorted perception of who they are; but they can't consistently do that at home. Their spouses and children will see right through them. Second, marriage and family relationships (and in Paul's letter, the slave-master relationship) have always been considered lifetime commitments. Rather than run away from the pressures of living together, we are supposed to stay committed and grow up. Where better are we going to learn to love one another, accept one another, forgive one another and bear with one another? Notice that Titus chapter 2 begins with an appeal for sound doctrine and ends with appeal to godliness (see vv. 1,12-14). Within that context Paul discusses the family and social relationships, just as he does in Ephesians and Colossians.

It is critically important to distinguish between who we are in Christ and our role responsibilities in life. When Paul led the runaway slave to Christ, he sent Onesimus back to his earthly master. Paul appealed to Philemon to receive Onesimus as a brother in Christ (see Philem. 10-11). In the time of Christ, a slave was more like a lifetime employee, and a slave often lived better than the self-employed who were quite poor. In the case of Onesimus, being a slave was only his social role; he was first and foremost a child of God. This distinction can be clearly seen in Colossians 3:11,22: In verse 11 Paul says in Christ there is neither slave or free; then in verse 22 he talks about the role responsibility of slaves.

The same truth holds for husbands and wives. Husbands are to respect their wives as heirs with them of the gracious gift of life (see 1 Pet. 3:7). In other words, Christian wives are children of God and equal in status with their Christian husbands. But they don't have the same calling in life. In our passage for today, Paul gives specific instructions for older men, older women, younger women, young men and slaves; he concludes by admonishing all to live godly lives (see Titus 2).

In a general sense, Paul's Epistles are divided into halves. The first half of each epistle is often considered theological, and the second half is practical. The tendency is to skip the first half and look to the second half for practical instruction for daily living. The result is a subtle form of Christian behaviorism: "You shouldn't do that; you should do this. Or that isn't the best way to do it; here is a better way." Committed Christians will try the best they can, but often fail or burnout trying.

Why isn't it working? Because they have not first been established in Christ. If we can get believers to enter into the first half of Paul's Epistles, they will be firmly rooted in Christ. Then they will be able to supernaturally live according to the second half.

> Therefore, as God's chosen people, holy and dearly loved, clothe yourselves with compassion, kindness, humility, gentleness and patience. Bear with each other and forgive whatever grievances you may have against one another (Col. 3:12-13).

Thought for the day: *Why did God intend for these character qualities to be worked out in our families and jobs?*

MARRIAGE, A COVENANT RELATIONSHIP

Malachi 2:13-16

The Lord wasn't pleased with the false worship of His covenant people and He explains why:

> You ask "Why?" It is because the LORD is acting as the witness between you and the wife of your youth, because you have broken faith with her, though she is your partner, the wife of your marriage covenant. Has not the LORD made them one? In flesh and spirit they are his. And why one? Because he was seeking godly offspring. So guard yourself in your spirit, and do not beak faith with the wife of your youth. "I hate divorce," says the LORD God of Israel (Mal. 2:14-16).

Divorcées hate divorce as well. Nobody feels good when they fail to keep their commitments. Marriage is like gluing two pieces of paper together. Any attempt to separate them leaves both sheets damaged. Each spouse has been badly wounded—and the children of divorce suffer as well. So God knew what He was doing when He established marriage as a lifetime covenant. Unless abuse is involved, the permanence of marriage protects the spouses and creates a healthy, stable environment in which to raise children. And God is seeking godly offspring that comes from a marriage between a man and woman who honor Him.

There are only two covenant relationships in this present age. Both are based on God's Word and rooted in His character. The first and foremost is our New Covenant relationship with God. The second is the marriage between a man and a woman. All other meaningful relationships are contractual or mutually convenient. Two people can have a covenant relationship with God, and consequently have fellowship or spiritual kinship one with the other. But they don't have a covenant relationship with each other unless they are married. While contractual relationships protect all parties in case one should default, marriage is not a contract that permits one spouse to leave when the other doesn't fulfill his or her expectations.

A covenant is a promise to fulfill irrespective of the other person involved and made to last regardless of circumstances. Wedding vows are a covenant commitment to stay faithful as a husband or wife, for better or for worse, for richer or for poorer, in sickness and in health, until death separates the two. What makes a marriage relationship unique is commitment. What makes a marriage relationship great is love, understanding and forgiveness. In marriage, a man and wife become one in Christ, and together they help each other conform to His image.

In Matthew 19:3-12, the Lord admonishes the Pharisees who had lost their commitment to stay married. They didn't want to commit adultery since that was a capital offense under the law, so they were divorcing their wives for any little reason (see also Matt. 5:31-32). They were actually proliferating adultery since they had no biblical grounds for divorce. Jesus said, "I tell you that anyone who divorces his wife, except for marital unfaithfulness, and marries another woman commits adultery" (Matt. 19:9).

> For this reason a man will leave his father and mother and be united to his wife, and the two will become one flesh. So they are no longer two, but one (Matt. 19:5-6).

Thought for the day: *In what way are a husband and a wife one?*

SEXUALITY IN THE END TIMES

1 Corinthians 7

The background for Paul's teaching on sexuality is his belief that the present form of the world was passing away, that the Second Coming of Christ was near (see 1 Cor. 7:29-31) and that life would get very distressful (see v. 26). Whether single, betrothed, married to another believer, married to a nonbeliever, in a difficult marriage or having been divorced or widowed—it is amazing how valuable and relevant his advice is to us who continue to live in the Last Days before the coming of the Lord.

Paul's main concern, no matter what our matrimonial state, was to secure our undistracted devotion to the Lord (see v. 35). To that end, Paul urges single people never to put their desire for marriage higher than their desire to serve God (see v. 26) and to view their singleness as a gift and perhaps a lifelong calling from God (see v. 7). He realizes that Christians are going to be attracted to people of the opposite sex and tempted into immorality (see vv. 1-2), so he places boundaries on available partners and on behavior (see v. 34). First, believers should not marry unbelievers (see 2 Cor. 6:14-16). He argues that the righteous have nothing in common with the unrighteous. They would be unequally yoked with different values, standards and direction in life. Spiritually, they are incompatible. Second, for the sake of Christian ministry, "It is good for a man not to marry. But since there is so much immorality, each man should have his own wife, and each woman her own husband" (1 Cor. 7:1-2).

To those already married, Paul says marriage is a gift and calling from God (see v. 7). They are not to withhold themselves from each other sexually. Their bodies not only belong to themselves but also to each other for the purpose of fulfilling their sexual needs. On the other hand, no spouse can satisfy the other spouse's lust. That can only be resolved in their relationship with God. Neither spouse has the right to violate the other person's conscience or defile them physically in any way since their bodies are the temples of God. "Marriage should be honored by all, and the marriage bed kept pure, for God will judge the adulterer and all the sexually immoral" (Heb. 13:4). Sexual intimacy and fulfillment in marriage can only happen in the context of mutually shared love and trust.

Paul advises Christian couples not to separate; but if they do, they must remain unmarried and work toward reconciliation. There are times when a relationship can be so strained that separation may be necessary for the good of the family. Ideally, they should stay together and work it out; but if one spouse becomes physically or mentally abusive, it may be advisable to separate, but not divorce. Scripture teaches that wives and children should be submissive, but Scripture also teaches that governing authorities have the right to punish wrongdoers (see Rom. 13:4). Those who are in authority have the responsibility to provide and protect. In cases of abuse, the State has the right to intervene, protect battered wives and abused children, and prosecute the offenders.

There are only two grounds for divorce and remarriage. The first is abandonment by an unbelieving spouse. Should a couple be unequally yoked, the believer must stay committed to the marriage for the purpose of his or her spouse's salvation. The unbeliever can leave; and if he or she does, the believer is not bound to the marriage (see 1 Cor. 7:15).

The second is adultery. Under the Law, the adulterer would have been stoned to death, so obviously the remaining spouse would be free to remarry. Under grace, forgiveness and reconciliation should be attempted; but if not successful, the faithful spouse has the right to divorce and remarry.

Submit to one another out of reverence for Christ (Eph. 5:21).

Thought for the day: *What are we to be subject to if not the needs of one another?*

TRAINING UP A CHILD

Proverbs 22:6

All the nurture in the world cannot make a rose out of a tulip. Parents have to train up children in the way the children should go, not the way the parents want them to go. Consequently, parents need to be students of their own children and assist them in being what God has intended them to be. To accomplish this, parents have to adopt the right parenting style. The following diagram depicts four different styles:

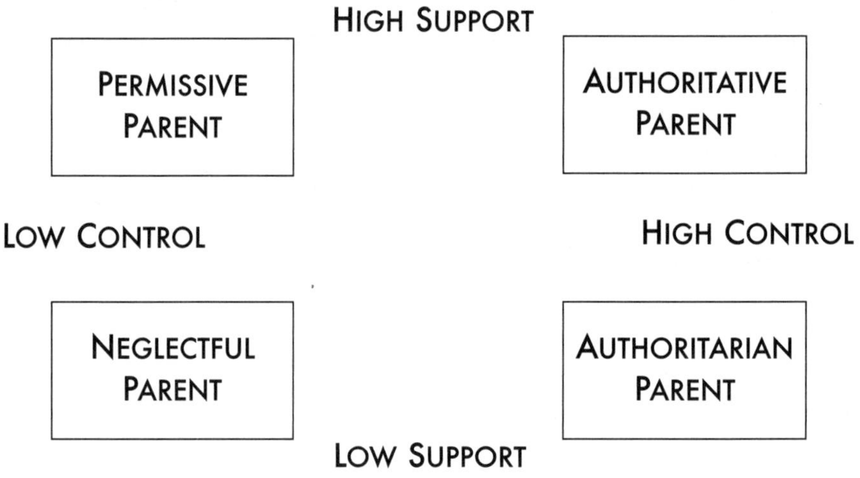

HIGH SUPPORT

PERMISSIVE PARENT		AUTHORITATIVE PARENT

LOW CONTROL **HIGH CONTROL**

NEGLECTFUL PARENT		AUTHORITARIAN PARENT

LOW SUPPORT

The two most powerful influences in parenting are control and support. Parental control is the parent's ability to manage a child's behavior. Parental support is the ability to make a child feel loved. By definition, *authoritative* parents have the ability to make their children feel loved and the ability to control their behavior. *Permissive* parents love their children, but fail to control their behavior. *Neglectful* parents do neither. *Authoritarian* parents try to control their children's behavior but fail to make them feel loved.

Research has shown that children of authoritative parents have the highest sense of worth, conform most easily to authority, are most likely to accept their parents' religion and are least likely to rebel against societal norms. Permissive parents produce children who rank second in all four categories just mentioned, and authoritarian parents produce children who rank last.

Obviously, it is more important that you make your children feel loved than it is to control their behavior. You may not always be able to control your children's behavior, but you can always love them because your ability to love is not dependent upon the children. Research reinforces what Paul wrote: "Fathers, do not exasperate your children; instead, bring them up in the training and instruction of the Lord" (Eph. 6:4).

Children ask two questions. Do you love me? and Can I get my own way? The permissive parent answers yes to both questions and potentially spoils the child. The child of a neglectful parent doesn't feel loved and gets his own way. The neglected child has the greatest potential to become a juvenile delinquent. The authoritarian parent answers no to both questions. Tragically, many parents resort to authoritarianism when problems surface in the home, which is the worst thing they can do. The overly controlled and underloved child is either riddled with guilt and shame and/or rebels against authority. Authoritative parents set boundaries and maintain discipline while demonstrating genuine love. They have the best chance of producing a well-adjusted child.

Fathers, do not embitter your children, or they will become discouraged (Col. 3:21).

Thought for the day: *Why does Scripture warn the father and not the mother about exasperating or embittering children?*

DISCIPLINING CHILDREN

Malachi 4:5-6

The prophecy concerning Elijah was probably fulfilled by the coming of John the Baptist who ministered "in the spirit and power of Elijah" (Luke 1:17). John prepared the way for Jesus who brought us new life. This new life in Christ is what will turn the hearts of parents and children toward each other. Parents play a role much like that of John the Baptist, who said, "He must become greater; I must become less" (John 3:30). Mothers and fathers play the dominant role in shaping the lives of their children when their children's only identity and heritage is physical. It is the goal of all Christian parents to lead their children to Christ, but they need to do more. They must help their children realize that they are children of God and have an inheritance in Christ.

Proverbs 29:17 says, "Discipline your son, and he will give you peace; he will bring delight to your soul." Discipline is a proof of our love; and there are many ways to discipline, but every child does not respond the same way to the same discipline. To know which of the following forms of discipline is appropriate for each child requires an understanding of your children, and seldom is it appropriate to apply the same discipline to each child all the time.

1. Communication: Communication is the most common form of discipline. Parents should make a clear statement of their expectations and the consequences for disobedience. A rule should be definable, defensible and enforceable. Verbal communication after disobedience is a powerful form of discipline. Even parental silence communicates volumes. Knowing they have disappointed their parents can be more painful than a spanking.
2. Natural consequences: Allowing children to experience the natural consequences of their disobedience and irresponsible behavior is very effective, especially for strong-willed children. Some children just have to learn the hard way. Rescuing the child from their own mistakes can seriously impede their growth. They need to understand the connection between cause and effect.

3. Logical consequences: Assigning chores or restricting privileges that are logically connected to the sin or disobedience effectively teaches them to be responsible.

4. Reinforcement: Reinforcement is catching your children doing something right and rewarding their good behavior. Good behavior that is rewarded is more likely to be repeated.

5. Extinction: Crying or throwing a temper tantrum can be a way of getting attention. If you just let them have their tantrum, they begin to realize that it isn't working. The children are training the parent when it works. The wise parent doesn't honor such manipulative techniques by paying attention to them.

6. Spanking: The Bible does teach that spanking can be used to discipline negative behavior. Spanking should not be used for punishment, but for the purpose of shaping future behavior. You don't spank children to get even; you spank them so they don't repeat a particular behavior again, and spanking should always be done in love, using an instrument other than your hand.

No discipline seems pleasant at the time, but painful. Later on, however, it produces a harvest of righteousness and peace for those who have been trained by it (Heb. 12:11).

Thought for the day: *What is the difference between punishment and discipline?*

SPIRITUAL DISCERNMENT

1 Kings 3:5-15

In a world saturated with deceiving spirits, false prophets and false teachers, the need for us as believers to exercise discernment cannot be overstated. In the Old Testament the Hebrew verb *bin* and its variations are used 247 times; it is translated as "discern," "distinguish" and "understand." It means "to make a distinction, or separate from." The New Testament counterpart *diakrino* also means "to separate or divide." The use of the word is applied primarily to judging or making decisions. The Holy Spirit enables us to distinguish right from wrong, truth from lies and God's thoughts from man's thoughts.

As believers, we think with our minds, but we discern with our spirits. Mentally we can know whether something is right or wrong in the natural realm by observation and inquiry. Theologically we can agree or disagree with a verbal or written statements based on our education, experience and understanding of God's word. However, the spiritual world is not always discernible by our natural senses. To chart our way in the spiritual world requires the presence of God. When the Holy Spirit takes up residence in our lives, He bears witness with our spirit and enables us to know right from wrong in the spiritual realm. This God-given ability to discern is like a sixth sense that enables us to know that something is right or wrong, even though we may not know intellectually what is right or what is wrong.

The interaction between God and Solomon is helpful in understanding spiritual discernment. David had died, and Solomon had taken his place as king of Israel. Solomon loved the Lord; but by his own admission, he was too young and inexperienced to be the king (see 1 Kings 3:7). The Lord appeared to Solomon in a dream at night, and God said, "Ask for whatever you want me to give you" (v. 5). Solomon asked, and the Lord gave him "a discerning heart to govern [his] people and to distinguish between right and wrong" (v. 9).

This passage reveals two key concepts about discernment. First, God gave Solomon the ability to discern because his motives were pure. Solomon wasn't asking for a wise and discerning heart for his own personal profit, not even to gain an advantage over his enemies. He wanted discernment in order to administer justice and know good from evil. Motive is crucial, since the power to discern can be misused in the Church. It is a powerful advantage to know something no one else knows.

Second, spiritual discernment is always concerned with the moral realm of good and evil. The Holy Spirit gives us a check in our spirit when something is wrong. Discernment is our first line of defense when our natural senses aren't able to register any danger or direction. However, the ability to discern spiritually does not negate the necessity of knowing God's Word.[1]

> I will ask the Father, and he will give you another Counselor to be with you forever—the Spirit of truth. The world cannot accept him, because it neither sees him nor knows him. But you know him, for he lives with you and will be in you (John 14:16-17).

Thought for the day: *Are you aware of God's presence in you?*

DISCERNING GOOD AND EVIL

Hebrews 5:12—6:3

In addition to the presence of the Holy Spirit, one of the Church's greatest assets is mature saints. They have put their faith into practice, and they understand the teaching about righteousness. They have had their senses trained to discern good and evil. The greatest liability, however, is saints who got old but didn't mature. They should be able to teach others, but instead they need to be taught the elementary truths of God's Word. These spiritual infants haven't successfully put God's Word into practice. They lack the skills and sensitivity that come from maturity.

Sound doctrine is like a skeleton in the body. It is absolutely essential for stability and structure. But a skeleton by itself is dead and so is orthodox teaching without the life of Christ (see 1 Cor. 2:14-16). The "elementary teaching" that the writer of Hebrews describes sounds like the summary of a good systematic theology book (see Heb. 5:12—6:3). Sound doctrine is essential, but learning to walk with God is more than an intellectual exercise. Those who put their faith into practice have trained themselves to distinguish good from evil. Experience is a good teacher if it is combined with a good theology empowered by the Holy Spirit.

Paul had a similar problem with the Church at Corinth. He wanted to give them solid food, but he could only give them milk because they were not able to receive it (see 1 Cor. 3:1-3). They were not able to receive it because of the jealousy and quarrels among them. They were acting like mere men instead of children of God.

There are many people sitting in our churches who cannot receive solid teaching, because they have never put into practice what they have already learned, and because they have unresolved personal and spiritual conflicts. Immature saints proceed without caution. They conduct business as usual in the Church; as a result, the spiritual atmosphere is clouded and members are operating in the flesh. The mature saint can sense the oppression and can alert the others while calling for prayer, but spiritually immature saints see no danger.

In the same way, spiritually immature parents see no visible signs that their children are in trouble. Discerning parents know when something is wrong, and they petition God on behalf of their children and share their discernment lovingly with their children without judgment. They let their children know that they are aware something is wrong, but they don't try to guess what is wrong if they don't know. They let the Holy Spirit bring that conviction, meanwhile keeping the communication lines open and remaining available to their children.

Those who are spiritually discerning can sense a false prophet before that prophet's false doctrine is exposed. They can sense a compatible spirit in another believer and discern an incompatible spirit in others. They know during and after an event whether something is their idea or God's idea. They know when they are living by faith in the power of the Holy Spirit and can sense when they aren't.

> But solid food is for the mature, who by constant use have trained themselves to distinguish good from evil (Heb. 5:14).

Thought for the day: *Have you ever sensed the presence of evil? What did you do, or what should you have done?*

LISTENING TO GOD

John 10:1-30

Jesus said, "My sheep listen to my voice; I know them, and they follow me. I give them eternal life, and they shall never perish; no one can snatch them out of my hand" (John 10:27-28). The eternal security that we have in Christ is not based on our ability to hang on to the hand of God. It is based on God's ability to hold on to us and protect us against the spiritual wolves that would try to snatch us out of His hand. Jesus is the great shepherd, and we are the sheep of His pasture. He calls every one of us by name and we listen to His voice (see v. 3). On His own authority, Jesus has laid down His life for us. He is not a hired hand who works for wages. He is the Great Shepherd who loves us.

God has spoken through His prophets and apostles who faithfully proclaimed His Word and wrote it down under the inspiration of the Holy Spirit. We listen to the voice of God when we read His Word, and when we hear it proclaimed by faithful servants who have been called as evangelists, pastors and teachers. We also listened to His voice when Jesus opened the gate and invited us in. Our acceptance of that invitation may have been in response to a gospel tract or an evangelistic meeting, an invitation at church or someone who simply shared his or her faith. We may have heard the Gospel proclaimed or have seen it in print, but there was an inner "voice" that persuaded us to come. We felt convicted of our sin, but at the same time we saw the open door because our eyes had been opened. We knew that somebody was calling us. It probably wasn't audible, but we heard it in our spirit and we responded. Somehow we knew the truth in a way we had never known before.

The *Friend's Book of Discipline* says:

> Our power to perceive the light of God is, of all our powers, the one which we need most to cultivate and develop. As exercise strengthens the body and education enlarges the mind, so the spiritual faculty within us grows as we use it in seeing and doing God's will.

We don't always hear with our ears the voice of God, nor do we see with our eyes. The spiritual world does not operate through our natural senses;

therefore, knowledge of it is not received through the normal channels of perception. Coupled with the written Word, which is hidden in our hearts, this inner voice nudges us in the right direction or gives us a check in our spirit against that which is wrong. We start thinking thoughts that are wise, insightful and in accordance with Scripture. Somehow we know what we are supposed to do or say—and with a sense of confidence that is not natural. He is leading us and we are following Him.

> The watchman opens the gate for him, and the sheep listen to his voice. He calls his own sheep by name and leads them out. When he has brought out all his own, he goes on ahead of them, and his sheep follow him because they know his voice (John 10:3-4).

Thought for the day: *Do you recognize the voice of God calling and leading you?*

SPIRITUAL DISCLOSURE

John 16:5-15

Because of the Holy Spirit within us, we have the power to live the Christian life, but that is not the only work and probably not the primary work of the Holy Spirit. We are never instructed to pursue power, because we already have it (see Eph. 1:18-19). Our Christian walk will be distorted if we pursue something we already have.

The Holy Spirit is the divine impetus behind our spiritual gifts, but that is probably not the primary work of the Holy Spirit. The Church at Corinth seemed to have all the gifts, but they were very immature. We are never instructed to seek spiritual gifts for ourselves, but we are instructed to seek the Giver and allow Him to gift us anyway He chooses.

No, the primary work of the Holy Spirit is to communicate God's presence to us. While it was good that Jesus was physically present with the disciples, it was better that He left, so He could be spiritually within every believer through the Holy Spirit. Jesus said, "When [the Holy Spirit] comes, he will convict the world of guilt in regard to sin and righteousness and judgment" (John 16:8). Sin is rebellion against God that reached its climax in the crucifixion of Christ. The greatest sin is unbelief (see John 3:18), and it is the unique work of the Holy Spirit to convict the world of sin so that people will turn to Christ. The Holy Spirit will bring glory to Jesus by making known within us His resurrection and ascension (see John 16:14). Finally, the Holy Spirit will also bear witness to the judgment of Satan. "The prince of this world now stands condemned" (John 16:11). Satan knows that his future is doomed and will do all that he can to take with him as many as he can.

Jesus promised that when the Holy Spirit came, He would guide us into all truth. He would not speak on His own initiative, but would teach only that which comes from the Father. If believed, that truth would set us free. Jesus said, "He will bring glory to me by taking from what is mine and making it known to you" (John 16:14). The Holy Spirit is bearing witness with our spirit that we are children of God (see Rom. 8:16). We have become partakers of the divine nature (see 2 Pet. 1:4). This is the great work of the Holy Spirit: to glorify the work of Jesus and make all this known to us in the inner person.

In the Bible, "mystery" means "that which has not been previously revealed." Paul tells us,

> I have become [the Church's] servant by the commission God gave me to present to you the word of God in its fullness—the mystery that has been kept hidden for ages and generations, but is now disclosed to the saints. To them God has chosen to make known among the gentiles the glorious riches of this mystery, which is Christ in you, the hope of glory (Col. 1:25-27).

This is why we rejoice: Our souls are in union with God. We are alive in Christ. We must learn to begin every day by acknowledging that the very presence of God is within us. Then we need to practice His presence throughout the day.

> All that belongs to the Father is mine. That is why I said the Spirit will take from what is mine and make it known to you (John 16:15).

Thought for the day: *How has God disclosed Himself to you?*

SPIRITUAL WISDOM

1 Corinthians 2:6-16

The Holy Spirit leads us into all truth, enables us to discern good from evil and empowers us to live righteous lives. How He does this is difficult for the finite mind to comprehend, but Paul offers some explanation of the process (see 1 Corinthians 2:6-16). First, the natural person cannot understand spiritual truth. The combined wisdom of the rulers of this world could never discern the wisdom of God. Had they been able to, they would not have crucified Christ. God's wisdom was hidden in the past, but is now being revealed in the ultimate revelation of Christ. "No eye has seen, no ear has heard, no mind has conceived what God has prepared for those who love him" (v. 9). It is humanly impossible to understand the wisdom of God through our natural channels of perception and our limited ability to reason, "but God has revealed it to us by his Spirit" (v. 10).

Second, the Holy Spirit knows all things and is capable of revealing the nature of God and His will. "The Spirit searches all things, even the deep things of God" (1 Cor. 2:10). Third, as believers we have not received the spirit of this world, but we have received the Spirit who is from God. The Spirit makes known to us the things freely given by God. Fourth, we have the mind of Christ, because the very presence of God is within us. Fifth, the Holy Spirit takes words (*logos*), that are not taught by human wisdom but by the Spirit; and He combines (brings together, compares or explains) them. What is actually being combined or compared is not clear. The original language literally reads "spirituals with spirituals." That phrase is translated in the *New International Version* of the Bible as, "words taught by the Spirit, expressing spiritual truth in spiritual words" (v. 13).

Recall that we are transformed by the renewing of our minds (see Rom. 12:2). Paul says, we are "to be made new in the attitude [literally, the spirit] of [our] minds" (Eph. 4:23). The Holy Spirit discloses to us the mind of Christ as we study God's Word. The Holy Spirit then enables our thoughts and renews our minds with the *Logos*. The peace of Christ rules in our hearts as the Words of Christ richly dwell within us (see Col. 3:15-16). Finally, the peace of God guards our hearts and our minds (see Phil. 4:7).

We may not fully understand how God does this, but we don't have to fully understand in order to believe that He does. For instance, nobody can fully explain the virgin birth of Jesus, the mystery of the incarnation, the Holy Trinity and the miracle of our new birth, but liberated Christians believe these truths. When we choose to believe what God says is true, the Holy Spirit renews our minds and we begin to understand and see more clearly. Those who refuse to believe God and His Word until they fully understand will never fully understand. Those who choose to trust God and live accordingly by faith are blessed and begin to understand more fully as they mature in Christ. Thomas saw the resurrected Jesus and believed, prompting Jesus to say, "Blessed are those who have not seen and yet have believed" (John 20: 29).

> And without faith it is impossible to please God, because anyone who comes to him must believe that he exists and that he rewards those who earnestly seek him (Heb. 11:6).

Thought for the day: *Do we know more in order to believe more, or do we believe more in order to know more? Are the two interrelated?*

SPIRITUAL GIFTS

1 Corinthians 12

The Holy Spirit indwells every born-again believer, enabling each one to live the Christian life and conform to the image of God. However, the ministry of the Holy Spirit is not just for individual edification. The sanctifying process requires that the whole Body of Christ work together. The Holy Spirit is the agent who equips individual members to serve one another in three ways (see 1 Cor. 12:4-11). First, each member has at least one gift of grace by which he or she ministers to the Body of Christ. Second, individual members are enabled to offer different kinds of service to the Church. Third, there are different kinds of workings within the Church, manifesting spiritual power in operation.

Paul argues that there is unity in diversity. All these manifestations of the Spirit have a unity in source. The "same Spirit" (1 Cor. 12:4), "same Lord [Jesus]" (v. 5), and "the same God works all of them in all men" (v. 6). There is also a unity of purpose. These gifts, services and manifestations are not given for personal edification; they are given so that we may build up one another: "Now to each one the manifestation of the Spirit is given for the common good" (v. 7). Paul lists a variety of ways that the Spirit may manifest Himself among the believers (see vv. 8-10). "All these are the work of one and the same Spirit, and he gives them to each one, just as he determines" (v. 11).

The Body of Christ is made up many parts, and all are necessary. Some members may feel like they are unwanted or unnecessary when other gifts or manifestations of the Spirit seem to take on a greater prominence. "But God has combined the members of the body and has given greater honor to the parts that lacked it, so that there should be no division in the body, but that its parts should have equal concern for each other" (1 Cor. 12:24-25). As the Body of Christ, we should eagerly desire the greater gifts to be manifested among us for the edification of all (see v. 31). We should not desire a greater gift for ourselves in order that we may be exalted above the others. God gives as He chooses, and we should gladly accept what He gives us and use it to the glory of God. We will never be fulfilled trying to become somebody we aren't or trying to acquire a gift that others have.

Paul gives no instruction for determining our own gifts. We should seek the Giver, not the gift; focus on being the person God intended us to be; and through love serve one another. In the process, our giftedness will become evident to all. Spiritual gifts are a means to an end, not an end in itself. The manifestations of the Spirit will come and go; but what remains are faith, hope and love—and the greatest of these is love (see 1 Cor. 13:13).

> Now you are the body of Christ, and each one of you is a part of it (1 Cor. 12:27).

Thought for the day: *Why did God distribute different gifts among His people?*

MOTIVATIONAL GIFTS

1 Peter 4:7-11

As the return of the Lord becomes even more imminent, we should become clear minded, self-controlled and committed to love one another. Love covers a multitude of sins, but love is not blind. If we are godly Christians, we see the faults and limitations of others and accept them for who they are in Christ. We not only love our friends, but we also offer hospitality, which is a love of strangers. Finally, we should use our gifts to serve others. Gift (*charisma*) stems from God's grace (*charis*). His grace is manifested to others as we use the gift that God has bestowed upon us to serve one another. We should do so with the strength that God provides.

Peter divides the gifts into two groups, service and speaking. Paul in Romans 12:4-8 gives a more complete list. You will be motivated by the grace of God to serve the Body of Christ in one of the following seven ways:

1. Gift of prophecy: "Prophecy" literally means "to speak forth the mind and counsel of God." It can mean to fore-tell (predict future events) or forth-tell (speak God's truth boldly to people). The primary emphasis is on the proclamation of God's Word. People with this gift are motivated to help people live righteous lives.
2. Gift of serving: This gift enables people to help others. People with this gift are motivated to respond to the needs of others in a practical way.
3. Gift of encouragement or exhortation: People with this gift encourage others to live out their faith according to God's Word. They are motivated to communicate God's Word in such a way that people listen and want to respond.
4. Gift of teaching. People with this gift are concerned about the authority of Scripture and doctrinal accuracy. They are motivated to rightly divide the word of truth and correct doctrinal error.
5. Gift of giving: People with this gift contribute to the financial needs of others, and to the mission of the Church. They are motivated to be good stewards of the financial resources necessary to complete the mission of the Church.
6. Gift of leadership or administration: People with this gift pro-

vide the leadership and organizational structure necessary for effective ministry. They are motivated to organize the efforts of the Church for maximum efficiency.

7. Gift of mercy: This gift causes those who have it to feel deeply the spiritual and emotional needs of others. They are motivated to relieve pain and suffering, and to provide comfort through prayer and personal assistance.

Every one of the above motivational gifts is needed in the Body of Christ. The different emphasis of each gift provides for a balanced ministry. We need to contribute to the Body of Christ by that which motivates us and receive from others that which motivates them.

We have different gifts, according to the grace given us (Rom. 12:6).

Thought for the day: *If we are motivated according to our gift, how can that be a blessing or a problem when working together?*

PUBLIC USE OF GIFTS

1 Corinthians 14

Paul is addressing a problem that had arisen in Corinth concerning public worship and the use of the gifts, specifically of prophecy and tongues. In earlier chapters Paul had been discussing how Christians should live out their freedom, which is qualified and regulated by love. A self-indulgent spirit that debauched the principle of freedom in other areas had found a similar expression in the use of gifts for public worship. Such selfishness produced disunity and chaos in public worship.

Whatever is done in the Church must be for the edification of all. Gifts are given for the common good (see 1 Cor. 12) and must be in agreement with the principle of love (see 1 Cor. 13). There was no problem with any of the service gifts being used excessively. The primary concern was the gift of prophecy and the gift of tongues—specifically their use in public worship. In response, Paul offered some prudent guidelines.

First, whatever is communicated in public worship must be intelligible. It must be spoken in the common language or at least be interpreted in the common language. Prophecy is more desirable than tongues (unless someone has the gift of interpretation), because prophecy is spoken in a language that can be understood by all present (see 1 Cor. 14:1-3).

Second, "Since you are eager to have spiritual gifts, try to excel in gifts that build up the church" (1 Cor. 14:12). These gifts would certainly include serving, mercy, giving, administration, exhortation and teaching, as well as prophecy. It seems to be part of our fallen nature to desire gifts that appear more supernatural and more noticeable by others. However, the exercise of any gift is supernatural, and its proper use is always noticed by God.

Third, tongues are a sign for unbelievers, and the gift of prophecy is for believers since it communicates truth to those who are open to receiving it (see 1 Cor. 14:22). Based on Paul's statement in verses 18 and 19, some would argue for the private use of tongues for their own edification. But even the private use of tongues without an interpretation is unintelligible. Therefore, the personal benefit is subjective, i.e. a sense of God's presence, or an emotional moment that enhances a love relationship. A prophetic message can always be understood and "the secrets of [their hearts] will be laid bare" leading to repentance (v. 25).

Fourth, "God is not a God of disorder but of peace" (1 Cor. 14:33). Paul has previously indicated that women can pray and prophesy in public worship as long as they are under authority (see 1 Cor. 11:5). In this chapter, Paul seems to be prohibiting them from speaking in Church. Some argue that a woman should be in submission at home and church and that this timeless order was established at creation. Others understand this instruction to be sensitive to current social practices. In that culture it was "disgraceful for a woman to speak in church" (1 Cor. 14:35), but they reason it may not be so in other cultures. Regardless of our understanding on this issue, we should always be respectful and "everything should be done in a fitting and orderly way" (v. 40).

So what shall I do? I will pray with my spirit, but I will also pray with my mind; I will sing with my spirit, but I will also sing with my mind (1 Cor. 14:15).

Thought for the day: *Does God bypass our minds, or does He work through them? Who does seek to bypass our minds?*

LIFE ENDOWMENTS

Matthew 25:14-30

We have all been given some capacity to invest in the kingdom of God, and we will give an account for our stewardship. In the parable of the talents, the man went on a journey and gave one of his servants five talents; to another he gave two talents; and the third servant got one talent. They were rewarded according to their ability (see Matt. 25:14-15).

The first two servants doubled their investment, but the servant who received one talent buried his. When the master returned, he praised the two servants who had wisely invested their talents. He put them in charge of greater things. They also got to share in their master's happiness (see Matt. 25:19-23). This is an important principle for those who wish to grow in grace and expand their influence. When God finds us faithful in the little things, He puts us in charge of greater things. If we are waiting for our ship to come in or for a big opportunity to come along, it may never happen. Those opportunities are created by our own industriousness. We get out of life what we invest in it.

The man who was given one talent only had excuses. He didn't invest his talent because his master was a hard man who reaped where he did not sow (see Matt. 25:24-25). He reasoned, *My master probably isn't coming back anyway.* His perception of his master was wrong; and his failure to trust him cost the wicked, lazy servant his eternal life (see v. 30). The master reasoned, "Even though you thought I was a hard man who reaped where I did not sow, you still should have invested my money so I could have received the interest" (see vv. 26-27). The heart of this principle is expressed well in the following poem.

"Father, where shall I work today?" And my love flowed warm and free.
Then He pointed out a tiny spot, and said, "Tend that for me."
I answered quickly, "Oh no, not that. Why, no one would ever see,
No matter how well my work was done, not that little place for me!"
And the word He spoke, it was not stern, He answered me tenderly,
"Ah little one, search that heart of thine; art thou working for them or me?
Nazareth was a little place, and so was Galilee."[1]

There are two types of people who will never realize their potential:

those who won't do what they are told, and those who won't do anything unless they are told. You may not have any outstanding gifts or talents, but what you have you can put to good use. A timely word or act of kindness will pay future dividends. You may not lead many to Christ, but you may lead one who later leads many. In the end, God will judge you fairly according to your ability. "From everyone who has been given much, much will be demanded; and from the one who has been entrusted with much, much more will be asked" (Luke 12:48).

So then, each of us will give an account of himself to God (Rom. 14:12).

Thought for the day: *Would you live differently if you knew you had to give an account of yourself?*

346 THE DAILY DISCIPLER

STEWARDSHIP

1 Corinthians 4:1-5

In Christ we have an entitlement. Paul says, "All things are yours . . . and you are of Christ, and Christ is of God" (1 Cor. 3:22). We have all things, because we are united to Christ and Christ with God the Father. But we don't have ownership. We belong to God, and everything we possess belongs to Him. We are stewards of the mysteries of God, i.e., the truth that has been revealed in the gospel of our Lord Jesus Christ. A steward is someone who manages a household or estate.

"Now it is required that those who have been given a trust must prove faithful" (1 Cor. 4:2). The use of our own lives and all that we possess has been entrusted to us, and someday we will give an account for how well we have managed the estate. There is no time that is ours and the rest is God's. There is no portion of money that is ours and the rest belongs to God. It all belongs to Him. He made it all and simply entrusted it to us for His service. It matters not what others think of our stewardship. It doesn't even matter what we think of ourselves. We can have a clear conscience, but that doesn't make us innocent. It is the Lord who judges us.

Jesus told a parable about a rich fool. The man produced such a good crop that he had to tear down his barns and build bigger ones. Thinking that he had stored up enough to last for many years, he decided to take it easy; eat, drink and be merry. "But God said to him, 'You fool! This very night your life will be demanded from you. Then who will get what you have prepared for yourself?' " (Luke 12:20). On another occasion, a rich young man asked Jesus how he could have eternal life. Jesus told him to keep the commandments. The rich man said that he already did. Then Jesus said, "If you want to be perfect, go, sell your possessions and give to the poor, and you will have treasure in heaven. Then come, follow me" (Matt. 19:21). The young man walked away, because he had great wealth. Jesus showed the rich young man that his righteousness was self-rightness and that his security was in his possessions and not in his eternal relationship with God.

"You may say to yourself, 'My power and the strength of my hands have produced this wealth for me.' But remember the LORD your God, for it is he who gives you the ability to produce wealth" (Deut. 8:17-18). It is not just the results of our labor that we are called to be stewards of, but the labor itself. Kingdom stewardship is like the Stradivari Society that entrusts these superb violins into the hands of the artists who make great music. God has given us time, talent and treasure, which remain His property but are intended to be used to glorify Him.

So we make it our goal to please him, whether we are at home in the body or away from it. For we must all appear before the judgment seat of Christ, that each one may receive what is due him for the things done while in the body, whether good or bad. Since, then, we know what it is to fear the Lord, we try to persuade men (2 Cor. 5:9-11).

Thought for the day: *Why and what are we persuading people to do?*

PRAYER AND PRAISE

Psalm 138

If you saw a giant man a mile away, he wouldn't look very big. But if you were standing right before him, you couldn't help but praise him. You wouldn't say, "Praise you!" You would at least think or perhaps even say, "My, you sure are big!" You would describe his dominant features. Worship is ascribing to God His divine attributes. But worship would not naturally flow from you if you were unaware of God's presence and you thought He was far off. If you were suddenly ushered into God's glorious presence, you would immediately and voluntarily burst forth in praise: beautiful, awesome, big, loving, kind, powerful. In fact no words could adequately describe His majesty.

When we practice God's presence, worshiping Him is a natural process as it was for David in Psalm 138. When we get entangled in the daily affairs of life, it is easy to lose a conscious sense of His presence. Then is when we need to worship God the most. God is seeking those who will worship Him in Spirit and in truth (see John 4:23), but God does not need us to tell Him who He is. He is fully secure within Himself. We need to worship God, because we need to keep the divine attributes of God continuously in our minds. There will be times in our Christian experience when we don't sense His presence. During these times we need to continue believing that He is omnipresent, omnipotent and omniscient.

When David prayed, God answered him. Being aware of God's presence made him bold and stouthearted (see Ps. 138:3). An awareness of God's presence and an acknowledgment of who He is are essential prerequisites for approaching God in prayer. Notice how Jesus taught us to approach God in the Lord's Prayer (see Matt. 6:9-13):

1. Saying "Our Father in heaven" implies that we have a relationship with Him. As children of God, we have the right to petition our heavenly Father. The crucifixion and resurrection of Christ made access to God possible.

2. Saying "hallowed be your name" is an act of praise. It is an acknowledgment that God is Holy. We approach a judge in a court of law by saying, "Your honor." If we show disrespect, we can be held for contempt and thrown out of court. We approach

God with even greater respect. The throne of God is the ultimate authority of the universe, and there is no other judge remotely like Him in glory and majesty.

3. Saying, "your kingdom come, your will be done, on earth as it is in heaven" means that His kingdom plans and priorities supersede ours. We try to ascertain God's will in prayer. We don't try to convince Him of our will. It is His kingdom we are trying to build, not ours. Prayer is a means by which we seek God's will.

4. "Give us today our daily bread" is a petition for real needs, not selfish wants.

Yet a time is coming and has now come when the true worshippers will worship the Father in spirit and truth, for they are the kind of worshippers the Father seeks (John 4:23).

Thought for the day: *What does it mean to worship God and why do we do it?*

LEVELS OF PRAYER

Psalm 95

Psalm 95 is a model for approaching God in prayer. It begins with praise and thanksgiving. The apostle Paul seldom mentioned prayer in the New Testament without an attitude of gratitude. "I have not stopped *giving thanks* for you, remembering you in my prayers" (Eph. 1:16, emphasis added). "Do not be anxious about anything, but in everything, by prayer and petition, *with thanksgiving*, present your requests to God" (Phil. 4:6, emphasis added). "Devote yourselves to prayer, being watchful and *thankful*" (Col. 4:2, emphasis added). "Be joyful always; pray continuously; *give thanks* in all circumstances" (1 Thess. 5:16-18, emphasis added). "Let us come before him *with thanksgiving*" (Ps. 95:2, emphasis added).

There are three levels of communicating with God in prayer. Each level incorporates praise and thanksgiving. The first level is petition, which Paul has mentioned in Philippians 4:6. James adds, "You do not have, because you do not ask" (4:2). However, he qualifies this by saying, "When you ask, you do not receive, because you ask with wrong motives, that you may spend what you get on your pleasures" (4:3). Petitions should be consistent with the Lord's Prayer discussed previously.

Petition is all too often one-way communication, and people tire of that. The next level of prayer is personal and more like a dialogue. As we personally and humbly approach God (see Ps. 95:6-7), the psalmist says, "Today, if you hear his voice, do not harden your hearts" (vv. 7-8). The word "hear" means "to listen so as to obey." If we heard from God, we may be inclined to "harden our hearts," since the first items on God's list are issues that concern our relationship with Him. So if there are unresolved moral issues that we have never confessed to God, rest assured that will be at the top of His list. All those distracting thoughts that we struggled with while petitioning Him in level one are from God or allowed by God to get our attention, even if they are from the enemy. The Lord wants us to actively deal with whatever comes to our minds during prayer. There is nothing we can't talk to God about, because He already knows the thoughts and attitudes of our hearts (see Heb. 4:12-13). These issues are critical since they relate to our relationship with God, which is always His first concern.

When prayer becomes this personal, we begin to pray continually (see

1 Thess. 5:17). This makes intercessory prayer possible, which is the next level. There are few true intercessors who are intimate enough with God to hear His voice and obey. Intercessors hear from God, sense the burden to pray and continue in prayer until the burden leaves. Seldom if ever is their prayer time in public. It is usually in the privacy of their homes and often late at night. God accomplishes much of His work through these dear saints who know how to pray.

If I had cherished sin in my heart, the Lord would not have listened (Ps. 66:18).

Thought for the day: *What will happen to our prayer life if we are not honest with God and won't deal with real issues in our lives?*

PRAYING BY THE SPIRIT

Jude 20

After warning us about false teachers and the ungodliness of the last days, Jude writes, "But you, dear friends, build yourselves up in your most holy faith and pray in the Holy Spirit" (Jude 20). Paul also exhorts us to "pray in the Spirit on all occasions with all kinds of prayers and [petitions]" (Eph. 6:18). We can only pray effectively as the Holy Spirit enables us, and we can only pray in the name of our Lord and Savior Jesus Christ. That does not mean that we simply end a prayer by saying, "in Jesus' name I pray." It means that we pray in a way that is consistent with the nature and purpose of Jesus. "In him and through faith in him we may approach God with freedom and confidence" (Eph. 3:12).

If we are going to pray in the Spirit, we need to be filled with the Spirit (see Eph. 5:18-20). Then the Holy Spirit enables us to pray as explained by Paul in Romans 8:26; "In the same way, the Spirit helps us in our weakness. We do not know what we ought to pray for, but the Spirit himself intercedes for us with groans that words cannot express."

The word "helps" is *sunantilambano* in the Greek language. It has two prepositions before the verb *lambano*, which means "take." Paul is saying that the Holy Spirit comes alongside, bears us up and takes us across to the other side—in other words, He takes us to God. The fact that we really don't know how or what to pray for demonstrates our weakness. The prayer that God the Holy Spirit prompts us to pray is the prayer that God the Father will always answer. He leads us to pray as He guides our thoughts. His guidance may be so deep that words cannot express what we sense in our hearts. The Holy Spirit knows our hearts, and He knows the will of God.

The Holy Spirit not only helps us to pray, He also intercedes on our behalf. Two members of the Trinity are continuously praying on our behalf. John says, "My dear children, I write this to you so that you will not sin. But if anybody does sin, we have one who speaks to the Father in our defense—Jesus Christ, the Righteous One" (1 John 2:1). According to Paul, "Christ Jesus, who died—more than that, who was raised to life—is at the right hand of God and is also interceding for us" (Rom 8:34). We have more help than we could ever comprehend, and there is no reason why we can't pray without ceasing.

So make a start today. Ask God to fill you with His Holy Spirit, and start thanking Him for all that He is and for all that He has done for you. Then let the Holy Spirit disclose to your mind the will of your heavenly Father. He knows what to pray for, and He will continue to lead you throughout your day as you practice the presence of God.[1]

And he who searches our hearts knows the mind of the Spirit, because the Spirit intercedes for the saints in accordance with God's will (Rom. 8:27).

Thought for the day: *If our prayer is going to be effective, why must we pray by the Spirit?*

EFFECTIVE PRAYER

1 Samuel 12:16-24

What no human can do in eternity, God can do in an instant—and He does it in response to our prayers. Thomas Chalmers said, "Prayer does not enable us to do a greater work for God. Prayer is a greater work for God." Samuel demonstrated this principle when he said, "Now then, stand still and see this great thing the LORD is about to do before your eyes!" (1 Sam. 12:16). God didn't move until "Samuel called upon the LORD" (v. 18). James said,

> The prayer of a righteous man is powerful and effective. Elijah was a man just like us. He prayed earnestly that it would not rain, and it did not rain on the land for three and a half years. Again he prayed, and the heavens gave rain, and the earth produced its crops (5:16-18).

Both Samuel and Elijah were righteous, and that is why they were effective in prayer; but in every other way they were no different from us.

We will never be effective in prayer if we go to God in emergencies and then return to managing our own lives when the crisis passes. That would make prayer a fourth-down punting situation instead of a first-down huddle. It is not appropriate to ask God to bless *our* plans; rather, we should humbly ask God to reveal *His* plans. God is capable of doing anything that is consistent with His nature. The question is, Will He? We may never know unless we ask. Prayer is not conquering God's reluctance but laying hold of God's willingness. "This is the confidence we have in approaching God: that if we ask anything according to his will, he hears us. And if we know that he hears us—whatever we ask—we know that we have what we asked of him" (1 John 5:14-15). Our prayers will always be effective if our petitions and intercessions are in agreement with the Word of God.

Paul has instructed us to be alert and pray in the Spirit for all the saints (see Eph. 6:18). Prayer is part of our divine protection as believers. We need to respond immediately in prayer to the Spirit's prompting and to the requests of our brothers and sisters in Christ. In addition Paul says, "I urge, then, first of all, that requests, prayers, intercession and thanksgiving be made for everyone—for kings and all those in authority, that we may live peaceful and quiet lives in all godliness and holiness" (1 Tim. 2:1-2).

Samuel considered it a sin against God not to pray for others (see 1 Sam. 12:23). However, we can only ask the Lord to do through others what we are willing for the Lord to do through us. Only to the degree that we have been tested and found approved can we request on behalf of others. Neither Christ nor the Holy Spirit can intercede through us on a higher level than that in which they have first had victory in us. Christ is the perfect intercessor, because He took the place of each one prayed for.

I urge, then, first of all, that requests, prayers, intercession and thanksgiving be made for everyone—for kings and all those in authority, that we may live peaceful and quiet lives in all godliness and holiness (1 Tim. 2:1-2).

Thought for the day: *Why should we pray for those in authority over us and what should we pray for (see 1 Tim. 2:3-4)?*

PRAYING FOR THE LOST

Jonah 4

God told Jonah to go to Nineveh and preach, but he refused (see Jon. 1:1-3). Because of his disobedience he found himself in the belly of a fish, praying for his own salvation (see Jon. 2). Jonah finally did go to Nineveh, and to his disappointment they did repent and God relented. Jonah knew that God would spare the Ninevites if they repented, and he did not want these enemies of Israel to be spared. Sensing his anger, God gave Jonah an object lesson. If Jonah was justified in being upset about the loss of a plant to whose existence he had contributed nothing, was not God justified in showing love and concern for the people of Nineveh, whom He had created? (See Jon. 4:5-11.)

The story of Jonah forces us to examine our own hearts. Do we want the judgment of God to fall on all the lost people of this world, or do we want them to repent and believe? If the lost are our enemies, the question becomes a test of our character. Do we have a heart like Jonah, or do we have a heart like God? We are not all called to be full-time missionaries or evangelists, but we are all called to share our faith and pray. There are two principles that we need to know in order to effectively pray for the lost.

First, Jesus tells us, "The harvest is plentiful but the workers are few. Ask the Lord of the harvest, therefore, to send out workers into his harvest field" (Matt. 9:37-38). If we have a burden to pray for someone or some group of people who don't know the Lord, then we should ask God to send them a messenger. God has to work through His established means of bringing salvation to the lost people of this world. In Romans 10:14-15, Paul explains what that process is:

> How, then, can they call on the one they have not believed in? And how can they believe in the one of whom they have not heard? And how can they hear without someone preaching to them? And how can they preach unless they are sent?

Second, John writes, "If anyone sees his brother commit a sin that does not lead to death, he should pray and God will give him life" (1 John 5:16). The context of this passage is clearly talking about spiritual life and death, not physical life and death. The lost people of this world are dead in their trespasses and sins. Jesus came that we might have life. So John is telling us to petition God to give them eternal life. Our prayers do not save them. They are saved by their own personal faith in the finished work of Christ. However, in His sovereignty, God has chosen to work out His plan of salvation through the Church. We choose to believe, but God saves us. It is in response to our prayers that God miraculously works—and the salvation of souls is His crowning achievement.

This is the confidence we have in approaching God: that if we ask anything according to his will, he hears us. And if we know that he hears us—whatever we ask—we know that we have what we asked of him (1 John 5:14-15).

Thought for the day: *How can we know that what we have asked for is consistent with His will?*

GOD'S WILL

Ruth 2—4

The book of Ruth is a love story about redemption. First there is Naomi's passage from emptiness to fullness made possible by the selfless love of Ruth and Boaz (see Ruth 2—3). Then Boaz functions like a kinsman-redeemer, a type of Christ (see Ruth 4). Finally, this episode in history is a critical link in the genealogy of David, which is the bloodline of Christ. What person could have orchestrated such a drama that would fit so perfectly into God's redemptive plan? History is His story, a joining of human responsibility and God sovereignty.

God's will for our lives is our sanctification (see 1 Thess. 4:3). His number one priority is that we conform to the image of God. He may even have to sacrifice our career or disrupt our plans if that is what it takes to accomplish His will. God accomplished His purpose with Ruth; because she left her pagan heritage and moved to a covenant nation under God, and because she was submissive, unselfish and loving. She became the person God had created her to be.

Jesus prayed, "Sanctify them by the truth; your word is truth" (John 17:17). To fully comprehend truth, we need to understand the biblical balance between reason and intuition (see the diagram on p. 359). Those who are above the horizontal line are the intuitive and rational persons who have trusted in Christ. The bell-shaped curve represents how humanity relates to truth, which is at the top and center of the curve. Throughout Scripture, we can see how God balances the two sides. Paul said, "Jews demand miraculous signs and Greeks look for wisdom . . . but to those whom God has called, both Jews and Greeks, Christ [is] the power of God and the wisdom of God" (1 Cor. 1:22-24).

Truth is both real and right, and those who have fully appropriated the truth have zeal and knowledge. We need to let the Word of Christ richly dwell within us (rational), but we also need to be filled with the Spirit (intuitive). Both have the same result (compare Eph. 5:18-20 with Col. 3:15-17), and both are required for balance.

In a general sense, rationalism has characterized the Western world, and intuition has characterized the Eastern world. In our humanity, some are more subjective while others are more cognitive. Some rely on feelings while others rely on facts. Some are personal and art oriented, while others are task and math oriented. For those who never come to Christ, some "are swayed by all kinds of evil desires" (2 Tim. 3:6), while others are "always learning but never able to acknowledge the truth" (2 Tim. 3:7).

Be strong in the Lord *and* in his mighty power (Eph. 6:10, emphasis added).

Thought for the day: *Why are we inclined to think either or instead of both and when it comes to the use of reason and intuition in the Body of Christ?*

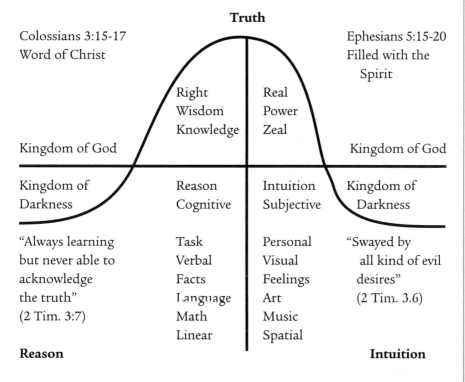

Truth

	Right Wisdom Knowledge	Real Power Zeal	
Colossians 3:15-17 Word of Christ			Ephesians 5:15-20 Filled with the Spirit
Kingdom of God			Kingdom of God
Kingdom of Darkness	Reason Cognitive	Intuition Subjective	Kingdom of Darkness
"Always learning but never able to acknowledge the truth" (2 Tim. 3:7)	Task Verbal Facts Language Math Linear	Personal Visual Feelings Art Music Spatial	"Swayed by all kind of evil desires" (2 Tim. 3.6)
Reason			**Intuition**

DO ALL TO THE GLORY OF GOD

1 Corinthians 10:23-33

Jesus said, "If anyone chooses to do God's will, he will find out whether my teaching comes from God or whether I speak on my own" (John 7:17). The essential prerequisite to knowing the will of God is the willingness to do it. Suppose God's will for your life is on the other side of a closed door and you ask, "What is it?" The critical question is, Why do you want to know? So you can decide whether or not you want to go through the door? If God is God, doesn't He have the right to decide what is on the other side of the door? If you don't give him that right, you have usurped the throne of God, and He is no longer the Lord of your life. George Muller said:

> I seek at the beginning to get my heart into such a state that it has no will of its own in regard to a given matter. Nine-tenths of the difficulties are overcome when our hearts are ready to do the Lord's will, whatever it may be. When one is truly ready in this state, it is usually but a little way to the knowledge of what His will is.[1]

If we desire to do the will of God, two other questions must be considered. First, we must ask, Will God be glorified if I do it? We glorify God when we bear fruit (see John 15:8). This includes the fruit of the Spirit as well as the fruit of reproduction. If what we are doing cannot be done without violating the fruit of the Spirit, then it is best that we don't do it. This is the greatest test of our faith in public. In the face of temptation or hostile opposition, can we continue living by the Spirit, or will we defer to the deeds of the flesh? We are in the will of God if we maintain our position in Christ and let the fruit of the Spirit be evident in our lives. As long as we are within the moral boundaries of God, Paul says, "'Everything is permissible'—but not everything is beneficial" (1 Cor. 10:23). In exercising our own freedom, we do not have the right to violate another person's conscience. We must restrict our freedom for the sake of the weaker Christian and always consider the good of others.

Second, we must ask, Can I do what I am doing and be a positive witness for the Lord Jesus Christ? Paul says,

> Though I am free and belong to no man, I make myself a slave to everyone. To the Jews I became like a Jew, to win the Jews. I have become all things to all men so that by all possible means I might save some. I do all this for the sake of the gospel, that I may share in its blessings (1 Cor. 9:19-20,22-23).

If we are compromising our witness, then we cannot be in the center of God's will. There are many morally neutral activities and games in which we can participate, but sometimes we don't have the maturity to do so without giving in to old flesh patterns. In such cases, it is best to not participate until we have reached enough maturity to stay in God's will and exhibit the fruit of the Spirit.

> So whether you eat or drink or whatever you do, do it all for the glory of God (1 Cor. 10:31).

Thought for the day: *Can you continue doing what you are doing and glorify God, being a positive witness for Him?*

DIVINE GUIDANCE

2 Kings 2

Elijah was a divinely guided man of God who was about to be taken home to heaven (see 2 Kings 2:1). Elisha wouldn't leave his master, because he knew that God was with Elijah and he wanted the same anointing. Elijah took Elisha to the other side of the Jordan, and he watched the chariots of God transport Elijah home (see vv. 6-12). Elisha picked up Elijah's mantle and struck the water, and he walked across the Jordan River to the other side (see vv. 13-14). The crowd wanted him to look for his master (see v. 16), but there was no need to search for Elisha's master, because God was now his master.

Like Elisha, we all have to discover God for ourselves if we are going to be divinely guided by Him. The seven following issues are commonly considered for discerning God's will:

1. *Conscience:* Should we let our consciences be our guide? Our conscience is a function of our mind, and it can be defiled (see Titus 1:15). The Holy Spirit is our guide. False guilt can produce a guilty conscience, and a poorly developed conscience would sense no guilt. Salvation and growth in Christ renews our minds and consciences. Paul says, "I strive always to keep my conscience clear before God and man" (Acts 24:16).

2. *Fleeces:* The idea of a fleece comes from the story of Gideon in Judges 6. Gideon was asking God for a sign to confirm what God had already revealed. Gideon wasn't demonstrating faith in God. How many times does God need to say something before we are sure He means it? How much confirmation do we need to do what is right?

3. *Circumstances:* Some people are guided by the circumstances of life. If the circumstances are unfavorable, they conclude it isn't God's will; and if the circumstances are favorable, they assume they are on the right path. Circumstances are not reliable guides. We need greater resolve to stay faithful when difficulties arise. Paul said, "I have learned to be content whatever the circumstances" (Phil. 4:11).

4. *The counsel of others:* "For lack of guidance a nation falls, but many advisers make victory sure" (Prov. 11:14). It is always wise to seek godly counsel and gain the perspective of others. However, "Blessed is the man who does not walk in the counsel of the wicked" (Ps. 1:1).

5. *Gifts and abilities:* God will always lead us in a way that is consistent with how He has equipped us. God will never ask us to be someone we aren't, nor will He ask us to do something we aren't qualified to do. Unfortunately, many never realize their potential by stepping out in faith, nor take the risks that faith requires.

6. *Duty:* Our calling is not to see what lies dimly ahead, but to do what clearly lies at hand. We don't need any special leading to do our Christian duty, nor a subjective confirmation for doing what is clearly taught in Scripture.

7. *Desires:* If we follow our natural desires, we can easily be led astray. However, if we "Delight [our]selves in the LORD . . . he will give [us] the desires of [our] heart" (Ps. 37:4); but we delight ourselves in the Lord first, and then our desires will be transformed.

Fear God and keep his commandments, for this is the whole duty of man (Eccles. 12:13).

Thought for the day: *How much of God's will is just sanctified common sense?*

MAKING WISE DECISIONS

Deuteronomy 32:28-29

The nation of Israel was showing little discernment, and they lacked the wisdom to know their own destiny (see Deut. 32:28-29). Moses, like all the great leaders in the Bible, was intimately acquainted with God, and acquiesced to His will in all things. The wise person knows the will of God; the successful person does it. If you are trying to discern God's will and make wise decisions, consider the following questions:

1. *Have I prayed about it?* The first thing a Christian does about anything is pray and seek His kingdom. Recall that the Lord's Prayer begins with a petition to establish His kingdom and do His will.

2. *Is it consistent with the Word of God?* The majority of God's will for our lives has already been revealed in His Word. According to the courts of our land, ignorance of the law is no excuse. Make it your habit to consult the Bible when making decisions.

3. *Does this decision or choice compromise my Christian witness?* If the choice you are considering requires you to compromise your witness or integrity, then the answer is no. The end does not justify the means.

4. *Will the Lord be glorified?* Are you seeking the glory of man or the glory of God? Can you do it and glorify God in your body? Are you concerned about God's reputation or yours? Will this build His kingdom or yours?

5. *Am I choosing and acting responsibly?* What are my responsibilities and what would be the most responsible course of action to take? You cannot be in God's will and shirk your responsibility.

6. *Is it reasonable?* God expects us to think. His guidance may transcend human reasoning, but it never excludes it. God doesn't bypass our minds. He operates through them. Our Lord is a rational God and His ways are reasonable.

7. *Does a realistic opportunity exist?* Closed doors are not meant to be broken down. If you have a hopeless scheme, let it go. If a realistic opportunity exists, and all the other factors are in

agreement, then step out in faith. God opens windows of opportunity, but they may close if not taken advantage of.

8. *Are unbiased, spiritually sensitive associates in agreement?* Be careful not to consult only with those who are inclined to agree with you, or those who are afraid to be honest with you. Give them permission to ask hard questions and the right to disagree without recrimination.

9. *Do I have a sanctified desire to do it?* The greatest joy in life is to serve God and be in His will. You should feel good about doing God's will and want nothing less. If you delight yourself in the Lord, His desires will be your desires.

10. *Do I have a peace about it?* You should sense an inner confirmation if you are in God's will and a troubled spirit if you aren't.

Devote yourselves to prayer, being watchful and thankful (Col. 4:2).

Thought for the day: *Before you make a decision, do you pray about it?*

GOD GUIDES A MOVING SHIP

Acts 16:1-10

In Acts 15:36, Paul decided to revisit the churches he had helped establish on his first missionary trip. The churches were being strengthened and increasing in numbers (see Acts 16:5). Suddenly the Holy Spirit kept them from preaching in Asia (see v. 6), and the Spirit of Jesus would not allow them to keep going the same direction (see v. 7). Then Paul received a vision to go to Macedonia (see v. 9). If God had wanted Paul to go to Macedonia in the first place, why didn't He guide Paul on a more direct path to Macedonia? Because God wanted Paul to start his second missionary trip by strengthening the Churches in Asia.

This midcourse correction underscores an important concept of divine guidance. God can only guide a moving ship. A rudder doesn't work if the ship isn't moving. Guidance comes when we are actively doing God's will. We are not empowered to do our will. A ship without power is helpless at sea. The helmsman can't do anything because the rudder only works if the ship is under way. Life is a journey that takes us through many bends in a river. Like a good river pilot, God guides us around obstacles and away from troubled waters. If we are actively serving God, we will experience many midcourse corrections. We may not know in advance where God is leading us, but we will never get there if we are not actively underway.

We also need to bloom where we have been planted. Rattling doors to find an open one is not God's way. We ought to be content where we are and prove ourselves faithful in what God has already assigned us to do. He will open the doors of opportunity at the right time. If we aren't bearing fruit now, it is unlikely that we will be fruitful in another time and place.

Isaiah wrote, "The LORD will guide you always" (58:11). In the context prior to that verse, the Israelites had been seeking God's leading by fasting (see vv. 2-3). But God revealed that their fasting had been a farce that ended in strife (see v. 4). Then He shares what a real spiritual fast should be, for those who are intent on discerning God's will.

Is not this the kind of fasting I have chosen: to loose the chains of injustice and untie the cords of the yoke, to set the oppressed free and break every yoke? Is it not to share your food with the hungry and to provide the poor wanderer with shelter—when you see the naked, to clothe him, and not to turn away from your own flesh and blood? Then your light will break forth like the dawn (vv. 6-8).

In other words, God is asking us, "Why are you fasting to know My ways when you have clearly not been faithful to do what I have already commanded you to do? If you will minister to your people the way I have instructed, then your next step will be clear."

I thank Christ Jesus our Lord, who has given me strength, that he considered me faithful, appointing me to his service (1 Tim. 1:12).

Thought for the day: *Describe Paul's life when God called him into service.*

FAITH APPRAISAL

Amos 7:7-8

A plumb line is a weight that hangs on the end of a line that carpenters use to ensure that the walls of a building are built straight. The Lord showed Amos that the nation of Israel was no longer true to His plumb line (see Amos 7:7-8). God's people were supposed to be built by His standards; but when tested, He found they were completely out of plumb.

God is testing us also to see if our walk of faith is true to His Word. The next nine studies will help you determine how true your plumb line is. Start by assessing your own walk of faith with the following appraisal by circling the number that best represents you and complete the statements:

	Low				High
1. How successful am I?	1	2	3	4	5

I would be more successful if _____

2. How significant am I?	1	2	3	4	5

I would be more significant if _____

3. How fulfilled am I?	1	2	3	4	5

I would be more fulfilled if _____

4. How satisfied am I?	1	2	3	4	5

I would be more satisfied if _____

5. How encouraged am I?	1	2	3	4	5

I would be more encouraged if _____

6. How happy am I?	1	2	3	4	5

I would be more happy if _____

7. How much fun am I having?   1   2   3   4   5

I would be having more fun if _____

8. How secure am I?   1   2   3   4   5

I would be more secure if _____

9. How peaceful am I?   1   2   3   4   5

I would be more peaceful if _____

However you completed those above sentences reflects what you presently believe, and you are right now living according to what you have chosen to believe. Does your belief about these issues line up with Scripture?

Maybe a more basic question needs to be asked: Does God want us to live successful, significant, fulfilled and satisfied lives? It is hard to image that a loving heavenly Father has called us to be failing, insignificant, unfulfilled and dissatisfied children of God. As we shall see, rating a five on all nine issues above has only to do with our relationship with God and our walk by faith. We can all become the people God has created us to be, regardless of the circumstances of life.

> For in the gospel a righteousness from God is revealed, a righteousness that is by faith from first to last, just as it is written: "The righteous will live by faith" (Rom. 1:17).

Thought for the day: *How does your life reflect what you believe?*

SUCCESS

Joshua 1:7-9

Success is related to goals, but how are you setting realistic and godly personal goals for your life? What may be a realistic goal for one person could be impossible for another. God has not given each person the same endowment of gifts, talents and intelligence. Besides, your identity and sense of worth are not determined by those qualities. Your sense of worth is based on your identity in Christ; and your growth in character, both of which are equally accessible to every child of God. Success is accepting God's goal for your life and by His grace becoming what He created you to be.

We can be successful in the eyes of the world and a complete failure in the eyes of God. Many a person has climbed the ladder of success only to realize that it was leaning against the wrong wall. Joshua gives us the first key to being successful in the eyes of God. God had promised the Israelites prosperity and success on only one condition, and it had nothing to do with the cooperation of the Philistines or favorable circumstances: They would be successful if they lived according to His ways. They were successful in crossing the Jordan by faith (see Josh. 3), and they were successful in defeating Jericho by faith (see Josh. 6). But they were defeated at Ai, because Achan violated God's command (see Josh. 7:10-12). This simple principle of success stretches our faith.

Do you believe that you could run for public office and win by staying true to His Word? Do you believe that you could be a successful business person and never violate the Word of God? Success may mean that you drive an inexpensive car and live in a modest home as an honest person.

Second, to be successful, we have to become the people God created us to be. We may not have enough time to accomplish what we want, but we have enough time to do God's will. We may not be able to reach the position we hoped for, but what position is higher than being seated with Christ in the heavenlies? We can try to make a name for ourselves in the world, but what name could we make for ourselves that is better than being called children of God. Scripture provides no instruction for determining a career, but it gives a lot of instruction concerning what kind of career person we should be.

Third, to be successful, we must be good stewards of what God has entrusted to us. Our time, talent and treasure belong to Him, and they must be used to the glory of God. The Lord wants us to prosper, but what is our definition of prosperity? God's definition begins with the prosperity of our souls. What material possession or social status would you exchange for love, joy, peace, patience, kindness, goodness, faithfulness, gentleness and self-control? No earthly possession or position can give us what we all desire and what is available to all of us if we would just abide in Christ.

Dear friend, I pray that you may enjoy good health and that all may go well with you, even as your soul is getting along (3 John 2).

Thought for the day: *Will earthly possessions and positions help our soul to "get along"?*

SIGNIFICANCE

Ecclesiastes 3:1-11

Significance is related to time and eternity. What is forgotten in time is of little significance. What is remembered for eternity is of great significance. According to this passage in Ecclesiastes, God has set eternity in our hearts and appointed a time for everything (see 3:1-11). If we want to increase our significance, then we should focus our energies on those activities that remain forever. Paul writes, "For physical training is of some value, but godliness has value for all things, holding promise for both the present life and the life to come" (1 Tim. 4:8).

There are two tragedies concerning the concept of significance. The first tragedy is the significance the world attaches to things that are irrelevant in eternity, such as sporting events and lunar landings. They certainly impact our present world at the time, but what countries participated in the World Cup 15 years ago, and who won the World Series 20 years ago? Who was the most valuable player? Who cares? The world tries to maintain the significance of athletic events by keeping records for years, but the general population soon forgets. It was a significant achievement for humankind when Neil Armstrong landed on the moon, but now flights into space barely make the headlines, and many young people don't know who Neil Armstrong is!

The second tragedy is the sense of insignificance that Christians feel concerning their service for God. The world makes such a big deal about "significant" events that quickly fade from our memories, and the daily events of one Christian or local church go relatively unnoticed. But what happens in heaven when one sinner repents? All the angels in heaven rejoice (see Luke 15:7). That person's name is now written in the Lamb's Book of Life, and he or she will live in the presence of God forever. Someone teaching a group of little children in church may feel insignificant compared to the stars of Hollywood, or the celebrities in music and sports. But what could be more significant than to teach a young child the truth? What a child chooses to believe will affect him or her for all eternity.

There is no need to search for significance, because there are no insignificant children of God. There are no insignificant Christian ministries—no matter how obscure—provided that they are doing God's will. We are in the significant business of laying up treasures in heaven. We will live very significant lives if we build upon the foundation that Christ has laid, but everything we build for ourselves in our own strength will be torn down. Someone once said, "There is only one life; it will soon be past, only what is done for Christ will last."

If what he has built survives, he will receive his reward (1 Cor. 3:14).

Thought for the day: *How long do treasures on Earth last compared to eternity?*

FULFILLMENT

Habakkuk 3:17-19

Fulfillment is discovering our own uniqueness in Christ, and using our gifts and talents to edify others and glorify the Lord. Fulfillment is related to our calling and the roles we play in life. God has a unique place of ministry for each of us. It is important to our sense of fulfillment that we realize our calling in life.

The key is to discover the roles you occupy in which you cannot be replaced, and then decide to be what God created you to be. For example, there are over 6 billion people in this world, but you are the only one who can be someone's sister, brother, father, mother, coworker, neighbor or special friend.

A mother was puzzled by young ladies who entered the marketplace to find their fulfillment in the world. She correctly thought, *What could be more fulfilling, challenging or rewarding than to raise godly children in this world?* A businessman wondered about his coworkers who stepped on each other's backs and neglected their families in order to get ahead so that they could be "fulfilled" in their work. He thought, *What can be more fulfilling than to be a good witness at work where I serve the Lord and make provision for my family?* Habakkuk had a sense of fulfillment as he concluded his book, even though it had resulted in no material blessings (see Hab. 3:17-18).

We all occupy a unique role as ambassadors for Christ where we live, work and play. These are our mission fields, and we are the workers that God has appointed for the harvest. Our greatest fulfillment comes from accepting and occupying God's unique place for us to the best of our ability. We can always pray for those around us and look for opportunities to share the love of Christ. We may be their only link to the Church and to the gospel of the Lord Jesus Christ.

As we search for our role in life and in the Church, we must be on the lookout for a potential cause for lack of fulfillment which is typified by the young student who quizzed his teacher, "What is my spiritual gift, prophecy or exhortation?" To which the teacher replied, "I don't think it is either one. If anyone has the gift of service, you certainly do. I have seen you move instinctively to meet the needs of others." The disappointed student replied, "I knew it." We will never be fulfilled trying to become somebody we aren't.

The only way to be fulfilled in life is to discover our own potential and uniqueness in Christ and become that to the glory of God.

Jesus fulfilled His calling even though there was so much more others wanted Him to do. In His last breath, He was able to say, "It is finished" (John 19:30). Paul also fulfilled his calling. "I have fought the good fight, I have finished the race, I have kept the faith" (2 Tim. 4:7). Paul said to Timothy, "But you, be sober in all things, endure hardship, do the work of an evangelist, fulfill your ministry" (2 Tim. 4:5, *NASB*).

He fulfills the desires of those who fear him; he hears their cry and saves them (Ps. 145:19).

Thought for the day: *How can life be more fulfilling for you?*

SATISFACTION

Ecclesiastes 5:10

Satisfaction is related to the quality of life. Satisfaction comes from living righteously and seeking to raise the level of quality in relationships, service and products. Jesus tells us, "Blessed are those who hunger and thirst for righteousness, for they will be [satisfied]" (Matt. 5:6). Do you believe that? If you did believe what Jesus has said, what would you be doing? If you aren't hungering and thirsting after righteousness, then you really don't believe it satisfies. What Jesus tells us is true, of course, because nothing else really satisfies. "Whoever loves money never has money enough; whoever loves wealth is never satisfied with his income. This too is meaningless" (Eccles. 5:10). You may be satisfied with a new car for a period of time, but you will become dissatisfied when the quality of the car deteriorates and the performance of new cars exceeds yours.

What causes individuals to be dissatisfied is seldom related to what enables them to be satisfied. When people complain about the holes in the roads, the hard chairs at church or the temperature of the auditorium, are they satisfied when their complaints are heard and the problems fixed? That is why it is so unproductive for church leaders to run around putting out fires. As soon as one is out, another one will start. They are investing their time in that which causes dissatisfactions and not on what causes people to be satisfied. What satisfies people is meaningful ministries that bear fruit and quality relationships with God and others. Seldom will you see a Christian bearing fruit who isn't satisfied.

Satisfaction is related to quality, not quantity. To raise the level of satisfaction, one has to focus on raising the quality. You will be a lot more satisfied if you do a few things well rather than a lot of things in a mediocre way. The same holds true for relationships. You don't need a lot of superficial friends. "A man of many companions may come to ruin, but there is a friend who sticks closer than a brother" (Prov. 18:24). We all need a few close friends who value a quality relationship. And what about your most important earthly relationship, your marriage relationship? If you are not satisfied in your marriage, you will not solve it with gifts or promises. You will only solve it by being reconciled to God and each other in a quality way.

Quality, not quantity, is what Jesus modeled for us. He occasionally taught the multitudes and He did equip 70 workers; but He invested most of His time with the Twelve. Out of those twelve, He selected only three to be with Him on the Mount of Transfiguration (see Mark 9:2) and the Garden of Gethsemane (see Mark 14:32-33). Finally there was only one who stayed with Jesus at the foot of the cross, John—and to him, Jesus entrusted the care of His mother (see John 19:26-27).

> "Martha, Martha," the Lord answered, "you are worried and upset about many things, but only one thing is needed. Mary has chosen what is better, and it will not be taken away from her" (Luke 10:41-42).

Thought for the day: *What is the one thing that is needed in order to be satisfied?*

ENCOURAGEMENT

Nehemiah 4

The world is filled with blessing snatchers. They can find something bad in everything. They feel called to play the role of devil's advocate even though the devil doesn't need any help. They are quick to object and always have a reason why it can't be done. Dripping with negativism, they put a damper on life. Many of these pessimistic people who see only the dark side of life probably don't realize how discouraging they are to others. People like Sanballat and Tobiah represent the worst, since they actually oppose the work of God. They ridicule those who are trying to do God's will: "What are they building—if even a fox climbed up on it, he would break down their wall of stones!"(Neh. 4:3).

Nehemiah was an encourager. Encouragers motivate others to courageously continue on. Hearing the insults of Sanballat and Tobiah, Nehemiah prayed (see Neh. 4:4), and the people continued working with all their hearts. This only caused the enemy to unite against them, but Nehemiah prayed again and stationed guards. The enemy continued to chip away by spreading lies. Propaganda is a very effective weapon in war. An army can be defeated without weapons if they become discouraged and believe the lies of the enemy. Listen to the discouraging tone of the rumor mill: "The strength of the laborers is giving out, and there is so much rubble that we cannot rebuild the wall. Also our enemies said, 'Before they know it or see us, we will be right there among them and will kill them and put an end to the work'" (vv. 10-11). Such is the work of terrorists in this world.

Nehemiah countered again by stationing half the people for defensive purposes and gave a speech to all the people. "Don't be afraid of them. Remember the Lord, who is great and awesome, and fight for your brothers, your sons and your daughters, your wives and your homes" (Neh. 4:14). Their fear was abated when they remembered the Lord, and they returned to their task of rebuilding the wall. God had frustrated the plans of the enemy (see v. 15). When the walls were completed and the enemy heard about it, "all the surrounding nations were afraid and lost their self-confidence, because they realized that this work had been done with the help of God" (Neh. 6:16).

We may not always have leaders like Nehemiah to encourage us, but we can always encourage ourselves in the Lord as David did (see 1 Sam. 30:6). When you feel discouraged, remember God is great and awesome. He will meet all your needs, and you can do everything through Christ who strengthens you (see Phil. 4:13,19). Therefore, "Let us not give up meeting together, as some are in the habit of doing, but let us encourage one another—and all the more as you see the Day approaching" (Heb. 10:25). When you encourage someone, you give that person the courage to run the race with endurance.

> Therefore encourage one another and build each other up, just as in fact you are doing (1 Thess. 5:11).

Thought for the day: *How can you encourage those around you?*

HAPPINESS

Ecclesiastes 11:7-10

Solomon encourages us to enjoy life while we are living (especially in our youth), because the darkness of death is coming. Earlier Solomon tells us that enjoying life includes eating and drinking (see Eccles. 2:24; 3:13; 8:15; 9:7); wearing nice clothes and pleasant lotions (see 9:8); enjoying marital bliss (see 9:9); and finding satisfaction in our work (see 2:24; 3:22; 5:18). We should do what our hearts desire, but first we must delight ourselves in the Lord so that our desires are in line with the joy of the Lord.

For believers, the key to happiness is wanting what we have. Think about it. All commercialization is based on the premise that we would be happy if we only had what they are selling. Never has there been a time in human history when so many people have had so many material possessions and entertainment options, and yet been so unhappy. God's concept of happiness is summed up in the simple little proverb "Happy are those who want what they have!" Then we will be happy all our lives. The problem is that we focus on what we don't have instead of on what we do have.

Consider first what we deserve. If God gave us what we deserved, we would all suffer eternal damnation in hell. Now consider what we have. We have eternal life in Christ Jesus. We have the forgiveness of sins. We have the internal presence of the Holy Spirit who leads us and enables us to live liberated lives in Christ. We have new life and a rich inheritance in Him. We have a God who will meet all our needs and will never leave us. We should count our blessings and thank God for what we have.

Happiness can be so fleeting because it is dependent upon the circumstances of life. But we can always be joyful in our spirit when we know that the joy of the Lord is our strength (see Neh. 8:10). Personal happiness is the wrong goal. The goal is to know God and become the person He has created us to be. That leads only to godliness and contentment: "But godliness with contentment is great gain. For we brought nothing into the world, and we can take nothing out of it. But if we have food and clothing, we will be content with that" (1 Tim. 6:6-8).

God is joyful, and joy is a fruit of the Spirit. The joy that comes from knowing God is the result of our being at one with Him. Only in Christ can we say, "Be joyful always; pray continually; give thanks in all circumstances, for this is God's will for you in Christ Jesus" (1 Thess. 5:16-18). "Though you have not seen him, you love him; and even though you do not see him now, you believe in him and are filled with an inexpressible and glorious joy, for you are receiving the goal of your faith, the salvation of your souls" (1 Pet. 1:8-9).

Nehemiah said, "Go and enjoy choice food and sweet drinks, and send some to those who have nothing prepared. This day is sacred to our Lord. Do not grieve, for the joy of the LORD is your strength" (Neh. 8:10).

Thought for the day: *How can the joy of the Lord be your strength?*

FUN

2 Samuel 6

Fun is uninhibited spontaneity. Life is fun when we feel uninhibited and allow ourselves to be spontaneous. Worldly people know how to have fun. Many have made it their chief ambition in life. They throw off their inhibitions by going where nobody cares how they act. Some believe they need to drink or take drugs to get rid of their inhibitions or escape from the dismal realities of their natural life. Many think that Christians can't have any fun, because our "rules" keep us from being spontaneous and our "religion" makes us feel inhibited. That is a false understanding of our relationship with God, as David clearly demonstrated.

David was bringing the Ark of the Covenant back to Jerusalem, and his joy was so great that he was "leaping and dancing before the LORD" (2 Sam. 6:16). This uninhibited spontaneity caused Michal, the daughter of Saul, to despise him in her heart. She said to David, "How the king of Israel has distinguished himself today" (v. 20). David had not been acting properly according to protocol, because he didn't have the typical inhibitions that plague those who are more concerned about what others think than with what God thinks. But God judged Michal not David (see v. 23).

As David danced before the Lord, it didn't bother him that he was undignified in Michal's eyes. He didn't even care if he was humiliated in his own eyes (see 2 Sam. 6:22). He was having fun in the presence of the Lord. Life will be a lot more fun if we can rid ourselves of unscriptural inhibitors. Chief among the inhibitors of Christian fun is our carnal tendency to keep up appearances. We don't want to look out of place or be thought less of by others, so we stifle our inhibitions and spontaneity with a form of false decorum. That is people pleasing, and Paul said that anybody who lives to please people is not a bondservant of Christ (see Gal. 1:10). As Christians we don't play for the grandstand; we play for the coach.

Too many Christians are sound in the faith but sour in the face. They claim to have the joy of the Lord, but you would never guess it by their countenance. Having fun in the presence of God is living with enthusiasm. "Enthusiasm" means "in God" and is derived from the words *en* and *theos*. So it is not inconsistent for Christians to have fun and be enthusiastic about life. We are not chained to contemporary cultural taboos; we are liberated children of God. There is no need to keep up with the Joneses, since they probably don't have a clue where they are going. They may be going to hell, but we're not. The world is getting worse, but we're not.

Then how are we supposed to act? Christianity is not an act. It is a real experience. A liberated life in Christ. We restrict our freedom for the weaker brother, but we don't act like the weaker brothers and sisters who can't be themselves.

A righteous [man] can sing and be glad (Prov. 29:6).

Thought for the day: *When was the last time you really enjoyed life?*

SECURITY

Psalm 23

At the beginning of this twenty-first century, it is apparent that God is shaking the foundations of this earth. Nations are rising and falling, uniting and dividing—and at a pace never observed before. Over 60 countries in this world are in political chaos, and many more are suffering from economic insecurity. The population of the world has doubled in the last 30 years. Of all the people who have ever lived on planet Earth, one half are alive today. The population is exploding, but our natural resources are decreasing. This trend cannot continue without serious ramifications for our overcrowded Earth. Consequently, there is a growing sense of insecurity all over the world. People are insecure, because they are depending upon temporal things they have no right or ability to control. In the midst of ensuing conflicts, we have a shepherd who will guide us even through the valley of the shadow of death.

Security is relating to that which is eternal, not the temporal and transitory things of this world. We are secure in Christ, and our security is found in our eternal relationship with Him. No one can snatch us out of our heavenly Father's hand (see John 10:35-39), and nothing can separate us from the love of God (see Rom. 8:35-39). We were marked in Christ with a seal, the promised Holy Spirit, who is a deposit guaranteeing our inheritance (see Eph. 1:13-14). Conflicts in this world are inevitable, but in the midst of them we can have a sense of security.

Consider the various approaches to conflict (see diagram on p 385).

Those who have a high regard for relationships and want to accomplish something seek to resolve conflicts. They yield for the sake of relationships if the need to achieve isn't that great. Those who have a high "need" to achieve but a low regard for relationships seek to win. Still others withdraw because they have no regard for relationships or achievement. The most secure people are those who seek to resolve conflicts or yield for the sake of relationships. That is because security is found in relationships, not achievements. You probably felt secure in your home if relationships were valued over achievements. Secure individuals don't always have to be right and win every time there is a conflict, nor do they walk away from meaningful relationships. They have found their security in their eternal relationship with God and others.

But the greatest of these is love (1 Cor. 13:13).

Thought for the day: *Do you value relationships over achievements?*

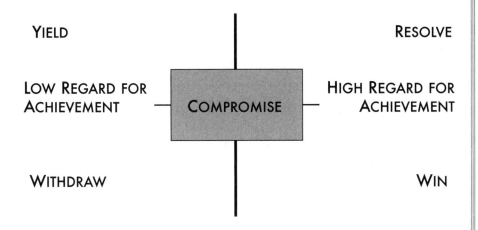

HIGH REGARD FOR RELATIONSHIPS

YIELD   RESOLVE

LOW REGARD FOR ACHIEVEMENT — COMPROMISE — HIGH REGARD FOR ACHIEVEMENT

WITHDRAW   WIN

LOW REGARD FOR RELATIONSHIPS

PEACE

Isaiah 32:17

Everybody wants world peace, but it may not always be possible. It is a desire that we all share, but it is not our primary objective. Suppose a wife seeks counsel with the goal of having more peace in her home. Nobody can guarantee that. To do so her counselor would have to be able to control every person in the home and that is impossible. Jesus said you should, "Seek first his kingdom and his righteousness, and all these things will be given to you as well" (Matt. 6:33). Isaiah said, "The fruit of righteousness will be peace" (32:17). That kind of peace is related to our internal order, not to the external order of this world. Jesus said, "I have told you these things, so that in me you may have peace. In this world you will have trouble. But take heart! I have overcome the world" (John 16:33).

Peace *with* God is something we already have (see Rom. 5:1). The peace *of* God that guards our hearts and our minds is something we need to appropriate on a daily basis (see Phil. 4:7). The only One who can give us that peace is the Prince of Peace. Jesus said, "Peace I leave with you; my peace I give you. I do not give to you as the world gives. Do not let your hearts be troubled and do not be afraid" (John 14:27). The peace of Christ that rules in our hearts stands in stark contrast to the false prophets of this world. "They dress the wound of my people as though it were not serious. 'Peace, peace,' they say, when there is no peace. Are they ashamed of their loathsome conduct? No, they have no shame at all; they do not even know how to blush" (Jer. 6:14-15).

We should pray for the peace of Jerusalem and for all the troubled spots of the world. We should seek to unite this world in peaceful reconciliation, because Jesus said, "Blessed are the peacemakers, for they will be called sons of God" (Matt. 5:9). Peace can be humanly negotiated so that we can coexist without destroying ourselves. That kind of peace only heals wounds superficially. The tension will always be there unless we resolve the inner conflicts. To accomplish inner peace we have to work toward righteousness, "the effect of righteousness will be quietness and confidence forever" (Isa. 32:17). We can have an inner peace in the midst of an external storm.

Peace comes when you quiet your heart before the Lord. In the midst of confusion, acknowledge God's presence in your life (the Quakers used to refer to this discipline as "centering down"). Then join one of America's most famous Quakers, John Greenleaf Whittier, in the following prayer.

> *Drop Thy still dews of quietness,*
> *Till all our strivings cease;*
> *Take from our souls the strain and stress,*
> *And let our ordered lives confess,*
> *The beauty of Thy peace.*[1]

Those who walk uprightly enter into peace (Isa. 57:2).

Thought for the day: *How would we feel if we allowed the Prince of Peace to rule in our hearts?*

SERVANT LEADERSHIP

Matthew 20:20-28

Secure Christian leaders have found their own identity and security in Christ. Insecure leaders try to establish their identity and sense of worth in titles, degrees, and positions of authority and power. Insecure parents promote their children to such attainments. Such was the case when the mother of Zebedee's sons approached Jesus. She wanted her children to sit on the right and left side of Jesus (see Matt. 20:20-21). The Lord said it was not His to offer, and then He asked if they were prepared to drink from the cup He was about to drink (see vv. 22-23). When the other 10 disciples heard about this, they became indignant (see v. 24).

When people clamor for power and position, it creates interpersonal problems in any organization. What are the others supposed to do when someone climbs over their backs to get ahead? They neither want those kind of people over them, nor do they want to succumb to the same self-serving tactics. Jesus exhorted His disciples not to be like the Gentiles who exercise their authority and lord it over others. Instead, they were to be like servants if they wanted to be great (see Matt. 20:25-26).

There is no position lower than that of a servant or a slave. Christian leaders are not supposed to rely on their position as the basis for their leadership. Christian leadership is not position based; it is character based. Those aspiring to the position of an overseer must show they are qualified by their character (see 1 Tim. 3 and Titus 1). The ability to lead may be somewhat dependent upon gifts, talents, intelligence or personality, but that is not what qualifies them to be a Christian leader. Even though some believers may be gifted, talented, intelligent and personable, they should be immediately disqualified if their character is deficient. Christian leaders should be an example to those under their authority and not lord it over them (see 1 Pet. 5:1-4).

Leaders are subject to the needs of those who are under their authority. All great leaders should sense the burden of being responsible for those who follow them. Jesus certainly did. He served us by giving His life to meet our greatest need. Jesus had no human position of authority in the religious establishment or the State. And yet, "the crowds were amazed at his teaching, because he taught as one who had authority, and not as their teachers of the law" (Matt. 7:28-29). They recognized His authority because of the quality and conduct of His life.

While Christian leaders are not to appeal to their position or demand loyalty to themselves, those who are under authority are required to respect their position. "Obey your leaders and submit to their authority. They keep watch over you as men who must give an account. Obey them so that their work will be a joy, not a burden, for that would be of no advantage to you" (Heb. 13:17).

> By this all men will know you that you are my disciples, if you love one another (John 13:35).

Thought for the day: *How easy is it to follow someone who loves you, and how hard is it to follow someone who doesn't?*

BALANCE OF POWER

Deuteronomy 17:14–18:21

In this passage, the Lord sets forth the roles and responsibilities of the prophet, priest and king (see Deut. 17:14–18:21). The concept of having checks and balances in government as well as the idea of having executive, legislative and judicial branches of government originated from this text. The prophet brought the law; the priest interpreted it; and the king executed it. The king would be roughly parallel to our executive branch of government. The Lord never told the Israelites to have a king, but He anticipated that they would ask for one in order to be like other nations (see Deut. 17:14-15).

The king must be chosen from one of the Israelites; he cannot be a foreigner. The president of the United States must also be born in the United States. The king was not to use his office as a means of personal gain, but Solomon, the third king of Israel, violated every one of this restrictions (see 1 Kings 10:21–11:3). Laws are also in place to make sure that U.S. presidents do not use their office for personal gain. Finally, the king was to keep for himself on a scroll a copy of the law so that he would revere God and follow carefully the word of the Lord. The king was not to interpret the law; he was to execute the law as interpreted by the priests (see Deut. 17:18-20).

The priests represented the judicial branch of government. They could not have an allotment or inheritance with Israel (see Deut. 18:1-2). In other words, they could not have any conflict of interest. Judges in the judiciary branch of the American government must recuse themselves if a particular case presents a conflict of interest.

The prophets were to speak the words of the Lord. They wrote the law. If they spoke presumptuously, they were to be removed and they were not to be feared if what they said did not come to pass (see Deut. 18:17-22). The legislative branch of government creates the laws of the land. In a representative form of government, legislators (senators and representatives) are supposed to speak on behalf of the people who put them into office. If they speak presumptuously and fail to represent the people, they are removed by the people in coming elections.

Only Christ is qualified to be prophet, priest and king. No person is good enough to rule without checks and balances. Under the New Covenant, we have pastors (pastor-teacher), shepherds (elders) and administrators (overseers). Although the terms pastor, elder and overseer refer to the same office, they do not describe the same function. They roughly parallel the roles of prophet (pastor), priest (elder) and king (overseer). They make up the leadership of the local church. The New Testament teaches a plurality of elders so that one person doe not hold all the authority. Christ is the head of the Church, and He alone rules. Elders collectively discern the will of God and lead the people by proclaiming the Word of God, caring for the people and by overseeing a ministry that ensures every member of the Body of Christ is contributing to the good of all.

Now the overseer must be above reproach (1 Tim. 3:2).

Thought for the day: *What happens in our churches when the integrity of the leadership is questioned?*

PURPOSEFUL LEADERSHIP

Genesis 11:1-9

If you know *how*, you will likely have a job, but you will work for the one who knows *why*. Why are we here, and why are we doing what we are doing? Those are the most basic questions in life. As Christians we should have a sense of purpose in life and a reason for doing what we are doing. Our purpose is to glorify God by manifesting His presence in this world, and then do all to the glory of God. We are to know Him and make Him known by fulfilling the Great Commission. All this is to be done in keeping with the Great Commandment, to love God with all our being and love one another in the same way we have been loved by God.

The descendants of Noah decided that they were going to build a tower that reached to heaven. The Lord said, "If as one people speaking the same language they have begun to do this, then nothing they plan to do will be impossible for them" (Gen. 11:6). What did God observe about these people that led Him to make such a statement?

These people had the first three out of four key ingredients that are essential for the success of any Christian ministry. First, they had a common objective. A well-defined purpose or mission statement keeps people moving in the same direction.

Second, there was unity among the people. They were one people. Leadership is the ability to unite the church to accomplish a mutually shared objective. When that objective is accomplished, all the members feel satisfied with their contribution.

Third, they had an effective communication system. They were one people speaking the same language. Very little will be accomplished if the members of a work crew cannot walk in the light and speak the truth in love with one another.

Let's take a closer look at the importance of communication. Fulfilling our purpose in our homes and churches requires us to keep the communication lines open. Building consensus requires good communication skills. People need to be heard, not just told. It is hard to get a commitment from people to do our will, but it is easy to get a commitment from others to do their will. People are already committed to do what they think is right. If they are heard and sense that they have contributed to the plans, they will get behind the leaders and support them. To disrupt their plans to build the tower, all God had to do was destroy their communication system (see Gen. 11:7-9). When they couldn't speak to each other, they scattered.

The fourth ingredient is the desire to do God's will. The men of the world never completed their task, because they had never consulted God. Building a tower and making a name for themselves was their idea. So let's learn from their mistake. Let's first collectively discern the will of God to determine a common objective. Then we will establish an effective communication system and unity among the people. Once we have taken these four steps, there is nothing we purpose to do that will be impossible for us.

> I pray also for those who will believe in me through their message, that all of them may be one, Father, just as you are in me and I am in you. May they also be in us so that the world may believe that you have sent me (John 17:20-21).

Thought for the day: *How will the world know that God the Father has sent God the Son?*

SHARED LEADERSHIP

Numbers 11

Every Christian leader has felt the burden of ministry. Some have felt so inadequate for the task that they have wished they were dead. Like Moses, they would rather die than to be around for their own demise. No matter how well the pastor preaches and teaches, there will always be some who say, "I'm not getting fed around here." Christian leaders who feel the burden of ministry should keep in mind that the two most powerful Kingdom figures in the Old Testament, Moses and Elijah, both requested to die during their ministry experience (see Num. 11:15; 1 Kings 19:3-4).

The Lord told Moses, "Bring me seventy of Israel's elders who are known to you as leaders and officials among the people" (Num. 11:16). The Lord would take of the Spirit that rested on Moses and put it on them, and they would carry the burden of the people. Jethro gave similar advice to Moses in Exodus 18:17-23. Jethro wasn't suggesting an authoritarian or hierarchical rule. The organizational structure was designed to appoint others to come alongside Moses so as to relieve his burden, since he had been trying to do it all by himself.

Why don't Christian leaders enlist the help of others who they know to be leaders and officials? Some are codependent and need to be needed. Others are overly conscientious, thinking, *I have been called to do this, so I better do it.* For some, it just never crossed their minds to enlist the help of others. Some have a Messiah Complex. They think they are the only ones who can do the ministry. Professionalism impedes the work of the Church if we believe that only the elite are qualified to help others. The purpose of Christian leadership is "to prepare God's people for works of service, so that the body of Christ may be built up until we all reach unity in the faith and in the knowledge of the Son of God and become mature" (Eph. 4:12-13). Paul wrote, "Carry each other's burdens, and in this way you will fulfill the law of Christ" (Gal. 6:2).

When the Spirit rested on the elders they prophesied only once, but Eldad and Medad continued prophesying. Joshua wanted them to stop prophesying. But Moses said, "Are you jealous for my sake? I wish that all the LORD's people were prophets and that the LORD would put his Spirit on them!" (Num. 11:29). As Christian leaders, do we want the Spirit of God to rest on others as He does on us? Do we want the Lord's anointing to rest as obviously on others as we would have it rest on us? Do we get as much delight when others have the spotlight in the kingdom of God as we do when it is our turn? Do we earnestly seek to help all the members of our churches reach their highest potential, even if it means that they are able to do some aspects of ministry better than us? Do we rejoice when others bear fruit and get more attention than we do? If we are servant leaders, we do.

> And the things you have heard me say in the presence of many witnesses entrust to reliable men who will also be qualified to teach others (2 Tim. 2:2).

Thought for the day: *How can we multiply ourselves for the purpose of ministry?*

HUMBLE INTERCESSION

Numbers 12—16

Moses was the most humble man on the face of the earth (see Num. 12:3). He showed his humility when his staff, congregation and elders challenged his authority and leadership. First Miriam and Aaron began to talk against Moses (see Num. 12:1-2). The Lord called all three out to the Tent of the Meeting and spoke to them. The Lord wanted to know why Miriam and Aaron weren't afraid to speak against Moses whom God had chosen to lead His people (see vv. 5-9). When the Lord departed, Miriam had leprosy (see v. 10). It would be human nature to agree with God's discipline, but Moses interceded on her behalf and God relented. The leprosy would last only for a week (see vv. 11-14).

In Numbers 14:1-4, the whole assembly was discouraged because of the bad report from 10 of the spies. They were ready to stone Moses, but then the Lord intervened again (see v. 10). God said He would strike them down with a plague for their unbelief and make Moses into an even greater nation (see vv. 11-12). How many Christian leaders would pass that test? If your congregation was about to stone you and God Himself said He was going to do away with them and give you an even greater ministry, wouldn't you feel just a little bit vindicated and maybe excited about having a bigger ministry? That is not how Moses felt. He was concerned about God's reputation. What would the pagan nations think if God brought these people out into the wilderness only to destroy them? Moses prayed that God would with-hold His judgment and God did (see vv. 13-20). Like Miriam, though, the people would have to suffer some consequences (see vv. 21-23).

In Numbers 16, Moses is tested again. This time the community leaders who had been appointed members of the council rose up against Moses. Again the Lord intervened; and He said to Moses and Aaron, "Separate yourselves from this assembly so I can put an end to them at once" (Num. 16:21). How many of us would be making a fast retreat? Moses again cried out to God, "O God, God of the spirits of all mankind, will you be angry with the entire assembly when only one man sins?" (Num. 16:22). Again God relented and the ground swallowed up only the leaders and their fam-ilies (see vv. 26-33).

If you are a pastor or leader and wonder why God doesn't intervene for you when the people reject your leadership, you have missed the point. Moses wasn't praying that God judge those who rebelled against him. He was praying that God would withhold judgment. Would your church profit more if you, their pastor, prayed for God's judgment upon his staff, board and congregation, or would they profit more if the pastor prayed that God would withhold His judgment? God said in Ezekiel 22:30, "I looked for a man among them who would build up the wall and stand before me in the gap on behalf of the land so I would not destroy it, but I found none." God is looking for more servant leaders like Moses.

Humble yourselves, therefore, under God's mighty hand, that he may lift you up in due time (1 Pet. 5:6).

Thought for the day: *What will happen if we don't humble ourselves?*

ESTABLISHING OUR FREEDOM IN CHRIST

James 4:1-12

James clearly reveals the ongoing battle that we have with the flesh (see Jas. 4:1-3), the world (see vv. 4-6) and the devil (see v. 7). To resolve these personal and spiritual conflicts, we need to draw near to God and repent of our old ways. If we try to resist the devil without first submitting to God, we will be attempting to set ourselves free by our own strength and resources. In the flesh we are no match for Satan. On the other hand, we can submit to God and still not resist the devil, thus remaining in bondage. The critical issue is our relationship with God, and the following seven issues need to be resolved in order to live a free and productive life in Christ (see the *Steps to Freedom in Christ*).

1. God said in Leviticus 20:6 that He would cut off from His people any who consulted mediums and spiritists. Those who have been falsely guided by and/or have made some commitment to any cult or occult teaching must specifically renounce that teaching and any pledges or vows they have made. We cannot draw near to God and stay attached to spiritual counterfeits.

2. We must recognize the ways that we have been deceived and choose the truth that will set us free. False prophets and teachers can deceive us; we can pay attention to deceiving spirits; and we can deceive ourselves. To get out of denial, we must face the truth about our own sinful condition, and learn how to overcome old flesh patterns, mental strongholds and defense mechanisms. The finished work of Christ is our defense.

3. We must forgive others from our hearts. Nothing will keep us more bound to the past than an unwillingness to forgive, and Satan will take advantage of it (see 2 Cor. 2:10-11). God Himself will turn us over to the tormentors if we refuse to forgive as we have been forgiven (see Matt. 18:21-35).

4. We must humble ourselves before God, because He is opposed to the proud (see Jas. 4:6). Humility is confidence properly placed in God. The truly humble believer worships God and

puts no confidence in the flesh (see Phil. 3:3). The proud cannot draw near to God.

5. We must be submissive to governing authorities (see Rom. 13:1-5). We cannot submit to God and rebel against the authority that He has established.

6. We must confess all known sins and renounce any use of our bodies as instruments of unrighteousness. The latter allows sin to reign in our mortal bodies (see Rom. 6:11-13). Then we must submit our bodies to God as living sacrifices (see Rom. 12:1).

7. We must renounce the sins and iniquities of our ancestors that have been passed on from one generation to the next and take our place in Christ (see Exod. 20:5).

Since we have these promises, dear friends, let us purify ourselves from everything that contaminates body and spirit, perfecting holiness out of reverence for God (2 Cor. 7:1).

Thought for the day: *If we want to experience our freedom in Christ, why is it essential to submit to God and resist the devil?*

RENOUNCING

2 Corinthians 4:1-2

In making a public profession of faith, the members of the Early Church would stand, face west and say, "I renounce you, Satan, and all your works and all your ways." This generic declaration is still practiced in many denominations of Christianity throughout the world. More specifically, the Early Church members would renounce every counterfeit religious experience they had ever had, every false vow or pledge they had made and every false teacher or doctrine in which they had believed. They would then face east and make a public declaration to follow Christ and believe the truth.

We read in the Old Testament, "He who conceals his sins does not prosper, but whoever confesses and renounces them finds mercy" (Prov. 28:13). In a similar way, Paul encouraged the Church to renounce secret and shameful ways and choose the truth. Renunciation involves giving up a claim or right. When we renounce, we are making a definite decision to let go of any past unrighteous commitments, pledges, vows, pacts and beliefs that are not Christian. We have not truly repented (changed our minds) if we make a decision for Christ, and then continue to hold on to the past and believe what we have always believed. That would make salvation an experience of addition rather than transformation. At salvation, we didn't just receive something new to be added on to what we already were. We are new creations in Christ and that potentially sets us free from our past. To decisively let go of the past is the first step in repentance. It is not enough to say we believe something to be true and at the same time continue to believe the lie. The truth will set us free only if it nullifies the lies that we have believed.

The apostle Paul reveals the close link between renouncing and not losing heart (that is, not being depressed or discouraged). Many new believers can easily lose heart if they simply add a little Christianity to their existing world experience. The finished work of Christ has eradicated our sin and given us new lives in Christ. But at the moment we were born again, we had not fully repented nor were our minds instantly renewed. We still needed the Holy Spirit within us to lead us to the truth that would set us free. Only through the grace of the Holy Spirit can we fully repent and be transformed by the renewing of our minds.

As new believers we can repent, because it is God who grants repentance leading to a knowledge of the truth. Only then can we come to our senses and escape the trap of the devil (see 2 Tim. 2:25-26). A failure to do so will leave many of us defeated and bound to our pasts. We are trying to have the best of both worlds and doing so has caused us heartache and pain. "It is for freedom that Christ has set us free. Stand firm, then, and do not let yourselves be burdened again by a yoke of slavery" (Gal. 5:1).

> Therefore since we are God's offspring, we should not think that the divine being is like gold or silver or stone—an image made by man's design and skill. In the past God overlooked such ignorance, but now he commands all people everywhere to repent (Acts 17:29-30).

Thought for the day: *What happens if we trust in Christ but don't repent?*

GOD'S SOVEREIGNTY AND OUR RESPONSIBILITY

2 Thessalonians 3

Paul prays that God would strengthen and protect us from the evil one (see 2 Thess. 3:3). Then he continues by saying we ought to carry out our own responsibilities and not become idle. Scripture draws a clear line between God's sovereignty and our responsibility.

God's Sovereignty		Our Responsibility

On the left side is what God and only God can do. If we try to play the role of God, we will invariably become frustrated and fail. We are not God, and we cannot save ourselves. We should not try to be someone else's conscience, and we cannot change another person. Nothing will interfere with Christian relationships and ministry more than our attempting to play the role of God in another person's life. The key to living the Christian life is to know God and His ways. If we choose to rebel against God and live another way, it leads to death (see Prov. 14:12).

The right side of the line depicts our responsibility, which is revealed in Scripture. God will not do for us what He has commanded us to do. God can only do that which is consistent with His nature and His Word. God cannot lie, and He will not change to accommodate us. We can't ask God to study His Word for us when He has required us to handle accurately the Word of truth (see 2 Tim. 2:15). God will enable us to do all that He has commanded, but He will not believe for us, forgive others for us, repent for us or assume any of our others responsibilities that He has clearly delegated to us. If we won't work, then neither should we eat (see 2 Thess. 3:10).

The devil has a field day when we fail to understand this simple truth. If we expect God to act a certain way, we are disappointed in Him when He doesn't respond the way we want. The same reasoning follows for unanswered prayer: "When you ask, you do not receive, because you ask with wrong motives" (Jas. 4:3).

Not recognizing who is responsible for what is even more devastating when it comes to resolving spiritual conflicts. Suppose a child suddenly becomes aware of a spiritual presence in her room, pulls the covers over her head and cries out, "God, do something!" But God doesn't seem to do anything. So she wonders, *Why don't you help me, God? You are all powerful. You can make it go away. Maybe You don't care, or maybe I'm not a Christian. Maybe that is why You're not helping.* That scenario is being played out all over the world in the lives of defeated believers.

God did do something. He defeated the devil, made us new creations in Christ and seated us with Him in the heavenlies (see Eph. 2:1-6). He has given us the authority and the responsibility to resist the devil (see Jas. 4:7). We also have the responsibility to put on the armor of God and take every thought captive and make it obedient to Christ (see Eph. 6:10-18; 2 Cor. 10:5). But what will happen if we don't assume our responsibility?

> But put on the Lord Jesus Christ, and make no provision for the flesh in regard to its lust (Rom. 13:14, *NASB*).

Thought for the day: *What will happen if you do make a provision for the flesh?*

404 THE DAILY DISCIPLER

ASSUMING OUR RESPONSIBILITY

James 5:13-16

This passage in James is the only place in the Bible that specifically says what we are supposed to do if we are sick or suffering (see Jas. 5:13-16). The Church has focused primarily on the role of the elders, while the responsibilities of the suffering and sick are often overlooked. There are three reasons why the prayer of a righteous person will not be very effective if the person in trouble is not assuming his or her responsibility.

We cannot ask other people to do our praying for us. If we are suffering, initially, we are the ones who should be praying (see Jas. 5:13). Intercessory prayer on our behalf is never intended to replace our responsibility to pray. The critical issue is our individual relationship to God, and there is only "one mediator between God and men, the man Jesus Christ" (1 Tim. 2:5). If you had a daughter who kept coming to you on behalf of your son, wouldn't you tell your daughter to advise her brother to come see you personally? We cannot have a second-hand relationship with God. Every child of God has the same access to Him. The only effective prayer at this stage is the prayer of a repentant heart. If we cherish sin in our hearts, the Lord will not hear us (see Ps. 66:18). The answer is to deal with the sin, not ask someone else to do our praying for us.

Second, we will never experience victory, wholeness, mental, emotional and spiritual health unless we assume our own personal responsibility for the same. God puts the responsibility on those suffering to take the initiative to call the elders, not vice versa. No one can be physically, spiritually or mentally healthy for someone else. Only God can change us, make us whole, bind up our broken hearts and set us free. Any lasting change will be directly related to what each individual person has chosen to believe and to do in response to God.

Understand that good health is not contagious, but bad health is. The same holds true spiritually: Just sitting by a spiritual giant will not have any effect on our spirituality, since there is no such thing as spiritual osmosis. On the other hand, "Do not be misled: 'Bad company corrupts good character' " (1 Cor. 15:33).

Third, confession, which is open and honest agreement with God, must come before healing (see Jas. 5:16). All too often elders are summoned to pray for the sick, only to discover later that those they prayed for have been living in bondage to sin, bitterness, pride and rebellion. They are probably sick because of these unresolved issues. The loving thing to do is to help them resolve their personal and spiritual problems by submitting to God and resisting the devil.

If we are sick and suffering for spiritual and psychosomatic reasons and if we truly repent, then the prayers of the righteous for us will be effective. We can't expect God to bless and heal us if we are rebelling against Him and His ways; but those who are righteous can pray with confidence for us if we are living righteously.

> When I kept silent [about my sin], my bones wasted away through groaning all day long. Then I acknowledged my sin to you and did not cover up my iniquity (Ps. 32:3,5).

Thought for the day: *Why must those who suffer due to sin pray themselves rather than have someone else pray for them?*

DO WE WANT TO GET WELL?

John 5:1-18

There are three types of people that cannot be helped. The first are those who will not acknowledge they have a problem or realize their need for God. The second are those who know they are in trouble, but their pride won't let them ask for the help they need. Their self-sufficiency is keeping them from finding their sufficiency in Christ. Life has a way of bringing these two types of people to the end of their resources. The overly confident Paul had to be struck down before He would turn to Christ.

The third type of people who cannot be helped are those who really don't want to get well. Such was the case of the man who was an invalid for 38 years. He would lie by the pool of Bethesda where the blind, the lame and the paralyzed came to be healed (see John 5:2-5). Supposedly an angel would come and stir the waters, and whoever was in it at the time was healed. The Lord asked him, "Do you want to get well?" (v. 6). That was a very profound question, not a cruel one. The invalid answered with an excuse. There was no one to put him in the water, and someone always got in ahead of him (see v. 7)! This man showed no faith in God, but the Lord in His sovereignty chose to heal him anyway (see vv. 8-9). Jesus warned him to stop sinning, for the eternal consequences of sin are far worse than his physical ailment (see v. 14). To show his gratitude, the man turned Him in for healing him on the Sabbath (see v. 15)!

Jesus took away this man's excuse and probably his source of income through begging. There are some people who really don't want to get well. They have a built-in excuse for not rising above the circumstances. Because of their illness, they get attention and pity from others. Many try to have their basic needs met through begging, welfare and charity.

Just as if the invalid had really wanted to get well, he would have found a way to get in that pool, so if we really want to get well, we would make whatever commitment it takes to overcome our infirmities. We wouldn't get mad at God or blame anybody else. We would choose to believe that we can overcome our deficiencies in Christ and that we can do all things through Him who gives us strength (see Phil. 4:13). If we have to swallow our pride and humble ourselves, we do it.

If we have to submit to a process that trusted people advise us to take, we do it. If we have to give up an unrighteous lifestyle, we do it. If we have to ask others to forgive us, we do it. If we need to forgive others, we do it. If we need to persevere under pressure, we do it. We do whatever it takes to become the person God created us to be, because Jesus did what it took for us to be alive and free in Him. The test of our character is determined by what it takes to stop us from pursuing our convictions: "As you know, we consider blessed those who have persevered" (Jas. 5:11).

So do not throw away your confidence; it will be richly rewarded. You need to persevere so that when you have done the will of God, you will receive what he has promised (Heb. 10:35-36).

Thought for the day: *Why is perseverance a test of our character?*

DISCIPLESHIP COUNSELING

Matthew 12

Chapter 12 of Matthew establishes Jesus as God's chosen Servant. He is the Lord of the Sabbath (see vv. 1-13) who fulfilled the prophecies of Isaiah (see vv. 15-21), and Jonah (see vv. 38-42), and demonstrated His authority over the kingdom of darkness (see vv. 22-32). He considered those who did His Father's will to be spiritually related to Him (see vv. 46-50). Jesus also showed total concern for the plight of His people. If His disciples were hungry, He saw that they were fed, even if it violated manmade religious traditions. If they were disabled, He healed them from their physical and spiritual bondage.

The demon-possessed man was blind and mute and the Lord "healed him" (Matt. 12:22). Healing the whole person and deliverance from demons have not always been seen or understood as part of the same process. The natural tendency is to establish physical or psychotherapeutic ministries that ignore the reality of the spiritual world or, conversely, to create some kind of one-dimensional deliverance ministry that sees human problems as only spiritual. But that wasn't the nature of Jesus. He ministered to the whole person, and He did so in the context of all reality.

Our lives are like our houses. If we haven't taken the garbage out in six months or cleaned up our spills, our homes will attract a lot of flies. Because flies are so distracting, we want to get rid of them. Some of us will be tempted to study the flight patterns of all the flies and determine their names and spiritual rank. Even if that were possible, it still wouldn't resolve the problem. We could exercise our authority over them and demand that they leave, but they would only come back and find the house empty, resulting in even greater bondage. The primary goal is not to get rid of the flies, but to get rid of the garbage. Repentance and faith in God have been and will continue to be the answer until Christ returns. Once we have submitted to God, resisting the devil and his demons is quite easy, because they no longer have any right to harass us.

Jesus confronted demons, but He didn't get into any dialogue with them. If we dialogue with demons in another person, we are bypassing the victim, who needs to repent and choose the truth. If we dialogue with demons and believe what they say, we will be deceived, because they all speak from their own nature and they are all liars (see John 8:44). Those who are captive to sin are only set free by the grace of God as they individually and personally respond to Him in repentance and faith.

The Church has been commissioned to continue Christ's ministry of setting captives free and binding up the brokenhearted. To be an effective instrument in His hand, we must be liberated in Christ ourselves and totally dependent upon Him, for apart from Christ we can do nothing.[1]

Therefore go and make disciples of all nations (Matt. 28:19).

Thought for the day: *How is counseling different from discipling in the Bible?*

THE TRUTH ENCOUNTER

Acts 20:13-38

Paul modeled what he taught, and his message to the elders at Ephesus was a summary of his message to us in the Epistles (see Acts 20:13-38). Under the gospel of grace we have been called to repent and have faith in our Lord Jesus Christ. We have also been warned that spiritual wolves will arise from our own numbers and distort the truth. This encounter with false prophets and teachers and deceiving spirits is better seen as a truth encounter rather than a power encounter. Truth is the liberating agent. There are no instructions to pursue power, because we already have all the power we need to live the Christian life and minister to others (see Eph. 1:18-19). Satan has been defeated and disarmed (see Col. 2:15); and the only way he continues to rule is through deception. When his lies are exposed, his power is broken. That is why we are admonished to know the truth, believe the truth, speak the truth and live the truth in love.

Before the Cross, Satan had not been defeated and God's people had not been redeemed. So it would take some specially endowed authority agent to expel demons. That is why Jesus gave his disciples "power and authority to drive out demons" (Luke 9:1). Spirit-filled disciples exercising their authority in Christ over demons were ministers of deliverance in the Gospels and the early chapters of Acts. Those who needed demons cast out would call these specially gifted ministers, who had the power through Christ Jesus, to cast out demons.

After the Cross, Satan was defeated and in this present Church Age every believer has the same power and authority to do God's will. That is why there are no instructions in the Epistles for casting out demons within the Church. It is no longer the outside minister's responsibility. The deliverer is Christ, and He has already come and we don't get our information from evil spirits. We get our information from the Holy Spirit, who is the Spirit of Truth. He will lead us into all truth and that truth will set us free. No outside agent can repent for us or believe for us. That is a choice we all have to make in order to live liberated lives in Christ.

The only power that Satan has is the power we give him through fear and unbelief. Satan roars likes a hungry lion, but in reality he has no teeth (see 1 Pet. 5:8). A lion roars for two reasons. First, to paralyze its prey in fear.

If fear is controlling our lives, then faith in God is not. Second, a lion will stand over its prey's burrow, nest or den, and roar. The poor creature will run out in fear and be consumed. To fear Satan more than God is to elevate him above God as an object of worship. He wants to be feared, because he wants to be worshiped. Those who overcome will inherit eternal life, but the cowardly and unbelieving will not (see Rev. 21:6-8).

> Jesus said, "If you hold to my teaching, you are really my disciples. Then you will know the truth, and the truth will set you free" (John 8:31-32).

Thought for the day: *What liberates us from Satan?*

SETTING CAPTIVES FREE

2 Timothy 2:22-26

This passage, 2 Timothy 2:22-26, is the pastoral model for helping others experience their freedom in Christ. Paul lists six qualifications for setting captives free:

1. *We must be the Lord's servants.* Christian counseling should be understood as an encounter with God; not just a technique learned through formal education. To be effective we must be totally dependent upon God, knowing that only He can set a captive free and bind up the brokenhearted.

2. *We must not be quarrelsome.* The goal is not to win the argument but to avoid it. The reason a nuclear physicist doesn't trust in Christ is the same reason a garbage collector doesn't. They don't want to. The primary problem is moral not intellectual. They don't want to give up control of their lives or change their lifestyle. We will accomplish little by pandering to someone's intellectual arrogance, but we must cater to their intellectual integrity by giving a reason for the hope we have in Christ (see 1 Pet. 3:15).

3. *We must be kind to all.* Jesus said, "Go and learn what this means: 'I desire mercy, not sacrifice'" (Matt. 9:13). Mercy comes from the Hebrew word *hesed* which is translated in the Old Testament as "lovingkindness" or "compassion." We are working with wounded people who cannot handle harsh treatment, criticism or rejection. They need to tell us their story, but they won't if we aren't the kind of people they would feel safe to share it with.

4. *We must be able to teach.* That means we must know the truth that will set them free. They are in bondage to the lies they have believed. They have no interest in sharing their problems just for the purpose of sharing them, but they will share their deepest secrets to the right person for the purpose of resolving their problem.

5. *We must not be resentful.* We can't bring our own problems into the counseling session and expect to help someone else. We

have to be free in Christ ourselves in order to be used by God to set others free.

6. *We must be gentle like Jesus.* The only time the Lord ever described himself was in Matthew 11:29: "I am gentle and humble in heart." We cannot run roughshod over people, move too fast or get ahead of God's timing. Patience is a virtue. We never have enough time to do it right, but we always have enough time to do it over again.

This passage does not teach us to confront demons in some kind of power encounter; it teaches a kind and gentle encounter with truth. We must be dependent upon God, because He is the One who grants repentance that leads to a knowledge of the truth, and that is what sets the captives free. The "Steps to Freedom in Christ" are based on this model.

They will come to their senses and escape from the trap of the devil, who has taken them captive to do his will (2 Tim. 2:26).

Thought for the day: *Where is the spiritual battle being waged and how can we win it?*

THE WONDERFUL COUNSELOR

Isaiah 61:1-3

Jesus quoted the first part of this passage when He stood up in a synagogue to read from God's Word on the Sabbath (see Luke 4:14-22). Jesus stopped reading in the middle of verse 2 after the word "favor," emphasizing what He would accomplish in His first advent. When He comes again, He will fulfill verses 2 and 3. Judgment will come for unbelievers and a garment of praise for those who trust in Him.

No passage better reveals the heart of God than these few verses. Jesus is the good news. He is the Alpha and the Omega, the beginning and the end. Jesus is the great I AM. To His children He is our Savior, our Lord and our life. Isaiah said He was anointed to preach the good news to the poor. Jesus said, "Blessed are the poor in spirit, for theirs is the kingdom of heaven" (Matt. 5:3). Isaiah said Jesus was sent to bind up the brokenhearted (see Isa. 61:1). Jesus said, "Blessed are those who mourn, for they will be comforted" (Matt. 5:4). Isaiah said Jesus came to proclaim freedom for the captives and release from darkness for the prisoners (see Isa. 61:1). Jesus said, "Blessed are the meek, for they will inherit the earth" (Matt. 5:5). This is the year of the Lord's favor, and we are the benefactors.

During this Church Age, God has committed Himself to work through His children as they minister one to another. So when we minister to the spiritual captive and the brokenhearted, we can be assured that Jesus is present, and He wants to set them free and bind up their broken hearts. As Christian disciplers and counselors, we are facilitators of a process that connects people to God. We are encouragers who acknowledge the presence of God and realize that apart from Christ, we can do nothing. We know in our hearts that the Spirit, the Sovereign Lord and the Messiah is the "Wonderful Counselor, Mighty God, Everlasting Father, Prince of Peace" (Isa. 9:6).

Discipleship counseling is the process of building the life of Christ into one another. It is a relational experience centered on the Word of God in the presence of Christ and one another. A good biblical discipler would be a good biblical counselor, and a good counselor would be a good discipler.

They are essentially the same pastoral roles in the New Testament. The goal of both is to work with God in the sanctifying process.

Therefore, "We proclaim him, admonishing and teaching everyone with all wisdom, so that we may present everyone perfect in Christ" (Col. 1:28). We do this "so that the body of Christ may be built up until we all reach unity in the faith and in the knowledge of the Son of God and become mature, attaining to the whole measure of the fullness of Christ" (Eph. 4:12-13).

He heals the brokenhearted and binds up their wounds (Ps. 147:3).

Thought for the day: *How effective can a counselor be if God is not included in the process?*

A CALL TO LIVE
A RIGHTEOUS LIFE

2 Peter 3

We don't know the day or the hour, but we do know that the Lord is coming again. In the Olivet discourse (see Matt. 24), Jesus gives us the signs of the end of the age. He warns us not to be deceived, because there will be false Christs and false prophets and there will be a coming apostasy before He returns. Peter said there would be scoffers (see 2 Pet. 3:2-4) who make fun of the Second Advent. With wars and rumors of wars, earthquakes and famine, and increasing lawlessness, many of us ask, Why doesn't the Lord come back now? Because He looks into the kingdom of darkness and sees millions who have never heard the Gospel. If He shut the door now, how many of your friends, relatives, neighbors and coworkers would be shut out of His kingdom for all eternity. He is waiting for "the gospel of the kingdom [to be] preached in the whole world as a testimony to all nations, and then the end will come" (Matt. 24:14). "The Lord is not slow in keeping his promise, as some understand slowness. He is patient with you, not wanting anyone to perish, but everyone to come to repentance" (2 Pet. 3:9). Listen to some of Paul's final words:

> In the presence of God and of Christ Jesus, who will judge the living and the dead, and in view of his appearing and his kingdom, I give you this charge: Preach the Word; be prepared in season and out of season; correct, rebuke and encourage—with great patience and careful instruction. For the time will come when men will not put up with sound doctrine. Instead, to suit their own desires, they will gather around them a great number of teachers to say what their itching ears want to hear. They will turn their ears away from the truth and turn aside to myths. But you, keep your head in all situations, endure hardship, do the work of an evangelist, discharge all the duties of your ministry (2 Tim. 4:1-5).

The only way to hasten the day of the Lord is to do the work of an evangelist, which we should do out of love for God and others anyway. "The day of the Lord will come like a thief" (2 Pet. 3:10) when we least expect it. Jesus could come tomorrow or next year or next century.

The real question is, What kind of person ought you to be? "You ought to live holy and godly lives as you look forward to the day of God and speed its coming" (2 Pet. 3:11-12). May the good Lord bless you and encourage you as you seek to be all that God has created you to be. "To him who is able to keep you from falling and to present you before his glorious presence without fault and with great joy—to the only God our Savior be glory, majesty, power and authority, through Jesus Christ our Lord, before all ages, now and forevermore! Amen" (Jude 24).

> At that time the sign of the Son of Man will appear in the sky, and all the nations of the earth will mourn. They will see the Son of Man coming on the clouds of the sky, with power and great glory. And he will send his angels with a loud trumpet call, and they will gather his elect from the four winds, from one end of the heavens to the other (Matt. 24:30-31).

Thought for the day: *Knowing that the Lord is returning, what two tasks should we be doing?*

FORCES OPPOSING OUR SANCTIFICATION

WORLDVIEW

Daniel 10

Worldview is what we have learned to believe about the world in which we live. It consists of the conscious and subconscious suppositions that we hold about reality. Rationalism and naturalism have dominated the Western world. From that philosophical perspective, reality is only that which can be perceived through the five senses. The reality of the spiritual world is not part of a natural worldview that only believes in what can be seen. A biblical worldview includes the reality of the spiritual world. That is why "We fix our eyes not on what is seen, but on what is unseen. For what is seen is temporary, but what is unseen is eternal" (2 Cor. 4:18).

From a biblical worldview, there are three enemies to our sanctification: the world, the flesh and the devil. We not only live in a fallen world that shapes our old nature; we also live in a world that is dominated by spiritual forces that are actively opposing the will of God. Satan is "the prince [ruler] of this world" (John 16:11), "the god of this age" (2 Cor. 4:4) and "the ruler of the kingdom of the air" (Eph. 2:2). Satan "leads the whole world astray" (Rev. 12:9), and "the whole world is under the control of the evil one" (1 John 5:19). If we honestly look at the world around us, we will see more evidence of the kingdom of darkness than we will of the kingdom of God. There is more immorality, injustice and bondage to sin, than there is righteousness, justice and freedom from sin. For this reason the Son of God appeared "to destroy the devil's work" (1 John 3:8).

This opposition to the will of God is illustrated in Daniel 10. Daniel prays, fasts and mourns for three weeks on behalf of Israel's captivity (see vv. 2-3). Finally, an angel comes to tell Daniel that his prayers have been heard, because of his humility and desire to gain understanding. The angel said that he would have come sooner, but "the prince of the Persian kingdom resisted me twenty-one days. Then Michael, one of the chief princes, came to help me because I was detained there with the king of Persia" (v. 13). Conservative scholars agree that the "prince of the Persian kingdom" is a spiritual enemy of God who is opposing God's plan to work with Daniel.

Opposition to the kingdom of God continues to this day. Even now, there is a fierce battle going on in the heavenlies—the spiritual realm—and it is affecting what is happening in the natural realm. A Christian worldview takes into account that "our struggle is not against flesh and blood, but against the rulers, against the authorities, against the powers of this dark world and against the spiritual forces of evil in the heavenly realms" (Eph. 6:12).

We live by faith, not by sight (2 Cor. 5:7).

Thought for the day: *Why must we live by faith and not by sight?*

THE KINGDOM OF GOD

Acts 28:31

Kingdoms have a ruler, a realm and a reign. God created Adam and Eve to rule over the birds of the sky, the beasts of the field and the fish of the sea. Under the sovereign rule of God, Adam and Eve's descendants were to have dominion over the earth (see Gen. 1:28-30). But Satan deceived Eve, and Adam sinned (see Gen. 3:6). Satan became the rebel holder of authority, the prince of this world. He would rule through his hierarchy of demons who would blind the minds of the unbelieving (see 2 Cor. 4:4), and deceive and lead astray the hearts and minds of all humankind. Satan is portrayed as possessing all the kingdoms of this world (see Luke 4:6). When the devil offered Jesus the kingdoms of this world in exchange for His worship, Jesus never corrected his claim nor did He succumb to the temptation.

Scripture clearly presents God as the King of kings and Lord of lords of the universe. God sits on His throne (see Ezek.1:26-28) where He is surrounded by the heavenly host who serve Him (see 1 Kings 22:19), and He watches over the whole earth (see Ps. 33:13). God is the eternal King (see Ps. 145:13) who overcomes the forces of chaos and disorder symbolized by the flood and the sea (see Pss. 29:10; 93:1-4). His reign is characterized by power and glory (see Ps. 145:11), but also by truth and righteousness (see Ps. 96:13). God alone is the judge of this world (see Ps. 96:10).

The "kingdom of God" and "the kingdom of heaven" are essentially synonymous. These terms describe any type of rulership God may assert over the earth at a given time. The apostles expected that the kingdom of God would be established through the nation of Israel (see Acts 1:6). John the Baptist, Jesus and the apostles announced to Israel that the Kingdom was at hand. However, the leadership of Israel rejected Jesus as their king. As a result, the kingdom of heaven in its earthly manifested form has been postponed until the Second Advent of Christ. Some Bible scholars see the Second Coming of Christ as the beginning of a millennial reign when the kingdom of God will be fully established on Earth. The final judgment will come after the millennium.

Satan may be the prince of this world, but he has been judged and now stands condemned (see John 16:11). That is one reason why Paul could boldly and without hindrance preach the kingdom of God. The full manifestation of God's kingdom on Earth is yet to come, but that does not mean that God is not King or that He is not ruling. On Earth, His realm consists of His children who are charged to fulfill the Great Commission. "And this gospel of the kingdom will be preached in the whole world as a testimony to all nations, and then the end will come" (Matt. 24:14). Satan knows his end is coming and he will do all he can to impede the progress of the gospel.

> Our Father in heaven, hallowed be your name, your kingdom come, your will be done on earth as it is in heaven (Matt. 6:9-10).

Thought for the day: *Why do you think we are instructed to pray this way concerning the kingdom of God?*

THE PRESENCE OF THE KINGDOM OF GOD

Matthew 13

The Lord often used parables to teach Kingdom truths. They are illustrative stories that Jesus drew from nature and human life. When asked why He spoke in parables, "He replied, 'The knowledge of the secrets of the kingdom of heaven has been given to you, but not to them'" (Matt. 13:11). Recall from Paul's teaching that the natural person cannot comprehend the Word of God (see 1 Cor. 2:14). In the parable of the sower, the message about the kingdom is received by some but not by others (see Matt. 13:18-23). The devil snatches the message away from some, others hear the good news but it doesn't take root. Still others are carried away by "the worries of this life and the deceitfulness of wealth" (v. 22). The good soil represents those who hear the Word and understand it. Only the latter bears fruit, which is the evidence that they have new life in Christ.

The parable of the weeds (see Matt. 13:36-40) reveals another truth about the kingdom of heaven. Whenever and wherever God sows good seed in the field, the devil comes along and sows a bad seed. The field is the world, and Jesus is the One who sows the good seeds who are the sons of the Kingdom. The devil sows the bad seeds who are the sons of the evil one. The bad seed is darnel or quack grass. It is very hard to distinguish from the other grain when it is young; but when it matures, it is very easy—the good seed produces fruit that can be seen, the darnel doesn't. The good seed propagates by spreading seed; the darnel sends out roots under ground. They will coexist until the final harvest when Jesus sends His angels to weed out His kingdom. They will throw those who do evil into the fiery furnace (see vv. 40-42).

The kingdom of God is not an action taken by humankind or a realm that we establish. The Kingdom is a divine act, not a human accomplishment. The word "Kingdom" also means the realm set up by God and the benefits that are associated with it. Humankind may enter the Kingdom (see Luke 16:16) or receive it as a gift (see Luke 12:32). Consequently, the message of the Kingdom is the good news. The present world is under the rule of Satan, but the action of God in Jesus means that Satan is being defeated, his rule is being brought to an end, and his captives are being set free. The coming of the Kingdom means the hour of judgment upon wicked people; it is also the hour of deliverance from demonic powers (see Matt. 12:28). The work of Jesus is a sign of the coming and the presence of the Kingdom. He rules in the hearts of those who are the sons and daughters of the kingdom. The kingdom of God is characterized by grace (see Matt. 20:1-16) and a compassion that binds up the brokenhearted. Notice how the Kingdom is associated with preaching (see Luke 9:1); with spiritual authority over demons (see Mark 1:39; 3:14-15); and with healing (see Luke 9:1-2,6,11; 10:9).

> When Jesus had called the Twelve together, he gave them power and authority to drive out demons and to cure diseases, and he sent them out to preach the kingdom of God and to heal the sick (Luke 9:1).

Thought for the day: *Why don't the miracles of healing and deliverance happen in our times?*

THE ESTABLISHMENT OF GOD'S FUTURE REIGN

Zechariah 14:9

Zechariah prophesied that the Lord would one day be King over all the earth (see Zech. 14:9). The coming of the Kingdom is a recurring theme in Scripture. Although the Kingdom was present in the ministry of Jesus, He also spoke of it as being in the future and told His disciples to pray for its coming (see Matt. 6:10), and to be ready when it comes (see Matt. 25:1-13). When Jesus said a number of times that it was coming soon (see Matt. 16:28; Mark 9:1), He was referring to the age yet to come (see Mark 10:30). The future Kingdom was associated with the second coming of Jesus, the resurrection of the dead and the setting up of an eternal peace in His presence. It is described as a banquet (see Matt. 8:11) or wedding feast (see Rev. 9:9).

If the presence of the Kingdom is closely associated with Jesus, then its future coming is associated with His Second Coming. The two events form a single future hope. Even though the future Kingdom is imminent for us, Jesus indicated an interval between His death and its arrival. During this time the disciples were given the keys to the kingdom (see Matt. 16:19) and were instructed to preach the gospel to all the nations (see Matt. 24:14). The Church Age was a mystery, which means that its existence had not been previously revealed. The purpose of the Church is given in Ephesians 3:8-11:

> This grace was given me: to preach to the Gentiles the unsearchable riches of Christ, and to make plain to everyone the administration of this mystery [the Church], which for ages past was kept hidden in God, who created all things. His intent was that now, through the church, the manifold wisdom of God should be made known to the rulers and authorities in the heavenly realms, according to his eternal purpose which he accomplished in Christ Jesus our Lord.

In the above passage, the rulers and authorities are in the spiritual realm (i.e., the heavenlies), not the natural realm. The Church triumphs over the kingdom of darkness when the children of God live righteous lives and speak the truth in love. They can do it, because Jesus is the head of the Church. "God placed all things under his feet and appointed him to be head over everything for the church, which is his body, the fullness of him who fills everything in every way" (Eph. 1:22-23).

We don't know when the Lord will come again.

But the day of the Lord will come like a thief. The heavens will disappear with a roar; the elements will be destroyed by fire, and the earth and everything in it will be laid bare. Since everything will be destroyed in this way, what kind of people ought you to be? You ought to live holy and godly lives as you look forward to the day of God and speed its coming (2 Pet. 3:10-12).

We should make plans to live long, productive lives on planet Earth, but we should live righteously as though Jesus were coming tomorrow.

For the Lord himself will come down from heaven, with a loud command, with the voice of the archangel and with the trumpet call of God, and the dead in Christ will rise first. After that, we who are still alive and are left will be caught up together with them in the clouds to meet the Lord in the air. And so we will be with the Lord forever. Therefore encourage each other with these words (1 Thess. 4:16-18).

Thought for the day: *How does this passage from 1 Thessalonians encourage you?*

GOOD VERSUS EVIL

Esther 3

There are no religious references in the book of Esther. God is never mentioned; neither is prayer, worship or sacrifice, and yet it clearly illustrates the eternal battle between good and evil. In the normal course of human events, Satan is working to destroy God's plan of redemption, and God controls and directs all the seemingly insignificant coincidences that result in deliverance for His Chosen People. Events in the Persian City of Susa threatened the continuity of God's plan in redemptive history. Had Haman successfully destroyed all of Mordecai's people, the Jews, it would have prevented the coming of the Messiah (see Esther 3:6). Devout Jews to this day celebrate the Feast of Purim to commemorate the deliverance of the Israelites in Persia (see Esther 9:26-28).

Think of all the times that the Messianic bloodline was threatened. Cain killed Abel, but Eve was granted another son to carry on the family line (see Gen. 4:17). A scapegoat was provided minutes before Abraham sacrificed Isaac his son (see Gen. 22:10-13). A caravan happened to come along when Joseph had been left to die (see Gen. 37:26-28). Moses was spared when all the male children were killed (see Exod. 2:1-10). Haman tried to annihilate the Jews (see Esther 3:6). The demonized Saul tried to kill David (see 1 Sam. 19:9-10). Herod ordered all the newborn male babies to be killed, which would have included Jesus; but Joseph and Mary were warned in a dream to flee to Egypt (see Matt. 2:13-18). Wars, diseases and natural disasters have threatened God's people, but God has always ensured that there would be a remnant.

The Jews were dispersed after the destruction of Jerusalem in 70 A.D. Throughout the Church Era, they have continued to be persecuted. Had Hitler been successful, he would have annihilated the Jews. It is a miracle that they have maintained their Jewish identity and have reestablished their home in Israel. As a nation, they did not accept Jesus as their Messiah. But, "God did not reject his people, whom he foreknew" (Rom. 11:2). As a result of their rejection, "Israel has experienced a hardening in part until the full number of the Gentiles has come in. And so all Israel will be saved" (Rom. 11:25-26). Israel continues to be God's timetable for the consummation of the ages.

The New Testament and the Early Church clearly understood that Satan and his demons were the instigators of evil in this world. The Western church is inclined to see the book of Esther as a battle only between good people and bad people. Such a deduction leaves one to think that evil is purely the product of natural people living in a fallen world and operating under the permissive will of God. That ignores the reality of Satan and his diabolical rule over the world. Satan interfered with God's plans in the Garden, and the battle continues all the way to the book of Revelation. The primary battle is still between the kingdom of God and the kingdom of darkness, between the Spirit of truth and the father of lies, between the Christ and the Antichrist.

> And we know that we are children of God, and that the whole world is under the control of the evil one (1 John 5:19).

Thought for the day: *How is Satan able to control the whole world?*

SATAN

Ezekiel 28:1-19

The word "satan" is only mentioned three times in the Old Testament (see 1 Chron. 21:1; Job 1:6-12; Zech. 3:1-10). However, conservative scholars identify the serpent in Genesis 3 as Satan, or at least a beast that was possessed by Satan. Scripture says the serpent is "more crafty than any of the wild animals the LORD God had made" (Gen. 3:1). Satan's designations as "tempter" (Matt.4:3) and the "ancient serpent" (Rev. 12:9) refer back to the Genesis passage. Orthodox Christianity has always understood that it was Satan who deceived Eve and caused the Fall of humankind.

Biblical scholars have noted that the characteristics about the king of Tyre in Ezekiel 28 do not seem applicable to a mere human being. He sees himself as being wise as a god (see v. 6) and wiser than Daniel (see v. 3). This proud person claims to be a god and sit on the throne of a god (see v. 2). This is what the Lord has to say about him:

> You were the model of perfection, full of wisdom and perfect in beauty. You were in Eden, the garden of God; . . . You were anointed as a guardian cherub, for so I ordained you. You were on the holy mount of God; you walked among the fiery stones. You were blameless in your ways from the day you were created till wickedness was found in you. . . . So I drove you in disgrace from the mount of God, and I expelled you. . . . Your heart became proud on account of your beauty, and you corrupted your wisdom because of your splendor (vv. 12-17).

The Church has understood this passage to be speaking about the fall of the king of Tyre and the fall of Satan. Ezekiel is making an historical as well as a cosmic point about Satan as a created angelic being. At one time Satan had a privileged position with God, but he fell due to his own rebellious choice. The full character of Satan's evil nature is not fully developed in the Old Testament.

However, in the New Testament the term "satan" occurs 36 times. Most references are preceded by the definite article "the" and refer to him as a personal devil. That means the devil is a personality who is crafty and deceptive, as opposed to an impersonal force. Orthodox Christianity has always professed to believe in a personal devil.

Satan holds a position of great influence in the spiritual world. He has personal access to the presence of God, a privilege that will be taken away from him in the future (see Rev. 12:9). Satan is the ruler over a powerful kingdom of evil that he executes with intelligent consistency. However, Satan is a created being and therefore does not have the attributes of God. Since he is not omnipresent, he rules over the kingdom of darkness by delegating responsibility to "his angels" (Matt. 25:41; Rev. 12:7).

In the pride of your heart you say, "I am a god" (Ezek. 28:2).

Thought for the day: *Is there any evidence that this same spirit is operating in this world today?*

THE FALL OF LUCIFER

Isaiah 14:1-23

This passage in Isaiah contains a prophecy against Sennacherib who proclaimed himself king after conquering Babylon (see Isa. 14:4). Though he is mighty now and able to inflict suffering and turmoil on his subjects (see v. 3), he shall be brought down to the grave and mocked (see vv. 9-11). Although the passage refers to the king of Babylon, the Church has also considered the verses that follow as a prophecy of the fall of Lucifer. Lucifer is Latin for "morning star" (v. 12). Lucifer is the symbolic representation of the king of Babylon in his pride, splendor and fall. Satan is the head of this present world system and the invisible power behind the successive world rulers of Tyre, Babylon, Persia, Greece and Rome.

This far-reaching passage goes beyond human history and marks the beginning of sin in the universe and the fall of Satan. The rule of Satan is not confined to his own person. All those who are dead in their trespasses and sins follow "the ways of this world and of the ruler of the kingdom of the air, the spirit who is now at work in those who are disobedient" (Eph. 2:2). Satan operates his kingdom through a hierarchy of evil spirits and unregenerate people.

In the same way, the rule of God is not confined to His own Person. Jesus says, "I tell you the truth, anyone who has faith in me will do what I have been doing. He will do even greater things than these, because I am going to the Father" (John 14:12). As long as Jesus remained on Earth, His kingdom rule was confined to himself. After being glorified, the Holy Spirit is present in every believer. As believers, we will do greater things, because the presence of Christ is manifested all over the world in our lives. God rules His kingdom through ministering angels and through the lives of His children who are filled (controlled) by the Holy Spirit.

Caught up with his own beauty, Lucifer challenged the throne of God. He expressed his pride by saying five times "I will" (see Isa. 14:13-14). But he was only a light bearer and not the source of light. As a created being, Satan could only reflect the glory of God. His pride and rebellion resulted in his expulsion from heaven. Now he is totally devoid of light. Satan is not some shady character who is naughty at times. He is the epitome of evil, the total absence of anything good.

In contrast, "God is light; in him there is no darkness at all" (1 John 1:5). At one time we were darkened in our understanding and separated from the life of God (see Eph. 4:18). Then came Jesus: "In him was life, and that life was the light of men" (John 1:4). "For you were once darkness, but now you are the light in the Lord. Live as children of light (for the fruit of the light consists in all goodness, righteousness and truth)" (Eph. 5:8-9).

> As for you, you were dead in your transgressions and sins, in which you used to live when you followed the ways of this world and of the ruler of the kingdom of the air, the spirit who is now at work in those who are disobedient (Eph. 2:1-2).

Thought for the day: *Is the natural person just following natural instincts, or is there a spiritual force behind his or her actions?*

THE WORK OF SATAN

Job 1:6-12

In the prologue to the book of Job, Satan appears with the angels who are gathering for their council meeting with the Lord (see Job 1:6). After roaming the earth, Satan is questioning the way God orders his creation. God invites Satan to consider his servant Job. Whether Job is serving God with a pure heart or for the fringe benefits of knowing Him is the question. To find out, God allows Satan to test Job by destroying everything he possesses, including his children and his own health (see 1:12-22; 2:6-8). Satan is not merely performing duties assigned to him as one member of the inner council of God. He came with the sons of God; he is not one of them. The fact that Satan is prohibited from taking Job's life tells us that God limits what Satan can do. God is not the author of evil, but He will allow it within limits for our testing. Neither did God create Satan. God created Lucifer with a free will to serve Him—Satan is the result of Lucifer's choice to rebel against God.

Satan described his activity as "roaming through the earth and going back and forth in it" (Job 1:7). He is engaged in worldwide, relentless conflict against God and His people. He is the "enemy" of God and truth (see Matt. 13:28, 39; 2 Thess. 2:9-12). He works through our weaknesses and limitations and employs the allurements of the world. He works in the realm of moral darkness (see Acts 26:18) as a tempter, enticing us to sin. His purpose is to get the children of God to live independently of God. When we sin, he changes his attack and acts as our accuser.

Jesus describes Satan's chief characteristic, which is also evident in the sons of the evil one.

> You belong to your father, the devil, and you want to carry out your father's desire. He was a murderer from the beginning, not holding to the truth, for there is no truth in him. When he lies, he speaks his native language, for he is a liar and the father of lies (John 8:44).

Deception is Satan's primary strategy, since he has succeeded in leading the whole world astray (see Rev. 12:9). Satan masquerades as "an angel of light," disguising his messengers of falsehood as messengers of truth (see

2 Cor. 11:13-15). Those who give themselves over to evil and become the agents of Satan to persuade others to do evil are children and servants of the devil (see John 6:70; Acts 13:10).

Satan is a counterfeiter. He sends false prophets and teachers. He sows counterfeit believers among the "sons of the kingdom" (see Matt. 13:25,38). Satan leads people away by counterfeiting the true gifts of God. Apostate workers engage in religious activities without accepting the power of God's truth (see 2 Tim. 3:1-9). He blinds the minds of unbelievers "so that they cannot see the light of the gospel of the glory of Christ, who is the image of God" (2 Cor. 4:4).

> The great dragon was hurled down—that ancient serpent called the devil, or Satan, who leads the whole world astray. He was hurled to the earth, and his angels with him (Rev. 12:9).

Thought for the day: *How does the devil lead the whole world astray?*

THE NAMES AND NATURE OF SATAN

Revelation 9:11

The term "satan" has the general meaning of "an adversary" or "an enemy." In 1 Samuel 29:4, it is used of David, who is considered an enemy in battle. In 1 Kings 11:14,23,25, it designates political adversaries of Solomon. In Psalm 109:6, the word "satan" is used to refer to a human accuser. After adding "the," the term "the adversary" becomes a proper name and denotes the person of Satan. He is referred to as "the devil" 33 times, which means "the slanderer." The terms "satan" and "devil" are essentially interchangeable. John called him "the angel of the Abyss, whose name in Hebrew is Abaddon, and in Greek, Apollyon" (Rev. 9:11). Both words mean "destruction" or "destroyer." The Abyss is the place of destruction. In the Bible names are often more than labels for identification. In the case of Satan they imply character and purpose as well. The following are additional names given to Satan in Scripture.

1. "The accuser of the brothers" (Rev. 12:10). Satan accuses Christians before God day and night, but Jesus always lives to make intercession saying, "My grace is sufficient," since He has died once for all our sins.
2. "Enemy" or "adversary" (1 Pet. 5:8). The adversary "prowls around like a roaring lion looking for someone to devour." Satan is the enemy of our souls.
3. "Belial" (2 Cor. 6:15). It means "worthlessness" or "wickedness." Satan is the personification of wickedness. There is no harmony between Christ and Belial.
4. "The great dragon" and "the ancient serpent" (Rev. 12:9). The word "dragon" is used figuratively of Satan to convey craft and power but also of the serpent's role as tempter in the Garden (see Gen. 3).
5. "The evil one" (Matt. 13:38). The evil one snatches away the good seed and sows the bad seed.
6. "The father of lies," "liar" and "murderer" (John 8:44). The devil

stands in direct opposition to the Spirit of Truth. God is the author of life, not death, and He cannot lie. The devil is a liar and is the author of death.

7. "The ruler of the kingdom of the air" (Eph. 2:2). Satan is no mere earthbound enemy. He is a spiritual being who roams the earth and pollutes the atmosphere.

8. "The prince [ruler] of this world" (John 12:31; 14:30; 16:11). This world is still dominated by the kingdom of darkness. Satan will rule all those who he manages to deceive until Jesus comes again.

9. "The tempter" (Matt. 4:3; 1 Thess. 3:5). The tempter came to Jesus to stop Him from continuing on His mission, and Paul is concerned that the tempter would make his converts useless.

At the name of Jesus every knee should bow, in heaven and on earth and under the earth (Phil. 2:10).

Thought for the day: *What is significant about a name?*

THE JUDGMENT AND DEFEAT OF SATAN

John 12:31

The explicit purpose of Christ's coming into this world was to "destroy the devil's work" (1 John 3:8). With that understanding, we have the assurance that Satan will be driven out (see John 12:31). According to Jesus, he already stands condemned (see John 16:11). The crucial battle between the kingdom of God and the kingdom of evil took place in the conflict between Christ and Satan. Satan's initial defeat came in the wilderness temptation at the beginning of our Lord's ministry (see Mark 1:12-13). Because Jesus did not succumb to the devil's temptations, He was able during His ministry to enter the strong man's house and plunder His goods (see Mark 3:27).

The crucifixion and resurrection of Christ was the decisive defeat of Satan. At the Cross, Satan was judged as a usurper and cast out, because he was no longer the legitimate ruler of this world. The Cross and the Resurrection broke the power of Satan over humankind. The finished work of Christ accomplished three immediate benefits to us. First we were made alive; second, we were forgiven; and, third, the powers and authorities were disarmed (see Col. 2:13-15). In so doing, Jesus destroyed "him who holds the power of death—that is, the devil" and continues to "free those who all their lives [have been] held in slavery by their fear of death" (Heb. 2:14-15). And for those of us who have put our trust in Him, Jesus Christ has delivered each one of us from Satan's power.

While judgment has already been pronounced upon him, Satan is still permitted to operate as a usurper until the time of his final imprisonment. As a dethroned monarch, he is still allowed to rule those who accept his authority. But as believers, we don't have to fear death or Satan. He no longer has authority over us, and he can do nothing to change our position in Christ. By putting our faith in the saving work of our Lord Jesus Christ, we have been delivered from the dominion of darkness and brought into the kingdom of the God (see Col. 1:12-13). All we have to do is stand firm in our faith.

Jesus asserted that "the eternal fire" had been prepared for "the devil and his angels" (Matt. 25:41). The book of Revelation describes the final judgment of the devil. At the return of Christ, the devil will be confined to the bottomless pit for 1,000 years, during which time the earth will be free from his deceptive and destructive influences (see Rev. 20:1-3). At the end of the 1,000 years, Satan will be loosed from his prison and will again deceive the inhabitants of the earth. This final rebellion will be summarily crushed by divine action. According to John's vision, "the devil, who deceived them, was thrown into the lake of burning sulfur, where the beast and the false prophet had been thrown. They will be tormented day and night for ever and ever" (Rev. 20:10). His doom will be to share the eternal punishment of those whom he deceived (see Rev. 20:12-14).

> And having disarmed the powers and authorities, he made a public spectacle of them, triumphing over them by the cross (Col. 2:15).

Thought for the day: *What power does Satan have over you—or any of God's children?*

ANGELS

Psalm 148:1-6

The word "angel" means "messenger." The term primarily refers to heavenly beings, although the term can mean a human messenger such as a prophet (see Hag. 1:13) or a priest (see Mal. 2:7). Other terms in the Bible refer to these angelic beings as "sons of God" (Gen. 6:2-4; see Job 1:6); "heavenly beings" (Ps. 29:1); "holy ones" (Ps. 89:5); "heavenly host" (Luke 2:13); and "hosts" as in the phrase "LORD of hosts" (1 Sam. 1:11, *KJV*). The seraphim in Isaiah 6 also belong to the order of angels.

Angels are spiritual and majestic in nature. They existed before the creation of Adam and Eve, and their purpose is to execute God's will (see Ps. 148:2-5). They can pass from the spiritual realm to the physical realm at will, unimpeded by natural boundaries (see Acts 12:7). Angels are stronger and more powerful than humans are (see 2 Pet. 2:11). But they are not omnipotent, and they are subservient to God (see Ps. 103:20). Angels also have superior intellect and wisdom (see 2 Sam. 14:17,20). But they are not omniscient (see Matt. 24:36). According to Jesus, they do not marry and they will live forever (see Luke 20:35-36).

In the Bible, good angels consistently appeared in human form on Earth. They never appear as animals, reptiles, birds or material objects. There is no biblical record showing that a good angel ever appeared to wicked people or warned them of any danger. They are "ministering spirits sent to serve those who will inherit salvation" (Heb. 1:14). Good angels always appeared to good people in human form as men. They never appeared as women or children, and they were always clothed. Just as Christ appeared in human form, so angels identified with man in form, speech and deed. Sometimes angels were so disguised as men that they were not at first recognizable as angels.

Abraham entertained "three men" as dinner guests. One remained to talk while the other two left to spend the night with Lot, who thought they were men (see Gen. 18:2; 19:1). Joshua did not know that the man standing before him was God's angel (see Josh. 5:13). Neither did Gideon realize that his guest was an angel until the angel made an offering of his meal (see Judg. 6:21-22).

Occasionally angels displayed themselves with a heavenly countenance and clothing that revealed the glory of God. While the two women were lingering at the empty tomb of Jesus, "suddenly two men in clothes that gleamed like lightning stood beside them" (Luke 24:4). Daniel gave a very colorful description of an angel (see Dan. 10:5-6). On numerous occasions, angels were described as "a man"—or at least having the appearance of a man (Ezek. 40:3; Dan. 10:18; Zech. 2:1).

> Do not forget to entertain strangers, for by so doing some people have entertained angels without knowing it (Heb. 13:2).

Thought for the day: *Have you ever thought that you might have encountered an angel? How would you know if you had?*

THE NATURE OF ANGELS

Judges 13

In the original creation all angels were good. But when Satan led a rebellion against God, he took a third of the angels with him (see Rev. 12:7-9). Now God commands His good angels, and Satan commands a hoard of bad angels who are also identified as evil spirits or demons. Contrary to the good angels, demons never appear in human form. They are spirits who serve the evil desires of Satan. This is how Satan functions as the ruler of this world. He is not omnipresent, so he reigns over his kingdom through rulers, authorities, powers of this dark world and "the spiritual forces of evil in the heavenly realms" (Eph. 6:12). This apparently describes a demonic hierarchy.

In contrast to the evil nature of demons, good angels are called "the holy angels" (Luke 9:26), "the angels of God" (Luke 12:8) and "God's angels" (Heb. 1:6). Jesus spoke of "His angels" (Matt. 16:27) and "angels in heaven" (Matt. 22:30). Paul referred to "His powerful angels" (2 Thess. 1:7). Of these good angels, only two are mentioned by name. First, Michael is called the archangel by Jude (see v. 9). Michael disputed with Satan concerning the body of Moses and invoked the name of the Lord to rebuke him. In Daniel, Michael is called "one of the chief princes" (10:13). In Revelation, Michael is portrayed as the commander of the army of good angels who defeated and expelled the bad angels from heaven (see 12:7-8).

Second, Gabriel is the chief messenger angel. He announced the births of John the Baptist and Jesus (see Luke 1:13,26-38). He interpreted Daniel's dream and delivered God's decree on the same mission (see Dan. 8:15-27).

Third, "the angel of the LORD" seems to be a unique angel in the Old Testament. This angel announces the birth of Samson (see Judg. 13:3-5) much like Gabriel did to Mary. Manoah asked the angel of the Lord what his name was. "He replied, 'Why do you ask my name? It is beyond understanding'" (v. 18). Using the definite article "the" has led some to speculate that this may be a pre-incarnate appearance of Christ. The same speculation has been made about the "man" who wrestled with Jacob and told him that he had struggled with God (see Gen. 32:22-31).

Several conclusions can be drawn from this angelic visitation to Manoah. First, angels have a specific assignment from God, which they strictly follow. Manoah prayed that God would send the angel again in order to teach them how to raise the child. The Lord granted a second visit, but the angel of the Lord simply repeated his earlier message. Second, they communicate audibly in the same language and through the same medium that humans do. Third, they take on a physical form that can be seen by any person present. Fourth, they may not always be recognized as an angelic being, but they are recognized as "[men] of God" (Judg. 13:6,16). Fifth, they can change their form as they depart from our presence (see v. 20). All this stands in stark contrast to demons.

> The angel of the LORD encamps around those who fear him, and he delivers them (Ps. 34:7)

Thought for the day: *When can we be assured of God's protection?*

THE MINISTRY OF ANGELS

Acts 12

The work of angels is to execute God's will in heaven and upon this earth. Their service can be summarized in the following five ways:

1. *They announce and forewarn.* An angel announced in advance to Abraham and Sarai the conception and birth of their son Isaac (see Gen. 18:9-14). The angel of the Lord foretold the birth of Samson (see Judg. 13:2-24). Gabriel announced the birth of John the Baptist and Jesus (see Luke 1:13,30). An angel announced the birth of Jesus to the shepherds, and suddenly a chorus of heavenly hosts joined them in praising God. Angels also forewarned the righteous of imminent danger. Abraham and Lot were forewarned by an angel about the destruction of Sodom and Gomorrah (see Gen. 18:16–19:29). Joseph was warned to flee to Egypt by an angel (see Matt. 2:13).

2. *They guide and instruct.* Abraham was repeatedly in conversation with angels and guided by them in his sojourn. He told Eliezer, God will "send his angel before you" (Gen. 24:7). When Moses led the Israelites out of Egypt, the angel of God guided them (see Exod. 14:19). In Exodus, God told them, "See, I am sending an angel ahead of you to guard you along the way and to bring you to the place I have prepared" (23:20). An angel gave instructions to Cornelius (see Acts 10:3-7).

3. *They guard and defend.* "The angel of the LORD encamps around those who take refuge in him" (Ps. 34:7). An angel made Balaam revise his prophecy and rewrite his sermon (see Num. 22:21-38). God's angelic army stood by to defend Elisha and his servant (see 2 Kings 6:17). An angel prevented Abraham from sacrificing Isaac (see Gen. 22:9-12). An angel protected the lives of Daniel and his three Hebrew friends (see Dan. 3:28; 6:22). The angel of death slew the first-born of Egypt to force the release of the Israelites (see Exod. 12:23). The angel of the Lord slew the army of Sennacherib to keep him from destroying Jerusalem (see 2 Kings 19:35). Jesus could have called upon 12 legions of angels

to save Himself (see Matt. 26:53).

4. *They minister to our needs.* Peter was in great need when an angel released his chains, and marched him out of prison. Angels are mediators of God's love and goodwill toward humankind, and their mission is always benevolent. An angel ministered to Elijah when he was exhausted by feeding him some hot cakes and water (see 1 Kings 19:5-7). After Jesus fasted for 40 days and was tempted by the devil, the "angels attended him" (Mark 1:13).

5. *They assist in judgment.* When the people shouted that Herod spoke as God, "Immediately, because Herod did not give praise to God, an angel of the Lord struck him down, and he was eaten by worms and died" (Acts 12:23). The sheep and the goats will be divided, "When the Son of Man comes in his glory, and all the angels with him" (Matt. 25:31).

Are not all angels ministering spirits sent to serve those who will inherit salvation (Heb. 1:14)?

Thought for the day: *Consider all the spiritual forces that are at work for your salvation and sanctification.*

THE NATURE OF DEMONS

Luke 11:24-26

After Jesus cast out a demon that had rendered a man dumb, His detractors accused Him of casting out demons by the power of "Beelzebul, the prince of demons" (Luke 11:15). The following discussion about demons reveals their nature and personality as deduced from verses 24-26:

1. *Demons can exist outside or inside of humans.* Demons have no physical means of expressing themselves except through human or animal agents. They seem to find a measure of rest in organic beings, preferring swine to nothingness (see Mark 5:12). Evil spirits may assert territorial rights and be associated with certain geographical locations.
2. *They are able to travel at will.* Being spiritual entities, demons are not subject to the physical barriers of the natural world. The walls of church buildings do not provide a sanctuary, nor does our skin serve as a spiritual barrier. That is why we put on the armor of God and find our sanctuary in our position in Christ.
3. *They are able to communicate with each other.* They can speak to humans through a human subject, such as the Gadarene demoniac (see Matt. 8:28-34). We can also pay attention to deceiving spirits in our minds (see 2 Cor. 11:3; 1 Tim. 4:1).
4. *Every evil spirit has a separate identity.* Notice the use of personal pronouns: "I will return to the house I left" (Luke 11:24). They are thinking personalities, not impersonal forces. Demons are like cockroaches. They operate under the cloak of darkness; and when the light is turned on, they scurry for the shadows. They don't like to be detected, preferring to remain under cover of darkness.
5. *They have the ability to remember and make plans.* They can leave a person, come back, remember their former state, evaluate their present state and plan reentry with others. They obviously have the ability to think strategically.
6. *They are able to evaluate and make decisions.* The demons found "the house swept clean and put in order" (Luke 11:25). They can

evaluate the condition of an intended victim and take advantage of a person's vulnerability.

7. *They are able to combine forces.* Notice that the one spirit joined with a group of seven other spirits, making the last state of the victim worse than before. In the case of the Gadarene demoniac, a number of them had united together—hence their name, "Legion" (Mark 5:9).

8. *They vary in degrees of wickedness.* The first demon brought back seven others "more wicked than itself." Jesus indicated degrees of wickedness and power when he said, "This kind can come out only by prayer" (Mark 9:29). These variations in power and wickedness fit the hierarchy described in Ephesians 6:12.

The next day an evil spirit from God came forcefully upon Saul (1 Sam. 18:10).

Thought for the day: *Can God use an evil spirit for His own purposes?*

THE WORK OF DEMONS

Revelation 12:9-12

The Bible records extreme cases in which demons actually possessed humans. In Mark 1:21-28, a demon spoke through a man in a synagogue. " 'Be quiet!' said Jesus sternly. 'Come out of him!' The evil spirit shook the man violently and came out of him with a shriek" (vv. 25-26). The Gadarene demoniac had many demons in him (see Mark 5:1-20). He exhibited supernatural strength by breaking the chains that bound him. No human was strong enough to subdue him. The demons begged Jesus not to send them out of the area and requested to go into a herd of pigs. Two thousand pigs rushed to their death in a lake. Somehow these demons were able to control the man's central nervous system, enabling them to speak through the man and direct the will of the pigs. When the evil spirits left, the man's rational capacities were restored.

Demons are also capable of inflicting severe illnesses on people. A man brought his son to Jesus saying, "A spirit seizes him and he suddenly screams; it throws him into convulsions so that he foams at the mouth. It scarcely ever leaves him and is destroying him" (Luke 9:39). This was not a natural epileptic seizure. Jesus rebuked the evil spirit, healed the boy and gave him back to his father (see v. 42). A woman in a synagogue "had been crippled by a spirit for eighteen years. She was bent over and could not straighten up at all" (Luke 13:11). This was not osteoporosis. Jesus said Satan had kept her bound (see v. 16). Demons can inflict physical illnesses on people who passively allow them. Over 25 percent of those physically healed in the gospel of Mark are the result of their having been set free from demonic influences.

It is more common for people to suffer from "mental illnesses" caused by demons than from physical illness caused by them. It is not uncommon for the secular world to diagnose certain individuals as being mentally ill when the real issue is the spiritual battle being waged for their minds. "The Spirit clearly says that in later times some will abandon the faith and follow deceiving spirits and things taught by demons" (1 Tim. 4:1). Paul tells us, "I am afraid that just as Eve was deceived by the serpent's cunning, your minds may somehow be led astray from your sincere and pure devotion to Christ" (2 Cor. 11:3). If we are deceived and believe a lie, it will affect our mental and emotional health, which often shows up physically as a psychosomatic illness.

Satan has led the whole world astray by using demons to tempt, accuse and deceive humanity (see Rev. 12:9). Satan and his demons have been judged and they will be thrown out in the final judgment. Irenaeus, an Early Church Father said, "The devil, however, as he is the apostate angel, can only go to this length, as he did at the beginning, to deceive and lead astray the mind of man into disobeying the commandments of God, and gradually to darken the hearts."

> We know that anyone born of God does not continue to sin; the one who was born of God keeps him safe, and the evil one cannot harm him (1 John 5:18).

Thought for the day: *How important is it to know this verse, should we find ourselves under spiritual attack?*

THE ENEMIES OF OUR SANCTIFICATION

Jeremiah 17:1-18

Jeremiah paints a bleak picture for those who trust in themselves and depend on their own strength and resources (see Jer. 17:5). Before Christ, our hearts were deceitful and beyond human cure (see v. 9). But if we trust in the Lord who searches our hearts, then we shall "be like a tree planted by the water" (v. 8). The consistent message in Scripture is that we need the Lord for healing and salvation (see v. 14), and we continue to need Him for our sanctification.

Every child of God is a diamond in the rough. We begin our Christian walk looking like a lump of coal. We may look pretty bad and be messy to work with; but given enough time and pressure, every lump of coal has the potential to become a brilliant diamond. If you remove coal from the pressures of the earth and introduce impurities into its chemical composition, it will never reach its potential. Staying pure and remaining under pressure is what makes a diamond out of coal. Unlike a lump of coal, we have a part to play in the sanctifying process. We cannot just "let go and let God" be the One who perfects us; we must also assume our responsibility and do our part. It is true that victory is only possible through the finished work of Christ, and so we can rest in the finished work of Christ. It is also true that progressive sanctification takes place when we abide in Christ and live by the power of the Holy Spirit, but Scripture presents the sanctification process as far more than a passive receptivity on our part.

You must "continue to work out your salvation with fear and trembling, for it is God who works in you to will and to act according to his good purpose" (Phil. 2:12-13). We don't work for our salvation, but working it out is a rigorous process that is being opposed by the world, the flesh and the devil. Whether we like it or not, we are in a battle against evil forces (see Eph. 6:10-16). The battle is described as a struggle, or literally, a "wrestling." The Greek word describes a "hand to hand fight." Paul admonishes us to "fight the good fight" (1 Tim. 1:18). Later in the epistle he adds, "But you, man of God, flee from all this, and pursue righteousness, godliness, faith, love, endurance and gentleness. Fight the good fight of the faith" (6:11-12).

We are able to enter the fray armed with Christ's victory, because we wage war "in Christ." Our ultimate victory is certain, but that doesn't eliminate the present battle. The battle often intensifies when we start bearing fruit. The power of sin is most evident when we seriously challenge it. Temptation is no struggle if we are continuously giving in to it. We sense the opposition when we seek to resolve personal and spiritual conflicts and strive to live righteous lives.

I have fought the good fight, I have finished the race, I have kept the faith (2 Tim. 4:7).

Thought for the day: *Wouldn't you like to be able to say the words of 2 Timothy 4:7 at the end of your life?*

DEFINING THE FLESH

2 John

One of the most dangerous heresies confronting the Early Church was Gnosticism. The Gnostics taught that the spirit is entirely good, and matter is entirely evil. Therefore, our natural bodies are evil, and God was good, because He is a Spirit. Salvation comes by special knowledge (*gnosis* is Greek for "knowledge") that enabled them to escape from the body. The fact that Christ came in the flesh was denied. Some people influenced by Gnosticism taught that Jesus only *seemed* to have a body—a heretical view called Docetism—or they held that the divine Jesus joined the man Jesus at his baptism and left before the man Jesus died—a heresy called Cerinthianism. Since the body was evil, it was to be treated harshly. Many of the Epistles addressed the problem of Gnosticism, as does 2 John. Anyone who did not acknowledge Jesus as coming in the flesh was a deceiver (see 1 John 4:1-3; 2 John 7).

The term "flesh" has many meanings in Scripture. In some instances it is referring to the physical body. At times it can refer to the whole person. The Son of God's willingness to take on humanity is described as "The Word became flesh and made his dwelling among us" (John 1:14). In such uses there is no concept of sinfulness or evil. Jesus never sinned, and His body was never evil. The common thread to the uses of "flesh" is the idea of weakness or transitoriness. Compared to the spirit, which denotes life and power, the flesh is weak. It is this concept of weakness that has contributed to the use of the term "flesh" for that which is sinful or contrary to God. Humanity, as flesh, is not only frail as creatures, but also morally. Apart from God, humanity is no match for the power of sin and consequently comes under its bondage.

The use of the word "flesh" (the *New International Version* translates "flesh" as "old nature," and sometimes as "sin nature") in reference to humankind's propensity to sin is prominent in the New Testament. It may be defined as existence apart from God. It represents our "old nature" before Christ when we were "in Adam" or "in the flesh." The old nature characterizes the history of fallen humanity (the old self) before Christ; and the coming of the creation in Christ (the new self) is characterized by the Spirit. As new believers we are no longer "in the flesh"; we are "in Christ," but we can still walk or live according to the flesh. The flesh and the Spirit are in opposition because the Holy Spirit is dependent upon God the Father (see Gal. 5:16). The flesh is self-centered and functions independently of God. The flesh seeks life on human terms and standards, rather than God's.

Our bodies are not sinful, but our minds retain certain flesh patterns that we learned before we came to Christ. And we still have certain physical cravings that we have to subdue. Satan will work through those mental flesh patterns and cravings to get us to live independently of God.

So I say, live by the Spirit, and you will not gratify the desires of the sinful nature (Gal. 5:16).

Thought for the day: *Why is the flesh in opposition to the leading of the Holy Spirit?*

OVERCOMING THE OLD NATURE

Haggai

God's people were exiled to Babylon for 70 years after the destruction of the Solomon's temple in 586 B.C. Haggai and Zechariah were prophets who encouraged them to rebuild the Temple after they returned to Jerusalem. The major obstacle was their lethargy. Haggai showed them the consequences of their disobedience (see Hag. 1:6,11; 2:16-17), and their obedience (see 2:7-9,19). They would be spiritually strengthened if they trusted and obeyed God (see 2:4-5). God would do His part, but His people would never experience health, wholeness and victory without assuming their individual responsibility. Good health is not contagious only bad health is—in the same way that ceremonial uncleanness was transmitted in contact with others but holiness wasn't (see 2:12-14). "Do not be misled: 'Bad company corrupts good character'" (1 Cor. 15:33). Simply being around good people is not enough to overcome the struggles with the flesh. There is no spiritual osmosis.

Like the Israelites, we have the responsibility to rebuild the temple, the dwelling place of God, which is now our bodies. Before Christ our total person was dominated by the flesh and oriented toward sin. Now that Christ dwells within us, we are oriented toward God, but we still have a remnant of propensity toward self-autonomy (flesh or old nature). This can be overcome by the power of the Spirit. The old "I" died with Christ and has risen a new "I" with a new heart and a new orientation. This new orientation toward God radiates outward to increasingly minimize the propensity of the old nature. The Holy Spirit dwells in the new heart and seeks to fill (control) the entire person.

At salvation, the old self was crucified (see Rom. 6:6). The finished work of Christ made that possible when we received it by faith. Paul says to the new believer, "Those who belong to Christ Jesus have crucified the sinful nature with its passions and desires" (Gal. 5:24). The old self was crucified with Christ, but it is our responsibility to crucify the old nature, to put the old nature (flesh) to death. In repentance we crucified everything we knew to be wrong. We took our old self-centered nature with all its passions and desires and nailed it to the cross.

The reality of our actions is experienced only in accord with the faith in which it is done. We crucified everything we knew to be wrong with all the faith we had at that time. But our knowledge of the truth and our response in faith were not yet mature and complete. We grow as we appropriate more and more of Christ's life by the power of the Holy Spirit. As we grow, the reality of what we did in principle (that is, crucifying the flesh and its old self-centered influence) becomes increasingly more real in our experience. As long as we choose to believe the truth and live by faith in the power of the Holy Spirit, the flesh will be rendered inoperative.

> Those who live according to the sinful nature [flesh] have their minds set on what that nature desires; but those who live in accordance with the Spirit have their minds set on what the Spirit desires (Rom. 8:5).

Thought for the day: *Where do we win this battle against the old self?*

DEFINING THE WORLD

Zephaniah

Zephaniah preached the coming of the day of the Lord (see 1:14). God would be merciful to His people, but the world would be judged (see 3:8) and all the godless nations in it (see 2:1-15). The term "world" (in Greek, *kosmos*) basically means "order" or "system." "Kosmos" can mean the entire created universe (see Acts 17:24), the earth (see Mark 8:36) and frequently the world of humanity (see John 3:16,19), which is under the dominion of sin. Consequently, "the world" is a term used to speak of the complex system of humanity apart from God. The institutions, structures, values and mores of this world are organized without God.

The evil character of this fallen world system and its animosity toward God can be seen in what Jesus said to His disciples: "If the world hates you, keep in mind that it hated me first. If you belonged to the world, it would love you as its own. As it is, you do not belong to the world, but I have chosen you out of the world" (John 15:18-19). As Christians, we live in this world, but we are not of this world. The wisdom of the world looks at the cross of Christ as foolishness and is antithetical to the wisdom of God (see 1 Cor. 1:18-24). The nature of this world is evil because it is the domain of Satan's rule (see 1 John 5:19).

The true characteristics of the world are seen in 1 John 2:16: "For everything in the world—the cravings of sinful man, the lust of his eyes and the boasting of what he has and does—comes not from the Father but from the world." The "cravings of sinful man" are the sinful desires of our fallen human nature. The "lust of the eyes" relates to looking only on the outward appearance of people or things without seeing their real value. It is the love of beauty divorced from the love of goodness. Eve saw the forbidden fruit as "pleasing to the eye" (Gen. 3:6). Achan said, "I saw in the plunder a beautiful robe from Babylonia, two hundred shekels of silver and a wedge of gold weighing fifty shekels, I coveted them and took them" (Josh. 7:21). David saw that "the woman was very beautiful" (2 Sam. 11:2) and sinned grievously.

The Greek term for boasting describes those who make more of themselves than reality justifies. Fallen humanity and the world system do not seek the will of God; rather, they choose to exercise their own sovereign right to decide the shape of their lives. This attitude is not limited to the braggart; John indicates it is the attitude of anyone who lives their lives apart from God (see 1 John 2:16). These characteristics are not from the Father, but from the world. If God is not included in all that we do, then it is from the world. "Such 'wisdom' does not come down from heaven, but is earthly, unspiritual, of the devil" (Jas. 3:15).

> Brothers, I could not address you as spiritual, but as worldly—mere infants in Christ (1 Cor. 3:1).

Thought for the day: *Paul acknowledges that new believers will act carnally (fleshly), but how does he see those who have had the opportunity to grow but didn't?*

OVERCOMING THE WORLD

Nahum

Nineveh was a worldly city characterized by the godless nature of its people. Nahum communicated to the inhabitants that God was "slow to anger" (1:3) and a refuge "for those who trust in him" (1:7), but He would not leave the guilty unpunished (see 1:3). They never overcame their worldliness and therefore were doomed. We, too, can let our affections be drawn to the world. Thus we are warned, "Do not love the world or anything in the world. If anyone loves the world, the love of the Father is not in him" (1 John 2:15). As Christians we are betrothed to Christ, but we are tempted to commit adultery with the world: "You adulterous people, don't you know that friendship with the world is hatred toward God? Anyone who chooses to be a friend of the world becomes an enemy of God" (Jas. 4:4).

The world seeks to weaken our love for Christ by appealing to our old nature, which desires to live according to the world's values. The temptation of the world is to satisfy our pleasures and not seek that which pleases God. The world system promotes self-sufficiency, but we have all the resources we need to withstand these threats. "For everyone born of God overcomes the world. This is the victory that has overcome the world, even our faith" (1 John 5:4). In the first sentence, "overcomes" is present tense, indicating not that believers never succumb to the temptation of the world, but that victory rather than defeat generally characterizes our lives as believers. In the second sentence, "has overcome" is in the past tense, indicating that the action is finished. This is consistent with the truth that when we came to Christ, we were joined to the One who could say, "Take heart! I have overcome the world" (John 16:33). Christ's triumph over the powers of sin belongs to every believer who is alive "in Him."

"Who is it that overcomes the world? Only he who believes that Jesus is the Son of God" (1 John 5:5). John switches back to the present tense, indicating an ongoing sense of overcoming—that is, the daily experience of our victory over the world because we are alive in Christ. When we placed our faith in Christ, we became overcomers, and we continue to live like overcomers when we continue to believe all that God says is true. In Christ we have overcome the evil spirit of this world. "You, dear children, are from God and have overcome [false prophets], because the one who is in you is greater than the one who is in the world. We are from God, and whoever knows God listens to us; but whoever is not from God does not listen to us" (1 John 4:4,6).

> Do not deceive yourselves. If any one of you thinks he is wise by the standards of this age, he should become a "fool" so that he may become wise. For the wisdom of this world is foolishness in God's sight (1 Cor. 3:18-19).

Thought for the day: *Why are we so easily swayed by the "wisdom" of the world?*

THE BATTLE FOR OUR MINDS

1 Chronicles 21

The mind is the focal point for spiritual warfare. The fact that Satan is capable of putting thoughts in our minds is clearly taught by Scripture. In the Old Testament, "Satan rose up against Israel and incited David to take a census of Israel" (1 Chron. 21:1). What is wrong with taking a census? Shouldn't David know the strength of his military? Joab knew it was wrong and tried to stop David (see v. 3). Thousands died as a result of David's sin. This passage reveals the subtle nature of Satan and his strategies. Satan knew that David had a whole heart for God and would not willingly or knowingly defy the Lord. The strategy was to get David to put his confidence in his resources rather than God's resources, which is a major issue to this day.

How did Satan incite David? Did he talk audibly to him? No, the idea for the census came from David's mind—it was his idea. At least he thought it was. Therein lies the deception. These deceptive thoughts come to us in "first person singular" in such a way that we think they are our thoughts. If we knew the true source of the thoughts, then we would no longer be deceived. The origin of our negative "self-talk" may not always be our old nature or the world. Some of our negative thinking can originate from Satan. Judas, who was one of the chosen disciples, also believed the devil's lies. "The evening meal was being served, and the devil had already prompted Judas Iscariot, son of Simon, to betray Jesus" (John 13:2). We may be tempted to think this was just a bad decision prompted by the flesh, but Scripture literally says, "the devil having put into the heart." When Judas realized that he had been deceived, he took his own life.

In the earliest days of the Church, God struck down Ananias and Sapphira, because they had kept back half of their property and allowed the Church community to think they had given it all (see Acts 5:1-2,5-10). The judgment seems rather severe for the crime, but Peter reveals why the Lord intervened. "Ananias, how is it that Satan has so filled your heart that you have lied to the Holy Spirit?" (Acts 5:3). God had to send a powerful message to the Early Church, because He knew what the real battle was. If Satan and his demons can deceive us into believing a lie, they can control our lives with disastrous results. Any lie we believe, regardless of its source, will have a negative effect on how we live. Ananias and Sapphira sadly discovered that whatever source you yield yourself to, by that source you shall be filled or controlled. The word "filled" in Acts 5:3 is the same word used in Ephesians 5:18, where we are admonished to be "filled" with the Holy Spirit. This strategy is not new, since the mother of us all, Eve, was deceived, having believed a lie.

> He was a murderer from the beginning, not holding to the truth, for there is no truth in him. When he speaks, he speaks in his native language, for he is a liar and the father of lies (John 8:44).

Thought for the day: *What is implied in identifying Satan as the father of lies?*

SATAN'S SCHEMES

2 Corinthians 2:1-11

Paul instructs the Church to forgive after carrying out church discipline. The body of believers needs to forgive for their own sake and for the sake of the one being disciplined. We remain bound to the past if we don't forgive, and Satan will take advantage of our unforgiveness. Paul said, "I have forgiven in the sight of Christ for your sake, in order that Satan might not outwit us. For we are not unaware of his schemes" (2 Cor. 2:10-11). To understand Satan's "schemes," we need to understand the Greek word that it is derived from, *noema*. In Scripture, "noema," which is also translated as "mind" or "thought," is used as follows:

1. "[Satan] has blinded the [noema] of unbelievers, so that they cannot see the light of the gospel of the glory of Christ, who is the image of God" (2 Cor. 4:4). Those who live under the law and cannot see their need for Christ have had their minds blinded by Satan. We would understand the need for prayer and pray differently if we understood how Satan blinds the minds or thoughts of unbelievers. Evangelism was more effective in the Early Church when they understood how to free people from demonic influences. Being able to do so became a test of righteousness and orthodoxy.

2. "We demolish arguments and every pretension that sets itself up against the knowledge of God, and we take captive every [noema] to make it obedient to Christ" (2 Cor. 10:5). It doesn't make any difference whether the negative and lying thoughts we are thinking are coming from our old nature, from the world or from the father of lies. We examine every thought. If it is not true, then we don't think it and we certainly don't believe it. Some of these thoughts are so evident that they sound like a voice or voices in people's minds. Tragically they are often perceived as a sign of mental illness in our modern world, when in reality it is a spiritual battle for the mind.

3. "I am afraid that just as Eve was deceived by the serpent's cunning, your [noema] may somehow be led astray from your sin-

cere and pure devotion to Christ" (2 Cor. 11:3). Recall that Satan deceived Eve, and she believed his lies. The tendency is to believe that if we are nice people, such deception can't happen to us; but Eve was sinless at the time she was deceived. Good people can be deceived.

4. Another use of the word "noema" in Scripture is Philippians 4:7: "And the peace of God, which transcends all understanding, will guard your hearts and your [noema] in Christ Jesus." To stand against Satan's mental assaults, we must choose to think on "whatever is true, whatever is noble, whatever is right, whatever is pure, whatever is lovely, and whatever is admirable—if anything is excellent or praiseworthy—think about such things" (Phil. 4:8). Then we must put our righteous thoughts into practice, "And the God of peace will be with [us]" (Phil. 4:9).

But their minds [or, noema] were made dull, for to this day the same veil remains when the old covenant is read. It has not been removed, because only in Christ is it taken away (2 Cor. 3:14).

Thought for the day: *How are we going to reach those who are lost and living under the law if Satan has blinded their minds?*

LED ASTRAY

2 Corinthians 11:1-13

False prophets had invaded the Corinthian church. Satan masquerades as an angel of light, so we should not be surprised to find Satan's servants masquerading as servants of righteousness (see 2 Cor. 11:14-15). Paul was concerned that comparing his own ministry with that of the false prophets could appear as foolish boasting. His main concern, however, was given in verse 3: "But I am afraid that just as Eve was deceived by the serpent's cunning, your minds may somehow be led astray from your sincere and pure devotion to Christ." Clearly, Satan has the capacity to lead our minds astray if we let him. Therefore, "Let us fix our eyes on Jesus, the author and perfecter of our faith" (Heb. 12:2).

The following verse in 2 Corinthians 11 reveals the basis for Paul's concern: "For if someone comes to you and preaches a Jesus other than the Jesus we preached, or if you receive a different spirit from the one you received, or a different gospel from the one you accepted, you put up with it easily enough" (v. 4). These false prophets were talking about the same historical Jesus but were preaching Him a different way. The primary doctrine that separates Christianity from the cults is Christology. Orthodox Christianity asserts that Jesus is the Son of God, the second Person of the Trinity, the promised Messiah. Jesus said, "I told you that you would die in your sins; if you do not believe that I am the one I claim to be, you will indeed die in your sins" (John 8:24).

To believe in Jesus wrongly is to receive the wrong spirit. If what we have received is not the Holy Spirit, then it can only be an evil spirit. Like their leader, demons can masquerade as angels of light. These spirit guides will seldom reveal their true nature as long as we continues to believe a lie.

Such demons are behind cults, which do the work of Satan as the cult leaders masquerade as servants of righteousness. Consequently, many cult members can appear to live righteous lives. Their beliefs are typically very legalistic and their leadership extremely authoritarian.

If you have the wrong Jesus and the wrong spirit, you will have the wrong gospel. If Jesus isn't who He said He is, then His sacrifice is not efficacious. His sacrificial death would be no different from the sacrifice of bulls and goats which do not take away sin (see Heb. 10:4). An erroneous gospel is not the gospel of grace, but a false gospel of works. If Jesus did not die for the sins of humankind, then cult members believe they must perform good works or religious services in order to receive forgiveness and eternal life.

At the other extreme, New Age philosophies see Jesus as the master psychic. New Agers believe that He had the "spiritual power" to see and hear things that others don't. That power and enlightenment is what they seek through mediums and spirit guides. New Age practitioners say we don't need a Messiah to die for our sins. We just need to be enlightened to the truth that we are gods. They have bought the original lie that Satan sold to Eve.

Those who are led by the Spirit of God are sons of God (Rom. 8:14).

Thought for the day: *How can we know which spirit is leading us?*

DECEIVING SPIRITS

1 Timothy 3:14—4:5

After speaking about the Church of the living God, the pillar and foundation of truth, Paul inserts a parenthesis about the historical visit of Jesus on planet Earth (see 1 Tim. 3:16). Then he says, "The Spirit clearly says that in later times some will abandon the faith and follow deceiving spirits and things taught by demons" (4:1). The parenthetical insertion in 1 Timothy 3:16 was to draw attention to Christ, which is the major work of the Holy Spirit (see John 16:14). Christians believe deeply in the ministry of the Holy Spirit. If there were no Holy Spirit, there would be no life, no power to live, no gifts, no guidance, no assurance and no Church. But we are to be Christ centered not spirit centered, and we are to be truth based not experienced based.

"The Spirit" is to be contrasted with "deceiving spirits." There is only one Holy Spirit, but there are many deceiving spirits who are demons or evil spirits. Paul is not telling us by way of parables or by signs and wonders; he is clearly saying there is a coming apostasy in the later days. Concerning the end times, Jesus said, "For false Christs and false prophets will appear and perform great signs and miracles to deceive even the elect—if that were possible. See, I have told you ahead of time" (Matt. 24:24-25; see also 2 Pet. 2:1-12).

Psychiatrists, psychologists, counselors, social workers and pastors routinely work with people who are struggling with their thoughts, having difficulty concentrating or hearing voices. Many cannot read their Bibles or concentrate when they pray or worship God. The voices are usually condemning or blasphemous. Such voices and thoughts cannot be fully explained as a neurological condition or a chemical imbalance. How can a chemical produce a personality or create a thought that we are opposed to thinking? Is there a natural explanation for this? Why not believe what Scripture has clearly taught and then take the appropriate measures to correct the problem? If the condemning, lying and blasphemous thoughts leave after submitting to God and resisting the devil (see Jas. 4:7), then the origin of the thoughts is not natural or neurological. Believers all over the world have found such relief from oppressive thoughts through genuine repentance (see the "Steps to Freedom in Christ"). The peace of God is now guarding their hearts and their minds in Christ Jesus (see Phil. 4:7).

Doctrines of demons "come through hypocritical liars, whose consciences have been seared as with a hot iron" (1 Tim. 4:2). They profess to believe one thing but live another way. They have no conscience. They are modern-day Gnostics who advocate an ascetic form of life (see also Col. 2:16-23). Their message is abstinence from marriage and food, but Paul counters by saying, "For everything God created is good, and nothing is to be rejected if it is received with thanksgiving" (1 Tim. 4:4).

Let the wicked forsake his way and the evil man his thoughts (Isa. 55:7).

Thought for the day: *How can you forsake your evil ways?*

MENTAL ILLNESS

Daniel 4

The spiritual nature of Nebuchadnezzar's mental illness cannot be denied. God warned him in a dream. Daniel encouraged him to repent (see Dan. 4:27), but 12 months later he was as proud as ever (see vv. 28-30). Finally, he raised his eyes toward heaven and his sanity was restored (see v. 34). People are generally considered mentally ill if they are out of touch with reality and relatively free from anxiety. Based on those standards, you would fail on both counts if you were experiencing a spiritual battle for your mind. What would secular mental health workers conclude if their clients told them that they were hearing voices or seeing things in their rooms that frightened them and the counselor didn't see or hear anything? They would conclude that their clients are out of touch with reality. Actually, the mental health workers may be the ones who are out of touch with reality, since what they are seeing and hearing is very real. Only it isn't "out there"—the battle is in their minds.

We can't physically hear anything unless there is a sound source that sends an audible signal through the medium of air to our eardrums. The eardrums pass the signals to our brains. In the same way, we don't see anything unless there is a physical light source sending a light ray that reflects off a material object to our optic nerve, which then sends a signal to our brains. Therefore, a spiritual attack that is seen or heard by one person will probably not be seen or heard by another person in the same setting. Spiritual battles for our minds do not involve any physical presence or source. "For our struggle is not against flesh and blood" (Eph. 6:12). People who are paying attention to deceiving spirits are afraid that they are losing their minds. Most are afraid to share with others what is going on inside themselves.

Our brains can only function the way they have been programmed by our minds. When we go to sleep at night, our brain continues to operate on stored information. The normal dreams we experience while sleeping are typically made up of people we already know and places we have been. The story can be rather creative, but the players and places have already been placed in our memory banks. If a child watches a horror movie in the afternoon and has a nightmare that night, chances are the nightmare will include the characters in the movie.

If the nightmares include grotesque images, figures and scenes never physically seen before, then the dreams are actually a spiritual assault on the mind and are coming from an external source (in other words, they are not coming from stored memory). Such spiritual attacks at night can be stopped by submitting to God and resisting the devil (see Jas. 4:7). This usually requires resolution of all known personal and spiritual conflicts (see the "Steps to Freedom in Christ").

Of course, the external and spiritual source of dreams can also be God, as it was for Nebuchadnezzar. But in such cases the dreams will always be true and lead to a healthy fear of the Lord, not a debilitating fear that excludes faith in God.

> So do not listen to your prophets, your diviners, your interpreters
> of dreams, your mediums or your sorcerers (Jer. 27:9).

Thought for the day: *How important is it that we understand from God's perspective what is happening in our minds?*

AUTHORITY AND POWER

Luke 10:17-23

"When Jesus had called the Twelve together, he gave them power and authority to drive out all demons and to cure diseases" (Luke 9:1). He sent these first 12 disciples out on a training mission to proclaim the kingdom of God. Jesus knew there would be spiritual opposition, so He gave them power and authority over demons. Then Jesus appointed 72 others and sent them out. "The seventy-two returned with joy and said, 'Lord, even the demons submit to us in your name'" (Luke 10:17). In proclaiming the kingdom of God, these missionaries were confronting the kingdom of darkness; and they discovered that demons were subject to them in the name of Jesus. They undoubtedly started out on their mission with some fear and apprehension, but they came back astonished at their victories over evil spirits.

Satan had suffered another defeat at the hands of these itinerant missionaries, because Jesus had given them authority to overcome all the power of the enemy. They were successful in taking back some of the ground that Satan had captured. In today's passage, the authority to trample on snakes and scorpions should be taken figuratively (see Luke 10:18-20). Jesus is probably alluding to the demonic hierarchy, since snakes and scorpions are not our enemies.

"Subjection" is a military term that means "to rank under." Authority is the right to rule. Power is the ability to rule. As believers, we have the right to rule over the kingdom of darkness because of our position in Christ. We also have the ability to rule, because of the indwelling power of the Holy Spirit. Therefore, we should, "be strong in the Lord and in his mighty power" (Eph. 6:10). It is critically important that we understand that the authority and power we possess in Christ is not our human or political authority and power, but His; and neither can be exercised apart from Him. We have the power and authority to do God's will, but nothing more.

Jesus must have found it necessary to dampen his disciples' enthusiasm about their victory over the kingdom of darkness. Flushed with victory, we, too, can easily lose our perspective and adopt a wrong focus. Jesus wants us to know that demons are subject to us, but our joy comes from knowing Him. We are to rejoice that we are children of God. We are to rejoice in the cause and not in the effect. To maintain our victory, we must be Christ centered, not demon centered. In doing so, we don't let the devil set the agenda. The devil has succeeded if he can get us to pay attention to him and what he is doing instead of fixing our eyes on Jesus and paying attention to what God is doing. We should never allow evil spirits to distract us from our devotion to Christ (see 2 Cor. 11:3).

Let us fix our eyes on Jesus, the author and perfecter of our faith (Heb. 12:2).

Thought for the day: *Why is it so important to be Christ and solution centered, rather than demon or problem centered?*

THE AUTHORITY OF CHRIST

Matthew 28:16-20

The 12 disciples were now 11. Satan had succeeded in deceiving Judas who had betrayed Christ (see John 13:2). To this small band of worshippers and doubters, Jesus gave the Great Commission. They were to make disciples of all nations and baptize them in the "name of the Father and of the Son and of the Holy Spirit" (Matt. 28:19). These first missionaries were to make disciples in every nation, not just converts, and they were to instruct them to obey all that Jesus had taught.

To accomplish this task, Jesus gave them two assurances. First, He would be with them until the end of the age; not in physical form, but in Spirit. This was made possible at Pentecost when the Holy Spirit was given to every believer (see Acts 1:4).

Second, Jesus assured His disciples that "All authority in heaven and on earth has been given to me" (Matt. 28:18). Jesus never appealed to His own authority until He had to delegate responsibility, even though His authority had been recognized. "The crowds were amazed at his teaching, because he taught as one who had authority, and not as their teachers of the law" (Matt. 7:28-29). If all authority has been given to Jesus, then Satan has no authority over any believer. Tragically many believers don't know their position in Christ, so evil spirits easily intimidate them. Satan can't do anything about our position in Christ; but if he can get us to believe it isn't true, we will live as though it's not true.

Satan wants to be feared, because he wants to be worshiped. If we consider his attributes to be equal to God's attributes, then we will believe we are caught in a battle between two equal but opposite powers. Anybody who believes that is defeated. God is omnipresent, omnipotent and omniscient. Satan and his demons have been defeated by Christ at the cross and are disarmed (see Col. 2:15). The children of God are spiritually alive and seated with Christ in the heavenlies. We have become joint-heirs with Jesus and have the authority to continue His work on planet Earth.

When we are confronted by evil forces, we can say with confidence, "I am a child of God, and the evil one cannot harm me" (see 1 John 5:18). They will try to intimidate us and that can easily happen if we don't know the truth. Satan wants us to respond to his attacks in fear, because then he is in control. If we respond in fear, we are operating in the flesh, which is on his level. The fear of anything other than God is not compatible with genuine faith in God. We have lost control if we start shouting and screaming. The authority we have in Christ does not increase with volume. We don't shout out the devil! We just calmly take our place in Christ.

> Then the end will come, when he hands over the kingdom to God the Father after he has destroyed all dominion, authority and power (1 Cor. 15:24).

Thought for the day: *Can two sovereigns be ruling in the same sphere at the same time?*

THE CONFERRING OF SPIRITUAL AUTHORITY AND POWER

Ephesians 1:1–2:7

"Praise be to the God and Father of our Lord Jesus Christ, who has blessed us in the heavenly realms with every spiritual blessing in Christ" (Eph. 1:3). In Christ we were chosen (see v. 4), in Him we have redemption (see v. 7), our hope lies in Christ (see v. 12), and we "were marked in him with a seal" (v. 13). The problem is we don't always see or understand this remarkable inheritance that we have in Christ, so Paul prays for us, and for all believers.

> I pray also that the eyes of your heart may be enlightened in order that you may know the hope to which he has called you, the riches of his glorious inheritance in the saints, and his incomparably great power [*dunameos*] for us who believe. That power [*energeian*] is like the working [*kratous*] of his mighty strength [*ischuos*], which he exerted in Christ when he raised him from the dead (vv. 18-20).

When we don't understand our spiritual heritage, we don't experience the freedom and the fruitfulness that is intrinsic to our position in Christ. To carry out our delegated responsibility, we have to know the authority we have in Christ and the power of the Holy Spirit who indwells us. Behind Christ's authority is the same power that raised Him from the dead and seated Him at the Father's right hand. That power source is so dynamic that Paul used four different Greek words to describe it (see italicized words in brackets in quote above). Behind the resurrection of the Lord Jesus Christ lies the mightiest work of power recorded in the Bible. The same power that raised Jesus from the dead and defeated Satan is available to us as believers.

The scope of Christ's authority is "far above all rule and authority, power and dominion, and every title that can be given, not only in the present age but also in the one to come" (Eph. 1:21). We share this same authority because we are seated with Christ in the heavenly realms (see vv. 4-7). We are not being made alive in Christ; we have been made alive in Christ. We are not being raised up with Christ; we have been raised up with Christ. We are right now together with Christ. The throne of God is the ultimate authority of the universe, and it is from this position of authority that we carry on our delegated Kingdom responsibilities.

Before Christ, we were dead in our transgressions and sins. We "followed the ways of this world and of the ruler of the kingdom of the air, the spirit who is now at work in those who are disobedient" (Eph. 2:2). But now we have received "the incomparable riches of his grace, expressed in his kindness to us in Christ Jesus" (2:7). "His intent was that now, through the church, the manifold wisdom of God should be made known to the rulers and authorities in the heavenly realms, according to his eternal purpose which he accomplished in Christ Jesus our Lord" (3:10-11).

> And God raised us up with Christ and seated us with him in the heavenly realms in Christ Jesus (Eph. 2:6).

Thought for the day: *What is the practical significance of being seated with Christ in the heavenlies (spiritual realm)?*

QUALIFICATIONS FOR SPIRITUAL AUTHORITY

Luke 9

Jesus gave the 12 disciples power and authority over demons and sent them out to proclaim the kingdom of God (see Luke 9:1), but they could not free a father's son from demonic control (see vv. 37-45). Jesus had to reveal to them several Kingdom-killing attitudes. First, Jesus had to deal with their *self-sufficiency*. When the disciples showed concern for the crowd, Jesus suggested they give them something to eat. They made the common error of thinking only of their resources and not God's. When Jesus took what they had and multiplied it, there was so much food left over that each disciple had a basket of their own. Mark 6:45-52 reveals that they had not gained any insight from that experience. When they struggled against the storm at sea, the Lord intended to pass them by (see Mark 6:48). Jesus intends to pass by the self-sufficient. If we want to row against the storms of life, He will let us row until our arms fall off. We must choose to be dependent upon God.

Second, Jesus warned them about being *ashamed of Him and His words* (see Luke 9:26). It is easy to imagine that Jesus could be ashamed of us, but how can any person who knows the truth be ashamed of Jesus? If we are ashamed of Jesus, He will be ashamed of us when He comes again.

The third Kingdom-killing attitude is *unbelief* (see Luke 9:37-45). The disciples were ineffective in helping the boy because they really didn't believe, and Jesus suggests some moral impurity on their part (see v. 41). The power we have in Christ is only effective when we believe (see Eph. 1:19).

Fourth, the 12 disciples were ineffective because of *pride* (see Luke 9:46-48). They were arguing among themselves as to who was the greatest. According to Jesus, the greatest are those who humble themselves and come to God with childlike faith. Humble people are confident in God and put no confidence in the flesh (see Phil. 3:3).

The fifth Kingdom-killing attitude is *possessiveness* (see Luke 9:49-50). We may be driving different cars in the kingdom of God, but we are all getting our gas from the same station. No one person or ministry is superior to another, and what God has given us we should freely share with others.

Sixth, the disciples displayed the *wrong spirit* (see Luke 9:51-56). What kind of spirit requests permission to use the power of God to destroy? It may be human nature to retaliate against those who reject us, but it is not God's nature or we would all be doomed.

The seventh Kingdom-killing attitude is a *false confidence* (see Luke 9:57-58). It is better to have a few followers who have counted the cost and will endure to the end than to have a crowd who will leave before the task is done.

The eighth Kingdom-killing attitude is *lame excuses* (see Luke 9:59-62). Jesus tells us, "No one who puts his hand to the plow and looks back is fit for service in the kingdom of God" (v. 62).

I begged your disciples to drive [a demon] out, but they could not (Luke 9:40).

Thought for the day: *Why couldn't the disciples drive out that demon in Luke 9:40? What lesson must we learn from this?*

THE LIMITATIONS OF SPIRITUAL AUTHORITY

Acts 19:13-20

If something seems to be working, the opportunists start jumping on board. Such was the case of some Jews who apparently thought they could perform exorcisms by some magical formula or by simply using the name of Jesus. The seven sons of Sceva, a Jewish chief priest, were doing this (see Acts 19:13-14). To their surprise, they got beat up and run out of the house by the demonized man (see v. 16). The demon knew Jesus and Paul, but not the seven sons of Sceva. The demon didn't beat them up, but the demonized man did. He was able to overpower them because of the adrenaline rush that had been stimulated by the evil spirit. It is the same phenomenon that gives people extraordinary strength to lift objects in order to save people, although in such instances their strength comes from a different spirit.

If a demonized person questioned who we are, all we would have to say is, "I am a child of God and you can't touch me" (see 1 John 5:18). All believers, young and old, have the same authority and power over demons, although mature saints may know better how to exercise it. People can get hurt when they misuse or fail to understand the power and authority we have in Christ. We only have the authority to do God's will. We are operating according to our old nature when we act independently of God. In the flesh we are no match for Satan and his demons. If we as believers operate independently of God, we will suffer defeat. But in Christ, demons are no match for us!

News of a person getting beat up by a demonized person created fear among the people, but fortunately they turned to the Jesus and His name was held in honor (see Acts 19:17). Many of the believers openly confessed their evil deeds (see v. 18). Those who were practicing sorcery brought the tools of their practice and openly burned them (see v. 19). The word of the Lord spread rapidly and grew in power (see v. 20). One of the major thrusts of Early Church evangelism was to free people from demonic influences. That will likely be the case again before the second coming of Christ.

It is human nature to see something work, and borrow the method, instead of understanding the message behind the method. There are no programs, rituals or formulas that can set anybody free. Who sets people free is Christ, and what sets people free is their response to God in repentance and faith. If God is in it, almost any program will work. It God isn't in it, then no program will work, no matter how biblical it may appear. But if God is in it, then a good program and strategy will bear more fruit than a bad program or strategy.

Apart from me you can do nothing (John 15:5).

Thought for the day: *What can we expect to accomplish for eternity if we try to do it by hard work and human ingenuity?*

THE ARMOR OF GOD

Ephesians 6:10-20

Satan's first objective is to blind the mind of the unbelieving (see 2 Cor. 4:3-4). Should he lose that battle, his next strategy is to deceive, tempt and accuse believers so that they will lead defeated lives. Satan's aim is to "prove" that Christianity doesn't work, that God's Word isn't true and that nothing of major consequence happened when we were born again. Since our struggle is against a Satan controlled demonic hierarchy, we need to know how to protect ourselves.

Our reaction to the spiritual forces of evil in the spiritual realm may be likened to our reaction to germs in the natural realm. Before the medical profession discovered the reality and nature of microbes, they saw no need to wear surgical masks, sterilize their equipment, scrub before surgery or use antibiotics. Consequently, a lot of people died needlessly. So we definitely need to know there are germs and viruses; but they can't be our focus or we will become hypochondriacs. The appropriate response is to live a healthy life. Generally speaking, our immune system will protect us if we get enough sleep, exercise regularly and eat a healthy diet. Demons are like little invisible germs looking for someone to infect. There is no need to be afraid of them or focus on their whereabouts, but we are to be aware of their existence and live righteous lives in Christ. Jesus is our immune system.

When we put on the armor of God we are putting on the Lord Jesus Christ (see Rom. 13:12-14). When we put on Christ, we take ourselves out of the realm of the flesh, where we are vulnerable. Satan can only touch that which is on his level and that is why we are to make no provision for the flesh. Satan has nothing on Christ (see John 14:30); and to the extent that we put on Christ, the evil one cannot touch us (see 1 John 5:18). There is no physical sanctuary or place where we are spiritually protected and there is no time when it is safe to take off the armor of God. Our only sanctuary is our identity and position in Christ (see Eph. 6:10).

Putting on the armor of God requires an active participation on our part. We cannot passively take our place in Christ. As Paul describes the armor of God, he admonishes us to "be strong" (Eph. 6:10); "put on" (v. 11); "take your stand" (v. 11); "stand firm" (v. 14); "take up" (v. 16); "take" (v. 17); "pray" (v. 18); and "be alert" (v. 18). "Therefore put on the full armor of God, so that when the day of evil comes, you may be able to stand your ground" (v. 13). The purpose for armor is to stop penetration, and we become vulnerable if we do not assume our responsibility to stand firm in our faith.

> The night is almost gone, and the day is near. Therefore let us lay aside the deeds of darkness and put on the armor of light (Rom. 13:12).

Thought for the day: *What will happen if we don't actively put on the armor of God?*

THE BELT OF TRUTH

John 17:13-19

Jesus is about to go to the Father and leave behind the 11 remaining disciples. Even though the devil is defeated, he is still prowling around like a roaring lion looking for someone to devour (see 1 Pet. 5:8). In this High Priestly Prayer (see John 17:13-19), Jesus doesn't ask that we be removed from the world. He asks that we be protected from the evil one. Being sanctified in God's Word is our first line of defense. The belt of truth is the first piece mentioned on the armor of God. It holds the other pieces of the armor in place.

The belt of truth helps us to combat lies. Sadly, lying is the most common defense mechanism employed by unbelievers. Those who have something to hide will seek to cover it up. They are playing right into the hands of Satan who is the father of lies. We will stay in bondage as long as we continue to believe his lies. Some don't want the truth to be known, because their deeds are evil and they don't want them exposed (see John 3:20). The first step in any recovery program is to face the truth and acknowledge the need for God, who alone has the power to overcome our sin. Those who turn to Christ find their sanctuary in Him, because Jesus is the truth (see John 14:6), the Holy Spirit is the Spirit of Truth (see John 14:17), He will lead us into all truth (see John 16:13) and that truth will set us free (see John 8:32).

If the devil tempted you, you would know it. If he accused you, you would know it. But if Satan deceived you, you wouldn't know it. If you knew it, you would no longer be deceived. That is why deception is the major tool of the devil. The fact that even good people can be deceived is evident in the sinless life of Eve before the Fall. She was deceived and believed a lie (see Gen. 3:1-6). Satan's strategy was deception in the Garden of Eden, and it is in the book of Revelation (see Rev. 12:9). Spiritual warfare will intensify in the end times with the coming of the false prophet and the Antichrist.

We don't overcome the father of lies by human reason or by scientific research. We overcome the deceiver by divine revelation. Jesus tells us, "Sanctify them by the truth; your word is truth" (John 17:17). We are admonished to walk in the light (see 1 John 1:7) and to speak the truth in love (see Eph. 4:25). The only thing we as Christians ever have to admit to is the truth. We never have to be afraid of the truth; it is a liberating friend. Therefore, "Trust in the LORD with all your heart and lean not on your own understanding; in all your ways acknowledge him, and he will make your paths straight. Do not be wise in your own eyes; fear the LORD and shun evil. This will bring health to your body and nourishment to your bones" (Prov. 3:5-8).

> Don't be deceived, my dear brothers. Every good and perfect gift is from above, coming down from the Father of the heavenly lights, who does not change like shifting shadows. He chose to give us birth through the word of truth (Jas. 1:16-18).

Thought for the day: *How can you keep from being deceived?*

THE BREASTPLATE
OF RIGHTEOUSNESS

Acts 24:10-16

When we put on Christ at salvation, we are justified before a Holy God (see Rom. 5:1). It is not our righteousness that saved us, but Christ's righteousness (see 1 Cor. 1:30). When we put on the armor of God, we are putting on the breastplate of righteousness, which is our defense against Satan's accusations. Every believer has struggled with condemning thoughts, because Satan is the accuser of the brethren. When that happens we can respond with Paul, "Who will bring any charge against those whom God has chosen? It is God who justifies" (Rom. 8:33). The breastplate of righteousness is the Lord's righteousness bestowed upon us. This righteousness is imputed at salvation. Imputed righteousness means that something that belongs to one person is put to the account of another.

God also imparts His righteousness within us. The Puritans called this imparted righteousness. Since we have become partakers of His righteous nature, we can live a holy life. "For it is God who works in you to will and to act according to his good purpose" (Phil. 2:13). Even though we stand in a righteous position in Christ, we should not commit or excuse any deeds of unrighteousness. We are saints who still have the capacity to sin and we will if we believe a lie or choose to live according to the old nature. Putting on the armor of light means that we walk in the light as God is in the light (see 1 John 1:6-7).

John wrote, "If we claim to be without sin, we deceive ourselves and the truth is not in us" (1 John 1:8). Therefore, walking in the light is not sinless perfection. It is simply agreeing with God and is essentially the same as confession, taken from the Greek *homologeo*, which means "to acknowledge or agree." In Paul's defense before Felix, he appealed to his orthodox beliefs and then added, "So I strive always to keep my conscience clear before God and man" (Acts 24:16). That is good advice for all of us. When we realize that we have done something wrong, we confess it. We don't have to ask for forgiveness, because we are already forgiven. Any residual guilt is a false guilt or Satan's accusations, since "there is now no condemnation for those who are in Christ Jesus" (Rom. 8:1).

You can walk in the light because you are already forgiven. You are the righteousness of God in Christ (see 2 Cor. 5:21). Your relationship with God and your eternal destiny are not at stake when you sin, but your daily victory is. Your confession of sin clears the way for the fruitful expression of righteousness in your daily life. "My dear children, I write this to you so that you will not sin. But if anybody does sin, we have one who speaks to the Father in our defense—Jesus Christ, the Righteous One. He is the atoning sacrifice for our sins, and not only for ours but also for the sins of the whole world" (1 John 2:1-2).

And the scripture was fulfilled that says, "Abraham believed God, and it was credited to him as righteousness," and he was called God's friend (Jas. 2:23).

Thought for the day: *What has been credited to you and on what basis?*

THE SHOES OF PEACE

Romans 16:17-20

There are a lot of divisive elements in this world, and Paul cautions us to watch out for them. Such divisive people are not serving our Lord Jesus Christ. "By smooth talk and flattery they deceive the minds of naïve people" (Rom. 16:18). Paul wrote in Titus 3:10-11, "Warn a divisive person once, and then warn him a second time. After that, have nothing to do with him. You may be sure that such a man is warped and sinful; he is self-condemned." They stand in stark contrast to true believers. Jesus tells us, "Blessed are the peacemakers, for they will be called sons of God" (Matt. 5:9).

The Lord is praying that we would all be one (see John 17:21); and Paul admonishes us to "Make every effort to keep the unity of the Spirit through the bond of peace" (Eph. 4:3). If we are going to keep the unity of the Spirit, then it must somehow be here already. Therefore, the basis for unity is not our common physical heritage, nor is it our religious traditions. The basis for our unity is our common spiritual heritage. Every believer is a child of God. We are brothers and sisters in Christ, and we ought to relate to one another as such.

When we receive Christ, we are united with the Prince of Peace. We already have positional peace with God (see Rom. 5:1); but the peace of Christ must rule in our hearts, and that is only possible if we let the Word of Christ richly dwell within us (see Col. 3:15-16). As the armor of God, the shoes of peace become our protection against the divisive schemes of the devil when we act as peacemakers among believers.

A tree split in half dies, but a tree that is pruned bears more fruit. Jesus prunes, but the devil divides—and it takes very little effort to divide a fellowship. All you have to do is start a whisper campaign, spread a few lies and accuse someone falsely. The book of Proverbs has a lot to say about malicious speech and gossip. "A gossip betrays a confidence but a trustworthy man keeps a secret" (11:13). "A perverse man stirs up dissension, and a gossip separates close friends" (16:28). "Without wood a fire goes out; without gossip a quarrel dies down" (26:20). Such is the divisive work of Satan and his false prophets.

But we have the promise that "The God of peace will soon crush Satan under [our] feet" (Rom. 16:20). If we want to be peacemakers, then we should "not let any unwholesome talk come out of [our] mouths, but only what is helpful for building others up according to their needs, that it may benefit those who listen. And [we should] not grieve the Holy Spirit of God, with whom [we] were sealed for the day of redemption" (Eph. 4:29-30).

Let us therefore make every effort to do what leads to peace and to mutual edification (Rom. 14:19).

Thought for the day: *How can you be a better peacemaker?*

THE SHIELD OF FAITH

Psalm 7:10-16

As a young shepherd, David had protected his sheep from lions (see 1 Sam. 17:34-35). Now as an adult, enemies surrounded David, so he took refuge in the Lord. He knew in his heart that God was the only One who could save him. David wrote, "My shield is God Most High, who saves the upright in heart" (Ps. 7:10). As a New Testament believer, you have to "take up the shield of faith, with which you can extinguish all the flaming arrows of the evil one" (Eph. 6:16). The Greek word for shield, *thureos*, conveys the idea of a large shield. It was a shield that the infantry would hide behind when the enemy shot their arrows.

These "flaming arrows" are nothing more than smoldering lies, burning accusations and fiery temptations bombarding our minds. Whenever we discern a deceiving, accusing or tempting thought, we meet it head-on with what we know to be true. We take every thought captive and make it obedient to Christ (see 2 Cor. 10:5). We overcome Satan's attacks by choosing the truth. This is what Jesus did when tempted by the devil. He simply quoted Scripture. Every time we memorize a Bible verse, listen to a sermon or participate in a Bible study, we increase our knowledge of God and enlarge our shield of faith. "Every word of God is flawless; he is a shield to those who take refuge in him" (Prov. 30:5).

Recall from a previous study that putting on the armor of God is essentially putting on the Lord Jesus Christ. He is our sanctuary. Therefore, our faith is not our shield. The object of our faith is our shield, since faith has no validity without an object. The same holds true for our faith in our police and fire departments. The fact that we believe we can call upon them is not what provides us with protection. The police and fire department provide physical protection; but if we didn't believe they could, and *would*, we would never call them.

No passage describes better the sanctuary we have in God than Psalm 91. "He who dwells in the shelter of the Most High will rest in the shadow of the Almighty" (v. 1). He will deliver us from the fowler's snare (see v. 3). He will cover us with His shield (see v. 4). "You will not fear the terror of night, nor the arrow that flies by day" (v. 5). "For he will command his angels concerning you to guard you in all your ways" (v. 11). Satan knew the spiritual significance of this last verse when he tempted Jesus (see Matt. 4:6), but Jesus would not be tempted to put God to the test. We are protected when we do God's will, not Satan's will. "'Because he loves me,' says the LORD, 'I will rescue him; I will protect him, for he acknowledges my name'" (Ps. 91:14).

> For surely, O LORD, you bless the righteous; you surround them with your favor as with a shield (Ps. 5:12).

Thought for the day: *How can you enlarge your shield of faith?*

THE HELMET OF SALVATION

Psalm 27

The helmet of salvation is part of our Christian armor. In the metaphor of armor, the helmet secures coverage of the most critical part of our anatomy, our mind, where spiritual battles are won or lost. The temptation is to doubt our salvation when we come under spiritual attack. The mental assault is fairly predictable. *How can you even think you are a Christian given the way you act and feel? God doesn't love you. You don't believe this Christian stuff do you?* But we can stand firm knowing that our salvation is not based on our good works, but on the good works of Christ. We are children of God by the grace of God, and nothing can separate us from His love (see Rom. 8:35).

Christian warriors wear the helmet of salvation in the sense that they are possessors of deliverance, clothed and armed in the victory of Jesus Christ. Since we are joined to the Lord Jesus Christ, the devil has no legitimate claim on us, and there is no reason to fear him. David said, "The LORD is my light and my salvation—whom shall I fear? The LORD is the stronghold of my life—of whom shall I be afraid?" (Ps. 27:1). We have faith and love as a breastplate, and the hope of salvation as a helmet. "For God did not appoint us to suffer wrath but to receive salvation through our Lord Jesus Christ" (1 Thess. 5:9).

The best way to keep Satan's thoughts out is to keep Christ's thoughts in. As surely as Satan can fill our hearts if we let him, so much more can the Lord fill our minds with His thoughts. Satan's thoughts may penetrate a leaky helmet, but we have the mind of Christ within us. Unlike Satan, the Lord does not intrude where not invited. That is why it is up to us to invite Him in at salvation (see John 1:12). As children of God, the Lord will never disown us or leave us. Even if we willfully walked away, we would still be His children. Our salvation is not based on our ability to hang on to God, but His ability to hang on to us.

Satan cannot do anything about our relationship with God; but if he can get us to doubt our salvation, we will struggle in our daily life. Defeated Christians typically have one thing in common. They don't know who they are in Christ and they don't understand what it means to be a child of God. As victorious Christians, we know, "that neither death nor life, neither angels nor demons, neither the present nor the future, nor any powers, neither height nor depth, nor anything else in all creation, will be able to separate us from the love of God that is in Christ Jesus our Lord" (Rom. 8:38-39).

> Yet to all who received him, to those who believed in his name, he gave the right to become children of God—children born not of natural descent, nor of human decision or a husband's will, but born of God (John 1:12-13).

Thought for the day: *Was it God's will or your will that you be God's child?*

THE SWORD OF THE SPIRIT

Psalm 119:89-112

God's Word is eternal (see Ps. 119:89), a lamp to our feet and a light to our path (see v. 105). The Word of God is the only offensive weapon in the armor of God. It is the "sword of the Spirit" (Eph. 6:17). Paul uses *rhema* instead of *logos* for "word" because the Greek word "rhema" carries the idea of proclamation. Our defense against the direct attacks from the evil one is to speak aloud God's truth. In addition to thinking and believing God's Word, we need to speak it because Satan is not omniscient, and he doesn't perfectly know what we are thinking. By observing us, he can know reasonably well what we are thinking, just as any student of human behavior can.

If you are paying attention to a deceiving spirit (see 1 Tim. 4:1), he is putting thoughts in your mind, and he will know whether you buy his lies by how you behave. It isn't hard for Satan to know what you are thinking if he has given you the thought. You are ascribing too much power to Satan if you think he can perfectly read your mind and know the future. Occult practitioners claim to be able to read minds (or influence them) or predict the future. But Satan doesn't perfectly know either what we're thinking or what the future holds. We should never ascribe the divine attributes of God to Satan.

It is not uncommon for people to come under a spiritual attack at night (see Job 4:12-16). The usual experience is an intense feeling of fear and the inability to speak or move. It may feel like a pressure on our chest or something grabbing our throat. Such spiritual attacks can easily be resolved by submitting to God first, and then resisting the devil (see Jas. 4:7). We can always silently and inwardly call upon the name of the Lord, because God knows the thoughts and attitudes of our hearts (see Heb. 4:12). As soon as we acknowledge God, He will enable us to resist the devil. All we would have to say is, "Jesus," and the evil spirit will flee; but we would need to verbally express it. Trying to respond physically wouldn't work, because we don't wage war as the world does (see 2 Cor. 10:3-4). Spiritual battles have to be won spiritually.

"If you confess with your mouth, 'Jesus is Lord,' and believe in your heart that God raised him from the dead, you will be saved. For it is with your heart that you believe and are justified, and it is with your mouth that you confess and are saved" (Rom. 10:9-10). Since you know your own thoughts and God also knows them, why does verbal confession result in salvation? Paul could be saying that saving faith is not complete until the will is exercised, but he could also be implying the need for the god of this world to hear our commitment.

Amid disquieting dreams in the night, when deep sleep falls on men, fear and trembling seized me and made all my bones shake. A spirit glided past my face, and the hair on my body stood on end (Job 4:13-15).

Thought for the day: *What would you do if you encountered a spirit (as described in Job. 4:13-15)?*

PRAYING WITH PERSEVERANCE FOR ALL THE SAINTS

Luke 18:1-8

Paul's discussion on the armor of God concludes with an admonition to, "pray in the Spirit on all occasions with all kinds of prayers and requests. With this in mind, be alert and always keep on praying for all the saints" (Eph. 6:18). We cannot engage in spiritual warfare without praying. Praying on "all occasions" means we are to pray when we feel like it and when we don't feel like it. If we realize our dependence upon God, we will pray often and be ready all the time. The preeminence of prayer needs to be settled in our minds. Prayer doesn't precede a greater work of God. Prayer *is* our greater work.

The Holy Spirit will lead us to pray for all the saints all the time. Our prayers will then be effective because the Holy Spirit has prompted them. Prayer has preceded every great movement of God. Pentecost was preceded by prayer as were the Great Awakenings in America. There has never been an outpouring of the divine Spirit from God without a previous outpouring of the human spirit toward God through prayer.

If the Holy Spirit is guiding our prayers, we will be prompted to ask for divine protection for others. Such prompting can come at any time of the day. We may never know the trouble another believer is in, but the Holy Spirit does. When the Lord puts someone on our mind, we need to stop whatever we're doing, and lift him or her up in prayer. We need to ask God to place a hedge of protection around that person. And we must keep praying until we sense the peace of God.

The Holy Spirit may also prompt you to pray for those who are in trouble. We have the spiritual authority in Christ to stand against Satan and his attacks. When the disciples were unsuccessful in driving out a demon in a boy, the Lord said, "This kind can come out only by prayer" (Mark 9:29). The disciples may have tried to do it by copying what they saw Jesus do, but they didn't have the same degree of dependence on their heavenly Father that Jesus did, nor the same degree of faith.

Jesus told the parable of the unjust judge so that his disciples would learn to be persistent in prayer (see Luke 18:1-8). The widow only wanted justice against her adversary, and she wasn't going to stop petitioning the judge until she got it. Her persistence finally won over the judge, who gave her justice. If a judge who doesn't care for that which is right or wrong is compelled by persistence to deal justly with a helpless individual, certainly we can expect God to answer prayer. He will not put us off, and He will quickly answer our cry for justice concerning our adversaries.

Before the Lord returns, there will be a coming apostasy. During this time of spiritual decline and persecution, the Lord asks whether He will find faith on the earth (see Luke 18:8). Presumably He means the kind of faith that perseveres in prayer and never wavers under fire.

> Be diligent in these matters; give yourself wholly to them, so that everyone may see your progress. Watch your life and doctrine closely. Persevere in them, because if you do, you will save both yourself and your hearers (1 Tim. 4:15-16).

Thought for the day: *Why is perseverance in prayer so important for our lives and ministry?*

PRAYING WITH AUTHORITY

1 Kings 18

James said, "Elijah was a man just like us. He prayed earnestly that it would not rain, and it did not rain on the land for three and a half years. Again he prayed, and the heavens gave rain, and the earth produced its crops" (Jas. 5:17-18). Elijah was a prophet of God, but he was just a mortal like us; and we have the same spiritual authority, because of our position in Christ. The key to Elijah's success is summarized in 1 Kings 18:36-38. He desired that God be known in Israel and that the hearts of the people would be turned back to Him. His confidence and faith in God were so great that he could see the answer to prayer before there was any visible evidence (see vv. 41-45). He was sure of what he hoped for and certain of what he did not see (see Heb. 11:1).

Every believer has the spiritual authority to do God's will and carry on the ministry of Christ. Jesus summarized His ministry when He read Isaiah 61:1-2 in the synagogue and applied it to Himself: "The Spirit of the Lord is on me, because he has anointed me to preach good news to the poor. He has sent me to proclaim freedom for the prisoners and recovery of sight for the blind, to release the oppressed" (Luke 4:18). In this present Church Age, God works through the prayers and faith of His children whom He has commissioned to make disciples of all nations. We have authority over Satan and his demons who have blinded the minds of the unbelieving (see 2 Cor. 4:4), and captivated many people to do his will (see 2 Tim. 2:26).

Satan's power has been broken (see Heb. 2:14-15; Col. 2:15), but he will not turn loose anything he thinks he can keep. Jesus came to undo the works of Satan (see 1 John 3:8), and it is part of our calling to recapture lost ground. We need to stand firm in our faith and pray with the authority delegated to us by the Lord Jesus Christ. We are not trying to enlist God in our service. Prayer is joining God in His service. Praying with authority is not expressing to God our will; it is discerning God's will and claiming with confidence the answer. "This is the confidence we have in approaching God: that if we ask anything according to his will, he hears us. And if we know that he hears us—whatever we ask—we know that we have what we asked of him" (1 John 5:14-15). We have the right to claim by faith the property that Satan has his hands on but which rightfully belongs to God. We need to persevere in faith until Satan turns loose those whom God has directed us to pray for. The evil one will hold on to his captives until we take our place in Christ and demand that he release them in the name of Jesus!

"O unbelieving and perverse generation," Jesus replied, "how long shall I stay with you? How long shall I put up with you? Bring the boy here to me." Jesus rebuked the demon, and it came out of the boy, and he was healed from that moment (Matt. 17:17-18).

Thought for the day: *Jesus had perfect faith and holiness, and He spoke with authority. How much more fruitful would we be in ministry if we believed the truth, lived righteous lives and exercised our authority in Christ as He led us?*

BINDING AND LOOSING

Matthew 16:13-23

God revealed to Peter that Jesus was the "Christ, the Son of the living God" (Matt. 16:16). A short time later Peter found himself speaking for the devil and Jesus rebuked him. "Get behind me, Satan! You are a stumbling block to me; you do not have in mind the things of God, but the things of men" (v. 23). Jesus' rebuke seems severe, but the fact that he identified Satan as the source of Peter's words was precise and appropriate. The devil's aim is to promote self-interest as the chief end of humankind. Satan is called the prince of this world because self-interest rules this world. He is called the accuser, because he does not believe that we have a higher motive than self-service. Satan's creed sounds like this: *Save yourself at all costs. Sacrifice duty to self-interest, the cause of Christ to personal convenience. All people are selfish at heart and have their price. Some may hold out longer than others, but in the end people choose their own will over the will of God.*

God has given the keys of the Kingdom to those who deny themselves, pick up their cross daily and follow Jesus. Whatever they bind on Earth will be bound in heaven, and whatever they loose on Earth will be loosed in heaven (see Matt. 16:19). A similar passage can be found in Matthew 18:18, but verses 19 and 20 add, "Again, I tell you that if two of you on earth agree about anything you ask for, it will be done for you by my Father in heaven. For where two or three come together in my name, there am I with them." Three points need to be noted.

First, since truth sets people free, the keys of the Kingdom may mean the keys of knowledge (see Luke 11:52). Second, both passages on binding and loosing are difficult to translate. Following the rules of Greek grammar, both passages can be translated: "Whatever you bind on earth shall have been bound in heaven, and whatever you loose on earth shall have been loosed in heaven" (Matt. 16:19, *NASB*). The same Greek language structure is found in John 20:23: "If you forgive anyone his sins, they are forgiven; if you do not forgive them, they are not forgiven" (*NIV*). That passage could also be translated: "If you forgive the sins of any, their sins have been forgiven them; if you retain the sins of any, they have been retained" (John 20:23, *NASB*). Notice the subtle differences between the two translations. Linguistically, they can be translated either way, but the *New American*

Standard Version is to be preferred. Most theologians agree that the Church does not have the power and right to bind, loose and forgive whomever it wishes.

Third, what the two or three gathered together in Jesus' name are agreeing on is God's will. The ideas to bind, loose and forgive originated in heaven, not in the independent mind of humanity. God is able to communicate in such a way that discerning Christians have the keys to the Kingdom. They are announcing what God has ordained.

> For I have come down from heaven not to do my will but to do the will of him who sent me (John 6:38).

Thought for the day: *Where does truth originate, from us or from God?*

THE LURE OF KNOWLEDGE AND POWER

Deuteronomy 18:9-16

The lure of the occult is almost always on the basis of acquiring knowledge and power. In a very real sense, knowledge is power. For example, precognition means to know about something before it happens. Imagine the power you would have if you knew events before they happened. You could be a billionaire just by betting at the racetrack. You could manipulate world events and have incredible political power. To know something before time means that you have access to some kind of power that can arrange future events. Satan has a limited capacity to do that by manipulating people who will pay attention to his deceiving spirits.

Everything Satan does is a counterfeit of Christianity. Clairvoyance, which is the power to see what our normal five senses cannot see, is a counterfeit of divine revelation. Precognition is a counterfeit of prophecy. Telepathy, which is the ability to communicate from one mind to another by extrasensory means, is a counterfeit of prayer. Psychokinesis, which is the manipulation of physical matter without the use of physical means, is a counterfeit of God's miracles. Spirit guides, or deceiving spirits, are counterfeits of divine guidance. Why would people want a spirit guide if they could have the Holy Spirit as their guide?

These finite longings for the infinite can be fulfilled by the knowledge and power that come from an intimate relationship with God. However, Satan is trying to pass off his counterfeits as the real thing. He will gain a foothold in our lives if he can lure us into the deceptive world of psychic knowledge and power. Moses' words of warning in Deuteronomy 18:9-13 are as viable today as they were for the Israelites under his leadership. We live in a contemporary Canaan in which it is socially acceptable to consult spiritists, mediums, palm readers, psychic counselors and horoscopes for guidance and esoteric knowledge.

Since Satan has the capacity to deceive the whole world, it is possible for him to arrange future events—but never perfectly. Only God can prophesy something and guarantee that it will come true. This is one way that we can know whether a prophet is true or false: "If what a prophet proclaims in the name of the LORD does not take place or come true, that is a message the LORD has not spoken. That prophet has spoken presumptuously" (Deut. 18:22). All the false prophets, psychic counselors and spiritual mediums have superhuman knowledge, but they are getting it from Satan and it is never perfectly accurate. Since they seem to know more than what is humanly possible, a gullible public pays attention to them, and they are being deceived.

> For false Christs and false prophets will appear and perform great signs and miracles to deceive even the elect—if that were possible. See, I have told you ahead of time (Matt. 24:24-25).

Thought for the day: *Why is God telling us this ahead of time?*

ESOTERIC KNOWLEDGE

Leviticus 19:31

The craving for esoteric, "extra" knowledge has led many people to seek out mediums and spiritists. God strictly forbids this practice: "Do not turn to mediums or seek out spiritists, for you will be defiled by them. I am the LORD your God" (Lev. 19:31). God is not restricting us from having knowledge that we need. He has made Himself and His ways known so that we can live productive lives. But ignorant people don't want to take the time to seek God and study His word, so they settle for a word of knowledge from some "spiritual advisor."

> When men tell you to consult mediums and spiritists, who whisper and mutter, should not a people inquire of their God? Why consult the dead on behalf of the living? To the law and to the testimony! If they do not speak according to this word, they have no light of dawn (Isa. 8:19-20).

Not much is known about the biblical terms "medium" and "spiritist." Since "medium" (taken from *ob*, meaning "witch" or "necromancer") is feminine, and "spiritist" (taken from *yidd oni*, from the root "to know") is masculine, some scholars think they are the male and female counterparts of the same role. Their role is to introduce false guidance. The Lord does not take lightly those who give false guidance or those who seek it out. "I will set my face against the person who turns to mediums and spiritists to prostitute himself by following them, and I will cut him off from his people" (Lev. 20:6). God takes an even tougher stand against those who would lead his people astray: "A man or woman who is a medium or spiritist among you must be put to death. You are to stone them; their blood will be on their own heads" (Lev. 20:27). We don't stone mediums today because we no longer live under Old Testament theocratic law—we are under Christ's New Covenant. However, our culture tends to make them celebrities and puts them on talk shows and schedules them for entertainment. Late night television is loaded with psychic hotlines promising divine guidance and spiritual help.

Many Christians have dabbled in the occult and suddenly found themselves in spiritual bondage to the lies they believed. God doesn't want their false guidance to pollute the Church so He cuts them off. Paul says, "We have renounced secret and shameful ways; we do not use deception, nor do we distort the word of God" (2 Cor. 4:2). To resolve spiritual conflicts arising from false guidance, it is necessary to renounce all involvement and association with false teachers, false prophets, and any and all cult and occult practices. That would include all vows or pledges made to anyone or anything other than Christ. The need to do this also applies to the children and grandchildren whose ancestors participated in any type of cult or occult practices, since these sins can be passed on from one generation to the next (see Exod. 20:4-5).[1]

Let us purify ourselves from everything that contaminates body and spirit, perfecting holiness out of reverence for God (2 Cor. 7:1).

Thought for the day: *Why do people seek esoteric knowledge?*

THE SPIRITUAL DEMISE OF SAUL

1 Samuel 28

Saul had sinned, causing God to turn away from him. The closest Saul came to repentance was 1 Samuel 15:24-31. After much prodding by Samuel, Saul used words that sounded good and made it seem like he was truly repentant. Like many who disobey God, he tried to rectify his mistake, but it was too late: "For the Spirit of the Lord had departed from Saul, and an evil spirit from the Lord tormented him" (1 Sam. 16:14).

This can appear to be a troublesome passage for two reasons. First, some could conclude that we can lose the Holy Spirit; but under the Old Covenant, the presence of the Holy Spirit was a temporary gifting, just like God's blessings were conditional. Under the New Covenant the Holy Spirit permanently takes up residence in those who believe. Second, it could seem as if the evil spirit was of God, but God only sent him. God reigns supreme, and He can use Satan and his emissaries as a means to discipline His people, as He did with Saul. He used the godless nation of Assyria to discipline His people (see Isa. 10:5-6). Even the Church is advised to turn grossly immoral people over to Satan for the destruction of their flesh so their souls may be saved (see 1 Cor. 5:5).

After Samuel had died, Saul's twisted thirst for spiritual knowledge led him to seek guidance from a medium. Having previously purged the nation of mediums and spiritists (see 1 Sam. 28:9), Saul decided to pay a visit to the witch of Endor. Coming to the witch in disguise, Saul persuaded her to call up Samuel (see vv. 11-19). But the scheme backfired when God permitted Samuel himself to return, terrifying the medium. Samuel's message to Saul was nothing but bad news, foretelling the imminent capture of Israel by the Philistines and the death of Saul and his son (see v. 19).

God expressly forbids the practice of necromancy, which is an attempt to bring up the spirits of the dead (see Isa. 8:19-20). The story of the rich man and Lazarus teaches the present-day impossibility of communicating with the dead (see Luke 16:19-31). When a secular psychologist claims to have regressed a client back to a former state of existence through hypnosis, don't believe it. When a psychic claims to have contacted the dead, don't believe it. When a New Age medium purports to channel a person from the past into the present, realize that it is nothing more than a demonic spirit or the fraudulent work of a con artist. Hypnosis bypasses the conscious use of the mind and is not a practice that Christians should participate in. Mediums have to reach a passive state of the mind in order to channel spirits. That is the most dangerous thing we can do spiritually. God never bypasses our minds. He works through them. "Brothers, stop thinking like children. In regard to evil be infants, but in your thinking be adults" (1 Cor. 14:20).

> Once when we were going to the place of prayer, we were met by a slave girl who had a spirit by which she predicted the future. She earned a great deal of money for her owners by fortune-telling (Acts 16:16).

Thought for the day: *What is the motive of those who practice witchcraft?*

THE RISE OF THE NEW AGE

Acts 8:4-25

From the day of Pentecost, all believers who knew the gospel received the Holy Spirit. Persecution in Jerusalem caused the gospel to spread to surrounding regions. The believers in Samaria had only an incomplete Gospel, which the apostles now graciously supplied in full (see Acts 8:14-17), and they too received the Holy Spirit. The disciples of Jesus were performing miracles, and evil spirits were coming out of many (see v. 7). At the same time in Samaria, a man named Simon amazed people with his sorcery. The people called him the "Great Power" (v. 10), and they followed him because he amazed them with his magic. But when they heard the good news from Philip, they believed and Simon also professed to believe and was even baptized (see vv. 12-13).

Then Simon tried to offer money to have the same "magical" power the disciples had—a practice called simony to this day (see Acts 18:18-19). Peter immediately rebuked him for thinking that he could buy the gift of God with money. Peter called for him to repent because he could tell that Simon was full of bitterness and captive to sin, indicating that Simon was probably not a true believer (see vv. 20-23). This account clearly reveals that the spiritual battle continued after Pentecost. The thirst for knowledge and power still lures a gullible public to seek false guidance. There are many customers like those in Acts 16:16-18 who sought guidance from a demonized slave girl, and there are many who will make a profit from them.

In our present time, the New Age movement cloaks the occultic message of enlightenment: "You don't need God; you are God. You don't need to repent of your sins and depend on God to save you. You just need to be enlightened. So turn off your mind and tune in to the great cosmic oneness through some mystical harmonic convergence." The New Age pitch is the oldest lie of Satan: "You will be like God" (Gen. 3:5). New Age practitioners change the names from "medium" to "channeler," "demon" to "spirit guide," and a gullible public buys it and spends big money doing so.

The harlots of the New Age movement may well represent the mystery religion of Babylon. "With her the kings of the earth committed adultery and the inhabitants of the earth were intoxicated with the wine of her adulteries" (Rev. 17:2). Every country has opened its doors to paranormal and psychic research. What the rulers of the countries of the world don't know is that they have embraced the religion of the Antichrist—which is masquerading under the guise of science. Such kings are like Jeshurun. "He abandoned the God who made him and rejected the Rock his Savior. They sacrificed to demons, which are not God—gods they had not known, gods that recently appeared, gods your fathers did not fear. You deserted the Rock, who fathered you; you forgot the God who gave you birth" (Deut. 32:15,17-18).

You have no part or share in this ministry, because your heart is not right before God (Acts 8:21).

Thought for the day: *How important are our motives when we seek to help others?*

COUNTERFEIT GIFTS

Exodus 7—11

The Pharaoh was not willing to let God's people go, so the Lord sent one plague after another. It is interesting to note that Pharaoh hardened his own heart several times before the Lord finally hardened Pharaoh's heart (see Exod. 9:12). He probably could have turned his heart to God at one time, but now he no longer could. This sequential hardening of our own hearts will lead to a depraved mind, a mind devoid of logic that leads to extreme depravity (see Rom. 1:28-32). After the tenth plague, Pharaoh finally relented and let God's people go for self-preservation (see Exod. 12:31), but he never repented.

Pharaoh summoned his magicians and sorcerers and at first, by their secret arts, they were able to duplicate what Moses had done (see Exod. 7:11,22; 8:7). "But when the magicians tried to produce gnats by their secret arts, they could not . . . The magicians said to Pharaoh, 'This is the finger of God' " (vv. 8:18-19). Their magical powers could only go so far. They could mimic what Moses did until God created gnats out of dust. Satan has no power to create, so the rest of the plagues went unmatched. The magicians knew it was the finger of God when they couldn't counterfeit what He was doing. Spiritual counterfeiters will continue throughout the Church Age, culminating with "terrible times in the last days" (2 Tim. 3:1). "Just as Jannes and Jambres opposed Moses, so also these men oppose the truth—men of depraved minds, who, as far as the faith is concerned, are rejected" (2 Tim. 3:8).

Practicing magic in the Old Testament is not the same thing as the entertaining tricks that our modern magicians do. Magicians who seek to entertain us have the ability to create illusions by using clever tricks and slight of hand. In a similar way, some "psychics" are only doing "cold readings." These clever charlatans ask the naïve a few leading questions. They observe their clients speech, mannerisms, appearance and dress. Based on these observations, such "psychics" make general statements that can appear to be accurate. But the gullible are so impressed with the accuracy of their "revelations" that they start giving more information, which these charlatans fabricate into a "reading." This is not demonic; it's just "verbal slight of hand," but they do reveal how easy it is for people to be deceived.

But the mediums and spiritists that God spoke against in Leviticus and Deuteronomy were not con artists, but people who possessed real spiritual power. They were channels for the demonic and knew in their own ranks who the true psychics were. Today, while the charlatans, with their phony cold readings, are only interested in bilking us out of our money, the true medium and spiritist wants to enslave us and expand the control of Satan. The evil one will also counterfeit many of the spiritual gifts that God has endowed the Church with. This is especially true for the gifts of tongues and prophecy. Both are not that uncommon in false religions and in various cults around the world.

Therefore, my brothers, be eager to prophesy, and do not forbid speaking in tongues. But everything should be done in a fitting and orderly way (1 Cor. 14:39-40).

Thought for the day: *Why did Paul give extra instruction regarding the gifts of tongues and prophecy?*

TEMPTATION

Matthew 4:1-11

Eventually Jesus would have to confront the rebel prince of this world, but it was not a contest the devil was looking forward to. The Holy Spirit, who led Jesus into the wilderness to be tempted by the devil, initiated the confrontation. The Lord even made himself vulnerable by fasting for forty days, which left Him on the verge of starvation. Taking advantage of His vulnerability, the devil said, "If you are the Son of God, tell these stones to become bread" (Matt. 4:3). The devil wanted Jesus to use His own divine attributes independently of God the Father to save Himself. That was essentially the advice that Peter later gave Jesus which prompted the stern rebuke, "Get behind me, Satan!" (Matt. 16:23). The role of the tempter is to get us to live our lives independently of God. Jesus responded by declaring His dependence upon God the Father.

Then the devil took Jesus to Jerusalem and stood him on the highest point of the temple. "Throw yourself off," he said, "because if You are the Son of God the angels will protect You" (see Matt. 4:6). The devil was tempting God by quoting Scripture, but Jesus would have no part of it (see v. 7). Finally, the devil took Jesus to a high mountain to show Him the kingdoms of the world. He offered these kingdoms to Jesus if the Lord would only worship him (see vv. 8-9). But Jesus would only worship the Lord our God and serve Him only (see v. 10). Jesus was tempted in the same way the first Adam and Eve had been. They failed the test and plunged the whole world into sin. Jesus passed the test and proved to be the Savior of the world and an example for us to follow. "For we do not have a high priest who is unable to sympathize with our weaknesses, but we have one who has been tempted in every way, just as we are—yet was without sin" (Heb. 4:15).

John describes the three channels of temptation that we will have to overcome. "For everything in the world—the cravings of sinful man, the lust of his eyes and the boasting of what he has and does—come not from the Father but from the world" (1 John 2:16). In Christ we have the resources and the power to conquer every temptation that Satan throws at us. The basis for temptation is legitimate needs that we all have. When we don't perceive that our basic needs are being met, we are much more vulnerable to temptation. God promises to meet all our needs according to his glorious riches in Christ Jesus (see Phil. 4:19). Remember, our life, identity, accept-ance, security and significance are all found in Christ.

> No temptation has seized you except what is common to man. And God is faithful; he will not let you be tempted beyond what you can bear. But when you are tempted, he will also provide a way out so that you can stand up under it (1 Cor. 10:13).

Thought for the day: *How does God provide a way of escape and how do we choose it?*

LUST OF THE FLESH

Deuteronomy 8:3

Satan first appealed to the lust of the flesh in Eve. The serpent planted a doubt in her mind when he asked, "Did God really say, 'You must not eat from any tree in the garden'?" (Gen. 3:1) Notice that the devil said "any tree" when God said only "the tree of the knowledge of good and evil" (Gen. 2:17). Satan distorts and questions the Word of God when he attacks the mind. Such tempting thoughts need to be taken captive and made obedient to Christ.

The key to winning the battle for the mind is to recognize tempting thoughts for what they are and never entertain them. Practice threshold thinking by not letting your mind go where it shouldn't. It is no sin to be tempted, but entertaining those thoughts will lead to sin. If you consider them in your mind, your emotions will be stimulated in the wrong direction, and they drive the will. Neither should you get into any discussion with Satan, but Eve did when she answered, "God did say, 'You must not eat fruit from the tree that is in the middle of the garden, and you must not touch it, or you will die' " (Gen. 3:3). Notice that she added the restriction "do not touch."

Satan had piqued her appetite for the forbidden fruit, and she saw "that the fruit of the tree was good for food" (Gen.3:6). Yielding to the lust of the flesh led to her downfall. It was through this channel of temptation that the devil wanted Jesus to turn a rock into bread, prompting Jesus to quote Deuteronomy 8:3: "Man does not live on bread alone." There would be nothing wrong with eating bread at the end of His fast, *except it wasn't the Father's will for Him to do so.* No matter how desirable the idea may have seemed to Jesus in His state of hunger, He was not about to act independently of the Father's will.

Eating is necessary and right, but eating too much, eating the wrong kinds of foods or allowing food to rule our lives is wrong. Food sustains life; but it does not guarantee life, which is God's gift to those who trust in and live by His Word. When we fast, we suppress the most powerful appetite we have, because food is necessary to sustain life. Sex as intended by God is beautiful and good, but sex outside of marriage, homosexual behavior and selfish sex are out-of-bounds and enslaving. If we give in to the temptation to meet our own fleshly desires independently of God, we are yielding to the lust of the flesh.

We all have residual flesh patterns that become our points of vulnerability, and Satan seems to know just what buttons to push. What could be very tempting to one person may not be at all to another. It is important that we recognize our weaknesses and not subject ourselves to unnecessary temptation. We should also restrict our freedom for the sake of the weaker Christian.

> When one is tempted, no one should say, "God is tempting me." For God cannot be tempted by evil, nor does he tempt anyone; but each one is tempted when, by his own evil desire he is dragged away and enticed (Jas. 1:13-14).

Thought for the day: *What is the difference between the Lord's testing and the devil's tempting?*

LUST OF THE EYES

Deuteronomy 6:4-19

The second channel of temptation through which Satan came to Adam and Eve related to his lie concerning the consequences of disobeying God. God said that death would accompany disobedience, but Satan said, "You will not surely die" (Gen. 3:4). He was appealing to Eve's sense of self-preservation by falsely assuring her that God was wrong about the issue of sin's consequences. "Don't listen to God, do what is right in your own eyes," he hissed. But Eve saw that the food was "pleasing to the eye" (Gen. 3:6), so she and Adam ignored God's command in order to do what appeared to serve their own best interests.

The lust of the eyes subtly draws us away from the Word of God and eats away at our confidence in God. We see what the world has to offer and desire it above our relationship with God. We begin to place more credence in our perspective of life than in God's plans and promises. Fueled by the lust for what we see, we grab for all we can get, believing that we need it, trying to justify the idea that God wants us to have it. Wrongly assuming that God will withhold nothing from us, we lustfully pursue material prosperity.

Instead of trusting God, we adopt a "prove it to me" attitude. That was the essence of Satan's second temptation of Jesus. "Prove that Scripture is right by throwing Yourself off the temple" (see Matt. 4:6). But Jesus wasn't about to play Satan's "show me" game. His response to this temptation was taken from a text that followed a passage every Hebrew child would know (see Deut. 6:4-9). The *Shema* (see Deut. 6:4-9; *Shema* is Hebrew for hear) is still recited daily by orthodox Jews. We are to walk in God's ways and not test the Lord our God (see v. 16). God is under no obligation to us; He is under obligation only to Himself. There is no way that we can cleverly word a prayer so that God must respond to our will. That only distorts the meaning of prayer and puts us in the position of trying to manipulate God. The righteous live by faith in the written Word of God and do not demand that God prove Himself in response to our whims or wishes, no matter how noble we think our cause may be.

Counterfeit gifts of knowledge and prophecy spoken through false prophets and deceived Christians can destroy our confidence in God. If they give us a "word from the Lord" and it doesn't prove to be true, then we conclude that God can no longer be trusted. The same thing happens if we pay attention to a deceiving spirit and think it is God. Paul says we will fall away from the faith if we pay attention to deceiving spirits and things taught by demons (see 1 Tim. 4:1). Such satanic temptations keep chipping away at the Word of God, eventually destroying our confidence in God if we believe the lies.

> My prayer is not that you take them out of the world but that you protect them from the evil one. Sanctify them by the truth; you word is truth (John 17:15,17).

Thought for the day: *How can we protect ourselves from the evil one?*

PRIDE OF LIFE

Proverbs 16:16-24

The third channel of temptation is to direct our own destiny, to rule our own world, to be our own god. Satan seduced Eve with the forbidden fruit: "For God knows that when you eat of it your eyes will be opened, and you will be like God, knowing good and evil" (Gen. 3:5). Satan's offer was an exaggerated appeal to our God-instilled propensity to rule. Satan was saying in effect, "Don't be satisfied living under God, when you have the potential to be like God." Because Eve saw that the tree was "desirable for gaining wisdom, she took some and ate it" (Gen. 3:6). Satan's promise that the couple would become like God was a lie. When Adam and Eve yielded to his temptation, they lost their lives and their position with God. Satan usurped their role and became the prince of this world.

Satan tried the same ploy with Jesus when he offered Him the kingdoms of this world if He would only worship him. Jesus didn't challenge Satan's rule over the kingdoms of the world and their glory. Since Satan is the prince of this world, they were his to offer, Adam and Eve having forfeited them to him. But Jesus was not about to settle for anything less than the defeat of Satan. So He commanded Satan to leave, declaring that He would worship and serve God only (see Matt. 4:10).

By appealing to the pride of life, Satan intends to steer you away from the worship of God and thereby destroy your obedience to Him. Whenever you think you don't need God's help or direction, that you can handle your life without consulting Him, that you don't have to bow your knee to anyone, beware: That is the pride of life. You may think you are serving yourself; but whenever you stop worshiping and serving God, you are in reality worshiping and serving Satan—and that is what he wants more than anything else.

Remember that there are three critical issues reflected in the channels of temptation. First, the lust of the flesh will draw us away from the will of God, and destroy our dependence upon Him. Second, the lust of the eyes will draw us away from the Word of God and destroy our confidence in Him. Third, the boastful pride of life will draw us away from our worship of God and destroy our humble obedience to Him. Every temptation that Satan throws at us will challenge one or all of these commitments to God.

The temptation to have power and influence apart from God has destroyed many ministries. We have to build God's kingdom, not ours. We have to glorify the Lord and not seek glory for ourselves. We have to find our worth in our relationship with God and not in human accomplishments. When we do, the King of kings and the Lord of lords will bless us.

Pride goes before destruction, a haughty spirit before a fall (Prov. 16:18).

Thought for the day: *Why do some people exhibit such pride?*

TOO MUCH OF A GOOD THING

Proverbs 25:16

Most committed Christians will not be tempted to do perverse and grossly immoral deeds. Satan is too clever and subtle for that. He knows that we will recognize the flagrant wrong in such temptations and refuse to act on them. His tactic is to push something good beyond the will of God until it becomes sin. He treats us like the proverbial frog in the pot of water: gradually turning up the heat of temptation, hoping we don't notice that we are approaching the boundary of God's will and jump out before it becomes sin.

"If you find honey, eat just enough—too much of it, and you will vomit" (Prov. 25:16). This Old Testament proverb suggests that we should do all things in moderation. Paul writes, "'Everything is permissible for me'—but not everything is beneficial. 'Everything is permissible for me'—but I will not be mastered by anything" (1 Cor. 6:12). He sees nothing but green lights in every direction of the Christian life. Everything is good and lawful for us because we are free from sin and no longer under the condemnation of the law. But Paul also knows that if we irresponsibly floorboard our lives in any of these good and lawful directions, we will eventually run the red lights of God's will, and that is sin.

The following statements reveal the sinful results in a number of areas when we are tempted to take the good things that God has created beyond the boundary of God's will.

> Physical rest becomes laziness.
> Quietness becomes noncommunication.
> Ability to profit becomes avarice or greed.
> Enjoyment of life becomes intemperance.
> Physical pleasure becomes sensuality.
> Interest in the possessions of others becomes covetousness.
> Enjoyment of food becomes gluttony.
> Self-care becomes selfishness.
> Self-respect becomes conceit.

Communication becomes gossip.
Cautiousness becomes insensitivity.
Anger becomes a bad temper and rage.
Lovingkindness becomes overprotection.
Judgment becomes criticism.
Same-sex friendships become homosexuality.
Sexual freedom becomes immorality.
Conscientiousness becomes perfectionism.
Generosity becomes wastefulness.
Self-protection becomes dishonesty.
Carefulness becomes fear.

Keep falsehood and lies far from me; give me neither poverty nor riches, but give me only my daily bread (Prov. 30:8).

Thought for the day: *Is Proverbs 30:8 your prayer?*

ACCUSATION

Zechariah 3:1-10

The Lord revealed to Zechariah a heavenly scene in which Satan's accusations of God's people are put in perspective (see Zech. 3:1-10). The cast of characters resembles a heavenly courtroom. The judge is God the Father. The prosecuting attorney is Satan. The accused is Joshua, the high priest who represents all of God's people. Under the Law, the high priest would enter the Holy of Holies once a year on the great Day of Atonement. It was an awesome experience to go before a manifestation of a Holy God. They would go through elaborate purification rites so that they could enter God's presence ceremonially undefiled. It became their practice to tie bells around the hem of their garments and ropes around their legs. The other priests would stay outside the veil and listen for the bells, if they heard no movement they would use the rope to pull the priest out, since no one else dared to enter.

Now Joshua was standing before God in filthy clothes. Not a good thing! But "The LORD said to Satan, 'The LORD rebuke you, Satan! The LORD, who has chosen Jerusalem, rebuke you! Is not this man a burning stick snatched from the fire?'" (Zech. 3:2). It was the devil who got rebuked, not God's people. "For the accuser of our brothers, who accuses them before our God day and night, has been hurled down" (Rev. 12:10). What the devil didn't count on was Jesus being our defense attorney. Because of His work on the Cross, there is no way we are going to lose this court case. Every born-again child of God has been snatched from the fires of hell.

Satan is not the judge. He cannot decide a verdict or pronounce a sentence; he can only bring accusations. While Satan is bringing charges against us in heaven, his emissaries also accuse us personally by bombarding our minds with false thoughts about our unworthiness and unrighteousness: *How could you do that and be a Christian? You're not really a child of God. God doesn't love you and He isn't going to save you.* If that doesn't work, his evil spirits will pepper us with blasphemous or foul thoughts that we think are our own thoughts, causing us to question our salvation.

The reason Satan's accusations are groundless is because God has solved the problem of our filthy garments. He has removed them and clothed us in Christ's righteousness. To those who have received His pardon, He says, "If you will walk in my ways and keep my requirements, then you will govern my house and have charge of my courts, and I will give you a place among these standing here" (Zech. 3:6-7). The pardoning is unconditional, but our ability to govern with Him in His house is conditional upon our willingness to trust and obey.

> When they hurled their insults at him, he did not retaliate; when he suffered, he made no threats. Instead, he entrusted himself to him who judges justly (1 Pet. 2:23).

Thought for the day: *How should we respond when judged and accused by others?*

JESUS OUR ADVOCATE

Hebrews 7:23-28

The book of Hebrews was written to present Jesus as greater than the angels and all other mortals. The writer wanted to get the Church out from under the Old Covenant of law and under the New Covenant of grace. Under the Law, the priests would continue offering sacrifices for those who committed sins. The old way of sacrificing animals for sins was replaced by a one-time sacrifice made by Jesus (see Heb. 7:23-24). We cannot sin and then offer another sacrifice. There is no other provision, and none is necessary.

The priests appointed under the law were weak and died. Being imperfect, they had to make sacrifices for themselves before they could offer them for others. But Jesus is eternal and perfect (see Heb. 7:28). His priesthood is permanent, and He sacrificed Himself one time for all the sins of everyone. "For God so loved the world that he gave his one and only Son, that whoever believes in him shall not perish but have eternal life" (John 3:16). That means that our sins are forgiven past, present and future. Don't buy the lie that only our past sins are forgiven and that future sins will be forgiven only if we confess them. When Jesus died for our sins, all our sins were future at that time. That is not a license to continue sinning but it is our defense against Satan's accusations.

Our Lord's work isn't done. He always lives to intercede on our behalf. When the devil accuses us day and night before God, we must remember that Jesus is seated at His right hand. He is saying, "Look at My feet where they drove the nails. Look at My side where they thrust the spear. My grace is sufficient and My sacrifice completely covers their sin."

It is interesting that the resurrected Christ continued to bear the marks of His crucifixion. When the disciples reported that they had seen the resurrected Jesus, Thomas said, "Unless I see the nail marks in his hands and put my finger where the nails were, and put my hand into his side, I will not believe it" (John 20:25). A week later, the Lord suddenly appeared in the midst of his disciples and told them to fear not. "Then he said to Thomas, 'Put your finger here; see my hands. Reach out your hand and put it into my side. Stop doubting and believe.' Thomas said to him, 'My Lord and my God!'" (John 20:27-28). The doubting Thomas believed because he had seen and felt the wounds of Jesus, prompting Jesus to say to him, "Because you have seen me, you have believed; blessed are those who have not seen and yet have believed" (John 20:29).

What a blessing to know that Jesus has died for our sins and continues to live as our defense attorney! By faith we put up the shield of faith and stand against Satan's fiery darts. His accusations fall on deaf ears when we know the truth and choose to believe God. Since we are no longer under the law, he has no basis for his accusations.

Who will bring any charge against those whom God has chosen? (Rom. 8:33).

Thought for the day: *What is our defense?*

THE NARROW WAY

Matthew 7:13-23

Jesus warns that "small is the gate and narrow is the road" to eternal life, and "only a few find it" (see Matt. 7:13-14). The path of life is like a small mountain road that has a steep cliff on one side and a roaring forest fire on the other. The path leads to a church, but along the path there is a lion seeking someone to devour. The devil will tempt us to jump off the steep cliff, which appeals to our many appetites. Imagine the exhilaration of sailing off that cliff. That is the path of license, which looks good, but it results in death. What the tempter offers looks good, or we wouldn't be tempted.

Another option is the roaring forest fire of legalism and its flames of condemnation. "Such regulations indeed have an appearance of wisdom, with their self-imposed worship, their false humility and their harsh treatment of the body, but they lack any value in retraining sensual indulgences" (Col. 2:23). Remember that the law kills, but the Spirit gives life. All the sanctuary we need is right ahead of us; and the Holy Spirit will lead us there, but it is not a building—it is our position in Christ. The tempter will speak to our minds: "Go ahead and do it, you know you want to, everybody is doing it, and you will get away with it." If we give in to the tempter, he immediately changes roles and becomes the accuser: "How can you call yourself a Christian and do that? You will never get away with it."

The struggle in our minds is like walking through a narrow door and seeing Jesus ahead of us. Lining the narrow street are buildings with people popping their heads out of doors and windows tempting and accusing us: "You don't believe this religious garbage do you? Come on in with the rest of us and have a good time." The most defeated Christians pay attention to them. They believe the lies and readily give in to the temptations. They are sitting in the street, and their progress toward Christ is stopped and His voice is drowned out by the deceivers. The second-most defeated Christians think they are fighting the good fight by dialoguing with the voices: "No, you're not going to entice me. That's not true. You can't accuse me." The problem is they are letting the devil set the agenda. They are standing in the street, but they aren't making any progress toward Christ.

Victorious Christians fix their eyes on Jesus and keep walking by faith in the power of the Holy Spirit. They don't pay attention to deceiving spirits and they will not be distracted by them. At first the battle for the mind is intense; but as they continue walking by faith the narrow path gets broader and broader, and the mental assault gets less and less intense as they draw closer to Christ.

> Enter through the narrow gate. For wide is the gate and broad is the road that leads to destruction, and many enter through it. But small is the gate and narrow the road that leads to life, and only a few find it (Matt. 7:13-14).

Thought for the day: *Why do people choose the broader path, and why are believers tempted to do so?*

THE UNPARDONABLE SIN

Mark 3:22-30

Teachers of the Law came from Jerusalem to accuse Jesus of being possessed by Beelzebub, whose name means "lord of the flies." That is an apt description of the devil and his demons who are like flies with great big mouths. They thought Jesus was driving out demons through the power of this prince of demons who dwelt within Him. Jesus answered this absurd charge by saying, "How can Satan drive out Satan?" (Mark 3:23). How can Satan act against himself? Any house or kingdom that is divided against itself cannot stand; therefore, "if Satan opposes himself and is divided, he cannot stand; his end has come" (v. 26). Obviously his kingdom of darkness continues to function.

Another argument given by Jesus relates to the strong man's house. Satan is the strong man; and his house is the realm of sin, sickness and death. His possessions are the people he holds captive to do his will. No one can enter his realm and plunder his possessions unless they first bind the strong man—in other words, prove themselves to be stronger. But Jesus can bind the strong man, rob the realm and release the captives. Jesus demonstrated His superiority over Satan when He was tempted and by His ability to cast our demons.

Many believers struggle with the false belief that they have committed the unpardonable sin by blaspheming the Holy Spirit. Those who are tormented by this fear usually suffer in silence. Jesus said, "All the sins and blasphemies of men will be forgiven them. But whoever blasphemes against the Holy Spirit will never be forgiven; he is guilty of an eternal sin" (Mark 3:28-29). Matthew adds to this statement: "Anyone who speaks a word against the Son of Man will be forgiven, but anyone who speaks against the Holy Spirit will not be forgiven, either in this age or the age to come" (12:32).

Why can we blaspheme one member of the Trinity and not another? It has to do with the unique works of Christ and the Holy Spirit. The work of the Holy Spirit is to draw all people to Christ. If you reject that witness, then you will never come to Christ and experience salvation. The work of Christ is to forgive all who come to Him by faith. Those who do come to Christ are children of God, and their sins and blasphemies are forgiven because they are in Christ. If you reject the witness of God's Spirit, then you never come to Christ in the first place.

That is why Christians cannot commit the unpardonable sin—because they are already pardoned. The Jewish leaders were in danger of committing the unpardonable sin, because they were ascribing the spiritual power of Christ to Beelzebub. Christians who question the work of the Holy Spirit in some people or ministries are not committing the unpardonable sin. They may be wisely testing the spirit, or wrongly quenching or grieving the Spirit; but neither of these is unpardonable.

So we see that they were not able to enter, because of their unbelief (Heb. 3:19).

Thought for the day: *What is the only thing that can keep us from entering?*

BETRAYAL AND RESTORATION

John 21:15-19

Many Christians struggle with a deep-seated sense of self-deprecation. They don't feel important, qualified or good for anything. They are paralyzed in their witness and productivity by thoughts and feelings of inferiority and worthlessness. Satan's lies and accusations have left them questioning their salvation and God's love.

The truth is we are important to God, we are qualified to serve Him, and we are unconditionally loved and accepted by Him. God's love and acceptance is unconditional, because His love is based on who He is and not on who we are or how well we behave.

Peter must have struggled with condemning thoughts and feelings, since he had betrayed Christ three times. How gracious of Jesus to give him the opportunity to say three times that he loved Him, once for each time he had betrayed Him (see John 21:15-17). There is a stark contrast between Peter and Judas. Peter was overcome by fear, and to save himself he denied Jesus. But Peter came under the conviction of the Holy Spirit and was restored. He became the spokesperson for the Early Church and glorified God by dying a martyr's death for the cause of Christ (see v. 19). Judas was a thief who allowed Satan to fill his heart to betray Christ, and he sold Him out for 30 pieces of silver (see Luke 22:3-5). There was no restoration for this son of perdition. He hung himself and died in shame. The conviction of the Holy Spirit leads to life without regret, but the sorrow of the world leads to death (see 2 Cor. 7:9-10).

God wants us to have the assurance of His love and eternal life, even if we have failed Him like Peter did. Consider the following declaration and verbally express it if you agree.

I believe there is no other name given under heaven by which I may be saved. I believe in my heart that Jesus died for my sins and that God raised Him from the dead in order that I may have eternal life. I confess with my mouth that Jesus is Lord. I renounce any efforts on my part to save myself. I choose to believe that I am saved by the grace of God through faith and that I am now a child of God because of His great mercy. I believe that God has transferred me out of the kingdom of darkness and into the kingdom of His beloved Son. I renounce the lies and accusations of Satan that would rob me of my full assurance of eternal life. I choose to take every thought captive and make it obedient to Christ. I put on the helmet of salvation and lift up the shield of faith against Satan's fiery darts. I submit myself to God and ask Him to fill me with His Holy Spirit. In the name of the Lord Jesus Christ, I command Satan and all his evil spirits to depart from me. I belong to God for all eternity.

If you confess with your mouth, "Jesus is Lord," and believe in your heart that God raised him from the dead, you will be saved (Rom. 10:9).

Thought for the day: *If Romans 10:9 describes you, why would you ever question your salvation again?*

DECEPTION

James 1:13-25

God will never tempt us nor accuse us. Those are Satan's roles. As crippling as they are, they are not the father of lies' most insidious weapon. Deception is the deadliest tool in his arsenal because if we are deceived we don't know it. Satan has succeeded in leading the whole world astray (see Rev. 12:9). That is why truth sets us free and why the belt of truth is the first piece of our protective armor. Jesus prayed that we would be kept from the evil one by being sanctified in the truth of God's Word (see John 17:15-17). James admonished us not to be deceived (see Jas. 1:16). There are three primary avenues through which we can be deceived: self-deception, false prophets/teachers and deceiving spirits.

Scripture identifies the following ways that we can deceive ourselves:

1. *We deceive ourselves if we listen to the word of God, but don't do it* (see Jas. 1:22-25). "All Scripture is God-breathed and is useful for teaching, rebuking, correcting and training in righteousness" (2 Tim. 3:16). We can't forget what we see in God's Word; we can't ignore His teaching, or we will be deceived.

2. *We deceive ourselves if we say we have no sin* (see 1 John 1:8). Having sin and being sin are two different issues. We are not sinless saints; we are saints who sin and we must confess and repent of any discrepancy between who we are and what we do.

3. *We deceive ourselves if we think we are something when we are not* (see Rom. 12:3; Gal. 6:3). We are children of God by the grace of God, who are living our lives before God, not people.

4. *We deceive ourselves when we think we are wise in this age* (see 1 Cor. 3:18-19). In professing ourselves to be wise we become fools (see Rom. 1:22). "The foolishness of God is wiser than man's wisdom" (1 Cor. 1:25). Wisdom is seeing life from God's perspective, not ours.

5. *We deceive ourselves when we think we are religious but do not keep a tight rein on our tongue* (see Jas. 1:26). Spirit-filled Christians exhibit self-control and only use their tongues to build up others.

6. *We deceive ourselves when we think we will not reap what we sow* (see Gal. 6:7). Everything we think and do has consequences and we will give an account.

7. *We deceive ourselves when we think the unrighteous will inherit the kingdom of God* (see 1 Cor. 6:9-10). We cannot defend a sinful lifestyle and claim to be Christians by calling sin something other than what it is.

8. *We deceive ourselves we when we associate with bad company and think it will not corrupt us* (see 1 Cor. 15:33). We will be known by the company we keep.

A truthful witness does not deceive, but a false witness pours out lies (Prov. 14:5).

Thought for the day: *How can we be sure that we are not deceiving ourselves or being deceived?*

FALSE PROPHETS AND TEACHERS

Jeremiah 23:14-32

Every true prophet of God in the Old Testament was similar to a New Testament evangelist. The prophet drew people back to God and His Word. The call to righteous living separated the genuine prophet from the false prophet. Through the prophet Jeremiah, God warns His people not to pay attention to false prophets who were speaking words of encouragement to those who despised God (see Jer. 23:16-17). God said His prophets "would have proclaimed my words to my people and would have turned them from their evil ways and from their evil deeds" (v. 22).

Those who prophesied lies in God's name were professing to have received their messages from dreams, but their messages were delusions from their own minds. "'For what has straw to do with grain?' declares the LORD" (Jer. 23:28). God had spoken through dreams, but the false prophets' dreams were like straw that had no nutritional value at all compared to the grain of God's Word.

Straw is good for bedding the livestock, but they will die if that is all you feed them. We get our spiritual nutrition from God's Word. If a prophetic message were to come to your church, it wouldn't be comforting to those church members who were living in sin. His Word is "like a hammer that breaks a rock in pieces" (Jer. 23:29). The Spirit of God is not going to lull His people into a spirit of complacency, because judgment begins in the household of God (see 1 Pet. 4:17). A prophetic message should motivate us to live righteous lives, not placate us in our sin (see 1 Cor. 14:24-25).

God is also against those prophets who steal His words from each other (see Jer. 23:30). That is plagiarism: taking what God has given someone else and using it as though it were your own. God is also against "the prophets who wag their own tongues and yet declare, 'The LORD declares'" (v. 31). Saying that our words are directly from the Lord when they aren't is an offense to God. Manipulating people by claiming a word from the Lord is spiritual abuse. For man to tell a young lady that God has told him they are supposed to get married is incredibly manipulative. If she wrongly thinks he is a man of God, then to refuse marriage is to refuse God. If God wanted them to get married, why wouldn't He tell both of them?

False prophets may also try to guide our lives by giving specific instructions for daily living and decision making. As such, they are functioning as a medium rather than as a true prophet, and there is only "one mediator between God and men, the man Jesus Christ" (1 Tim. 2:5). True prophets announce God's word in such a way that we fall down and worship God. Then the Holy Spirit will guide each of God's children, not human agents who function like mediums between God and His children. However, others may confirm your decision if it is from the Lord.

> For there is one God and one mediator between God and men, the man Christ Jesus, who gave himself as a ransom for all men—the testimony given in its proper time (1 Tim. 2:5-6).

Thought for the day: *Why is it so important to know the truth in 1 Timothy 2:5-6 when people try to guide your life?*

SIGNS AND WONDERS

Deuteronomy 13

Jesus performed many miracles in His public ministry, and "The apostles performed many miraculous signs and wonders among the people" (Acts 5:12). The occurrence of a sign or wonder reveals some kind of supernatural presence, but that presence may not always be God. Speaking of the latter days, Jesus said, "For false Christs and false prophets will appear and perform signs and miracles to deceive the elect—if that were possible. So be on your guard; I have told you everything ahead of time" (Mark 13:22-23).

False prophecy is not just a last-days problem. Since the fall of humanity, false prophets have plagued the Chosen People, causing them to go after other gods. Moses wrote that what prophets say must come to pass if they are true prophets, but he also wrote of another test. False prophets could perform signs and wonders and what they prophesy could come to pass, *but their message is to follow other gods*. In such cases the Lord is testing us to find out whether we love Him with all our hearts and all our souls (see Deut. 13:1-3). Such false prophets were to be stoned to death, and it was to be members of their family who carried out the death sentence (see vv. 5-10).

False prophets could pollute an entire city. In such a case the whole city was to be annihilated (see Deut. 13:12-15). Obviously the world has not followed this law, or huge numbers of people and people groups would have been wiped out. And the Church has no mandate to stone false prophets, but these Old Testament passages reveal how serious we must take the warning that there will be false prophets who will "prove themselves" by great signs and wonders. There is no question that Satan and his demons can perform signs and wonders, and there is no question that the occult works. Whether or not the supernatural acts lead people toward or away from the one true God is the real question. Quack doctors, shamans, psychics and New Age practitioners can come under the spell of evil spirits and channel information about people and events that appear to be accurate. Undiscerning people are easily impressed by their spiritual insights and might assume they are getting good spiritual direction. When the undiscerning receive guidance through the occult, they usually don't know they are following other gods.

The level of deception will intensify before the Lord returns. In Paul's second letter to the Thessalonians, he warns them not to be deceived by anyone into thinking that the day of the Lord had already come. The Lord won't return until there has been a falling away from the faith and the man of lawlessness is revealed (see 2 Thess. 2:3). The man of lawlessness is probably the Antichrist of Revelation 13, and he will proclaim himself to be God (see 2 Thess. 2:4). "The coming of the lawless one will be in accordance with the work of Satan displayed in all kinds of counterfeit miracles, signs and wonders, and in every sort of evil that deceives those who are perishing. They perish because they refused to love the truth and so be saved" (2 Thess. 2:9-10).

You shall have no other gods before me (Exod. 20:3).

Thought for the day: *Why is Exodus 20:3 the first of the Ten Commandments?*

COUNTERFEITS WITHIN THE CHURCH

2 Peter 2:1-10

Federal agents who are assigned to catch counterfeiters spend of the bulk of their training studying real currency, not counterfeit currency. The more familiar they are with the real thing, the easier it is to spot the counterfeit. In the same way our focus is to know the Lord and understand His ways. That is the primary way our churches can detect false prophets and teachers and become cult-proof. Being a discerning Christian who knows the truth is critical since false prophets and teachers will arise from among us: "They will secretly introduce destructive heresies, even denying the sovereign Lord who bought them" (2 Pet. 2:1). These servants of Satan will be disguised as ministers of righteousness and profess to be Christians (see 2 Cor. 11:15).

The Holy Spirit will work to unite the Church, but false prophets and teachers will be divisive. The Holy Spirit will lead us into all truth, but the truth is not in these people. Asking them to sign a doctrinal statement won't smoke them out, because they have no problem lying. Many believers will follow their shameful ways and the truth will be maligned. Their followers will be captivated by their looks, personality, charm and charisma, but these are not the biblical criteria by which we validate a ministry or minister. The biblical standards are truth and righteousness, both of which are maligned by false teachers.

Peter identifies two primary ways that we can identify false prophets and teachers who operate within the Church. First, they will eventually reveal their immorality by following the corrupt desire of their sinful nature (see 2 Pet. 2:10). It is not likely that their immorality will be easy to spot at first, but it will eventually surface in their lives. They are con artists who work under the cover of darkness, not wanting to have their deeds exposed. Second, they despise authority (see v. 10). They have an independent spirit. They won't answer to anyone, and they are very critical of those who are over them. They set up smoke screens to keep attention away from themselves, and they put everyone else on the defensive.

Once they have sown their seeds of destruction in the Church, they are very difficult to remove. If we try to remove the sons of the evil one, we may root up the children of God with them (see Matt. 13:29). That is why we must be so careful about whom we ordain into ministry or ask to serve as elders and deacons. Paul gives the requirements for Christian leadership in 1 Timothy 3:1-13 and Titus 1:5-9, and they are all related to godly character. Although nobody is perfect, these are the standards to which we are to aspire. People should be disqualified if they appeal to a different standard or fail to exhibit the fruit of the Spirit. Being popular, smart, wealthy, influential, politically savvy, talented and clever are qualities the world may esteem, but they are not included in the requirements to be a spiritual leader. We need to remember to look for godliness above all else in those we are considering promoting to leadership roles.

> He must also have a good reputation with outsiders, so that he will not fall into disgrace and into the devil's trap (1 Tim. 3:7).

Thought for the day: *How would having a bad reputation with outsiders make an elder more vulnerable to Satan?*

TESTING THE SPIRITS

1 John 4:1-6

Jesus said, "By their fruit you will recognize them" (Matt. 7:16). To bear
fruit, we have to abide in Christ and walk by the Spirit. John said, "This is
how we know who the children of God are and who the children of the devil
are: Anyone who does not do what is right is not a child of God; nor is anyone who does not love his brother" (1 John 3:10). Living a righteous life,
bearing fruit and loving our neighbor as ourselves are the marks of a true
believer. The command to believe in the name of God's Son, Jesus Christ,
(see 3:23) is followed by a prohibition: "do not believe every spirit" (4:1).
John tells his readers to "test the spirits to see whether they are from God"
(4:1). He is urging us to test the spirit that is behind every human teacher
who claims to be speaking under spiritual inspiration. It takes as much spiritual maturity to not believe every spirit as it does to believe in the one true
God. There needs to be a balance between superstition that believes everything and suspicion that believes nothing.

A prophet is a mouthpiece of some spirit. True prophets are the mouthpiece of the "Spirit of God" (1 John 1:2). False prophets are the mouthpieces
of the "spirit of falsehood" (v. 6) or "the spirit of the antichrist" (v. 3). Behind
every prophet is a spirit either from God or from the devil. Before we can
trust any spirits, we must test them to see whether or not they are from God.
In testing spirits, we are trying to determine their origin. Paul wrote,
"Therefore I tell you that no one who is speaking by the Spirit of God says,
'Jesus be cursed,' and no one can say, 'Jesus is Lord,' except by the Holy
Spirit" (1 Cor. 12:3). "Every spirit that acknowledges that Jesus Christ has
come in the flesh is from God" (1 John 4:2).

John may have written primarily to correct the teachings of the
Gnostics, but what He says has broader application. The confession that
Jesus came in the flesh goes beyond recognizing Jesus as the Messiah; it is a
public profession of faith in Christ as Lord and Savior, spoken openly and
boldly. Evil spirits recognized Jesus during His public ministry, but they
did not confess Him as Lord. Demons will say that Jesus is Lord, but
they will not say Jesus is their Lord. "Every spirit that does not acknowledge
Jesus is not from God" (1 John 4:3).

True believers are from God and they overcome the false prophets, because the Spirit within them is greater than the spirit that is in the world. Those who are in the world listen to these false prophets, but those who know God listen to those who are from God: "This is how we recognize the Spirit of truth and the spirit of falsehood" (1 John 4:6).

Do not put out the Spirit's fire; do not treat prophecies with contempt. Test everything. Hold on to the good. Avoid every kind of evil (1 Thess. 5:19-22).

Thought for the day: *How can you be sure of the source of the prophecy?*

DEGREES OF SPIRITUAL VULNERABILITY

Acts 5:1-11

The story of Ananias and Sapphira is the first recorded sin in the Early Church. Barnabas had given the Church all the proceeds from what he had sold (see Acts 4:37), but Ananias and Sapphira kept back some of their profits and allowed others to think they had given it all (see Acts 5:1-3). Keeping some of the money was no sin, but lying about it was; and so the Lord struck them both dead (see vv. 5,10). The penalty for lying seems mercilessly severe, yet it was extremely important that the Early Church be sent a clear message. God knew that if Satan could get us to believe his lies, he would have some measure of control over our lives.

Satan had filled Ananias's heart to lie to the Holy Spirit and in so doing he was testing "the Spirit of the Lord" (Acts 5:9). He quickly discovered that whatever we yield ourselves to, to that we shall be filled (controlled). If we choose to believe a lie regardless of the source, it will have a negative effect on the way we think, feel and live. Even though the devil has been defeated, the book of Acts clearly reveals that believers still have to contend with the kingdom of darkness. Satan continues to tempt, accuse and deceive believers who don't know how to stand firm in their faith and win the battle for their minds. Satan lost the ultimate battle at the Cross, but he didn't pull in his fangs or curl up his tail. His goal now is to blind the mind of the unbelieving and to destroy the testimony of believers. He doesn't want the world to believe that Jesus is the answer and that divinely revealed truth will set us free.

To what degree then are we vulnerable to Satan's attacks? First, we must recognize that the possibility of being tempted, accused and deceived is a continuous reality (see Gal. 6:1). Second, the fact that we can be influenced by the devil is highly probable. That is why Peter advises us to "Be self-controlled and alert. Your enemy the devil prowls around like a roaring lion looking for someone to devour. Resist him, standing firm in the faith, because you know that your brothers throughout the world are undergoing the same kind of sufferings" (1 Pet. 5:8-9). Third, it is possible that we could surrender some degree of control over our lives if we were to yield to his temptations, or believe his accusations and lies. Remember, Satan can't do anything about our position in Christ; but if he can get us to believe it isn't true, we will live as though it isn't. We can gain a measure of control over another person if we can get that person to believe every word we say. Finally, we can never be owned by anyone other than the Lord Jesus Christ. We have been bought and purchased by the blood of the Lamb (see 1 Pet. 1:18-19), and Satan cannot touch who we are in Christ.

If a ruler listens to lies, all his officials become wicked (Prov. 29:12).

Thought for the day: *Who is the father of lies and what is his nature?*

DEMON POSSESSION

Mark 5:1-20

The story of the Gadarene demoniac (see Mark 5:1-20) is the worst case of demon possession recorded in the New Testament. No person was able to physically control him; but spiritually, he was no match for Jesus who demonstrated his authority over demons. The term "demon possessed" is the English translation for the single word *daimonizomai* (verb) or *daimonizomenos* (participle)—which is best transliterated as "demonized." To be demonized means to be under the control of one or more demons. The term never occurs in the Epistles, so we have no way of knowing how it would apply to believers in the Church Age. Possession implies ownership, and we do know that Satan and his demons cannot have or own a Christian who belongs to God. In that regard, as Christians we are Holy Spirit-possessed, but that does not mean that we are not vulnerable. If we open the door to his influence, Satan will invade and claim squatter's rights. He will resist eviction until the ground beneath him is removed through repentance and faith in God.

Another Greek phrase in the Gospels is *echein daimonion*, which means to "have a demon." The religious leaders used this phrase when they accused both John the Baptist and Jesus of be being demonized (see Luke 7:33; John 7:20). The Pharisees made these accusations because they knew that John's and Jesus' supernatural knowledge had to be communicated to them through some spiritual means. It was common in those days to have esoteric knowledge communicated by demons through human agents (mediums and spiritists). Unwilling to recognize Jesus as the Messiah, they wrongly assumed the source of his information was from demons instead of God.

The theological argument that the Holy Spirit and an evil spirit cannot coexist is often used to argue that we as Christians cannot be invaded by a demon. But that does not stand up for several reasons. First, Satan is the prince of this world and the "ruler of the kingdom of the air" (Eph. 2:2). Thus Satan and his demons are present in the atmosphere of this world, and so is the omnipresent Holy Spirit—which means they do coexist. Second, Satan still has access to our Father in heaven (see Rev. 12:10). Third, the Holy Spirit is in union—a coexistence—with our human spirit, and surely we don't consider our human spirit perfect. Fourth, spatial arguments don't apply to the spiritual realm. There are no natural barriers or physical boundaries for spirits. That is why we shouldn't think of a church building as a sanctuary. Our sanctuary is "in Christ," not some physical, man-made structure. Fifth, if we are paying attention to a deceiving spirit, the spirit's presence cannot be external only. The battle is in the mind. If an evil spirit and the Holy Spirit cannot operate at the same time and in the same sphere, then there is no need for us to be alert and put on the armor of God. The purpose of armor is to stop penetration.

Put on the full armor of God (Eph. 6:11).

Thought for the day: *Why would we have to put on the armor of God unless we were somewhat vulnerable?*

SPIRITUAL BONDAGE

Luke 13:10-17

It is critical that Christians understand their vulnerability to demonic influences, so they may have an adequate biblical answer should they fall victim to the fowler's snare (see Ps. 91:3; 1 Tim. 3:7; 2 Tim. 2:26). We don't want Satan to outwit us, because we are ignorant of his schemes (see 2 Cor. 2:11). Those who don't understand their spiritual vulnerability will likely blame their old nature or God for their spiritual bondage. Attributing Satan's activities to the flesh, which is a common error in the Western church, leads only to self-condemnation and defeat. On the other hand, blaming the devil for our own carnal nature is a lame excuse and just as defeating. We have to crucify the flesh and grow out of old flesh patterns, and we must resist the devil and he will flee from us. We don't grow out of spiritual attacks, and we don't exercise our spiritual authority by telling the flesh to leave. To have the right answer requires us to know the nature of our problem. If we blame God, our confidence in Him is shattered, and we won't submit to Him and resist the devil (see Jas. 4:7).

In this passage from the Gospel of Luke (see Luke 13:10-17), Satan kept a "daughter of Abraham" (v. 16) in bondage for 18 years. She was a believer under the Old Covenant who was worshiping God in a synagogue. She was a God-fearing woman under spiritual bondage. As soon as Jesus released her from spiritual bondage, her physical problem was cured. This passage clearly indicates that Satan can affect a person physically. In the Gospel of Mark, for instance, over 25 percent of those who were delivered from demons by Jesus experienced a physical healing. Obviously not all our physical problems are caused by demons, but Scripture allows for the fact that some could be.

James teaches that the result of yielding to jealousy and selfish ambition will result in a "wisdom" that is earthly, natural and demonic (see 3:14-16). Paul warns that "some will abandon the faith and follow deceiving spirits and things taught by demons" (1 Tim. 4:1). In Ephesians 4:26-27, Paul writes, "'In your anger do not sin': Do not let the sun go down while you are still angry, and do not give the devil a foothold." The word "foothold" literally means "place." He is saying that we may allow the devil a place in our lives if we fail to speak the truth in love and be emotionally honest. Anger, which leads to bitterness and unforgiveness, is an open invitation to demonic influence (see 2 Cor. 2:10-11). Peter warned, "Your enemy the devil prowls around like a roaring lion looking for someone to devour" (1 Pet. 5:8). The word "devour" means "to consume or to swallow up." It is the same word used in 1 Corinthians 15:54: "Death has been swallowed up in victory." To be swallowed up by something conveys the thought of being controlled by it. The context of Peter's warning indicates that pride and failure to cast our anxiety onto Christ may leave us vulnerable to Satan.

> You, dear children, are from God and have overcome them, because the one who is in you is greater than the one who is in the world (1 John 4:4).

Thought for the day: *How can we maintain our confidence in God and be aware of our vulnerability at the same time?*

LOSS OF CONTROL

Luke 22:31-34

On what basis could Satan have demanded the right to sift Peter as wheat (see Luke 22:31)? The context (see v. 24) indicates that pride may have been the grounds for Satan's request. After all, God had kicked Satan out of heaven because of his pride (see Isa. 14:12; Luke 10:18), so it is no wonder that he is now demanding the same right over Peter. Notice how Jesus responded to Satan's request. He told Peter that he was going to pray that his faith would not fail; and when he had turned back from his arrogance and pride, he was to strengthen other believers (see v. 32). In other words, Jesus said, "Peter, you are going to suffer the consequences of your pride, and I'm praying that you don't lose your faith. After you have endured the trial and repented of your ways, use your experience to help others." Jesus did not say He would prevent Satan from having his way with Peter.

Peter said he was ready to die or go to prison for Jesus (see Luke 22:33). In spite of his attitude, Jesus said Peter would deny Him three times and Peter did (see v. 34). Peter had lost some measure of control in his life because of pride, and Jesus prayed for his successful recovery from the incident. The devil didn't make Peter do it. Peter denied Jesus because he allowed himself to become vulnerable due to his own pride. No Christian can say, "The devil made me do it," because we are all responsible for our own attitudes and actions. Satan simply takes advantage of the opportunities we give him. We have all the resources and protection we need to live victorious lives in Christ. When we leave a door open for the devil by not resisting temptation, accusation and deception, he will enter it. We won't lose our salvation, but his presence will affect our daily victory.

The army that goes to war unprepared will suffer terrible casualties. If we as Christians fail to use our armor, Satan will not stop short of invading our citadel. He will take us captive to do his will (see 2 Tim. 2:26). The world, the flesh and the devil are continually at war against the life of the Spirit within us. If we use our bodies as instruments of unrighteousness, we will allow sin to reign in our mortal bodies (see Rom. 6:12-14). If we fail to take every thought captive to the obedience of Christ (see 2 Cor. 10:5), we will end up being deceived. If we fail to forgive from our hearts, Jesus Himself will turn us over to the tormentors (see Matt. 18:34-35).

Choosing truth, living a righteous life and donning the armor of God are each believer's individual responsibility. We have a responsibility to one another, but not for one another. If a believer chooses to go into this world without his or her armor on, that believer may get hurt. As much as that may be a matter of concern for us, we still cannot make those decisions of responsibility for others. The choice is ours, but we do have a choice.

[Jesus] said, "According to your faith will it be done to you" (Matt. 9:29).

Thought for the day: *How much of what will happen to you will be according to what you choose to believe and how well you choose to live accordingly?*

SPIRITUAL CLEANSING

1 Corinthians 5:1-13

Paul was appalled by the lack of spiritual discipline in the church at Corinth (see 1 Cor. 5:1). A man was living an incestuous relationship with his father's wife (see v. 1). He was a man so deluded by Satan and controlled by immorality that he apparently flaunted his illicit relationship before the whole church (see v. 2). Paul's judgment on the matter was severe: "Hand this man over to Satan, so that the sinful nature may be destroyed and his spirit saved on the day of the Lord" (v. 5). Paul thought it best to allow Satan to have his way with the man in hopes that he would finally say, "I've had enough" and repent. God is not above using Satan to discipline us if that is what it takes to bring about repentance. Satan is tethered by the permissive will of God and can only do that which is permitted by Him.

Expelling the man from the church was Paul's way of handing him over to Satan. In the world he was severed from the church and the power of Christ. The world is Satan's territory where the man would have to suffer the consequences of his sins without the spiritual protection of the local church. The church was not meant to be a gathering place for sexually immoral believers. In fact believers in the Early Church were to expel the wicked from their fellowship (see 1 Cor. 5:13). Otherwise, these spiritually bound people would contaminate the church with the wrong spirit, and some would undoubtedly become sexual predators, defiling others.

God is more concerned about the Church's purity than He is about the Church's growth, because church growth is dependent upon church purity. The Holy Spirit is working in our midst to present the Bride of Christ "as a radiant church, without stain or wrinkle or any other blemish, but holy and blameless" (Eph. 5:27). If the wrong spirit controls professing believers and they in turn are controlling the Church, then the wrong spirit is controlling the Church. For the local church, this means just one unruly child can disrupt a family, a Christian camp or a Sunday School. One immoral, bitter or deceived adult can disrupt a board or church meeting. That is why church discipline is so necessary. When do we stop trying to nurture a bad apple back to health, and when do we get rid of the apple before the whole barrel is defiled? One of the most difficult decisions confronting spiritual leaders is how to ensure that the local church is under the lordship of Christ. The first priority is to carry out the ministry of reconciliation. If that should fail, the next priority is to expel from our fellowships those with a wrong spirit; we need to do this so that many others aren't defiled.

A growing church survives in an atmosphere of grace and in the context of trusting relationships. That makes the church vulnerable to those who would prey upon the good natures of committed believers. Discipline is a proof of our love, which must be tough enough to ensure church purity, but tender enough to set captives free and restore them to Christian fellowship.

> Husbands, love your wives, just as Christ loved the church and gave himself up for her to make her holy, cleansing her by the washing with water through the word, and to present her to himself as a radiant church, without stain or wrinkle or any other blemish, but holy and blameless (Eph. 5:25-27).

Final thought for the day: *How can you help your church be holy and pure?*

APPENDIX

Research Results of Discipleship Counseling

The Lord has called us to believe in Him and rely on the finished work of Christ. If we desire to experience our freedom in Christ, we must repent. This entails submitting to God and resisting the devil. Freedom in Christ Ministries has been endeavoring to help believers all over the world resolve their personal and spiritual conflicts through genuine repentance and faith in God. The message and method we use is written in my book *Discipleship Counseling* (Regal Books, 2003) and the tool we use is "The Steps to Freedom in Christ" (the Steps).

There have been several exploratory studies that have shown promising results regarding the effectiveness of the "Steps to Freedom in Christ." Judith King, a Christian therapist, did several pilot studies in 1996. All three of these studies were performed on participants who attended the Living Free in Christ Conference and received the "Steps to Freedom in Christ" during the conference. (The Living Free in Christ Conference materials are now available for all churches in a course entitled: *Beta, The Next Step in Discipleship*.)

The first study involved 30 participants who took a 10-item questionnaire before completing the Steps. The questionnaire was re-administered 3 months after their participation. The questionnaire assessed for levels of depression, anxiety, inner conflict, tormenting thoughts and addictive behaviors. The second study involved 55 participants who took a 12-item questionnaire before completing the Steps and then answered the questionnaire again 3 months later. The third pilot study involved 21 participants who also took a 12-item questionnaire before receiving the Steps and then again 3 months afterward. The following table illustrates the percentage of improvement in each category.

	Depression	Anxiety	Inner Conflict	Tormenting Thoughts	Addictive Behavior
Pilot Study 1	64%	58%	63%	82%	52%
Pilot Study 2	47%	44%	51%	58%	43%
Pilot Study 3	52%	47%	48%	57%	39%

Research was also conducted by doctoral students at Regent University under the supervision of Dr. Fernando Garzon (Doctor of Psychology) on the message and method of Freedom in Christ Ministries. Most people attending a Living Free in Christ Conference or a *Beta* course can work through the repentance process on their own using the "Steps to Freedom in Christ." In our experience, about 15 percent of the population can't, because of difficulties they have experienced. At two separate conferences, for those who could not work the Steps on their own, a personal session was offered them with a trained encourager. They were given a pretest before a Step session and a posttest three months later, which revealed the following improvement:

	Oklahoma City, OK	Tyler, TX
Depression	44%	57%
Anxiety	45%	54%
Fear	48%	49%
Anger	36%	55%
Tormenting Thoughts	51%	50%
Negative Habits	48%	53%
Sense of Self-Worth	52%	56%

Dr. Fernando Garzon at Regent University also conducted research on 24 Master of Divinity, Doctor of Psychology and Doctor of Ministry students taking a weeklong intensive class at Regent University. The students were taught the message of Freedom in Christ and went through the "Steps to Freedom in Christ." Dr. Garzon used the questionnaire that had been used for the above research as well as the Rosenberg Self-Esteem Inventory, the Beck Anxiety Inventory and the Symptom Checklist 90-R. The tests were administered at the beginning of the class and then again three weeks later. The results of the study were published in the *Journal of Psychology and Theology*. In summary, Dr. Garzon wrote:

Statistically significant reductions were found in several scales of the SCL-90 (global severity index, anxiety, depression, obsessive-compulsive, interpersonal sensitivity, hostility, somatization, paranoid ideation, and psychoticism). Anxiety was reduced as measured by the Beck Inventory, and statistically significant increases in self-esteem and spirituality items were also found.

Another quasi-experimental study under the supervision of Dr. Garzon randomly selected 46 participants to attend a Living Free in Christ Conference. The conference met for two hours Wednesday, Thursday, Friday evenings and all day Saturday. It ended with individuals being led, as a group, through the "Steps to Freedom in Christ." Subjects were given an SCL-90R. Measurements were taken two weeks before the conference, at the beginning of the conference, a few days after the conference, two weeks afterward and three months afterward. A statistically significant decrease in psychological distress for the subjects as measured by the Global Severity Index scale of the SCL-90R was observed. This decrease was sustained at levels below clinical concern at the three-month follow-up. An examination of mean trends for other SCL-90R scales revealed a similar pattern.

Dr. Garzon conducted further research on clients of Judy King. In these cases, Mrs. King integrated the message and method of Freedom in Christ Ministries as a key component of treatment. Psychological testing showed the benefits of including this material. The results are reported in *Released From Bondage* (Thomas Nelson Publishers, 2002), which is coauthored by Anderson, Garzon and King. The first part of this book includes testimonies of how Christians found their freedom in Christ with explanatory notes by Dr. Anderson. The second part has an introduction by Judy King and Dr. Garzon, along with the explanation of how Judy King integrated the "Steps to Freedom in Christ" in therapy.

Although God has used the Living Free in Christ Conference to help many believers all over the world, it is better accomplished through the local church. *Beta, The Next Step In Discipleship* (Gospel Light, 2004) is a 13-week curriculum designed for that purpose; and it is being used in Sunday School classes, small groups and home Bible studies. It will accomplish the same results as reported by the research shown above. If you desire to be better equipped to help others or desire more resources, please contact:

Freedom in Christ Ministries
9051 Executive Park Drive
Suite 503
Knoxville, TN 37923
(865) 342-4000
www.ficm.org and info@ficm.org

ENDNOTES

Sound Doctrine (Progressive Sanctification, p. 59)
1. For additional help on understanding justification and sanctification read Neil Anderson and Robert Saucy, *Unleashing God's Power Within You* (Eugene, OR: Harvest House, 2004).

A New Heart and a New Spirit (A New Heart, p. 128)
1. H. Wheeler Robinson, *The Christian Doctrine of Man* (Edinburgh: T & T Clark, 1926), p. 22.

Assurance of Salvation (The Test of Salvation, p. 141)
1. For additional help on overcoming a negative self-image, read Neil Anderson and David Park, *Overcoming a Negative-Self Image* (Ventura, CA: Regal Books, 2003).

The Nature of Faith (Living by Faith, p. 172)
1. For additional help on living by faith, read Neil Anderson, *Overcoming Doubt* (Ventura, CA: Regal Books, 2002).

The Fear of God (Freedom from Fear, p. 183)
1. For additional help on overcoming anxiety disorders, read Neil Anderson and Rich Miller, *Freedom from Fear* (Eugene, OR: Harvest House, 1999).

The Ministry of Reconciliation (The Ministry of Reconciliation, p. 205)
1. For further study on the ministry of reconciliation, read Neil Anderson and Charles Mylander, *Blessed Are the Peacemakers* (Ventura, CA: Regal Books, 2002).

Living by the Spirit (Overcoming Legalism, p. 217)
1. For help on overcoming legalism, read: Neil Anderson, Rich Miller and Paul Travis, *Breaking the Bondage of Legalism* (Eugene, OR: Harvest House, 2003).

Overcoming Anger (Righteous Indignation, p. 252)
1. For more help in dealing with your anger, read: Neil Anderson and Rich Miller, *Getting Anger Under Control* (Eugene, OR: Harvest House, 2002).

Overcoming Losses (Commitment to Overcome Depression, p. 284)
1. For more help on psychosomatic illnesses and health, read Neil Anderson and Joanne Anderson, *Overcoming Depression* (Ventura, CA: Regal Books, 2004); and Neil Anderson and Michael Jacobson, *The Biblical Guide to Alternative Medicine* (Ventura, CA: Regal Books, 2003).

Overcoming Sexual Bondage (Sin Dwelling in You, p. 307)
1. For more help on overcoming sexual lust and bondage, read Neil Anderson, *Finding Freedom in a Sex-Obsessed World* (Eugene, OR: Harvest House, 2003).

Understanding Chemical Addiction (Overcoming Addiction, p. 311)
1. For more help, read Neil Anderson, *Overcoming Addiction* (Ventura, CA: Regal Books, 2003).

Spiritual Discernment (Spiritual Discernment, p. 329)
1. For more help on discernment and knowing God's will (to be discussed in Chapter 34), read Neil Anderson, *Finding God's Will in Spiritually Deceptive Times* (Eugene, OR: Harvest House, 2003).

Prayer and Praise (Praying by the Spirit, p. 353)
1. To learn more about praying and walking by the Spirit, read Neil Anderson, *Praying by the Power of the Spirit* (Eugene, OR: Harvest House, 2003).

God's Will (Do All to the Glory of God, p. 360)
1. Basil Miller, *George Muller: Man of Faith and Miracles: A Biography of One of the Greatest Prayer-Warriors of the Past Century* (Minneapolis, MN: Bethany House Publishers, 1972), p. 50.

Encouragement (Peace, p. 387)
1. John Greenleaf Whittier, "Dear Lord and Father of Mankind," 1872, quoted at *The Cyber Hymnal.* http://www.cyberhymnal.org/htm/d/e/dearlord.htm (accessed March 2005).

Discipleship Counseling (Discipleship Counseling, p. 409)
1. For more instruction on helping others, read Neil Anderson, *Discipleship Counseling* (Ventura, CA: Regal Books, 2003).

The Lure of Knowledge and Power (Esoteric Knowledge, p. 503)
1. For more instruction, read Neil Anderson, *The Steps to Freedom in Christ* (Ventura, CA: Regal Books, 2004).

BOOKS AND RESOURCES BY
DR. NEIL T. ANDERSON

CORE MESSAGE AND MATERIALS

The Bondage Breaker and study guide and audiobook (Harvest House Publishers, 2000)—with well over 1 million copies in print, this book explains spiritual warfare, what our protection is, ways that we are vulnerable and how we can live a liberated life in Christ.

Breaking Through to Spiritual Maturity (Regal Books, 2000)—this curriculum teaches the basic message of Freedom in Christ Ministries.

Discipleship Counseling and videocassettes (Regal Books, 2003)—combines the concepts of discipleship and counseling, and the practical integration of theology and psychology, for helping Christians resolve their personal and spiritual conflicts through repentance.

The Steps to Freedom in Christ and interactive videocassette (Regal Books, 2000)—this discipleship counseling tool helps Christians resolve their personal and spiritual conflicts.

Victory Over the Darkness and study guide, audiobook and videocassettes (Regal Books, 2000)—with well over 1 million copies in print, this core book explains who you are in Christ, how you walk by faith, how your mind and emotions function and how to relate to one another in Christ.

SPECIALIZED BOOKS

The Biblical Guide to Alternative Medicine with Dr. Michael Jacobson (Regal Books, 2003)—develops a grid by which you can evaluate medical practices. It applies the grid to the world's most recognized philosophies of medicine and health.

Blessed Are the Peacemakers with Dr. Charles Mylander (Regal Books, 2002)—explains the ministry of reconciliation and gives practical steps for being reconciled with others.

Breaking the Bondage of Legalism with Rich Miller and Paul Travis (Harvest House Publishers, 2003)—an exposure and explanation of legalism and how to overcome it.

The Christ-Centered Marriage with Dr. Charles Mylander (Regal Books, 1997)—explains God's divine plan for marriage and the steps that couples can take to resolve their difficulties.

Christ-Centered Therapy with Dr. Terry and Julianne Zuehlke (Zondervan Publishing House, 2000)—a textbook explaining the practical integration of theology and psychology for professional counselors.

Daily in Christ with Joanne Anderson (Harvest House Publishers, 2000)—this popular daily devotional is being used by thousands of Internet subscribers every day.

Finding Hope Again with Hal Baumchen (Regal Books, 1999)—explains depression and how to overcome it.

Freedom from Addiction with Mike and Julia Quarles (Regal Books, 1997)—using Mike's testimony, this book explains the nature of chemical addictions and how to overcome them in Christ.

Freedom from Fear with Rich Miller (Harvest House Publishers, 1999)—explains fear, anxiety and disorders, and how to overcome them.

Freedom in Christ Bible (Zondervan Publishing House, 2002)—a one-year discipleship study with notes in the Bible.

Getting Anger Under Control with Rich Miller (Harvest House Publishers, 1999)—explains the basis for anger and how to control it.

God's Power at Work in You with Dr. Robert L. Saucy (Harvest House Publishers, 2001)—a thorough analysis of sanctification and practical instruction on how we grow in Christ.

Leading Teens to Freedom in Christ with Rich Miller (Regal Books, 1997)—this discipleship counseling book focuses on teenagers, their problems and how to solve them.

One Day at a Time with Mike and Julia Quarles (Regal Books, 2000)—this devotional helps those who struggle with addictive behaviors and how to discover the grace of God on a daily basis.

Released from Bondage with Dr. Fernando Garzon and Judith E. King (Thomas Nelson, 2002)—contains personal accounts of bondage with explanatory notes showing how people found their freedom in Christ, and how the message of Freedom in Christ can be applied to therapy with research results.

The Seduction of Our Children with Steve Russo (Harvest House Publishers, 1991)—explains what teenagers are experiencing and how parents can be equipped to help them.

Setting Your Church Free with Dr. Charles Mylander (Regal Books, 1994)—this book on Christian leadership also explains corporate bondage and how it can be resolved in Christ.

The Spiritual Protection of Our Children with Peter and Sue Vander Hook (Regal Books, 1996)—using the Vander Hook's experience, this book explains how parents can help their children.

A Way of Escape with Russ Rummer (Harvest House Publishers, 1998)—explains sexual strongholds and how they can be torn down in Christ.

Who I Am in Christ (Regal Books, 2001)—describes in 36 short chapters who you are in Christ and how He meets your deepest needs.

VICTORY OVER THE DARKNESS SERIES

Overcoming Negative Self-Image with Dave Park (Regal Books, 2003)
Overcoming Addictive Behavior with Mike Quarles (Regal Books, 2003)
Overcoming Depression with Joanne Anderson (Regal Books, 2004)
Overcoming Doubt (Regal Books, 2004)

THE BONDAGE BREAKER SERIES

Finding Freedom in a Sex-Obsessed World (Harvest House Publishers, 2004)

Finding God's Will in Spiritually Deceptive Times (Harvest House Publishers, 2003)

Praying by the Power of the Spirit (Harvest House Publishers, 2003)

YOUTH BOOKS

Awesome God with Rich Miller (Harvest House Publishers, 1996)

The Bondage Breaker—Youth Edition with Dave Park (Harvest House Publishers, 2001)

Extreme Faith with Dave Park (Harvest House Publishers, 1996)

Higher Ground with Dave Park and Dr. Robert L. Saucy (1999)[*]

Purity Under Pressure with Dave Park (Harvest House Publishers, 1995)

Radical Image with Dave Park and Dr. Robert L. Saucy (Harvest House Publishers, 1998)[*]

Real Life with Dave Park (Harvest House Publishers, 2000)[*]

Reality Check with Rich Miller (Harvest House Publishers, 1996)

Righteous Pursuit with Dave Park (Harvest House Publishers, 2000)

Stomping Out Depression with Dave Park (Regal Books, 2001)

Stomping Out Fear with Rich Miller and Dave Park (Harvest House Publishers, 2003)

Stomping Out the Darkness with Dave Park (Regal Books, 1999)

Ultimate Love with Dave Park (Harvest House Publishers, 1996)

[*] Available from Freedom in Christ Ministries only